The 10 Biggest Civil War Battles: Gettysburg, Chickamauga, Spotsylvania Court House, Chancellorsville, The Wilderness, Stones River, Shiloh, Antietam, Second Bull Run, and Fredericksburg

By Charles River Editors

Painting by Alfred Waud depicting a Confederate advance at Chickamauga

About Charles River Editors

Charles River Editors was founded by Harvard and MIT alumni to provide superior editing and original writing services, with the expertise to create digital content for publishers across a vast range of subject matter. In addition to providing original digital content for third party publishers, Charles River Editors republishes civilization's greatest literary works, bringing them to a new generation via ebooks.

Sign up here to receive updates about free books as we publish them, and visit Our Kindle Author Page to browse today's free promotions and our most recently published Kindle titles.

Introduction

The Battle of Shiloh (April 6-7, 1862)

"The turning point of our fate." – Jefferson Davis on the death of Albert Sidney Johnston at Shiloh

"Probably no single battle of the war gave rise to such wild and damaging reports." – William Tecumseh Sherman

After Union General Ulysses S. Grant captured Fort Henry and Fort Donelson in early 1862, Confederate General Albert Sidney Johnston, widely considered the Confederacy's best general, concentrated his forces in northern Georgia and prepared for a major offensive that culminated with the biggest battle of the war to that point, the Battle of Shiloh. On the morning of April 6, Johnston directed an all out attack on Grant's army around Shiloh Church, and though Grant's men had been encamped there, they had failed to create defensive fortifications or earthworks. They were also badly caught by surprise. With nearly 45,000 Confederates attacking, Johnston's army began to steadily push Grant's men back toward the river.

As fate would have it, the Confederates may have been undone by friendly fire at Shiloh. Johnston advanced out ahead of his men on horseback while directing a charge near a peach orchard when he was hit in the lower leg by a bullet that historians now widely believe was fired by his own men. Nobody thought the wound was serious, including Johnston, who continued to aggressively lead his men and even sent his personal physician to treat wounded Union soldiers taken captive. But the bullet had clipped an artery, and shortly after being wounded Johnston began to feel faint in the saddle. With blood filling up his boot, Johnston unwittingly bled to death. The delay caused by his death, and the transfer of command to subordinate P.G.T. Beauregard, bought the Union defenders critical time on April 6, and the following day Grant's reinforced army struck back and pushed the Confederate army off the field.

The Battle of Shiloh lasted two days, but the battle over the battle had just begun. Grant's army had just won the biggest battle in the history of North America, with nearly 24,000 combined casualties among the Union and Confederate forces. Usually the winner of a major battle is hailed as a hero, but Grant was hardly a winner at Shiloh. The Battle of Shiloh took place before costlier battles at places like Antietam and Gettysburg, so the extent of the casualties at Shiloh shocked the nation. Moreover, at Shiloh the casualties were viewed as needless; Grant was pilloried for allowing the Confederates to take his forces by surprise, as well as the failure to build defensive earthworks and fortifications, which nearly resulted in a rout of his army. Speculation again arose that Grant had a drinking problem, and some even assumed he was drunk during the battle. Though the Union won, it was largely viewed that their success owed to the heroics of General Sherman in rallying the men and Don Carlos Buell arriving with his army, and General Buell was happy to receive the credit at Grant's expense.

As a result of the Battle of Shiloh, Grant was demoted to second-in-command of all armies in his department, an utterly powerless position. And when word of what many considered a "colossal blunder" reached Washington, several congressmen insisted that Lincoln replace Grant in the field. Lincoln famously defended Grant, telling critics, "I can't spare this man. He fights."

The 10 Biggest Civil War Battles explains the campaign and events that led up to the decisive battle, what went right and wrong on both sides, and the aftermath of the battle. Accounts of the battle by important leaders like Sherman, Grant, and Braxton Bragg are included, along with analysis of the generals and fighting. Along with maps of the battle and pictures of important people, places, and events, you will learn about the Battle of Shiloh like you never have before.

The Second Battle of Bull Run (Second Manassas) (August 28-30, 1862)

"A splendid army almost demoralized, millions of public property given up or destroyed, thousands of lives of our best men sacrificed for no purpose. I dare not trust myself to speak of this commander as I feel and believe. Suffice to say...that more insolence, superciliousness, ignorance, and pretentiousness were never combined in one man." – Union II Corps Commander Alpheus Williams

The Second Battle of Bull Run (August 28-30, 1862) was one of the most decisive battles fought during the Civil War, and it was also one of the most unlikely. Less than three months before the battle, Joseph E. Johnston's Army of Northern Virginia had been pushed back nearly all the way to Richmond by George B. McClellan's Army of the Potomac, so close that Union soldiers could see the church steeples of the Confederate capital. And yet, at the end of Second Manassas, Robert E. Lee's Army of Northern Virginia found itself in the field unopposed about 20 miles away from the Union capital of Washington D.C. How could such a remarkable reversal of fortunes take place so quickly?

After Lee succeeded the wounded Johnston, he pushed McClellan's Army of the Potomac away from Richmond and back up the Peninsula in late June, only to then swing his army north to face a second Union army, John Pope's Army of Virginia. Needing to strike out before the Army of the Potomac successfully sailed back to Washington and linked up with Pope's army, Lee daringly split his army to threaten Pope's supply lines, forcing Pope to fall back to Manassas to protect his flank and maintain his lines of communication. At the same time, it left half of Lee's army (under Stonewall Jackson) potentially exposed against the larger Union army until the other wing (under James Longstreet) linked back up. Thus, in late August 1862, the Army of Northern Virginia and the Army of Virginia found themselves fighting over nearly the exact same land the South and North fought over in the First Battle of Bull Run 13 months earlier.

When Pope's army fell back to Manassas to confront Jackson, his wing of Lee's army dug in along a railroad trench and took a defensive stance. The battle began with the Union army throwing itself at Jackson the first two days. But the concentration on Stonewall's men opened up the Union army's left flank for Longstreet's wing, which marched 30 miles in 24 hours to reach the battlefield by the late afternoon of August 29. Lee used Longstreet's wing on August 30 to deliver a devastating flank attack before enough reinforcements from the retreating Army of the Potomac reached the field, sweeping Pope's Army from Manassas and forcing the Union soldiers into yet another disorderly retreat from Manassas to Washington D.C., a scene eerily reminiscent of the First Battle of Bull Run.

The 10 Biggest Civil War Battles comprehensively covers the campaign and the events that led up to the battle, the fighting itself, and the aftermath of the battle. Accounts of the battle by important participants are also included, along with maps of the battle and pictures of important people, places, and events. You will learn about the Second Battle of Bull Run like you never have before.

The Battle of Antietam (September 17, 1862)

"Those in whose judgment I rely tell me that I fought the battle splendidly and that it was a masterpiece of art. ... I feel I have done all that can be asked in twice saving the country. ... I feel some little pride in having, with a beaten & demoralized army, defeated Lee so utterly." - George McClellan

The bloodiest day in American history took place on the 75th anniversary of the signing of the Constitution. On September 17, 1862, Robert E. Lee's Confederate Army of Northern Virginia fought George McClellan's Union Army of the Potomac outside Sharpsburg along Antietam Creek. That day, nearly 25,000 would become casualties, and Lee's army would barely survive fighting the much bigger Northern army.

The fighting that morning started with savage fighting on the Confederate left flank near Dunker church, in a corn field and forests. The Confederates barely held the field in the north sector, but even still, Lee's army may have been saved by the Northern army's inability to cross the creek near "Burnside's Bridge". Ambrose Burnside had been given command of the "Right Wing" of the Army of the Potomac (the I Corps and IX Corps) at the start of the Maryland Campaign for the Battle of South Mountain, but McClellan separated the two corps at the Battle of Antietam, placing them on opposite ends of the Union battle line. However, Burnside continued to act as though he was a wing commander instead of a corps commander, so instead of ordering the IX corps, he funneled orders through General Jacob D. Cox. This poor organization contributed to the corps's hours-long delay in attacking and crossing what is now called "Burnside's Bridge" on the right flank of the Confederate line.

The delay allowed General A.P. Hill's Confederate division to reach the battlefield from Harpers Ferry in time to save Lee's right flank that afternoon. Fearing that his army was badly bloodied and figuring Lee had many more men than he did, McClellan refused to commit his reserves to continue the attacks. The day ended in a tactical stalemate

Although the battle was tactically a draw, it resulted in forcing Lee's army out of Maryland and back into Virginia, making it a strategic victory for the North and an opportune time for President Abraham Lincoln to issue the Emancipation Proclamation, freeing all slaves in the rebellious states.

The 10 Biggest Civil War Battles comprehensively covers the fighting, analyzes the decisions made by the battle's most important leaders, and explains the aftermath of the battle and the legacies that were made and tarnished by the battle. Along with a bibliography, maps of the battle, and pictures of important people and places, you will learn about the Battle of Antietam like you never have before.

The Battle of Fredericksburg (December 11-13, 1862)

"It is well that war is so terrible; otherwise we would grow too fond of it." – Robert E. Lee

The Army of the Potomac had pushed Robert E. Lee's army out of Maryland in September 1862 after the Battle of Antietam, but President Lincoln and his War Department wanted the army to continue going after the Army of Northern Virginia after it retreated back into Virginia. When George B. McClellan refused to do it, Lincoln fired him and installed Ambrose E. Burnside as the new commander. Burnside, who didn't believe himself capable of commanding the Army of the Potomac, only took the job because he was told Fighting Joe Hooker would get the spot if he refused.

With Washington urging Burnside to advance against Lee, Burnside launched an ill fated operation across the Rappahannock River near Fredericksburg in December 1862. From December 12-13, Burnside struggled to get his army across the river while it was under fire from Confederates in Fredericksburg, and things only got worse when they did. Although the Union almost broke the Confederate lines in the south on December 13, they were ultimately repulsed, and the battle is mostly remembered for the piecemeal attacks the Union army made on heavily fortified positions Longstreet's men took up on Marye's Heights. As they threw themselves at Longstreet's heavily fortified position along the high ground, the Northern soldiers were mowed down again and again. General Longstreet compared the near continuous fall of soldiers on the battlefield to "the steady dripping of rain from the eaves of a house." During the battle, Lee turned to Longstreet and commented, "It is well that war is so terrible, otherwise we should grow too fond of it."

As injured Northern soldiers lay freezing and dying on the field that night, the Northern Lights made a rare appearance. Southern soldiers interpreted it as a favorable omen from God and mentioned them frequently in their diaries, while Northern soldiers who saw something far less divine sparsely mentioned them. The following morning, Burnside extricated his army back behind the river, ending the fighting in 1862.

The 10 Biggest Civil War Battles comprehensively covers the campaign and the events that led up to the battle, the fighting itself, and the aftermath of the battle. Accounts of the battle by important participants are also included, along with maps of the battle and pictures of important people, places, and events. You will learn about the Battle of Fredericksburg like you never have before.

BATTLE OF STONE RIVER.

The Battle of Stones River (December 31, 1862-January 2, 1863)

"In all, fifty-eight pieces of artillery played upon the enemy. Not less than one hundred shots per minute were fired. As the mass of men swarmed down the slope they were mowed down by the score. Confederates were pinioned to the earth by falling branches." – G. C. Kniffin, aide to General Crittenden

Americans have long been fascinated by the Civil War and its biggest battles, particularly Gettysburg, Antietam, and Shiloh, all of which involved Robert E. Lee or Ulysses S. Grant. But one of the 6 biggest battles of the war, and the one that took the heaviest toll by % on both armies was fought at the end of 1862 in Tennessee, and it involved neither of those generals.

In late December 1862, William Rosecrans's Union Army of the Cumberland was contesting Middle Tennessee against Braxton Bragg's Army of Tennessee, and for three days the two armies savaged each other as Bragg threw his army at Rosecrans in a series of desperate assaults. Bragg's army was unable to dislodge the Union army, and he eventually withdrew his army after learning that Rosecrans was on the verge of receiving reinforcements. Though the battle was stalemated, the fact that the Union army was left in possession of the field allowed Rosecrans to declare victory and embarrassed Bragg.

Though Stones River is mostly overlooked as a Civil War battle today, it had a decisive impact on the war. The two armies had both suffered nearly 33% casualties, an astounding number in 1862 that also ensured Rosecrans would not start another offensive campaign in Tennessee until the following June. The Union victory also ensured control of Nashville, Middle Tennessee, and Kentucky for the rest of the war, prompting Lincoln to tell Rosecrans, "You gave us a hard-earned victory, which had there been a defeat instead, the nation could scarcely have lived over." The battle and its results also set into motion a chain of events that would lead to Rosecrans and Bragg facing off at the crucial battle of Chickamauga in September 1863, a battle that is often viewed as the last gasp for the Confederates' hopes in the West.

The 10 Biggest Civil War Battles comprehensively covers the campaign and the events that led up to the battle, the fighting itself, and the aftermath of the battle. Accounts of the battle by important participants are also included, along with maps of the battle and pictures of important people, places, and events. You will learn about the Battle of Stones River like you never have before.

The Battle of Chancellorsville (May 2-6, 1863)

"My God! It is horrible—horrible; and to think of it, 130,000 magnificent soldiers so cut the pieces by less than 60,000 half-starved ragamuffins!" – Horace Greeley, Editor of the *New York Tribune*

Of all the Civil War battles fought, and of all the victories achieved by Robert E. Lee at the command of the Confederate Army of Northern Virginia, the Battle of Chancellorsville is considered the most tactically complex and ultimately the most brilliant Confederate victory of the war.

In early May 1863, the Army of the Potomac was at the height of its power as it bore down on Robert E. Lee's Army of Northern Virginia near Fredericksburg, where the Confederates had defeated them the previous December. The Union behemoth had spent most of the winter season being reorganized and drilled by "Fighting Joe" Hooker, an aggressive commander who had fought hard at places like Antietam. With an army nearing 130,000 men, Hooker's Army of the Potomac was twice the size of the Army of Northern Virginia.

With that advantage, Hooker proposed a daring and aggressive two pronged attack that aimed to keep Lee's army occupied in front of Fredericksburg while marching around its left. Meanwhile a cavalry raid well in the rear was intended to cut Lee's lines of supplies and possibly retreat. Hooker's plan initially worked perfectly, with the division of his army surprising Lee. At the end of May 1, Lee was outnumbered 2-1 and now had to worry about threats on two fronts.

Incredibly, Lee once again decided to divide his forces in the face of the enemy, sending Stonewall Jackson to turn the Union army's right flank while the rest of the army maintained positions near Fredericksburg. The Battle of Chancellorsville is one of the most famous of the Civil War, and the most famous part of the battle was Stonewall Jackson's daring march across the Army of the Potomac's flank, surprising the XI Corps with an attack on May 2, 1863. Having ignored warnings of Jackson's march, the XI Corps was quickly routed. The surprise was a costly success, however, as Jackson was mortally wounded after being mistakenly fired upon by his own men.

Having seized the initiative, half of Lee's army launched desperate attacks on Hooker's forces near the Wilderness over the next 2 days, while simultaneously defending against Union attacks around Fredericksburg that pushed the other half of his army back several miles on May 3. Ultimately, Hooker, who may have suffered a concussion during the battle, decided to pull both parts of his army back across the Rappahannock River on May 4, requiring a careful extrication over the next few days as Lee's army tried to destroy them while they were still on the southern bank of the river.

Lee's heavily outnumbered army had just won the most stunning victory of the war, but it cost them Stonewall Jackson. Moreover, the reorganization of the armies and the battle itself played an influential role in the way the Pennsylvania Campaign and the Battle of Gettysburg unfolded later that summer.

The 10 Biggest Civil War Battles comprehensively covers the campaign and the events that led up to the battle, the fighting itself, and the aftermath of the battle. Accounts of the battle by important participants are also included, along with maps of the battle and pictures of important people, places, and events. You will learn about the Battle of Chancellorsville like you never have before.

Barlow Knoll, on the northernmost section of the battlefield

The Battle of Gettysburg (July 1-3, 1863)

The names of history's most famous battles still ring in our ears today, their influence immediately understood by all. Marathon lent its name to the world's most famous race, but it also preserved Western civilization during the First Persian War. Saratoga, won by one of the colonists' most renowned war heroes before he became his nation's most vile traitor. Hastings ensured the Normans' success in England and changed the course of British history. Waterloo, which marked the reshaping of the European continent and Napoleon's doom, has now become part of the English lexicon. In Charles River Editors' Greatest Battles in History series, readers can get caught up to speed on history's greatest battles in the time it takes to finish a commute, while learning interesting facts long forgotten or never known.

Without question, the most famous battle of the American Civil War took place outside of the small town of Gettysburg, Pennsylvania, which happened to be a transportation hub, serving as the center of a wheel with several roads leading out to other Pennsylvanian towns. From July 1-3, Robert E. Lee's Confederate Army of Northern Virginia tried everything in its power to decisively defeat George Meade's Union Army of the Potomac, unleashing ferocious assaults that inflicted nearly 50,000 casualties in all.

Day 1 of the battle would have been one of the 25 biggest battles of the Civil War itself, and it ended with a tactical Confederate victory. But over the next two days, Lee would try and fail to dislodge the Union army with attacks on both of its flanks during the second day and Pickett's Charge on the third and final day. Meade's stout defense held, barely, repulsing each attempted assault, handing the Union a desperately needed victory that ended up being one of the Civil War's turning points.

After the South had lost the war, the importance of Gettysburg as one of the "high tide" marks of the Confederacy became apparent to everyone, making the battle all the more important in the years after it had been fought. While former Confederate generals cast about for scapegoats, with various officers pointing fingers at Robert E. Lee, James Longstreet, and James Stuart, historians and avid Civil War fans became obsessed with studying and analyzing all the command decisions and army movements during the entire campaign. Despite the saturation of coverage, Americans refuse to grow tired of visiting the battlefield and reliving the biggest battle fought in North America.

The 10 Biggest Civil War Battles comprehensively covers the entire Pennsylvania campaign, analyzes the decisions made by the battle's most important leaders, and explains the aftermath of the Union victory and the legacies that were made and tarnished by the battle. Along with bibliographies, maps of the battle, and pictures of important people and places, you will learn about the Battle of Gettysburg like you never have before.

BATTLE OF CHICKAMAUGA

The Battle of Chickamauga (September 19-20, 1863)

"I know Mr. Davis thinks he can do a great many things other men would hesitate to attempt. For instance, he tried to do what God failed to do. He tried to make a soldier of Braxton Bragg." – General Joseph E. Johnston

Americans have long been fascinated by the Civil War and its biggest battles, particularly Gettysburg, Antietam, and Shiloh, all of which involved Robert E. Lee or Ulysses S. Grant. But the second biggest battle of the entire war mostly gets overlooked among casual readers, despite the fact it represented the last great chance for the Confederates to salvage the Western theater.

In mid-September, the Union Army of the Cumberland under General William Rosecrans had taken Chattanooga, but rather than be pushed out of the action, Army of Tennessee commander Braxton Bragg decided to stop with his 60,000 men and prepare a counterattack south of Chattanooga at a creek named Chickamauga. To bolster his fire-power, Confederate President Jefferson Davis sent 12,000 additional troops under the command of Lieutenant General James Longstreet, whose corps had just recently fought at Gettysburg in July.

On the morning of September 19, 1863, Bragg's men assaulted the Union line, which was established in a wooded area thick with underbrush along the river. That day and the morning of the next, Bragg continue to pummel Union forces, with the battle devolving from an organized succession of coordinated assaults into what one Union soldier described as "a mad, irregular battle, very much resembling guerrilla warfare on a vast scale in which one army was bushwhacking the other, and wherein all the science and the art of war went for nothing."

Late that second morning, Rosecrans was misinformed that a gap was forming in his front line, so he responded by moving several units forward to shore it up. What Rosecrans didn't realize, however, was that in doing so he accidentally created a quarter-mile gap in the Union center, directly in the path of Longstreet's men. Described by one of Rosecrans' own men as "an angry flood," Longstreet's attack was successful in driving one-third of the Union Army off the field, with Rosecrans himself running all the way to Chattanooga, where he was later found weeping and seeking solace from a staff priest.

As the Confederate assault continued, George H. Thomas led the Union left wing against heavy Confederate attack even after nearly half of the Union army abandoned their defenses and retreated from the battlefield, racing toward Chattanooga. Thomas rallied the remaining parts of the army and formed a defensive stand on Horseshoe Ridge, with more units spontaneously rallying to the new defensive line. Thomas and his men managed to hold until nightfall, when they made an orderly retreat to Chattanooga while the Confederates occupied the surrounding heights, ultimately besieging the city. Dubbed "The Rock of Chickamauga", Thomas's heroics ensured that Rosecrans' army was able to successfully retreat back to Chattanooga.

In the aftermath of the Battle of Chickamauga, several Confederate generals blamed the number of men lost during what would be the bloodiest battle of the Western Theater on Bragg's incompetence, also criticizing him for refusing to pursue the escaping Union army. General Longstreet later stated to Jefferson Davis, "Nothing but the hand of God can help as long as we have our present commander."

The 10 Biggest Civil War Battles comprehensively covers the campaign and the events that led up to the battle, the fighting itself, and the aftermath of the battle. Accounts of the battle by important participants are also included, along with maps of the battle and pictures of important people, places, and events. You will learn about the Battle of Chickamauga like you never have before.

The Battle of the Wilderness (May 5-7, 1864)

"Numbers meant little—in fact, they were frequently an encumbrance on the narrow trails. Visibility was limited, making it extremely difficult for officers to exercise effective control. Attackers could only thrash noisily and blindly forward through the underbrush, perfect targets for the concealed defenders." – Col. Vincent J. Esposito

With Robert E. Lee's Army of Northern Virginia continuing to frustrate the Union Army of the Potomac's attempts to take Richmond in 1862 and 1863, President Lincoln shook things up by turning command of all the armies of the United States to Ulysses S. Grant in March 1864. , Lee had won stunning victories at battles like Chancellorsville and Second Bull Run by going on the offensive and taking the strategic initiative, but Grant and Lincoln had no intention of letting him do so anymore. Attaching himself to the Army of the Potomac, Grant ordered Army of the Potomac commander George Meade, "Lee's army is your objective point. Wherever Lee goes, there you will go also."

From May 5-7, the two most famous generals of the Civil War squared off for the first time. The 100,000 strong Army of the Potomac was double the size of Lee's hardened but battered Army of Northern Virginia. It was a similar position to the one George McClellan had in 1862 and Joe Hooker had in 1863, and Grant's first attack, at the Battle of the Wilderness, followed a similar pattern. Nevertheless, Lee proved more than capable on the defensive.

The Battle of the Wilderness was fought so close to where the Battle of Chancellorsville took place a year earlier that soldiers encountered skeletons that had been buried in shallow graves in 1863. Moreover, the woods were so thick that neither side could actually see who they were shooting at, and whole brigades at times got lost in the forest. Both armies sustained heavy casualties while Grant kept attempting to move the fighting to a setting more to his advantage, but the heavy forest made coordinated movements almost impossible.

On May 5 and May 6, both armies attempted desperate attacks and counterattacks to strike a knockout blow, but they were ultimately unable to dislodge each other. Given the terrain and the nature of the fighting, it was one of the most horrendous battles of the war, with some wounded men literally burning to death in fires ignited by the battle that sparked the nearby underbrush and spread rapidly. The defending Confederates technically won a tactical victory by holding their ground, but they did so at a staggering cost, inflicting 17,000 casualties on the Army of the Potomac and suffering 11,000 of their own.

On May 7, Grant disengaged his army from the battle. His objective had been frustrated by Lee's skillful defense, the same position as Hooker at Chancellorsville, McClellan on the Virginian Peninsula, and Burnside after Fredericksburg. His men got the familiar dreadful feeling that they would retreat back toward Washington, as they had too many times before. This time, however, Grant made the fateful decision to keep moving south, inspiring his men by telling them that he was prepared to "fight it out on this line if it takes all Summer." The Battle of the Wilderness would only be the beginning of the Overland Campaign, not the end of it.

The 10 Biggest Civil War Battles comprehensively covers the campaign and the events that led up to the battle, the fighting itself, and the aftermath of the battle. Accounts of the battle by important participants are also included, along with maps of the battle and pictures of important people, places, and events. You will learn about the Wilderness like you never have before.

The Battle of Spotsylvania Court House (May 8-21, 1864)

"The appalling sight presented was harrowing in the extreme. Our own killed were scattered over a large space near the "angle," while in front of the captured breastworks the enemy's dead, vastly more numerous than our own, were piled upon each other in some places four layers deep, exhibiting every ghastly phase of mutilation. Below the mass of fast-decaying corpses, the convulsive twitching of limbs and the writhing of bodies showed that there were wounded men still alive and struggling to extricate themselves from the horrid entombment. Every relief possible was afforded, but in too many cases it came too late. The place was well named the "Bloody Angle." – Horace Porter, *Campaigning with Grant*

At the Battle of the Wilderness (May 5-7, 1864), Ulysses S. Grant and Robert E. Lee had fought to a standstill in their first encounter, failing to dislodge each other despite incurring nearly 30,000 casualties between the Union Army of the Potomac and the Confederate Army of Northern Virginia. Despite the fierce fighting, Grant continued to push his battered but resilient army south, hoping to beat Lee's army to the crossroads at Spotsylvania Court House, but Lee's army beat Grant's to Spotsylvania and began digging in, setting the scene for on and off fighting from May 8-21 that ultimately inflicted more casualties than the Battle of the Wilderness. In fact, with over 32,000 casualties among the two sides, it was the deadliest battle of the Overland Campaign.

Although the Battle of Spotsylvania technically lasted nearly 2 weeks, it is best remembered for the fighting that took place on May 12 at a salient in the Confederate line manned by Richard

S. Ewell's corps. Known as the Mule Shoe, a Union assault on the salient produced 24 hours of the most savage fighting conducted during the war, forever christening that point in the line as the Bloody Angle. Although Winfield Scott Hancock's II Corps established a temporary breakthrough, the Confederates were ultimately able to repulse the Union soldiers in bloody hand-to-hand fighting.

After their inability to break Lee's line on May 12, Grant continued to probe Lee's line for weaknesses, attempting to gain a perceptible advantage. However, by 1864 Civil War soldiers had become adept at digging in and building the kind of trenches that would dominate the fighting of World War I 50 years later. By winning the race to Spotsylvania, the Confederates had enough time to dig in and prepare for the kind of defensive fighting that made assaults futile. On May 20, Grant began the process of disengaging from his lines and marching the Army of the Potomac further south, forcing Lee into another race toward the North Anna River. The two armies had suffered a combined 50,000 casualties in about 15 days of fighting, but the Overland Campaign was still only half finished.

The 10 Biggest Civil War Battles comprehensively covers the events that led up to the battle, the fighting itself, and the aftermath of the battle. Accounts of the battle by important participants are also included, along with maps of the battle and pictures of important people, places, and events. You will learn about the Battle of Spotsylvania Court House like you never have before.

The Battle of Spotsylvania Court House

The Battle of Shiloh

Chapter 1: Johnston, Grant, and Sherman

In many ways, the Battle of Shiloh determined the Civil War careers of three of the most important generals in the Civil War.

Today Albert Sidney Johnston is one of the most overlooked generals of the Civil War, but in April 1862 he was widely considered the Confederacy's best general. After graduating from West Point, where he befriended classmates Jefferson Davis and Robert E. Lee, Johnston had a distinguished military career that ensured he would play a principal role in the Civil War.

Johnston

Resigning his Army commission out West in California at the beginning of the war, Johnston made his way to Richmond and arrived on September 5, 1861, just two days after the Confederates in the West had committed their first grievous mistake. After Virginia seceded, both the North and South hoped to have the border slave states on their side, particularly Kentucky and Missouri. Moreover, President Jefferson Davis decided early on upon a strategy that would have the Confederates defend as much Southern territory as they could, despite the fact that stretched their outnumbered forces thinner than they otherwise would have been had they concentrated.

As a result, Davis had forces stretched from the Mississippi River as far east as the Allegheny Mountains, with Tennessee being a crucial Confederate defensive location. However, Confederates under the command of Maj. Gen. Leonidas Polk and Brig. Gen. Gideon J. Pillow were moved into the capital of Kentucky on September 3, prompting Kentucky's governor to request Union assistance to drive the occupiers out of Columbus. With that, Kentucky was destined to remain in the Union fold, no doubt gratifying President Abraham Lincoln, who famously stated, "I hope to have God on my side, but I must have Kentucky."

As a remarkably experienced career Army officer, and a personal favorite of Jefferson Davis, it's no surprise that Johnston received an important post after arriving at Richmond. In fact, he was given command of almost the entire Western theater: "General Albert Sidney Johnston, Confederate States Army, is assigned to the command of Department No. 2, which will hereafter embrace the States of Tennessee and Arkansas, and that part of the State of Mississippi west of the New Orleans, Jackson & Great Northern and Central Railroad; also, the military operations in Kentucky, Missouri, Kansas, and the Indian country immediately west of Missouri and Arkansas. He will repair to Memphis, Tennessee, and assume command, fixing his headquarters at such point as, in his judgment, will best secure the purposes of the command." Along with that, Johnston was made the second most senior general in the Confederate Army, behind only Adjutant-General Cooper, ahead of Robert E. Lee, Joseph Johnston and P.G.T. Beauregard.

Due to the rash actions of more inexperienced officers, Johnston took command in the West at a tenuous time, as noted by his son: "General Johnston had hardly assumed command when he found the Federal armies in possession of nearly the whole of Missouri, and continually menacing Columbus, the left flank of his line in Kentucky, with heavy forces massed at Cairo." Johnston also quickly learned about the difficulties of trying to raise and organize an army in his department; the governors of the Confederate states were hesitant to marshal soldiers for purposes other than the defense of their native state.

Thus, when Johnston entered Kentucky with an army, it was a meager 4,000 strong army, and he still felt compelled to delicately address the state of Kentucky in the wake of Polk's and Pillow's mistakes:

"Proclamation. whereas, the armed occupation of a part of Kentucky by the United States, and the preparations which manifest the intention of their Government to invade the Confederate States through that territory, has imposed it on-these last as a necessity of self-defense to enter that State and meet the invasion upon the best line for military operations; and whereas, it is proper that the motives of the Government of the Confederate States in taking this step should be fully known to the world: now, therefore, I, Albert Sidney Johnston, General and commander of the Western Department of the army of the Confederate States of America, do proclaim that these

States have thus marched their troops into Kentucky with no hostile intention toward its people, nor do they desire or seek to control their choice in regard to their Union with either of the Confederacies, or to subjugate their State, or hold its soil against their wishes. On the contrary, they deem it to be the right of the people of Kentucky to determine their own position [in regard to the belligerents. It is for them to say whether they will join either Confederacy, or maintain a separate existence as an independent and sovereign State. The armed occupation of their soil, both as to its extent and duration, will, therefore, be strictly limited by the exigencies of self-defense on the part of the Confederate States. These States intend to conform to all the requirements of public law, and international amity as between themselves and Kentucky, and accordingly I hereby command all who are subject to my orders to pay entire respect to the rights of property and the legal authorities within that State, so far as the same may be compatible with the necessities of self-defense. If it be the desire of the people of Kentucky to maintain a strict and impartial neutrality, then the effort to drive out the lawless intruders who seek to make their State the theatre of War will aid them in the attainment of their wishes. If, as it may not be unreasonable to suppose, those people desire to unite their fortunes with the Confederate States, to whom they are already bound by so many ties of interest, then the appearance and aid of Confederate troops will assist them to make an opportunity for the free and unbiased expression of their will upon the subject. But if it be true, which is not to be presumed, that a majority of those people desire to adhere to the United States and become parties to the War, then none can doubt the right of the other belligerent to meet that War whenever and wherever it may be waged. But harboring no such suspicion, I now declare, in the name of the Government which I serve, that its army shall be withdrawn from Kentucky so soon as there shall be satisfactory evidence of the existence and execution of a like intention on the part of the United States."

Meanwhile, Johnston realized it was imperative to build and organize an army. When he had taken command of his large department, he only had about 40,000 total soldiers at his disposal, and they were stretched across a vast amount of territory. Furthermore, there was a general shortage of ammunition and resources. As his son would put it in his biography, "[I]t is thus apparent that the real question to be determined was not as between an offensive and a defensive campaign; this had already been settled by the physical and political considerations mentioned, and by the preponderance in the Federal strength, organization, and resources. The real questions were, how and where to maintain the semblance of a force sufficient for defense until an army could be created." In addition to taking up defensive positions, Johnston had to content himself to executing raids here and there, all in an attempt to mask his department's weakness.

At the beginning of 1862, Johnston had to deal with yet another setback, after inexperienced brigadier generals Felix Zollicoffer and Maj. Gen. George B. Crittenden rashly attacked Union troops along the Cumberland River at the Battle of Mill Springs. Soldiers under the command of Johnston's former subordinate George H. Thomas sharply repulsed them, inflicting casualties upon about 13% of the Confederate army. After that, Davis ordered P.G.T. Beauregard to the department, in the hopes that his fame from Fort Sumter and First Bull Run would help with recruiting. Around the same time, Johnston took the brigade Davis sent him, which was commanded by General John B. Floyd, and sent him to take command at Fort Donelson with orders to escape if the fort could not be held.

One of the men who knew Albert Sidney Johnston from the Mexican-American War was Ulysses S. Grant, who could at best be considered a failed businessman before the Civil War. After the attack on Fort Sumter, support for both the northern and southern cause rose. President Lincoln requested that each loyal state raise regiments for the defense of the Union, with the intent of raising an enormous army that would subdue the rebellion. At the outbreak of the Civil War, Grant felt he had an obligation to fight for the Union. Presiding over a war meeting in Galena, Illinois, called in response to President Lincoln's call-to-arms, Grant took responsibility for recruiting, equipping, and drilling the Jo Daviess Guards, a unit named in honor of Major Joseph Hamilton Daviess, who was killed in 1811 at the Battle of Tippecanoe. Grant then accompanied them to Springfield, the state capital, where Governor Richard Yates appointed him an aide and assigned him to duty in the state adjunct general's office, where his knowledge of military practice helped establish the area units' mustering procedure.

On June 15, 1861, Governor Yates appointed Grant colonel of a decidedly "unruly" regiment called the 21st Illinois Volunteers, which had already driven a lesser-qualified commander into early retirement. Assigned to northeastern Missouri, Grant was then promoted to brigadier general by President Lincoln, even before he'd engaged the enemy, due to the influence of U. S. Congressman Elihu B. Washburne, from Galena. Grant chose John A. Rawlins, a local lawyer, to serve as his chief-of-staff. Rawlins soon became Grant's closest advisor, critic, defender, and friend.

Grant

In February 1861 while waiting for assignment, William Tecumseh Sherman observed to fellow officers, "Whatever nation gets control of the Ohio, Mississippi, and Missouri Rivers, will control the continent."[1] He was, of course, referring to the strategic advantage these rivers served, flowing north to south into the very heart of the Confederacy; rivers wide enough to ferry vast armies, weapons, and provisions. In early 1861, however, all eyes were on the East, since the capital cities of Washington D.C. and Richmond were within less than 100 miles of each other. After Fort Sumter, the Lincoln Administration pushed for a quick invasion of Virginia, with the intent of defeating Confederate forces and marching toward the Confederate capitol of Richmond. Lincoln pressed Irvin McDowell to push forward. Despite the fact that McDowell knew his troops were inexperienced and unready, pressure from the Washington politicians forced him to launch a premature offensive against Confederate forces in Northern Virginia.

---

[1]   Gaffney, P. and D. Gaffney. *The Civil War: Exploring History One week at a Time*. Page 103.

Sherman will forever be associated with the Western theater of the Civil War, a legacy that has obscured the fact he first distinguished himself at the First Battle of Bull Run. Once again, fortuitous family connections ensured that Sherman, who had no real combat experience in the Mexican-American War or the 1850s, was placed in command of a brigade, an awfully lofty rank for his background.

Sherman

Nevertheless, Sherman's natural affinity for logistics helped place him at the head of the 13th U.S. Infantry in General Irvin McDowell's army. Subsequently, Sherman was present at the first major land battle of the war, the First Battle of Bull Run, when McDowell launched his overly-ambitious plan for a surprise flank attack against Confederate Brigadier General P.G.T. Beauregard. McDowell's strategy during the First Battle of Bull Run was grand, and in many respects it was similar to the tactics Lee used at the Battle of Chancellorsville. McDowell's plan called for parts of his army to pin down Confederate soldiers in front while marching another wing of his army around the flank and into the enemy's rear, rolling up the line.

Beauregard

Lee's seasoned Army of Northern Virginia could carry that battleplan out in May 1863, but in July 1861, this proved far too difficult for McDowell's inexperienced troops to carry out effectively. The Union had few bright spots come out of the First Battle of Bull Run, but Sherman was one of them, or at least so they thought. However, Sherman hardly felt distinguished as a result of the battle. Due to his inability to reform his brigade during the initial retreat, and the overall rout of Union forces as a whole, Sherman questioned his own competence, as well as his responsibility, in the defeat.

Sherman may have doubted himself, but his actions at Bull Run earned him recognition and a promotion to the rank of brigadier-general. Sherman was sent to Kentucky in August 1861 to serve as second-in-command to General Robert Anderson, who had been in command of Fort Sumter when the first shots of the war were fired. Sherman wrote, "Of course, I always wanted to go West, and was perfectly willing to go with Anderson, especially in a subordinate capacity."

However, in October 1861 Sherman was promoted to the command of the Department of the Cumberland, replacing Anderson, and the feeling of responsibility hit Sherman like a ton of bricks. In his Memoirs, Sherman explained some of the reasons he felt so uneasy in Kentucky. To start, it was a border state that had seen violence between Southern and Northern partisans, including John Brown, in the 1850s, and Sherman was not sure the state was actually pro-Union. Moreover, the Confederates in the area were commanded by Albert Sidney Johnston, who at the time was widely considered one of the best generals on either side, if not the best. Sherman began telling government officials of his concerns, which was at odds with their views, and he reported to his commanding officers that he needed 200,000 men for the Kentucky campaign, a request all his commanders viewed as being out of touch with reality.

By early November, Sherman was actually asking to be relieved of command, which the War Department was only too happy to oblige. Relieved of his post, rumors about his mental stability began to circulate; his so-called "eccentric" behavior and suspicion of news reporters leading some newspapers to write articles questioning his sanity and trustworthiness to lead men into battle. The *New York Times* reported that "[Sherman's] 'disorders' had removed him, perhaps permanently from his command." Sherman's wife, in a message to her brother, noted Sherman seemed to be struck by "that melancholy insanity to which your family is subject." And after being relieved from command, Sherman wrote a disturbing message to his brother John that seemed to confirm the general consensus: "I am so sensible of my disgrace in having exaggerated the force of our enemy in Kentucky that I do think I should have committed suicide were it not for my children. I do not think that I can again be trusted with command."[2]

Today, historians speculate that Sherman suffered a nervous breakdown. Thankfully for the general and the North, he regained his senses over the next month. Before the end of 1861, Sherman was placed in the Department of Missouri under General Henry Halleck.

Chapter 2: Fort Henry and Fort Donelson

Despite the loss of Fort Sumter, the North expected a relatively quick victory, and their expectations weren't unrealistic, given the Union's overwhelming economic advantages over the South. At the start of the war, the Union had a population of over 22 million. The South had a population of 9 million, nearly 4 million of whom were slaves. Union states contained 90% of the manufacturing capacity of the country and 97% of the weapon manufacturing capacity. Union states also possessed over 70% of the total railroads in the pre-war United States at the start of the war, and the Union also controlled 80% of the shipbuilding capacity of the pre-war United States.

However, while the Lincoln Administration and most Northerners were preoccupied with trying to capture Richmond in the summer of 1861, it would be the little known Ulysses S. Grant who delivered the Union's first major victories, over a thousand miles away from Washington. Grant's new commission led to his command of the District of Southeast Missouri, headquartered at Cairo, after he was appointed by "The Pathfinder", John C. Fremont, a national celebrity who had run for President in 1856. Fremont was one of many political generals that Lincoln was saddled with, and his political prominence ensured he was given a prominent command as commander of the Department of the West early in the war before running so afoul

---

[2]   Gaffney, P. and D. Gaffney. *The Civil War: Exploring History One week at a Time.* Page 85.

of the Lincoln Administration that he was court-martialed.

Regardless of how Grant got to the position he did, he immediately began to reveal his strategic military competence. On September 6, 1861, Grant quickly seized a strategic position at Paducah, Kentucky at the mouth of the Tennessee River. Grant's men first fought at Belmont, Missouri on November 7, a diversionary attack that proved inconclusive after the Union forces were initially successful but the Confederates were able to quickly rally and hold the field. But had it not been for Grant's decisiveness, his men may not have gotten out alive. He was credited with demonstrating exceptional independent initiative, quick decision-making, and fought aggressively to protect his men.

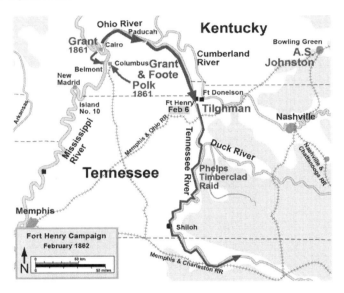

Map of the Fort Henry and Fort Donelson Campaign

Unhappy that his regiment was being used only for defensive and diversionary purposes, in January of 1862, Grant persuaded General Halleck to allow his men to launch a campaign on the Tennessee River. As soon as Halleck acquiesced, Grant moved against Fort Henry, in close coordination with the naval command of Flag Officer Andrew Hull Foote. The tag team of infantry and naval bombardment helped force the capitulation of Fort Henry on February 6, 1862.

"Old Brains" Halleck

The surrender of Fort Henry was followed immediately by an attack on Fort Donelson on the Cumberland River that earned Grant his famous nickname "Unconditional Surrender". Grant's forces enveloped the Confederate garrison at Fort Donelson, which included Confederate generals Simon Buckner, John Floyd, and Gideon Pillow. In one of the most bungled operations of the war, the Confederate generals tried and failed to open an escape route by attacking Grant's forces on February 15. Although the initial assault was successful, General Pillow inexplicably chose to have his men pull back into their trenches, ostensibly so they could take more supplies before their escape. Instead, they simply lost all the ground they had taken, and the garrison was cut off yet again.

During the early morning hours of February 16, the garrison's generals held one of the Civil War's most famous councils of war. Over the protestations of cavalry officer Nathan Bedford Forrest, who insisted the garrison could escape, the three generals agreed to surrender their army, but none of them wanted to be the fall guy. General Floyd was worried that the Union might try him for treason if he was taken captive, so he turned command of the garrison over to General Pillow and escaped with two of his regiments. Pillow had the same concern and turned command over to General Buckner before escaping alone by boat. Meanwhile, Forrest successfully rallied about 700 troops and fought through the siege across the river.

Despite all of these successful escapes, General Buckner decided to surrender to Grant. As a long-standing legend describes, when asked for terms of surrender, Grant sent a letter stating,

"No terms except an unconditional and immediate surrender." [3]

Forrest

Floyd

[3]   Grant, U. S. (John. Y. Simon, editor). *Ulysses S. Grant: Memoirs and Selected Letters.* Page 208.

Buckner

Pillow

Grant's campaign was the first major success for the Union, which had already lost the disastrous First Battle of Bull Run in July 1861 and was reorganizing the Army of the Potomac in anticipation of the Peninsula Campaign, which would fail in the summer of 1862. It also exposed the weakness of the outmanned Confederates, who were stretched too thin. But rather than admit weakness in public, Johnston instead personally took the blame. After he had to withdraw from Nashville in late February and let it fall to Don Carlos Buell's Union army on February 25, 1862, there were public calls for Johnston's removal. Naturally, his friend Jefferson Davis had his back, stating, "If Sidney Johnston is not a general, we had better give up the war, for we have no general."

Privately, Johnston wrote a memorandum detailing some of the problems that were plaguing his command in late 1861 and early 1862:

"I took command at Bowling Green on the 28th day of October, 1861, the force being nearly 12,000 men. From the best information we could get, the forces of the enemy were estimated at nearly twice the number of our own when I assumed command. There were many reasons why Bowling Green was held and fortified. It was a good base of military operations; was a proper depot for supplies; was capable, if fortified, of being held against largely superior numbers. If the army should be such that a forward movement was practicable, it could be held by a garrison, and our effective force be left free to operate against an enemy in the field. It was in supporting distance of Tennessee, from and through which reinforcements and munitions must come, if the people of Kentucky should be either hostile or neutral. My force was too weak and too illy appointed to advance against greatly superior numbers, perfectly equipped and provided, and being much more rapidly reinforced than my own. Our advance into Kentucky had not been met by the enthusiastic uprising of friends, which we, and many in and out of that State, had believed would take place. Arms were scarce, and we had none to give them. No prudent commander would thus hazard the fate of an entire army, so much weaker than the enemy, and dependent upon support not certain to come, and wanting in arms and discipline if it should.

Muldrough's Hill possessed no strategic importance, was worthless as a base of operations, and I had ordered General Buckner, in the first place, not to advance to that position, because the Green River, flowing directly across the line between Bowling Green and Muldrough's Hill, and being navigable, gave the enemy every desirable facility to cut the line in two in the rear of any force at Muldrough's Hill. Buckner's force was small, was illy armed, had no transportation except by rail, was deficient in many necessary appointments for making a campaign, and many of his men were fresh from home and wholly undisciplined. The enemy's forces increased much more rapidly than Buckner's; and the ratio of increase was fully preserved after I took command."

Chapter 3: The Armies Catch Their Breath

Grant had just secured Union command of precious control over much of the Mississippi River and much of Kentucky and Tennessee, but that would prove to be merely a prelude to the Battle of Shiloh, which at the time would be the biggest battle ever fought on the continent. After the victories at Fort Henry and Fort Donelson, Grant was now at the head of the Army of the Tennessee, which was about 45,000 strong and firmly encamped at Pittsburg Landing on the western side of the Tennessee River. And despite all the negative rumors about Sherman, Grant placed him at the head of a a new division of recruits assigned to accompany Grant's army to Pittsburg Landing, Tennessee. Grant had just salvaged Sherman's career, and Sherman was about to return the favor.

With Grant situated along the Tennessee River, his department head, Henry "Old Brains" Halleck, ordered Don Carlos Buell's army to join Grant's, thereby concentrating their armies before launching an offensive. Before they could launch their offensive, however, the Confederates, under the command of Johnston, would launch their own. The losses of the two forts had dismayed the Confederates, making President Davis too eager to try to regain momentum by quickly launching an offensive in an attempt to wrest control of Tennessee from the Union.

Near the end of February, Johnston reported his dispositions to the Confederate government:

"Headquarters, Western Department, Murfreesboro, Tennessee, February 27, 1862.

Sir: The fall of Fort Donelson compelled me to withdraw the forces under my command from the north bank of the Cumberland, and to abandon the defense of Nashville, which, but for that disaster, it was my intention to protect to the utmost. Not more than 11,000 effective men were left under my command to oppose a column of General Buell's of not less than 40,000 troops moving by Bowling Green, while another superior force under General Thomas outflanked me to the east, and the armies from Fort Donelson, with the gunboats and transports, had it in their power to ascend the Cumberland, now swollen by recent floods, so as to interrupt all communications with the south.

The situation left me no alternative but to evacuate Nashville or sacrifice the army. By remaining, the place would have been unnecessarily subjected to destruction, as it is very indefensible, and no adequate force would have been left to keep the enemy in check in Tennessee.

Under the circumstances I moved the main body of my command to this place on the 17th and 18th instant, and left a brigade under General Floyd to bring on such stores and property as were at Nashville, with instructions to remain until the approach of the enemy, and then to rejoin me. This has been in a great measure effected, and nearly all the stores would have been saved, but for the heavy and unusual rains which have washed away the bridges, swept away portions of the railroad, and rendered transportation almost impossible. General Floyd has arrived here. The rear-guard left Nashville on the night of the 23d. Edgefield, on the north bank of the Cumberland, opposite the city, was occupied yesterday by the advanced pickets of the enemy. I have remained here for the purpose of augmenting my forces and securing the transportation of the public stores. By the junction of the command of General Crittenden and the fugitives from Fort Donelson, which have been reorganized as far as practicable, the force now under my command will amount to about 17,000 men. General Floyd, with a force of some 2,500 men, has been ordered to Chattanooga to defend the approaches toward North Alabama and Georgia, and the communications between the Mississippi and the Atlantic, and with the view to increase his forces by such troops as may be sent forward from the neighboring States. The quartermaster's, commissary's, and ordnance stores which are not required for immediate use have been ordered to Chattanooga, and those which will be necessary on the march have been forwarded to Huntsville and Decatur. I have ordered a depot to be established at Atlanta for the manufacture of supplies for the quartermaster's department, and also a laboratory for the manufacture of percussion-caps and ordnance-stores, and, at Chattanooga, depots for distribution of these supplies. The machinery will be immediately sent forward.

Considering the peculiar topography of this State, and the great power which the enemy's means afford them upon the Tennessee and Cumberland, it will be seen that the force under my command cannot successfully cover the whole line against the advance of the enemy. I am compelled to elect whether he shall be permitted to occupy Middle Tennessee, or turn Columbus, take Memphis, and open the valley of the Mississippi. To me the defense of the valley seems of paramount importance, and consequently I will move this corps of the army, of which I have assumed the immediate command, toward the left bank of the Tennessee, crossing the river near Decatur, in order to enable me to cooperate or unite with General Beauregard for the defense of Memphis and the Mississippi. The department has sent eight regiments to Knoxville for the defense of East Tennessee, and the protection of that region will be confided to them and such additional forces as may be hereafter sent from the adjacent States. General Buckner was ordered by the department to take command of the troops at Knoxville, but, as at that time he was in presence of the enemy, the order was not fulfilled.

As it would be almost impossible for me under present circumstances to superintend the operations at Knoxville and Chattanooga, I would respectfully suggest that the local commanders at those points should receive orders from the department directly, or be allowed to exercise their discretion.

I have the honor to remain, very respectfully, your obedient servant,

A. S. Johnston, General C. S. A.

In the middle of March, Johnston was in the process of linking up the armies in his department and consolidating them into one fighting force that would approach about 55,000 soldiers, making his army nearly the equal of Grant's. The Confederate forces were linking up at Corinth,

Georgia, only about 20 miles away from Grant's army. Thus, it would not take much time for Johnston to launch his offensive north against Grant, hopefully before Buell could link up with his army. On March 18, Johnston wrote to Davis:

"The enemy are now at Nashville, about 50,000 strong, advancing in this direction by Columbia. He has also forces, according to the report of General Bragg, landing at Pittsburg, from 25,000 to 50,000, and moving in the direction of Purdy.

This army corps, moving to join Bragg, is about 20,000 strong. Two brigades, Hindman's and Wood's, are, I suppose, at Corinth. One regiment of Hardee's division (Lieutenant-Colonel Patton commanding) is moving by cars to-day (20th March), and Statham's brigade (Crittenden's division). The brigade will halt at Iuka, the regiment at Burnsville; Cleburne's brigade, Hardee's division, except regiment, at Burnsville; and Carroll's brigade, Crittenden's division, and Helm's cavalry, at Tuscumbia; Bowen's brigade at Cortland; Breckinridge's brigade, here; the regiments of cavalry of Adams and Wharton, on the opposite bank of the river; Scott's Louisiana regiment at Pulaski, sending forward supplies; Morgan's cavalry at Shelbyville, ordered on.

To-morrow, Breckinridge's brigade will go to Corinth; then Bowen's. When these pass Tuscumbia and Iuka, transportation will be ready there for the other troops to follow immediately from those points, and, if necessary, from Burnsville. The cavalry will cross and move forward as soon as their trains can be passed over the railroad-bridge.

I have troubled you with these details, as I cannot properly communicate them by telegram.

The test of merit in my profession with the people is success. It is a hard rule, but I think it right. If I join this corps to the forces of Beauregard (I confess a hazardous experiment), then those who are now declaiming against me will be without an argument. Your friend,

A. S. Johnston."

Davis responded to that letter:

My dear General: Yours of the 18th inst. was this day delivered to me by your aide, Mr. Jack. I have read it with much satisfaction. So far as the past is concerned, it but confirms the conclusions at which I had already arrived. My confidence in you has never wavered, and I hope the public will soon give me credit for judgment, rather than continue to arraign me for obstinacy.

You have done wonderfully well, and now I breathe easier in the assurance that you will be able to make a junction of your two armies. If you can meet the division of the enemy moving from the Tennessee before it can make a junction with that advancing from Nashville, the future will be brighter. If this cannot be done, our only hope is that the people of the Southwest will rally en masse with their private arms, and thus enable you to oppose the vast army which will threaten the destruction of our country.

I have hoped to be able to leave here for a short time, and would be much gratified to confer with you, and share your responsibilities. I might aid you in obtaining troops; no one could hope to do more unless he underrated your military capacity. I write in great haste, and feel that it would be worse than useless to point out to you how much depends upon you.

Johnston's son William summed up the situation at the beginning of April, just before the climactic Battle of Shiloh: "Grant felt safe at Shiloh, because he knew he was numerically stronger than his adversary. His numbers and his equipment were superior to those of his antagonist, and the discipline and morale of his army ought to have been so. The only infantry of the Confederate army which had ever seen a combat were some of Polk's men, who were at Belmont; Hindman's brigade, which was in the skirmish at Woodsonville; and the fugitives of Mill Spring. In the Federal army were the soldiers who had fought at Belmont, Fort Henry, and Donelson- 30,000 of the last. There were many raw troops on both sides. Some of the Confederates received their arms for the first time that week."

As he began to move his army north on April 2, Johnston issued general orders to be read to his army:

"I have put you in motion to offer battle to the invaders of your country. With the resolution and discipline and valor becoming men fighting, as you are, for all worth living or dying for, you can but march to a decisive victory over the agrarian mercenaries sent to subjugate you and to despoil you of your liberties, your property, and your honor. Remember the precious stake involved; remember the dependence of your mothers, your wives, your sisters, and your children, on the result; remember the fair, broad, abounding land, and the happy homes that would be desolated by your defeat.

The eyes and hopes of eight millions of people rest upon you; you are expected to show yourselves worthy of your lineage, worthy of the women of the South, whose noble devotion in this war has never been exceeded in any time. With such incentives to brave deeds, and with the trust that God is with us, your generals will lead you confidently to the combat-assured of success."

When Johnston began moving his army of about 45,000 north towards Grant's position, he hoped to catch Grant by surprise, a plan that his principal subordinate Beauregard thought had no chance of success. The element of surprise seemed even more unlikely when their initial plan of attacking on April 5 was ruined by stormy weather. Adding to Beauregard's consternation, the Confederates' weapons were so poor and their recruits so raw that many of them had to test-fire their weapons for the sake of practicing, something Beauregard figured would cost them the element of surprise anyway. Others yelled loudly at the sight of a deer.

There were other serious problems that forced the Confederate officers to debate whether or not to make an attack at all. In a biography of his father, Johnston's son William Preston Johnston explained:

"It was now learned that many of the troops had improvidently thrown away or consumed their provisions, and at the end of three days were out of subsistence. General Bragg promised, however, to remedy this from his alleged well-stocked commissariat. But General Beauregard earnestly advised the idea of attacking the enemy should be abandoned, and that the whole force should return to Corinth, inasmuch as it was scarcely possible they would be able to take the Federals unawares, after such delay and the noisy demonstrations which had been made meanwhile. He urged the enemy would be now found formidably intrenched and ready for the attack; that success had depended on the power to assail them unexpectedly, for they were superior in number, and in large part had been under fire. On the other hand, few comparatively of the Confederates had that advantage, while a large part were too raw and recently enrolled to make it proper to venture them in an assault upon breastworks which would now be thrown up. And this unquestionably was the view of almost all present.

General Johnston, having listened with grave attention to the views and opinions advanced, then remarked, in substance, that he recognized the weight of the objections to an attack under the circumstances involved by the unfortunate loss of time on the road. But, nevertheless, he still hoped the enemy was not looking for offensive operations, and that he would yet be able to surprise them; and that, having put his army in motion for a battle, he would venture the hazard."

Despite Beauregard's suggestion not to attack Grant, Johnston rejected his principal subordinate's advice, telling him he would "attack them if they were a million." Beauregard predicted, "In the struggle tomorrow we shall be fighting men of our own blood, Western men, who understand the use of firearms. The struggle will be a desperate one."

As it turned out, Union forces somehow did not hear any of the sounds coming from the firing or marching of Johnston's army, even as it camped just 3 miles away from them on April 5, the night before the Battle of Shiloh. That same night, Grant telegraphed his department head, Henry Halleck, "I have scarcely the faintest idea of an attack (general one) being made upon us, but will be prepared should such a thing take place." In actuality, Grant was considerably overstating the preparedness of his army, and he had discounted such a possibility so much that he would be 10 miles away from the battlefield when the Battle of Shiloh started at dawn the next morning. He had been injured days earlier when his horse fell on him, and he could not move without crutches, so he was downriver convalescing when Johnston's army threatened to overrun his on the morning of the 6th.

Chapter 4: The Beginning of the Battle

"Men of Arkansas! They say you boast of your prowess with the bowie-knife. Today you wield a nobler weapon — the bayonet. Employ it well." – Albert Sidney Johnston

The men who became Civil War generals had been taught the art of war employed by Napoleon over 50 years earlier during their West Point days, so naturally they used Napoleonic tactics. In the early 19th century, those tactics saw Napoleon dominate the European continent and win crushing victories against large armies. However, the weapons available in 1861 were far more accurate than they had been 50 years earlier. In particular, new rifled barrels created common infantry weapons with deadly accuracy of up to 100 yards, at a time when generals were still leading massed infantry charges with fixed bayonets and attempting to march their men close enough to engage in hand-to-hand combat.

By the end of the Civil War, the generals and the soldiers had learned so many bloody lessons that the warfare at places like Petersburg resembled the trench warfare of World War I more than Waterloo. In fact, the first thing armies would do after establishing their defensive line was to begin digging, fortifying their positions with earthworks, abates, trenches, and anything that could protect them. Positions became unassailable if an army was allowed to work on their defensive line for more than 24 hours.

Unfortunately, Grant's army had yet to learn that lesson in April 1862. Despite having been camped out along the western bank of the Tennessee River for a considerable period of time, his army did not dig in and established no defensive fortifications to prepare for a potential Confederate attack. That failure to prepare was all the more ironic because the position was so strong defensively, with water guarding both flanks of Grant's army and making it extremely difficult to attack. Like the rest of Grant's army, Sherman's division was initially ill-prepared for the confrontation, and the Confederate attack would end up smashing his division hard. Sherman may have avoided building up defensive fortifications to avoid being called overly cautious, and he had written a letter to his wife worrying "they'd call me crazy again".

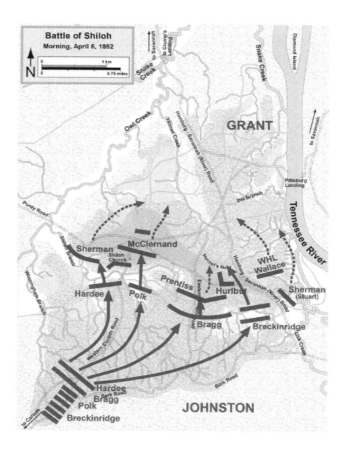

Early on the morning of April 6, Johnston deployed his army for battle along the Corinth Road with the intent of striking Grant's army and confidently told his men, "Tonight we will water our horses in the Tennessee River." In his report to the Confederate government after the battle, Beauregard explained how the lines were drawn up for the attack:

"It was then decided that the attack should be made on the next morning, at the earliest hour practicable, in accordance with the orders of movement; that is, in three lines of battle, the first and second extending from Owl Creek, on the left, to Lick Creek, on the right, a distance of about 3 miles, supported by the third and the reserve. The first line, under Major-General Hardee, was constituted of his corps, augmented on his right by Gladdens brigade, of Major-General Bragg's corps, deployed in line of battle, with their respective artillery following immediately by the main road to Pittsburg and the cavalry in rear of the wings. The second line, composed of the other troops of Bragg's corps, followed the first at a distance of 500 yards in the same order as the first. The army corps under General Polka followed the second line, at a distance of about 800 yards, in lines of brigades deployed, with their batteries in rear of each brigade, moving by the Pittsburg road, the left wing supported by cavalry. The reserve, under Brigadier-General Breckinridge, followed closely the third line in the same order, its right wing supported by cavalry.

These two corps constituted the reserve, and were to support the front lines of battle, by being deployed, when required, on the right and left of the Pittsburg road, or otherwise act according to the exigencies of the battle."

At about 5:00 a.m., a Union reconnaissance party comprised of the 25th Missouri made contact with Johnston's army and engaged in a brief skirmish around 5:15 a.m., which could have destroyed the element of surprise right then and there. While that certainly woke up nearby Union soldiers, the senior officers around Pittsburg Landing discredited the notion that the Confederate army was nearby. William Tecumseh Sherman, who was the senior Union officer on the field that morning, reacted dismissively when told the Confederates were preparing to attack, telling the messenger, "There is no enemy nearer than Corinth."

Meanwhile, miscommunication between Beauregard and Johnston hampered the Confederate attack before it even started. Johnston had telegraphed President Davis his plan, "Polk the left, Bragg the center, Hardee the right, Breckinridge in reserve." But Johnston's main focus was the attack on the Union left, which he hoped would interpose his army between Grant's army and the Tennessee River, which would cut off its supply line and its path to retreat. Johnston instructed Beauregard to direct the logistics from the rear while he was at the front, but Beauregard thought the battle plan should be to attack in three waves and try to drive Grant's army eastward into the Tennessee River, a plan wildly at odds with Johnston's. On top of that, Beauregard had fallen so ill that he was all but confined to a hospital bed in an ambulance in the rear the entire first day of the battle, even when command would fall upon him.

The Battle of Shiloh began in earnest around 6:00 a.m. with an attack on the Union right by the William Hardee's division and an attack on the Union left by Braxton Bragg's divisions. Their divisions were formed in one line about 3 miles long, but the length of their line and its lack of depth would quickly lead to their men getting intermingled, and officers would gradually lose command over their soldiers. That wasn't the only difficulty confronting the Confederate troops, as explained by Hardee's post-battle report:

"By the order of battle our troops were arranged in two parallel lines, the first, under my command, being composed of my corps, consisting of the brigades of Brigadier-Generals Hindman, Wood, and Cleburne, numbering 6,789 effective men, and the brigade of Brigadier-General Gladden, which was attached to my command to till the interval between my right and Lick Creek. The second was composed of five brigades, under Major-General Bragg, 1,000 yards in rear of mine, while four brigades, under Major-General Polk, supported the left, and three under Brigadier-General Breckinridge supported the right of the lines.

The order was given to advance at daylight on Sunday, April 6. The morning was bright and bracing. At early dawn the enemy attacked the skirmishers in front of my line, commanded by Major (now Colonel) Hardcastle, which was handsomely resisted by that promising young officer. My command advanced, and in half an hour the battle became fierce.

Hindman's brigade engaged the enemy with great vigor in the edge of a wood and drove him rapidly back over the field toward Pittsburg, while Gladden's brigade, on the right, about 8 o'clock, dashed upon the encampments of a division under the command of General Prentiss. At the same time Cleburne's brigade, with the Fifteenth Arkansas, deployed as skirmishers, and the Second Tennessee, en échelon on the left, moved quickly through the fields, and though far outflanked by the enemy on our left, rushed forward under a terrific fire from the serried ranks drawn up in front of the camp. A morass covered his front, and being difficult to pass, caused a break in the brigade. Deadly volleys were poured upon the men as they advanced from behind bales of hay, logs, and other defenses, and after a series of desperate charges the brigade was compelled to fall back."

Bragg's division encountered similar difficulties, as Bragg would note in his official report after the battle:

"The night was occupied by myself and a portion of my staff in efforts to bring forward provisions for a portion of the troops then suffering from their improvidence. Having been ordered to march with five days' rations, they were found hungry and destitute at the end of three days. This is one of the evils of raw troops, imperfectly organized and badly commanded; a tribute, it seems, we must continue to pay to universal suffrage, the bane of our military organization. In this condition we passed the night, and at dawn of day prepared to move.

The enemy did not give us time to discuss the question of attack, for soon after dawn he commenced a rapid musketry fire on our pickets. The order was immediately given by the commanding general and our lines advanced. Such was the ardor of our troops that it was with great difficulty they could be restrained from closing up and mingling with the first line. Within less than a mile the enemy was encountered in force at the encampments of his advanced positions, but our first line brushed him away, leaving the rear nothing to do but to press on in pursuit. In about one mile more we encountered him in strong force among almost the entire line. His batteries were posted on eminences, with strong infantry supports.

Finding the first line was now unequal to the work before it, being weakened by extension and necessarily broken by the nature of the ground, I ordered my whole force to move up steadily and promptly to its support. The order was hardly necessary, for subordinate commanders, far beyond the reach of my voice and eye in the broken country occupied by us, had promptly acted on the necessity as it arose, and by the time the order could be conveyed the whole line was developed and actively engaged.

From this time, about 7.30 o'clock, until night the battle raged with little intermission. All parts of our line were not constantly engaged, but there was no time without heavy firing in some portion of it. My position for several hours was opposite my left center Ruggles' division), immediately in rear of Hindman's brigade, Hardee's corps. In moving over the difficult and broken ground the right brigade of Ruggles' division, Colonel Gibson commanding, bearing to the right, became separated from the two left brigades, leaving a broad interval."

Bragg

Despite the Confederates' difficulties, however, the element of surprise was so strong that the initial assault couldn't help but be successful. Like Johnston's army, Grant's army was full of raw recruits, and when they were caught by surprise without adequate defensive works, many of them broke and ran toward Pittsburg Landing. Those that fought had to do so without the benefit of any semblance of orders from their officers, leading to a complete breakdown on the Union left. Grant took pains to describe his army's inexperience, writing in his memoirs, "Three of the five divisions engaged on Sunday were entirely raw, and many of the men had only received their arms on the way from their States to the field. Many of them had arrived but a day or two before and were hardly able to load their muskets according to the manual. Their officers were equally ignorant of their duties. Under these circumstances it is not astonishing that many of the regiments broke at the first fire. In two cases, as I now remember, colonels led their regiments from the field on first hearing the whistle of the enemy's bullets. In these cases the colonels were constitutional cowards, unfit for any military position; but not so the officers and men led out of danger by them. Better troops never went upon a battle-field than many of these, officers and men, afterwards proved themselves to be, who fled panic stricken at the first whistle of bullets and shell at Shiloh."

Grant and Sherman would play down how badly they were caught offguard by simply referencing the Confederates driving in their pickets and advanced guard that morning, but the truth was that the Confederate attack came bearing down upon the Union's defensive line almost immediately. Bragg would later note, "Contrary to the views of such as urged an abandonment of the attack, the enemy was found utterly unprepared, many being surprised and captured in their tents, and others, though on the outside, in costumes better fitted to the bed-chamber than to the battle-field."

Even still, Sherman would later claim in his official report that he was unsure of the Confederates' designs until about 2 hours into the battle:

"Shortly after 7 a.m., with my entire staff, I rode along a portion of our front, and when in the open field before Appler's regiment the enemy's pickets opened a brisk fire on my party, killing my orderly, Thomas D. Holliday, of Company H, Second Illinois Cavalry. The fire came from the bushes which line a small stream that rises in the field in front of Appler's camp and flows to the north along my whole front. This valley afforded the enemy a partial cover, but our men were so posted as to have a good fire at him as he crossed the valley and ascended the rising ground on our side.

About 8 a.m. I saw the glistening bayonets of heavy masses of infantry to our left front in the woods beyond the small stream alluded to, and became satisfied for the first time that the enemy designed a determined attack on our whole camp."

As Bragg and Hardee moved forward with a disorganized but successful attack on both flanks of the Union army, Johnston was exposing himself at so many points along the front that his men began to grow nervous that he might get himself killed. One Confederate officer recalled: "Colonel Preston then carried the order to Hindman's brigade, who made a splendid and victorious charge. . . It was while under this fire that Captain Brewster expostulated with General

Johnston against his exposing his person. I was not near enough to hear his reply, but it had no effect, for he smilingly rode to the brow of the hill where we could distinctly see the enemy retreating." In addition to putting himself in harm's way, Johnston's position at the front meant that Beauregard had to make important command decisions from the rear. About an hour and a half into the battle, at about 7:30 a.m., Beauregard plugged the holes in the Confederates' line by sending Polk's corps in on the left and Breckinridge's corps in on the right. While the timing was fortuitous in plugging gaps, especially in Bragg's line, it meant the attack continued to move forward in one line, with no secondary lines truly in reserve that could sustain an advance if one part of the line started to falter.

At the time, though, it wasn't clear whether strategic depth would even be necessary as the Confederates continued pushing a general rout of the Union forces in their front. Union General Jesse Hildebrand would note that whole regiments in his brigade got separated in the general confusion and retreat, and Sherman verified it, noting, "Hildebrand's brigade had substantially disappeared from the field, though he himself bravely remained." Sherman, who would suffer two wounds during the day and have a third bullet pass through his cap, later noted of the initial retreat:

"Although our left was thus turned, and the enemy was pressing our whole line, I deemed Shiloh so important, that I remained by it and renewed my orders to Colonels McDowell and Buckland to hold their ground; and we did hold these positions until about 10 a.m., when the enemy had got his artillery to the rear of our left flank and some change became absolutely necessary. Two regiments of Hildebrand's brigade—Appler's and Mungen's—had already disappeared to the rear, and Hildebrand's own regiment was in disorder. I therefore gave orders for Taylor's battery—still at Shiloh—to fall back as far as the Purdy and Hamburg road, and for McDowell and Buckland to adopt that road as their new line. I rode across the angle and met Behr's battery at the cross-roads, and ordered it immediately to come into battery, action right. Captain Behr gave the order, but he was almost immediately shot from his horse, when drivers and gunners fled in disorder, carrying off the caissons, and abandoning five out of six guns, without firing a shot. The enemy pressed on, gaining this battery, and we were again forced to choose a new line of defense. Hildebrand's brigade had substantially disappeared from the field, though he himself bravely remained. McDowell's and Buckland's brigades maintained their organizations, and were conducted by my aides, so as to join on General McClernand's right, thus abandoning my original camps and line. This was about 10 1/2 a.m., at which time the enemy had made a furious attack on General McClernand's whole front. He straggled most determinedly, but, finding him pressed, I moved McDowell's brigade directly against the left flank of the enemy, forced him back some distance, and then directed the men to avail themselves of every cover-trees, fallen timber, and a wooded valley to our right. We held this position for four long hours, sometimes gaining and at others losing ground; General McClernand and myself acting in perfect concert, and struggling to maintain this line."

Meanwhile, when Grant heard the sounds of artillery that morning, he headed toward Pittsburg Landing via boat, and he reached the battlefield around 8:30 a.m. to find his army in a precarious position. Once he arrived he immediately went about trying to order reinforcements to bolster his retreating line, including Bull Nelson's division (several miles away at Savannah) and Lew Wallace's division, which had been held in reserve at Crump's Landing.

Lew Wallace was considered a rising star in the Union Army, but his career was ruined by the events of April 6. After being ordered into battle by Grant, confusion in the battle plans and the rapid retreat of the Union army resulted in Wallace taking a different route than the one Grant ordered, and when Wallace arrived he found himself in the rear of the advancing Confederate army. Before Wallace could take advantage of that position in the Confederate rear, however, he was ordered to countermarch back toward Pittsburg Landing. Wallace's division would arrive there at about 7:00 p.m., around the end of the first day's fighting. Grant would later blame Wallace in his memoirs, writing, "I never could see and do not now see why any order was necessary further than to direct him to come to Pittsburg landing, without specifying by what route. His was one of three veteran divisions that had been in battle, and its absence was severely felt. Later in the war General Wallace would not have made the mistake that he committed on the 6th of April, 1862. I presume his idea was that by taking the route he did he would be able to come around on the flank or rear of the enemy, and thus perform an act of heroism that would redound to the credit of his command, as well as to the benefit of his country."

Lew Wallace

Grant was circumspect in discussing the effectiveness of the Confederates' initial assault:

"The Confederate assaults were made with such a disregard of losses on their own side that our line of tents soon fell into their hands. The ground on which the battle was fought was undulating, heavily timbered with scattered clearings, the woods giving some protection to the troops on both sides. There was also considerable underbrush. A number of attempts were made by the enemy to turn our right flank, where Sherman was posted, but every effort was repulsed with heavy loss. But the front attack was kept up so vigorously that, to prevent the success of these attempts to get on our flanks, the National troops were compelled, several times, to take positions to the rear nearer Pittsburg landing."

Chapter 5: The Hornet's Nest

"There was no hour during the day when there was not heavy firing and generally hard fighting at some point on the line, but seldom at all points at the same time. It was a case of Southern dash against Northern pluck and endurance." – Ulysses S. Grant

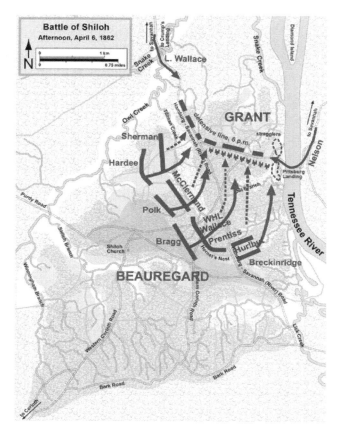

As the Union soldiers fell back, their center took up a defensive position in a field full of natural features ideal for maintaining a defensive posture. The Hornet's Nest was a field that ran along an open road, but trying to advance up the road exposed attackers to an enfilading fire from the side, so Confederate soldiers would end up throwing themselves against Union defenders from the divisions led by Benjamin M. Prentiss and W. H. L. Wallace over the course of several hours. In the biography of his father, William Preston Johnston described the Hornet's Nest: "Here, behind a dense thicket on the crest of a hill, was posted a strong force of as hardy troops as ever fought, almost perfectly protected by the conformation of the ground, and by logs and other rude and hastily prepared defenses. To assail it an open field had to be passed, enfiladed by the fire of its batteries. It was nicknamed by the Confederates, by a very mild metaphor, 'The Hornets' nest.'"

The road on the left and Hornet's Nest to the right of it.

Further evidence of the inexperience on both sides would be found in the action around the
Hornet's Nest. Historians estimate that the Confederates made somewhere between 8-14 separate
assaults against the Union line in the Hornet's Nest, even though the position could be turned if
the Confederates on their left or right pushed back one or both of the Union army's flanks, which
was eventually what happened.

Wallace

Once again, officers struggled to maintain any sense of control over their men in the Hornet's Nest, with units making their own arbitrary decisions down to the regimental and battalion levels. For the Union this was further complicated by the fact that division commander Wallace was mortally wounded in the struggle. Ultimately, Confederates led by Brig. Gen. Daniel Ruggles brought nearly 50 cannons to bear on the Hornet's Nest and were able to provide withering fire, compelling Union defenders, some of whom had been in the Hornet's Nest for 7 hours, to fall back.

However, as the Union line generally began to crumble and retreat, not everyone got the message. In the center of the line was Prentiss's division, and his men became a salient in the Union line when the units on their flanks fell back. Grant explained in his memoirs:

"In one of the backward moves, on the 6th, the division commanded by General Prentiss did not fall back with the others. This left his flanks exposed and enabled the enemy to capture him with about 2,200 of his officers and men. General Badeau gives four o'clock of the 6th as about the time this capture took place. He may be right as to the time, but my recollection is that the hour was later. General Prentiss himself gave the hour as half-past five. I was with him, as I was with each of the division commanders that day, several times, and my recollection is that the last time I was with him was about half-past four, when his division was standing up firmly and the General was as cool as if expecting victory. But no matter whether it was four or later, the story that he and his command were surprised and captured in their camps is without any foundation whatever. If it had been true, as currently reported at the time and yet believed by thousands of people, that Prentiss and his division had been captured in their beds, there would not have been an all-day struggle, with the loss of thousands killed and wounded on the Confederate side."

Prentiss

It was also during the fighting around the Hornet's Nest that the Confederates suffered their worst casualty of all. As the Union army kept retreating, Johnston began planning for his army to wheel on its left, thereby advancing his left flank toward Pittsburg Landing and the Tennessee River. Riding near Colonel Munford while watching the advancing Confederates attacking the retreating Federals. Munford later recalled their exchange: "We sat on our horses, side by side, watching that brigade as it swept over the ridge; and, as the colors dipped out of sight, the general said to me, 'That checkmates them.' I told him I was glad to hear him announce 'checkmate,' but that 'he must excuse so poor a player for saying he could not see it.' He laughed, and said, 'Yes, sir, that mates them.' The completion of this movement faced the troops at an angle of about 45° toward the left, when the forward movement became uniform."

At this point, Johnston again exposed himself to danger by riding to an advanced spot near the front of the line. Munford recounted, "Their bodies were almost entirely protected, but their position enabled them to see the entire persons of our troops, who, when they came in sight, were within easy musket-range and wholly unprotected. They opened upon us a murderous fire. General Johnston moved forward with his staff to a depression about thirty yards behind our front line, where the bullets passed over our heads; but he could see more than half of his line, and, if an emergency arose, could meet it promptly."

After being told by one of his officers that one of the man's brigades wouldn't charge forward, Johnston personally inspired them and prepared to lead a charge: "General Johnston rode out in front, and slowly down the line. His hat was off. His sword rested in its scabbard. In his right hand he held a little tin cup, the memorial of an incident that had occurred earlier in the day. As they were passing through a captured camp, an officer had brought from a tent a number of valuable articles, calling General Johnston's attention to them. He answered, with some sternness: 'None of that, sir; we are not here for plunder!' And then, as if regretting the sharpness of the rebuke, for the anger of the just cuts deep, he added, taking this little tin cup, 'Let this be my share of the spoils to-day.'"

Johnston then began directing an advance against the Union left in a cotton field along a peach orchard, riding in the center of his men's front. While ordering them to prepare to use bayonets during the charge, the two sides exchanged a fierce volley of gunfire and artillery. The Union defenders began to fall back, but Johnston's horse had been shot in 4 places, and one of the bullets had cut a hole in the sole of his boot, a seemingly insignificant wound. But as it turned out, the minie ball, which historians now believe was friendly fire, had clipped an artery, and unbeknownst to Johnston, he was bleeding heavily in his boot.

Governor Harris, who was with Johnston at the time, recalled the general's final moments:

"As I approached him, he said 'Governor, they came very near putting me hors de combat in that charge,' holding out and pointing to his foot. Looking at it, I discovered that a musket-ball had struck the edge of the sole of his boot, cutting the sole clear across, and ripping it off to the toe. I asked eagerly: 'Are you wounded? Did the ball touch your foot?' He said, 'No;' and was proceeding to make other remarks, when a Federal battery opened fire from a position which enfiladed our line just established. He paused in the middle of. a sentence to say, 'Order Colonel Statham to wheel his regiment to the left, charge, and take that battery.' I galloped to Colonel Statham, only about two hundred yards distant, gave the order, galloped back to the general where a moment before I had left him, rode up to his right side, and said, 'General, your order is delivered, and Colonel Statham is in motion;' but, as I was uttering this sentence, the general reeled from me in a manner that indicated he was falling from his horse. I put my left arm around his neck, grasping the collar of his coat, and righted him up in the saddle, bending forward as I did so, and, looking him in the face, said, 'General, are you wounded?' In a very deliberate and emphatic tone he answered, 'Yes, and I fear seriously.' At that moment I requested Captain Wickham to go with all possible speed for a surgeon, to send the first one he could find, but to proceed until he could find Dr. Yandell, the medical director, and bring him. The general's hold upon his rein relaxed, and it dropped from his hand. Supporting him with my left hand, I gathered his rein with my right, in which I held my own, and guided both horses to a valley about 150 yards in rear of our line, where I halted, dropped myself between the two horses, pulling the general over upon me, and eased him to the ground as gently as I could. When laid upon the ground, with eager anxiety I asked many questions about his wounds, to which he gave no answer, not even a look of intelligence.

Supporting his head with one hand, I untied his cravat, unbuttoned his collar and vest, and tore his shirts open with the other, for the purpose of finding the wound, feeling confident from his condition that he had a more serious wound than the one which I knew was bleeding profusely in the right leg; but I found no other, and, as I afterward ascertained, he had no other. Raising his head, I poured a little brandy into his mouth, which he swallowed, and in a few moments I repeated the brandy, but he made no effort to swallow; it gurgled in his throat in his effort to breathe, and I turned his head so as to relieve him.

In a few moments he ceased to breathe. I did not consult my watch, but my impression is that lie did not live more than thirty or forty minutes from the time he received the wound."

As Johnston's son would note in his biography, the wound "was not necessarily fatal. General Johnston's own knowledge of military surgery was adequate for its control by an extemporized tourniquet, had he been aware or regardful of its nature." Unfortunately for the Confederates, the severity of the wound was only discovered upon their commander's death. Johnston's body was wrapped up so that his fate was hidden from his troops as the officers on the scene raced back toward the rear to inform Beauregard. At a critical juncture in the fighting, with the Union army still on the ropes and the Confederates seeking to deal it a death blow, the Confederates had lost their commander.

The monument to Johnston on the Shiloh battlefield

Chapter 6: Holding the Line

As the Confederate commander fell dead, the Union line had fallen back to a more condensed line around Pittsburg Landing itself, with a three mile front from the Tennessee River on their left to the River Road on their right, intentionally keeping the road open for Lew Wallace's lost division. By this time, Don Carlos Buell's army was getting near enough that an advanced brigade of his under Col. Jacob Ammen was ferried across the Tennessee River and took up a spot on the left of the Union's defensive line. The new position, so close to the river, allowed for the use of Union gunboats in the defense as well.

Braxton Bragg summed up the situation in the late afternoon in his report:

"It was now probably past 4 o'clock, the descending sun warning us to press our advantage and finish the work before night should compel us to desist. Fairly in motion, these commands again, with a common head and a common purpose, swept all before them. Neither battery nor battalion could withstand their onslaught. Passing through camp after camp, rich in military spoils of every kind, the enemy was driven headlong from every position and thrown in confused masses upon the river bank, behind his heavy artillery and under cover of his gunboats at the Landing. He had left nearly the whole of his light artillery in our hands and some 3,000 or more prisoners, who were cut off from their retreat by the closing in of our troops on the left under Major-General

Polk, with a portion of his reserve corps, and Brigadier-General Ruggles, with Anderson's and Pond's brigades of his division.

The prisoners were dispatched to the rear under a proper guard, all else being left upon the field that we might press our advantage. The enemy had fallen back in much confusion and was crowded in unorganized masses on the river bank, vainly striving to cross. They were covered by a battery of heavy guns, well served, and their two gunboats, which now poured a heavy fire upon our supposed positions, for we were entirely hid by the forest. Their fire, though terrific in sound and producing some consternation at first, did us no damage, as the shells all passed over and exploded far beyond our positions."

Despite the strength of the Union's defensive position, two Confederate brigades made a desperate charge only to be repulsed. Around 6:00 p.m., Beauregard made one of the war's most controversial decisions by calling off the Confederate advance against the tightly huddled Union army, which was in the position of being forced to either defend successfully or be driven into the river and destroyed. At the time, Beauregard figured that he had the battle won anyway, having surrounded Grant's men along the river, and he didn't want to risk a confusing night attack against Grant's line, which was concentrated with artillery as a result of being so tightly encircled. That night, the overconfident Beauregard wired Richmond to inform authorities that the Confederates had won a "complete victory":

"The battle commenced on the 6th of April. We attacked the enemy in a strong position in front of Pittsburg; and, after a severe battle of ten hours, duration, thanks be to the Almighty, we gained a complete victory, driving the enemy from every position. The loss on both sides is heavy, including the commander-in-chief, General A. S. Johnston, who fell gallantly leading his troops into the thickest of the fight.

The chief command then devolved upon me, though at the time I was greatly prostrated and suffering from the prolonged sickness with which I had been afflicted since early in February. The responsibility was one which, in my physical condition, I would have gladly avoided, though cast upon me when our forces were successfully pushing the enemy back upon the Tennessee River, and though supported on the immediate field by such corps commanders as Major-Generals Polk, Bragg, and Hardee, and Brigadier-General Breckinridge commanding the reserve.

It was after six o'clock, P. M., as before said, when the enemy's last position was carried, and his force finally broke and sought refuge behind a commanding eminence, covering the Pittsburg Landing, not more than half a mile distant, and under the guns of the gunboats, which opened on our eager columns a fierce and annoying fire with shot and shell of the heaviest description. Darkness was close at hand. Officers and men were exhausted by a combat of over twelve hours, without food, and jaded by the march of the preceding day through mud and water; it was, therefore, impossible to collect the rich and opportune spoils of war scattered broadcast on the field left in our possession, and impracticable to make any effective dispositions for their removal to the rear."

Beauregard would later be forced to explain, "I thought I had General Grant just where I wanted him and could finish him up in the morning." Beauregard was terribly wrong because he was unaware that Don Carlos Buell's Army of the Ohio was within marching distance of Grant's men. That night, 18,000 more soldiers slipped into Pittsburg Landing, heavily bolstering Grant's forces and leaving Beauregard's men well outnumbered. At the same time, Grant's army was so disorganized that he didn't even attempt to reestablish his soldiers in their proper regiments, noting in his memoirs, "The nature of this battle was such that cavalry could not be used in front; I therefore formed ours into line in rear, to stop stragglers—of whom there were many. When there would be enough of them to make a show, and after they had recovered from their fright, they would be sent to reinforce some part of the line which needed support, without regard to their companies, regiments or brigades."

Buell

Grant also recalled his first meeting with Buell that night:

On one occasion during the day I rode back as far as the river and met General Buell, who had just arrived; I do not remember the hour, but at that time there probably were as many as four or five thousand stragglers lying under cover of the river bluff, panic-stricken, most of whom would have been shot where they lay, without resistance, before they would have taken muskets and marched to the front to protect themselves. This meeting between General Buell and myself was on the dispatch-boat used to run between the landing and Savannah. It was brief, and related specially to his getting his troops over the river. As we left the boat together, Buell's attention was attracted by the men lying under cover of the river bank. I saw him berating them and trying to shame them into joining their regiments. He even threatened them with shells from the gunboats near by. But it was all to no effect. Most of these men afterward proved themselves as gallant as any of those who saved the battle from which they had deserted. I have no doubt that this sight impressed General Buell with the idea that a line of retreat would be a good thing just then. If he had come in by the front instead of through the stragglers in the rear, he would have thought and felt differently. Could he have come through the Confederate rear, he would have witnessed there a scene similar to that at our own. The distant rear of an army engaged in battle is not the best place from which to judge correctly what is going on in front. Later in the war, while occupying the country between the Tennessee and the Mississippi, I learned that the panic in the Confederate lines had not differed much from that within our own. Some of the country people estimated the stragglers from Johnston's army as high as 20,000. Of course this was an exaggeration."

Buell wasn't the only one to express serious concern about the state of Grant's army. A news correspondent with the *Cincinnatti Gazette* reported about the scene he saw that night:

"Our whole army is crowded in the region of Wallace's camps, and to a circuit of one-half to two-thirds of a mile around the landing. We have been falling back all day. We can do it no more. The next repulse puts us into the river; and there are not transports enough to cross a single division till the enemy would be upon us. .... We have lost nearly all our camps and camp-equipage. We have lost nearly half our field-artillery. We have lost a division general, and two or three regiments of our soldiers as prisoners. We have lost --how dreadfully we are afraid to think — in killed and wounded. The hospitals are full to overflowing. A long ridge-bluff is set apart for surgical uses. It is covered with the maimed, the dead, and the dying. And our men are discouraged by prolonged defeat. . . . Meanwhile, there is a lull in the firing. For the first time since sunrise you fail to catch the angry rattle of musketry or the heavy booming of the field-guns. . . . On the bluffs above the river is a sight that may well make our cheeks tingle. There are not less than 5,000 skulkers lining the banks… Remember the situation. It was half-past 4 o'clock-perhaps a quarter later still. Every division of our army on the field had been repulsed. The enemy were in the camps of four out of five of them. We were driven to within little over half a mile of the landing. Behind us was a deep, rapid river. Before us was a victorious enemy. And still there was an hour for fighting. 'Oh, that night or Blucher would come!' 'Oh, that night or Lew Wallace would come!'

Nelson's division of General Buell's army evidently couldn't cross in time to do us much good. We didn't yet know why Lew Wallace wasn't on the ground. In the justice of our cause, and in that semicircle of twenty-two guns in position, lay all the hope we could see."

However, those who were aware of Buell's location were a lot more confident about the Union's chances, including some of the Confederates. As Buell's army began to cross the Tennessee River, Confederate cavalry under the legendary cavalier Nathan Bedford Forrest detected the presence of Buell's reinforcements and reported the intelligence to Beauregard, but that contradicted other intelligence Beauregard had received that claimed Buell's army was not marching toward Pittsburg Landing. While Beauregard remained confident about his chances the next day, Forrest confided to brigadier Patrick Cleburne, "If the enemy comes on us in the morning, we'll be whipped like hell."

Grant famously shared Forrest's confidence as well, later writing in his memoirs, "So confident was I before firing had ceased on the 6th that the next day would bring victory to our arms if we could only take the initiative, that I visited each division commander in person before any reinforcements had reached the field. I directed them to throw out heavy lines of skirmishers in the morning as soon as they could see, and push them forward until they found the enemy, following with their entire divisions in supporting distance, and to engage the enemy as soon as found. To Sherman I told the story of the assault at Fort Donelson, and said that the same tactics would win at Shiloh. Victory was assured when Wallace arrived, even if there had been no other support. I was glad, however, to see the reinforcements of Buell and credit them with doing all there was for them to do."

Grant's confidence wasn't simply a matter of hindsight. That evening, as the cries of the wounded pierced the air and kept soldiers on both sides awake, and as a thunderstorm passed through and brought a downpour, Sherman found Grant sitting under a tree. Sherman turned to the commander and said, "Well, Grant, we've had the devil's own day, haven't we?" Grant looked up at Sherman and replied, "Yes. Lick 'em tomorrow though."

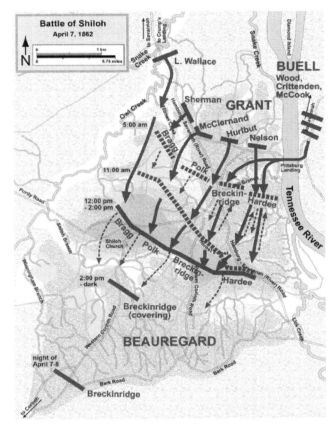

The Confederates had suffered over 8,000 casualties on April 6, including their commanding general, and the disorder and number of stragglers left Beauregard with an estimated 20,000 soldiers fit for combat the following morning. Meanwhile, Buell's army had added nearly 20,000 men to Grant's army, bringing its effective fighting numbers up to about 45,000. On top of that, many Confederates had retired to their rear for lack of supplies, with some of Polk's men reportedly retiring as far back as their bivouac site on the night before the battle.

Beauregard was still unaware that he was badly outnumbered and planned to advance in the morning, only to be surprised that Grant's army began a general advance along their entire line at dawn. Indicative of the back-and-forth sniping that would take place after the battle, Buell and

Grant were operating their men independently, with Buell insisting on controlling his own army. Of course, the Confederates had suffered a similar state of disorganization, with little command control above the brigade level, and there was even a delay bringing Polk's division back to the battlefield, where he was supposed to represent the center of the line. It wasn't until 10:00 a.m. that Beauregard had a stable defensive line.

Ironically, it was Lew Wallace's lost division, which had found its way to the right of the Union line, that saw the first major fighting as it began driving back a Confederate brigade led by Col. Preston Pond around 7:00 a.m. Sherman later noted of the fighting around there that it was "the severest musketry fire I ever heard." On the other side of the line, Bull Nelson's division advanced as far as the Hornet's Nest by the late morning, along with Crittenden's and McCook's divisions, where they first met serious resistance from Beauregard's army.

By noon, Beauregard was aware of his precarious predicament. In addition to being heavily outnumbered, he was running critically low on supplies and ammunition. Realizing that he could no longer take the offensive, Beauregard launched diversionary counterattacks near Shiloh Church, which gave the Union officers pause and made them more cautious, and he then began an orderly retreat of his army, using Breckinridge's 5,000 men as a rearguard. As the Confederates began heading back toward Corinth, the exhausted Union soldiers were only too happy not to give serious chase, except for Lew Wallace's relatively fresh division, which kept up an unsupported chase until nightfall.

With the fighting of April 7 over, Grant and Buell began arguing over whether or not to continue the pursuit of the Confederates, given that there was about an hour of daylight still to use. But Grant had made his decision, arguing that his men were too exhausted. With that, the Battle of Shiloh was over.

Chapter 8: The Aftermath of Shiloh

On April 8, Grant had Sherman conduct a cautious pursuit of the Confederates, which led to a brief skirmish at Fallen Timbers that nearly changed the course of the Civil War. Sherman sent forth skirmishers from the 77th Ohio, which was approaching a Confederate field hospital until it got tangled up among fallen trees. The Confederate rearguard consisted of cavalry led by Forrest, who surprised the 77th Ohio and Sherman with a daring charge led personally by Forrest himself. Sherman explained:

> "As we approached the ridge, down came, with a yell, Forrest's cavalry firing left and right with pistols, over the skirmish line, over the supports, and right among me and my staff. Fortunately, I had sent my adjutant, Hammond, back to the brigade to come forward into line quickly. My Aide-de-Camp, McCoy, was knocked down, horse and rider, into the mud, but I and the rest of my staff ingloriously fled, pell mell, throught he mud, closely followed by Forrest and his men, with pistols already emptied. We

sought safety behind the brigade in the act of forming 'forward into line,' and Forrest and his followers were in turn 'surprised' by a fire of the brigade which emptied many a saddle, and gave Forrest himself a painful wound, but he escaped to the woods on the south of the road."

As it turned out, Forrest had charged out far in advance of his own men and only became aware of it when Sherman's soldiers started yelling out, "Kill him! Kill him and his horse!" From point blank range, a Union soldier on the ground pushed his musket right up to Forrest's side and fired a shot that struck him above the hip and nearly into his spine. Somehow Forrest managed to lift up the soldier and shield his own body with the man as he began riding toward the Confederate line. Forrest would later be credited with killing 30 Union soldiers and losing 29 horses, and Fallen Timbers gave him one of the many wounds he would suffer during the war. Sherman later noted that had Forrest's pistols not been empty, "my career would have ended right there."

Once Beauregard's army had safely made it back to Corinth, the post-battle analysis and accusations began in earnest. Grant's army had just won the biggest battle in the history of North America, with nearly 24,000 combined casualties among the Union and Confederate forces. Usually the winner of a major battle is hailed as a hero, but Grant was hardly a winner at Shiloh. The Battle of Shiloh took place before costlier battles at places like Antietam and Gettysburg, so the extent of the casualties at Shiloh shocked the nation. Moreover, at Shiloh the casualties were viewed as needless; Grant was pilloried for allowing the Confederates to take his forces by surprise, as well as the failure to build defensive earthworks and fortifications, which nearly resulted in a rout of his army. Speculation again arose that Grant had a drinking problem, and some even assumed he was drunk during the battle. Though the Union won, it was largely viewed that their success owed to the heroics of General Sherman in rallying the men and Don Carlos Buell arriving with his army, and General Buell was happy to receive the credit at Grant's expense.

Grant himself was not above playing the blame game. Miscommunication between Grant and division commander Lew Wallace resulted in Wallace failing to properly march his men into the fight while the Confederates were advancing on the first day. For the rest of his life, Grant blamed Wallace for the failure, but historians do not believe the miscommunication was actually his fault. Nevertheless, with Grant and Halleck heaping the blame Wallace for the near loss at Shiloh, it permanently tarnished Wallace's military career, and he was removed from his command in June 1862. Still, it's likely that any military accomplishments Lew Wallace may have lost out on during the Civil War would have been eclipsed by his authorship in 1880 of the classic *Ben-Hur* anyway.

Although Halleck agreed with Grant that Lew Wallace deserved the blame Grant was giving him, Grant was ultimately the fall guy. As a result of the Battle of Shiloh, General Halleck demoted Grant to second-in-command of all armies in his department, an utterly powerless position. And when word of what many considered a "colossal blunder" reached Washington, several congressmen insisted that Lincoln replace Grant in the field. Lincoln famously defended Grant, telling critics, "I can't spare this man. He fights."

Lincoln may have defended Grant, but he found precious few supporters, and the negative attention bothered Grant so much that it is widely believed he turned to alcohol again. While historians still debate that, what is known is that he considered resigning his commission, only to be dissuaded from doing so by General Sherman. While Grant was at the low point of his career, Sherman's career had been resurrected, and he was promoted to major-general the following month. With rumors that Grant was falling off the wagon with alcohol, Sherman tried to reassure Grant not to quit the war, telling him "some happy accident might restore you to favor and your true place." Sherman's appreciation of Grant's faith in his abilities cemented his loyalty and established a friendship between the two that would last a lifetime. In later years Sherman would say, "General Grant is a great general! He stood by me when I was crazy, and I stood by him when he was drunk; and now, sir, we stand by each other always."

Although Grant stayed in the army, it's unclear what position he would have held if Lincoln had not called Halleck to Washington to serve as general-in-chief in July 1862. At the same time, Halleck was given that position in large measure due to Grant's successes in the department under Halleck's command. Thankfully for the Union, Halleck's departure meant that Grant was reinstated as commander.

Sherman captured the essence of it all in his memoirs:

"Probably no single battle of the war gave rise to such wild and damaging reports. It was publicly asserted at the North that our army was taken completely by surprise; that the rebels caught us in our tents; bayoneted the men in their beds; that General Grant was drunk; that Buell's opportune arrival saved the Army of the Tennessee from utter annihilation, etc. These reports were in a measure sustained by the published opinions of Generals Buell, Nelson, and others, who had reached the steamboat-landing from the east, just before nightfall of the 6th, when there was a large crowd of frightened, stampeded men, who clamored and declared that our army was all destroyed and beaten. Personally I saw General Grant, who with his staff visited me about 10 a.m. of the 6th, when we were desperately engaged. But we had checked the headlong assault of our enemy, and then held our ground. This gave him great satisfaction, and he told me that things did not look as well over on the left. He also told me that on his way up from Savannah that morning he had stopped at Crump's Landing, and had ordered Lew Wallace's division to cross over Snake Creek, so as to come up on my right, telling me to look out for him. He came again just before dark, and described the last assault made by the rebels at the ravine, near the steamboat-landing, which he had repelled by a heavy battery collected under Colonel J. D. Webster and other officers, and he was convinced that the battle was over for that day. He ordered me to be ready to assume the offensive in the morning, saying that, as he had observed at Fort Donelson at the crisis of the battle, both sides seemed defeated, and whoever assumed the offensive was sure to win. General Grant also explained to me that General Buell had reached the bank of the Tennessee River opposite Pittsburg Landing, and was in the act of ferrying his troops across at the time he was speaking to me."

Naturally, Grant wasn't the only one to come under fire. In the aftermath of the battle, Beauregard's judgment came under heavy scrutiny from President Davis and his commanders for choosing not to exploit the tactical advantage presented the first day, which ultimately resulted in major losses. To outside observers and many Confederates, Johnston's men had been gloriously and successfully advancing until his mortal wounding, only for Grant's forces to turn the tide the following day with Beauregard in command. Jefferson Davis would bemoan that Johnston's loss was a turning point not just in the battle but the entire war itself.

Naturally, Johnston was revered in his death as a national hero. Beauregard issued a general order to the army after Shiloh mourning his death and praising Johnston:

"Soldiers: Your late commander-in-chief, General A. S. Johnston, is dead; a fearless soldier, a sagacious captain, a reproachless man, has fallen-one who, in his devotion to our cause, shrank from no sacrifice; one who, animated by a sense of duty, and sustained by a sublime courage, challenged danger, and perished gallantly for his country while leading forward his brave columns to victory. His signal example of heroism and patriotism, if imitated, would make his army invincible.

A grateful country will mourn his loss, revere his name, and cherish his many virtues."

Before learning of the disastrous second day of the Battle of Shiloh, Davis announced the victory and the death of Johnston to the Confederate Congress:

"The great importance of the news just received from Tennessee induces me to depart from the established usages, and to make to you this communication in advance of official reports. From official telegraphic dispatches, received from official sources, I am able to announce to you, with entire confidence, that it has pleased Almighty God to crown the Confederate arms with a glorious and decisive victory over our invaders.

On the morning of the 6th, the converging columns of our army were combined by its commander-in-chief, General Albert Sidney Johnston, in an assault on the Federal army, then encamped near Pittsburg, on the Tennessee River.

After a hard-fought battle of ten hours, the enemy was driven in disorder from his position, and pursued to the Tennessee River, where, under the cover of the gunboats, he was at the last accounts endeavoring to effect his retreat by aid of his transports. The details of this great battle are yet too few and incomplete to enable me to distinguish with merited praise all of those who may have conspicuously earned the right to such distinction, and I prefer to delay our own gratification in recommending them to your special notice, rather than incur the risk of wounding the feelings of any by failing to include them in the list. When such a victory has been won over troops as numerous, well disciplined, armed, and appointed, as those which have been so signally routed, we may well conclude that one common spirit of unflinching bravery and devotion to our country's cause must have animated every breast, from that of the commanding general to that of the humblest patriot who served in the ranks. There is enough in the continued presence of invaders on our soil to chasten our exultation over this brilliant success, and to remind us of the grave duty of continued exertion until we shall extort from a proud and vainglorious enemy the reluctant acknowledgment of our right to self-government.

But an All-wise Creator has been pleased, while vouchsafing to us his countenance in battle, to afflict us with a severe dispensation, to which we must bow in humble submission. The last, long, lingering hope has disappeared, and it is but too true that General Albert Sidney Johnston is no more! The tale of his death is simply narrated in a dispatch from Colonel William Preston, in the following words:

General Johnston fell yesterday, at half-past 2 o'clock, while leading a successful charge, turning the enemy's right, and gaining a brilliant victory. A Min16-ball cut the artery of his leg, but he rode on until, from loss of blood, he fell exhausted, and died without pain in a few moments. His body has been intrusted to me by General Beauregard, to be taken to New Orleans, and remain until instructions are received from his family.

My long and close friendship with this departed chieftain and patriot forbid me to trust myself in giving vent to the feelings which this intelligence has evoked. Without doing injustice to the living, it may safely be said that our loss is irreparable. Among the shining hosts of the great and good who now cluster around the banner of our country, there exists no purer spirit, no more heroic soul, than that of the illustrious man whose death I join you in lamenting.

In his death he has illustrated the character for which through life he was conspicuous — that of singleness of purpose and devotion to duty with his whole energies. Bent on obtaining the victory, which he deemed essential to his country's cause, he rode on to the accomplishment of his object, forgetful of self, while his very life-blood was ebbing away fast. His last breath cheered his comrades on to victory. The last sound he heard was their shout of victory. His last thought was his country, and long and deeply will his country mourn his loss."

Albert Sidney Johnston was one of the most experienced leaders the Confederates had, but historians judging his decisions in the Western department have found plenty to criticize. Grant's memoirs continue to be celebrated and critically acclaimed for their candor, and he gave a rather candid opinion of Albert Sidney Johnston's generalship:

> "I had known Johnston slightly in the Mexican war and later as an officer in the regular army. He was a man of high character and ability. His contemporaries at West Point, and officers generally who came to know him personally later and who remained on our side, expected him to prove the most formidable man to meet that the Confederacy would produce.
>
> I once wrote that nothing occurred in his brief command of an army to prove or disprove the high estimate that had been placed upon his military ability; but after studying the orders and dispatches of Johnston I am compelled to materially modify my views of that officer's qualifications as a soldier. My judgment now is that he was vacillating and undecided in his actions.
>
> All the disasters in Kentucky and Tennessee were so discouraging to the authorities in Richmond that Jefferson Davis wrote an unofficial letter to Johnston expressing his own anxiety and that of the public, and saying that he had made such defence as was dictated by long friendship, but that in the absence of a report he needed facts. The letter was not a reprimand in direct terms, but it was evidently as much felt as though it had been one. General Johnston raised another army as rapidly as he could, and fortified or strongly intrenched at Corinth. He knew the National troops were preparing to attack him in his chosen position. But he had evidently become so disturbed at the results of his operations that he resolved to strike out in an offensive campaign which would restore all that was lost, and if successful accomplish still more. We have the authority of his son and biographer for saying that his plan was to attack the forces at Shiloh and crush them; then to cross the Tennessee and destroy the army of Buell, and push the war across the Ohio River. The design was a bold one; but we have the same authority for saying that in the execution Johnston showed vacillation and indecision. He left Corinth on the 2d of April and was not ready to attack until the 6th. The distance his army had to march was less than twenty miles. Beauregard, his second in command, was opposed to the attack for two reasons: first, he thought, if let alone the National troops would attack the Confederates in their intrenchments; second, we were in ground of our own choosing and would necessarily be intrenched. Johnston not only listened to the objection of Beauregard to an attack, but held a council of war on the

subject on the morning of the 5th. On the evening of the same day he was in consultation with some of his generals on the same subject, and still again on the morning of the 6th. During this last consultation, and before a decision had been reached, the battle began by the National troops opening fire on the enemy. This seemed to settle the question as to whether there was to be any battle of Shiloh. It also seems to me to settle the question as to whether there was a surprise.

I do not question the personal courage of General Johnston, or his ability. But he did not win the distinction predicted for him by many of his friends. He did prove that as a general he was over-estimated."

Despite Grant's estimation, there's no question that Johnston's deaths was one of the great what-ifs of the Civil War, if only because the Confederate commanding generals in the West that followed would prove to be wildly inept. Pemberton would surrender tens of thousands of soldiers to Grant the following year at Vicksburg, Bragg would prove himself not up to the challenge of commanding an army at Chickamauga and Chattanooga, Joseph Johnston would be relieved of command during Sherman's 1864 Atlanta Campaign, and John Bell Hood would all but destroy his own army against George H. Thomas in the Franklin-Nashville Campaign. Albert Sidney Johnston may not have been as great a general as his friend Jefferson Davis thought he was, but it's likely that he would have provided far more competent leadership in the critical Western theater than the Confederates otherwise had received. And with Robert E. Lee's Army of Northern Virginia constantly frustrating the Army of the Potomac in the East, the results of the Civil War may have been far different had Grant and Sherman not been so successful throughout the West.

At the same time, Johnston's death early in the war has also had the effect of obscuring his name and legacy among those who read about and study the Civil War. Despite being the most senior officer to die in battle and one of only two commanding generals to be killed in action during the Civil War, Americans are far less familiar with the Confederacy's highest ranking field officer than they are with men who were his junior in rank and ability.

Johnston's tomb in Austin, Texas

Bibliography

Shiloh: Bloody April. Wiley Sword. William Morrow & Company, Inc., 1974

Tennessee's War 1861-1865. ed. by Stanley F. Horn. Tennessee Civil War Centenial Commission, 1965.

The Shiloh Campaign: March - April 1862. David G. Martin. Combined Books, 1996

Guide To The Battle Of Shiloh. ed. by Jay Luvaas, Stephen Bowman, Leonard Fullenkamp. University of Kansas Press, 1996

Chris Emmett. The General and the Poet: Albert Sidney Johnston and Sidney Lanier: A Luminary Follows a Star. San Antonio, TX: Naylor. 1937.

William Preston Johnston. The Life of Gen. Albert Sidney Johnston, Embracing his Services in the Armies of the United States, the Republic of Texas, and the Confederate States. New York: D. Appleton. 1878.

Avery C. Moore. Destiny's Soldier: General Albert Sidney Johnston. San Francisco, CA: Fearon. 1958.

Charles P. Roland. Albert Sidney Johnston: Soldier of Three Republics. Austin, TX: University of Texas Press. 1964.

Brown, Dee. (Stan Banash, editor). *Dee Brown's Civil War Anthology*. Santa Fe: Clear Light Publishers, 1998.

Davis, Burke. *Sherman's March*. New York: Random House, 1980.

Fellman, Michael. *Citizen Sherman*. Kansas: University Press of Kansas, 1997.

Gaffney, P. and D. Gaffney. *The Civil War: Exploring History One week at a Time*. New York: Hyperion, 2011.

Gallagher, Gary W. *The Union War*. Cambridge: Harvard University Press, 2011.

Grant, U. S. (John. Y. Simon, editor). *Ulysses S. Grant: Memoirs and Selected Letters*. The Library of America, 1984.

Hart, Liddell, B. H. *Sherman: Soldier, Realist, American*. Dodd, Mead & Co., 1929.

Hesseltine, William B. *Ulysses S. Grant, Politician*. Dodd, 1935.

Hirshson, Stanley P. *The White Tecumseh: A Biography of General William T. Sherman*. John Wiley & Sons, 1997.

Lewis, Lloyd *Sherman: Fighting Prophet*. University of Nebraska Press, 1993.

Marszalek, John F. *Sherman: A Soldier's Passion for Order*. Southern Illinois University Press, 2007.

New York Times: "BENJAMIN HARRISON. 'SORROW AT THE CAPITAL: FORMAL ANNOUNCEMENT BY THE PRESIDENT--EULOGIES IN THE SENATE'" (1857-1922), February 15, 1891. Retrieved on 4.07.2012 via ProQuest Historical.

Porter, Horace. *Campaigning With Grant*. New York: University Press, 1961.

Sherman, W. T. (Charles Royster, notes). *Memoirs of General William T. Sherman*, Vol. I and II. The Library of America, 1990.

Wright, Mike. *What They Didn't Teach You About the Civil War*. Novato, CA: Presidio Press, 1998.

The Second Battle of Bull Run

Chapter 1: The Impact of the Peninsula Campaign

The Second Battle of Bull Run would be fought in late August about 25 miles outside of Washington D.C., but the Confederacy was facing a potential disaster around Richmond a few months earlier. The Union Army of the Potomac under "The Young Napoleon", George McClellan, had pushed the heavily outnumbered Army of Northern Virginia under Joseph Johnston to the outskirts of Richmond, seeking to capture the Confederate capital and possibly end the war.

During the Civil War, one of the tales that was often told among Confederate soldiers was that Joseph E. Johnston was a crack shot who was a better bird hunter than just about everyone else in the South. However, as the story went, Johnston would never take the shot when asked to, complaining that something was wrong with the situation that prevented him from being able to shoot the bird when it was time. The story is almost certainly apocryphal, used to demonstrate the Confederates' frustration with a man who everyone regarded as a capable general. Johnston began the Civil War as one of the senior commanders, leading (ironically) the Army of the Potomac to victory in the Battle of First Bull Run over Irvin McDowell's Union Army. But Johnston would become known more for losing by not winning. Johnston was never badly beaten in battle, but he had a habit of "strategically withdrawing" until he had nowhere else to go. Johnston continued to gradually pull his troops back to a line of defense nearer Richmond as McClellan advanced. In conjunction, the U.S. Navy began moving its operations further up the James River, until it could get within 7 miles of the Confederate capital before being opposed by a Southern fort. McClellan continued to attempt to turn Johnston's flank, until the two armies were facing each other along the Chickahominy River. McClellan's Army of the Potomac got close enough to Richmond that they could see the city's church steeples.

McClellan

By the end of May, Stonewall Jackson had startlingly defeated three separate Northern armies in the Valley, inducing Lincoln to hold back the I Corps from McClellan. When McClellan was forced to extend his line north to link up with troops that he expected to be sent overland to him, Johnston learned that McClellan was moving along the Chickahominy River. It was at this point that Johnston got uncharacteristically aggressive. Johnston had run out of breathing space for his army, and he believed McClellan was seeking to link up with McDowell's forces. Moreover, about a third of McClellan's army was south of the river, including Hancock's brigade in the IV Corps, while the other parts of the army were still north of it, offering Johnston an enticing target. Therefore he drew up a very complex plan of attack for different wings of his army, and struck at the Army of the Potomac at the Battle of Seven Pines on May 31, 1862.

Like McDowell's plan for First Bull Run, the plan proved too complicated for Johnston's army to execute, and after a day of bloody fighting little was accomplished from a technical standpoint. At one point during the Battle of Seven Pines, Confederates under General James Longstreet marched in the wrong direction down the wrong road, causing congestion and confusion among other Confederate units and ultimately weakening the effectiveness of the massive Confederate counterattack launched against McClellan.

By the time the fighting was finished, nearly 40,000 had been engaged on both sides, and it was the biggest battle in the Eastern theater to date (second only to Shiloh at the time). However, McClellan was rattled by the attack, and Johnston was seriously wounded during the fighting, resulting in military advisor Robert E. Lee being sent to assume command of the Army of Northern Virginia. McClellan confided to his wife, "I am tired of the sickening sight of the battlefield, with its mangled corpses & poor suffering wounded! Victory has no charms for me when purchased at such cost."

Lee

Although the Battle of Seven Pines was tactically inconclusive, McClellan's resolve to keep pushing forward vanished. He maneuvered his army so that it was all south of the Chickahominy, but as he settled in for an expected siege, Lee went about preparing Richmond's defenses and devising his own aggressive attacks.

From his first day in command, Lee faced a daunting, seemingly impossible challenge. McClellan had maneuvered nearly 100,000 troops to within seven miles of Richmond, three Union units were closing in on General Jackson's Confederates in Virginia's Shenandoah

Valley, and a fourth Union army was camped on the Rappahannock River ostensibly ready to come to McClellan's aid. On June 12, as McClellan sat on Richmond's eastern outskirts waiting for reinforcements, Lee began to ring the city with troop entrenchments.

However, with more Confederate troops swelling the ranks, Lee's army was McClellan's equal by late June, and on June 25, Lee commenced an all-out attempt to destroy McClellan's army in a series of fierce battles known as the Seven Days Battles. After a stalemate in the first fighting at Oak Grove, Lee's army kept pushing ahead, using Stonewall Jackson to attack McClellan's right. Although Stonewall Jackson was unusually lethargic during the week's fighting, the appearance of his "foot cavalry" spooked McClellan even more, and McClellan was now certain he was opposed by 200,000 men, more than double the actual size of Lee's army. It also made McClellan think that the Confederates were threatening his supply line, forcing him to shift his army toward the James River to draw supplies.

On June 26, the Union defenders sharply repulsed the Confederate attacks at Mechanicsville, in part due to the fact that Stonewall Jackson had his troops bivouac for the night despite the fact heavy gunfire indicating a large battle was popping off within earshot.

Stonewall Jackson

McClellan managed to keep his forces in tact (mostly through the efforts of his field generals), ultimately retreating to Harrison's Landing on the James River and establishing a new base of operation. Feeling increasingly at odds with his superiors, in a letter sent from Gaines' Mills, Virginia dated June 28, 1862, a frustrated McClellan wrote to Secretary of War Stanton, "If I save the army now, I tell you plainly that I owe no thanks to any other person in the Washington. You have done your best to sacrifice this army." McClellan's argument, however, flies in the face of common knowledge that he had become so obsessed with having sufficient supplies that he'd actually moved to Gaines' Mill to accommodate the massive amount of provisions he'd accumulated. Ultimately unable to move his cache of supplies as quickly as his men were needed, McClellan eventually ran railroad cars full of food and supplies into the Pamunkey River rather than leave them behind for the Confederates.

Despite the fact all of Lee's battle plans had been poorly executed by his generals, particularly Stonewall Jackson, he ordered one final assault against McClellan's army at Malvern Hill. Incredibly, McClellan was not even on the field for that battle, having left via steamboat back to Harrison's Landing. Biographer Ethan Rafuse notes McClellan's absence from the battlefield was inexcusable, literally leaving the Army of the Potomac leaderless during pitched battle, but McClellan often behaved coolly under fire, so it is likely not a question of McClellan's personal courage.

Ironically, Malvern Hill was one of the Union army's biggest successes during the Peninsula Campaign. Eventually, the Union artillery had silenced its Confederate counterparts, but there was then some miscommunication among the Confederate high command regarding whether or not the proposed assault should go forward. Lee abandoned his intention to assault, and Longstreet was informed, but those that didn't receive orders countermanding the assault went ahead with it, starting with D.H. Hill's division, which never got within 100 yards of the Union line. After the war, D.H. Hill famously referred to Malvern Hill, "It wasn't war. It was murder." Later that evening, as General Isaac Trimble (who is best known for leading a division during Pickett's Charge at Gettysburg) began moving his troops forward as if to attack, he was stopped by Stonewall Jackson, who asked "What are you going to do?" When Trimble replied that he was going to charge, Jackson countered, "General Hill has just tried with his entire division and been repulsed. I guess you'd better not try it."

After Malvern Hill, McClellan withdrew his army to Harrison's Landing, where it was protected by the U.S. Navy along the James River and had its flanks secured by the river itself. At this point, the bureaucratic bickering between McClellan and Washington D.C. started flaring up again, as McClellan refused to recommence an advance without reinforcements. After weeks of indecision, the Army of the Potomac was finally ordered to evacuate the Peninsula and link up with John Pope's army in northern Virginia, as the Administration was more comfortable having their forces fighting on one line instead of exterior lines. Upon his arrival in Washington, McClellan told reporters that his failure to defeat Lee in Virginia was due to Lincoln not sending sufficient reinforcements.

During the Seven Days Battles, Longstreet was more effective. In command of an entire wing of Lee's army, Longstreet aggressively attacked at Gaines' Mill and Glendale. Historians have credited Longstreet for those battles and criticized Stonewall Jackson for being unusually lethargic during the Seven Days Battles, ultimately contributing to Lee's inability to do more damage or capture McClellan's Army of the Potomac. Jackson's performance was not lost on

Longstreet, who pointed out that he performed poorly at the Seven Days Battles to defend charges that he was slow at Gettysburg. By the end of the campaign, Longstreet was one of the most popular and praised men in the army. Like Longstreet's father, Sorrel considered him a "rock in steadiness when sometimes in battle the world seemed flying to pieces." General Lee himself called Old Pete "the staff in my right hand." Though it is often forgotten, Longstreet was now Lee's principle subordinate, not Stonewall Jackson.

James Longstreet

Meanwhile, Porter Alexander, the artillery chief for Longstreet's corps, was extremely critical of Stonewall Jackson's lethargy, writing in his memoirs:

"This will be even more evident in the story of Jackson's column, now to be told. His command had always before acted alone and independently. Lee's instructions to him were very brief and general, in supreme confidence that the Jackson of the Valley would win even brighter laurels on the Chickahominy. The shortest route was assigned to him and the largest force was given him. Lee then took himself off to the farthest flank, as if generously to leave to Jackson the opportunity of the most brilliant victory of the war.

His failure is not so much a military as a psychological phenomenon. He did not try and fail. He simply made no effort. The story embraces two days. He spent the 29th in camp in disregard of Lee's instructions, and he spent the 30th in equal idleness at White Oak Swamp. His 25,000 infantry practically did not fire a shot in the two days."

At Richmond, Lee reorganized the Army of Northern Virginia into the structure it is best remembered by. Jackson now took command of a force consisting of his own division (now commanded by Brig. General Charles S. Winder) and those of Maj. General Richard S. Ewell,

Brig. General William H. C. Whiting, and Maj. General D. H. Hill. The other wing of Lee's army was commanded by Longstreet. On July 25, 1862, after the conclusion of the Seven Days Battles had brought the Peninsula Campaign to an end, JEB Stuart was promoted to Major General, his command upgraded to Cavalry Division, a promotion earned by his famous cavalry ride around McClellan's army earlier in the Peninsula Campaign.

JEB Stuart

Chapter 2: John Pope and the Army of Virginia

Lee and his army had pushed McClellan's Army of the Potomac away from Richmond, but there was little time for celebration in July 1862. While McClellan was trying to extricate his army from a tricky spot on the Virginian Peninsula, about 50,000 Union soldiers were menacing the Confederates in Northern Virginia, outnumbering Lee's army. If McClellan's Army of the Potomac linked up with the army now being gathered in Northern Virginia, they would vastly outnumber Lee and begin yet another drive toward Richmond. For Lee, the best option (and it was hardly a good one) was to try to prevent the two Union armies from linking up, and the only way to do that would be to inflict a decisive defeat upon the army in Northern Virginia before it was joined by McClellan's men.

Thus, even before McClellan had completely withdrawn his troops, Lee sent Jackson northward to intercept the new army President Abraham Lincoln had placed under Maj. General John Pope, which was formed out of the scattered troops in the Virginia area, including those who Stonewall Jackson had bedeviled during the Valley Campaign. Pope had successfully commanded Union soldiers in victories at Island No. 10 and during the Siege of Corinth, earning himself a promotion to Major General in March 1862.

However, Pope was also uncommonly brash, and he got off to a bad start with his own men by issuing one of the most notorious messages of the Civil War:

"Let us understand each other. I have come to you from the West, where we have always seen the backs of our enemies; from an army whose business it has been to seek the adversary and to beat him when he was found; whose policy has been attack and not defense. In but one instance has the enemy been able to place our Western armies in defensive attitude. I presume that I have been called here to pursue the same system and to lead you against the enemy. It is my purpose to do so, and that speedily. I am sure you long for an opportunity to win the distinction you are capable of achieving. That opportunity I shall endeavor to give you. Meantime I desire you to dismiss from your minds certain phrases, which I am sorry to find so much in vogue amongst you. I hear constantly of 'taking strong positions and holding them,' of 'lines of retreat,' and of 'bases of supplies.' Let us discard such ideas. The strongest position a soldier should desire to occupy is one from which he can most easily advance against the enemy. Let us study the probable lines of retreat of our opponents, and leave our own to take care of themselves. Let us look before us, and not behind. Success and glory are in the advance, disaster and shame lurk in the rear. Let us act on this understanding, and it is safe to predict that your banners shall be inscribed with many a glorious deed and that your names will be dear to your countrymen forever."

Pope

Pope's arrogance and patronization of soldiers in the Eastern theater turned off many of the men in his new command, and it even caught the notice of Lee, who uncharacteristically called his opponent a "miscreant".

Pope's Army of Virginia was officially consolidated on June 26, 1862, comprised of soldiers in various war departments who had been engaged in Northern Virginia earlier in the year. The army, about 50,000 strong, included three corps under Franz Sigel, Nathaniel Banks, and Irvin McDowell. Sigel replaced John Frémont, who outranked Pope and thus refused to be Pope's subordinate, while Banks had been bested in the Shenandoah Valley by Jackson and McDowell had lost the First Battle of Bull Run. Soldiers of the IX Corps under Ambrose Burnside, who would lead men disastrously at Antietam and Fredericksburg, would eventually link up with Pope's army ahead of the Second Battle of Bull Run

Each corps in Pope's army also had their own cavalry brigade, instead of centralizing the cavalry under one command, an organizational mistake that would not be fixed until after the battle. Conversely, Lee's cavalry were organized into one division under JEB Stuart and attached to Stonewall Jackson's wing of the Army of Northern Virginia. As a result of the Union army's organization, the smaller brigades of cavalry were both ineffective at traditional cavalry duties like screening the army's movements and performing reconnaissance, and their force was diluted in actual battle.

In addition to threatening Lee's army and Richmond, Pope's army was an immediate threat to the Virginian civilians in the area, and Pope's army began employing methods of appropriating resources that infuriated the Confederacy. Pope's General Order No. 5 instructed his men to "subsist upon the country," giving them the ability to take civilian supplies in exchange for vouchers that "loyal citizens of the United States" could turn in after the Civil War for reimbursement. General Orders 7 and 11 instructed soldiers to destroy any building that Confederate soldiers or partisans used to shoot at Union soldiers, and Pope also ordered his army to "arrest all disloyal male citizens within their lines or within their reach." While these policies were tame in comparison to the total warfare and scorched earth used in 1864 by William Tecumseh Sherman and Phil Sheridan, in the early years of the war they were still considered unconventional, and Lee was so incensed by them that he stated Pope "ought to be suppressed."

After the war, Pope would write about the campaign in a way that sought to defend his conduct, and he portrayed himself as far less arrogant in taking command of the Army of Virginia:

> "It became apparent to me at once that the duty to be assigned to me was in the nature of a forlorn-hope, and my position was still further embarrassed by the fact that I was called from another army and a different field of duty to command an army of which the corps commanders were all my seniors in rank. I therefore strongly urged that I be not placed in such a position, but be permitted to return to my command in the West, to

which I was greatly attached and with which I had been closely identified in several successful operations on the Mississippi. It was not difficult to forecast the delicate and embarrassing position in which I should be placed, nor the almost certainly disagreeable, if not unfortunate, issue of such organization for such a purpose.

It was equally natural that the subordinate officers and the enlisted men of those corps should have been ill-pleased at the seeming affront to their own officers, involved in calling an officer strange to them and to the country in which they were operating, and to the character of the service in which they were engaged, to supersede well-known and trusted officers who had been with them from the beginning, and whose reputation was so closely identified with their own. How far this feeling prevailed among them, and how it influenced their actions, if it did so at all, I am not able to tell."

Of course, if Pope had truly felt that way in 1862, it's unclear why he would have issued the patronizing message he had upon taking command.

Chapter 3: Cedar Mountain

Lee had taken a risk by sizing up McClellan and splitting his forces while the Army of the Potomac was still in the vicinity, but it was calculated and ultimately proved correct. With that, Lee decided upon trying to strike and hopefully destroy Pope's army before McClellan sailed his army back toward Washington D.C. However, shortly after sending Jackson north to take up a defensive stance against Pope near Gordonsville, Lee learned of intelligence suggesting Burnside's command was heading to unite with Pope, so he ordered A.P. Hill's 12,000 man "Light Division" to join Jackson. Despite the fact Lee now had only about 30,000 men at most opposing McClellan, the Union general continued to believe he was outnumbered and informed the Lincoln Administration he would need 50,000 more men to advance again. Then, despite having his request rejected and being given orders on August 3 to begin withdrawing his men from the Peninsula and head back to join Pope's army, McClellan protested before putting the withdrawal in motion on August 14.

McClellan has since been accused of intentionally delaying his evacuation out of spite and his disdain for Pope. McClellan was not in command at Second Bull Run, but he generated substantial controversy over whether he moved with speed to come to Pope's aid. What is unmistakable is that McClellan would feel vindicated if and when Pope was embarrassed, at one point mentioning that one possibility for the campaign is to let Pope attempt to get out of "his scrape." Lincoln would later accuse McClellan flat out of "acting badly" during the campaign.

On June 26, General Pope deployed his forces in an arc across Northern Virginia; its right flank (Sigel's corps) was around Sperryville on the Blue Ridge Mountains, the center consisted of Banks's corps at Little Washington, and its left flank (McDowell's corps) was outside Fredericksburg along the Rappahannock River. As Lee had anticipated, on August 6 Pope marched his forces south to capture the rail junction at Gordonsville, which meant to both threaten the Confederates from the north and distract Lee from McClellan's withdrawal from the Peninsula.

Just like in the Valley, Jackson's men were outnumbered by Pope's army, but Pope's corps were divided in three locations and none of them outnumbered Jackson individually. Jackson was thus determined to try to deal with them all separately before they could overwhelm him collectively.

Setting out on August 7, Jackson began marching his men toward the Union's isolated center, which consisted of about 8,000 men under Banks. However, his march was immediately hampered by a severe heat wave, which slowed his progress. On top of that, Jackson's insistence on keeping his marching plans secret messed up coordination among his principal subordinates, who were confused over which route they were supposed to take themselves. The delays allowed Pope to start shifting Sigel's corps to link up with Banks and form a defensive line around Cedar Run.

On August 9, Jackson's advancing column came into contact with the Union defenders posted on a ridge around Cedar Run, and they began forming a battle line while engaging in a general artillery duel with the Union forces. Jubal Early, whose brigade was in Jackson's vanguard, later explained, "No infantry had yet been seen, but the boldness with which the cavalry confronted us and the opening of the batteries, satisfied me that we had come upon a heavy force, concealed behind the ridge on which the cavalry was drawn up, as the ground beyond was depressed. I therefore halted the brigade, causing the men to cover themselves as well as they could by moving back a little and lying down, and then sent word for General Winder to come up."

However, the tempo of the battle changed on a dime after the mortal wounding of Confederate General Charles Winder, whose absence from the battlefield left the command of his division disorganized. A gap in the Confederate line opened up due to a misunderstanding by William Taliaferro, who had succeeded Winder, and that provided a chance for Banks to launch an attack. As Union soldiers came crashing down on the Confederates' right flank, another advance flanked the Confederates on their left and began rolling up their line.

Worried about losing control of his men and determined to inspire them, Jackson suddenly rode into the battlefield and attempted to brandish his sword, but the man who had once warned his VMI cadets to be ready to throw the scabbards of their swords away found that due to the infrequency with which he had used it, it had rusted in its scabbard. Waving his sword in its scabbard above his head, the Stonewall Brigade headed forward to reinforce the line.

However, the day wasn't saved for the Confederates until A.P. Hill's Light Division stabilized the Confederates' left flank and launched a counterattack. Jackson, who had not reconnoitered properly, was in danger of being beaten back by the vanguard of Banks's force when Hill came rushing in and changed the course of the battle, leading to a collapse of the Union right. Though outsiders thought Hill and Jackson worked like a "well oiled war machine," in reality, the two were maintaining an increasingly contentious relationship. The fact the two generals were at each other's throats was somewhat ironic, given that both of them were stern men. One of the men in his regiment recalled Hill's actions during the battle:

> "I saw A.P. Hill that day as he was putting his "Light Division" into battle, and was very much struck with his appearance. In his shirtsleeves and with drawn sword he sought to arrest the stragglers who were coming to the rear, and seeing a Lieutenant in the number, he rode at him and fiercely inquired: "Who are you, sir, and where are you going?" The trembling Lieutenant replied: "I am going back with my wounded friend." Hill reached down and tore the insignia of rank from his collar as he roughly said: "You are a pretty fellow to hold a commission -- deserting your colors in the presence of the enemy, and going to the rear with a man who is scarcely badly enough wounded to go himself. I reduce you to the ranks, sir, and if you do not go to the front and do your duty, I'll have you shot as soon as I can spare a file of men for the purpose." And then clearing the road, he hurried forward his men to the splendid service which was before them."

A.P. Hill

The Confederates had won the battle, but at a surprisingly staggering cost. Banks, who had attempted to take the offensive despite being outnumbered 2-1, lost over a quarter of his command, while Jackson had suffered nearly 1500 casualties himself. Jackson knew not to attempt the offensive anymore since Pope's army was beginning to link up, while the Lincoln Administration was ordering Pope to cancel his thrust towards Gordonsville.

Once certain McClellan was in full retreat, Lee began the process of reuniting his own army, still hoping to strike Pope before McClellan's troops could arrive as reinforcements. Lee wrote in his official post-campaign report:

> "The victory at Cedar Run effectually checked the progress of the enemy for the time, but it soon became apparent that his army was being largely increased. The corps of Major-General Burnside fromNorth Carolina, which had reached Fredericksburg, was reported to have moved up the Rappahannock a few days after the battle to unite with General Pope, and a part of General McClellan's army was believed to have left Westover for the same purpose. It therefore seemed that active operations on the James were no longer contemplated, and that the most effectual way to relieve Richmond from any danger of attack from that quarter would be to re-enforce General Jackson and advance upon General Pope.

> Accordingly on August 13 Major-General Longstreet, with his division and the two brigades under General Hood, were ordered to proceed to Gordonsville. At the same time General Stuart was directed to move with the main body of his cavalry to that point, leaving a sufficient force to observe the enemy still remaining in Fredericksburg and to guard the railroad. General R. H. Anderson was also directed to leave his position on James River and follow Longstreet."

Meanwhile, Pope was apparently now convinced that he did not have enough strength to take the offensive, despite the fact his numbers were at least equal to the Army of Northern Virginia and he was being promised further reinforcements from Burnside's corps and McClellan's army. After the war, he wrote, "It is only necessary to say that the course of these operations made it plain enough that the Rappahannock was too far to the front, and that the movements of Lee were too rapid and those of McClellan too slow to make it possible, with the small force I had, to hold that line, or to keep open communication with Fredericksburg without being turned on my right flank by Lee's whole army and cut off altogether from Washington."

Lee was determined to attack Pope, Pope was being ordered to cancel his forward movements, and Pope was apparently of the mind that he had to take the defensive. The ball was now in Lee's court, and it would lead the two armies to very familiar ground.

Chapter 4: Moving Toward Manassas

Once Lee had united his army in mid-August, he was initially determined to try to slip around Pope's left flank, not his right. Lee explained in his post-campaign report:

> "On the 16th the troops began to move from the vicinity of Gordonsville toward the

Rapidan, on the north side of which, extending along the Orange and Alexandria Railroad in the direction of Culpeper CourtHouse, the Federal Army lay in great force. It was determined with the cavalry to destroy the railroad bridge over the Rappahannock in rear of the enemy, while Longstreet and Jackson crossed the Rapidan and attacked his left flank. The movement, as explained in the accompanying order, was appointed for August 18, but the necessary preparations not having been completed, its execution was postponed to the 20th. In the interval the enemy, being apprised of our design, hastily retired beyond the Rappahannock. General Longstreet crossed the Rapidan at Raccoon Ford and, preceded by Fitzhugh Lee's cavalry brigade, arrived early in the afternoon near Kelly's Ford, on the Rappahannock, where Lee had a sharp and successful skirmish with the rear guard of the enemy, who held the north side of the river in strong force. Jackson passed the Rapidan at Somerville Ford and moved toward Brandy Station, Robertson's brigade of cavalry, accompanied by General Stuart in person, leading the advance. Near Brandy Station a large body of the enemy's cavalry was encountered, which was gallantly attacked and driven across the Rappahannock by Robertson's command."

Whether Lee's initial plan could have been successful if not for bad luck is unclear, but his plan was intercepted during a Union cavalry raid and brought to Pope, who used the news to withdraw to a tighter defensive line around the Rappahannock River. Rising waters made it far more dangerous for the Confederates to attempt to cross the Rappahannock with Union artillery on the other side of it. Moreover, Pope was biding his time in the hopes of receiving reinforcements from the Army of the Potomac that would greatly swing the numbers to the Union's advantage. He explained, "On the 21st of August, being then at Rappahannock Station, my little army confronted by nearly the whole force under General Lee, which had compelled the retreat of McClellan to Harrison's Landing, I was positively assured that two days more would see me largely enough reënforced by the Army of the Potomac to be not only secure, but to assume the offensive against Lee, and I was instructed to hold on "and fight like the devil."

Lee's next strategic shift was also a result of luck. Cavalry leader JEB Stuart had been concocting a plan to ride around Pope's army, just like he had done to McClellan's, only to be almost captured in the Union cavalry raid that had not only stolen Lee's orders but also one of his famous plumed hats. On August 22, Stuart's men conducted a raid on Pope's camp that bagged a bunch of valuables, as Longstreet explained in his memoirs:

"General Stuart was ordered over, with parts of his brigades, to investigate and make trouble in the enemy's rear. He crossed at Waterloo and Hunt's Mill with fifteen hundred troopers and Pelham's horse artillery, and rode to Warrenton. Passing through, he directed his ride towards Catlett's Station to first burn the bridge over Cedar Creek.

Before reaching Catlett's a severe storm burst upon him, bogging the roads and flooding the streams behind him. The heavy roads delayed his artillery so that it was after night when he approached Catlett's. He caught a picket-guard and got into a camp about General Pope's Headquarters, took a number of prisoners, some camp property, and, meeting an old acquaintance and friend in a colored man, who conducted him to General Pope's tents, he found one of the general's uniform coats, a hat, a number of official despatches, a large amount of United States currency, much of the general's personal equipments, and one of the members of his staff, Major Goulding. He made several attempts to fire the bridge near Catlett's, but the heavy rains put out all fires that could be started, when he sought axes to cut it away. By this time the troops about the camps rallied and opened severe fire against him, but with little damage. The heavy rainfall admonished him to forego further operations and return to the army while yet there was a chance to cross Cedar Creek and the Rappahannock before the tides came down. On the night of the 23d he reached Sulphur Springs, where he met General Jackson's troops trying to make comfortable lodgement on the east bank, passed over, and resumed position outside General Lee's left. The despatch-book of General Pope gave information of his troops and his anxiety for reinforcements, besides mention of those that had joined him, but General Stuart's especial pleasure and pride were manifested over the possession of the uniform coat and hat of General Pope. Stuart rode along the line showing them, and proclaiming that he was satisfied with the exchange that made even his loss at Verdierville before the march; but the despatch lost at Verdierville [Lee's orders] was the tremendous blow that could not be overestimated."

With information about Pope's dispositions, his strategic thinking, and the news about impending reinforcements, Lee now changed tack and decided to try to turn Pope's right, as he explained in his report:

"As our positions on the south bank of the Rappahannock were commanded by those of the enemy, who guarded all the fords, it was determined to seek a more favorable place to cross higher up the river, and thus gain the enemy's right. Accordingly, General Longstreet was directed to leave Kelly's Ford on the 21st and take the position in front of the enemy in the vicinity of Beverly Ford and the Orange and Alexandria Railroad bridge, then held by Jackson, in order to mask the movement of the latter, who was instructed to ascend the river.

On the 22d Jackson crossed Hazel River at Welford's Mill and proceeded up the Rappahannock, leaving Trimble's brigade near Freeman's Ford to protect his trains. In the afternoon Longstreet sent General Hood, with his own and Whiting's brigade, under Colonel Law, to relieve Trimble. Hood had just reached the position when he and Trimble were attacked by a considerable force which had crossed at Freeman's Ford. After a short but spirited engagement the enemy was driven precipitately over the river with heavy loss. General Jackson arrived at the Warrenton Springs Ford in the afternoon, and immediately began to cross his troops to the north side, occupying the

Springs and the adjacent heights. He was interrupted by a heavy rain, which caused the river to rise so rapidly that the ford soon became impassable for infantry and artillery."

While Lee was sending Jackson stealthily past Pope's right, the two armies skirmished around the Rappahannock River from August 22-25, which preoccupied Pope and helped keep his army in place and vulnerable to Jackson's turning movement. Meanwhile, Jackson's wing of the Army of Northern Virginia was heading toward Bristoe Station and the railroad junction at Manassas, where he would be positioned not only to destroy Pope's supply lines but also potentially cut off Pope's line of retreat.

Pope learned about Jackson's turning movement on August 26, and his initial response was to try to coordinate the dispositions of the reinforcements he thought he was due to receive imminently:

"I accordingly held on till the 26th of August, when, finding myself to be outflanked on my right by the main body of Lee's army, while Jackson's corps having passed Salem and Rectortown the day before were in rapid march in the direction of Gainesville and Manassas Junction, and seeing that none of the reënforcements promised me were likely to arrive, I determined to abandon the line of the Rappahannock and communications with Fredericksburg, and concentrate my whole force in the direction of Warrenton and Gainesville, to cover the Warrenton pike, and still to confront the enemy rapidly marching to my right.^

Stonewall Jackson's movement on Manassas Junction was plainly seen and promptly reported, and I notified General Halleck of it. He informed me on the 23d of August that heavy reënforcements would begin to arrive at Warrenton Junction on the next day (24th), and as my orders still held me to the Rappahannock I naturally supposed that these troops would be hurried forward to me with all speed. Franklin's corps especially, I asked, should be sent rapidly to Gainesville. I also telegraphed Colonel Herman Haupt, chief of railway transportation, to direct one of the strongest divisions coming forward, and to be at Warrenton Junction on the 24th, to be put in the works at Manassas Junction. A cavalry force had been sent forward to observe the Thoroughfare Gap early on the morning of the 26th, but nothing was heard from it."

By the time Pope was aware of Jackson's move on his right, the Confederates were well into his rear. On the night of August 26, Jackson's men slipped through Thoroughfare Gap and headed for the railroad at Bristoe Station, cutting up the line. The following morning, Jackson moved on the Union supplies stored at Manassas Junction, where he met one sole Union brigade led by George W. Taylor and easily pushed it aside, mortally wounding Taylor in the process. McClellan would later cite the defeat of Taylor's force as justification for not sending more infantry reinforcements to Pope without corresponding artillery and cavalry for their protection.

However, by the end of August 27, Jackson's men were being chased by a Union division under the command of "Fighting Joe" Hooker, forcing Jackson to conduct a rearguard action while he retreated and dug in behind an unfinished railroad near Bull Run creek. Jackson had posted his men about a mile away from where he had become a Confederate hero the year before during First Manassas, when his brigade had rallied the Confederates on Henry Hill and turned the tide of that battle. Now he was digging in right on a spot that Union soldiers opposing him had stood on 13 months earlier. Lee later reported, "General Jackson's force being much inferior to that of General Pope, it became necessary for him to withdraw from Manassas and take a position west of the turnpike road from Warrenton to Alexandria, where he could more readily unite with the approaching column of Longstreet. Having fully supplied the wants of his troops, he was compelled, for want of transportation, to destroy the rest of the captured property. This was done during the night of the 27th, and 50,000 pounds of bacon, 1,000 barrels of corned beef, 2,000 barrels of salt pork, and 2,000 barrels of flour, besides other property of great value, were burned."

On August 27, Jackson routed a Union brigade near Union Mills (Bull Run Bridge), inflicting several hundred casualties and mortally wounding Union Brig. Gen. George W. Taylor. Maj. Gen. Richard S. Ewell's Confederate division fought a brisk rearguard action against Maj. Gen. Joseph Hooker's Union division at Kettle Run, resulting in about 600 casualties. Ewell held back Union forces until dark. That night, Jackson marched his divisions north to the Bull Run battlefield, where he took position behind an unfinished railroad grade. Pope explained the outlook on the night of August 27, "The movement of Jackson presented the only opportunity which had offered to gain any success over the superior forces of the enemy. I determined, therefore, on the morning of the 27th of August to abandon the line of the Rappahannock and throw my whole force in the direction of Gainesville and Manassas Junction, to crush any force of the enemy that had passed through Thoroughfare Gap, and to interpose between Lee's army and Bull Run. Having the interior line of operations, and the enemy at Manassas being inferior in force, it appeared to me, and still so appears, that with even ordinary promptness and energy we might feel sure of success."

Picture of a train derailed near Manassas Junction by the raiding Confederates

With the Confederate army divided and Pope's army inbetween them, Pope was now positioned to prevent them from linking up by blocking the Thoroughfare Gap. Ultimately he opted not to, later claiming that when he saw smoke from the flames shooting near Manassas, he figured he had Jackson in trouble and could annihilate the Confederates before Longstreet reunited with them. In fact, those flames were coming from his own supplies, after Jackson's men began torching what they couldn't carry. As a result, Longstreet's wing of the army would suffer only a slight harassment from Union cavalry and one Union division before they gave way at Thoroughfare Gap.

With the path established for Longstreet's wing to march and reunite with Jackson's wing, the race was now on. Could Pope's army fall on Jackson's wing and destroy it before Longstreet rejoined it?

Chapter 5: August 28

Although Pope was now planning to thrust at Jackson's army, the Second Battle of Bull Run actually began on the evening of August 28 with Jackson's men taking the offensive. Pope was in the process of gathering all his men at Centreville, just above Bull Run and a few miles away from Jackson's men, because he thought Jackson's men were at Centreville itself. As Jackson's men kept their defensive line along the unfinished railroad cut, they watched a Union column marching along the Warrenton Turnpike near Brawner's farm, and it turned out to be soldiers from Brig. Gen. Rufus King's division (of McDowell's corps) marching toward Centreville to meet up with the rest of Pope's army and hopefully discover Jackson. Unbeknownst to the column, they were actually marching right past Jackson's entire wing of the army.

Emboldened by the news that Longstreet was passing through Thoroughfare Gap around the same time, Jackson got characteristically aggressive, and figuring that this Union column was retreating behind Bull Run to link up with Pope's army and perhaps even reinforcements from the Army of the Potomac, he decided to try to annihilate the column.

In the late afternoon, Jackson ordered his principal officers, "Bring out your men, gentlemen." With that, he ordered his artillery to open up on the column marching conspicuously across their front. As fate would have it, the part of the column in Jackson's front at this time was John Gibbon's brigade, which could be identified by their Black Hats. This "Black Hat Brigade" was destined to become one of the most famous Union brigades of the war after being christened the Iron Brigade by McClellan during the subsequent Maryland Campaign and fighting heroically at Gettysburg, but they had never seen action before Jackson's grizzled veterans opened fire on them that night around 6:30 p.m.

John Hatch's brigade of King's division had already marched past Jackson's front, so Gibbon worked to get reinforcements from Abner Doubleday's brigade and formed a battle line. Due to Pope's belief that Jackson was at Centreville, Gibbon mistakenly thought that the artillery being fired at them was coming from JEB Stuart's cavalry, and that two brigades could sweep them aside and end the harassment of their march. The Black Hat Brigade had never fought before, and now they were about to make a general advance against half of the Army of Northern Virginia.

Gibbon

While Gibbon formed his line along the turnpike, he used the 2nd Wisconsin regiment to advance through woods on the Confederates' right flank. In fact, when Gibbon convened with the regiment in the woods, he instructed them to capture the artillery. In reality, he was posting a lone regiment on the right flank of Richard S. Ewell's entire division, which was supported in the rear by William Taliaferro's division.

With his line formed, Gibbon's previously untested men began moving forward, only to come face to face with Confederates at nearly point blank range in Brawner's farm. Major Rufus Dawes, who would become a hero on Day 1 at Gettysburg in command of the 6th Wisconsin, described the fighting the 6th Wisconsin endured that night, "Our men on the left loaded and fired with the energy of madmen, and the 6th worked with equal desperation. This stopped the rush of the enemy and they halted and fired upon us their deadly musketry. During a few awful moments, I could see by the lurid light of the powder flashes, the whole of both lines. The two …

were within ... fifty yards of each other pouring musketry into each other as fast as men could load and shoot."

Meanwhile, the 2nd Wisconsin came through the woods and found themselves squarely on the Confederates' right flank at an angle that also happened to expose their own right flank. Thankfully for the Union, the 2nd Wisconsin was one of the few veteran regiments on the field that night, and they stood firm even after the Stonewall Brigade unleashed the first volley, firing a volley of their own and thus starting a general musketry exchange. Out of the nearly 430 men fighting for the 2nd Wisconsin, nearly 60% would become casualties.

The fact that daylight was running out likely contributed to the confusion that induced Gibbon to stand firm against the artillery assault, but it would also prove to be his saving grace. Gibbon shored up the right of his line with men from Doubleday's brigade and kept plugging in gaps in his line, and the fighting was so hot that Jackson actually started directing single regiments into the fighting. While Jackson was ordering multiple regiments into the fray, the unwitting Gibbon was countering by ordering up single regiments. Jackson described the fighting, "In a few moments our entire line was engaged in a fierce and sanguinary struggle with the enemy. As one line was repulsed another took its place and pressed forward as if determined by force of numbers and fury of assault to drive us from our positions."

By the time Jackson ordered up Isaac Trimble's brigade, it was so dark that all semblance of command coordination vanished. The Confederates started making piecemeal assaults instead of a general advance, allowing the heavily outnumbered Union regiments to repulse the attacks one at a time. By 9:00, the Union soldiers fought a gradual retreat back to the turnpike, leaving the field to Jackson's men. The fighting had produced a remarkable number of casualties in just 2 hours, with 1,150 Union and 1,250 Confederate casualties. Nevertheless, the Union soldiers had held their ground despite being outnumbered 3-1, and furthermore the Confederate casualties included Ewell and Taliaferro, two of Jackson's division commanders.

Ewell

Pope later wrote about where he was and what he was thinking when he heard about the fighting on the night of the 28th.

"The engagement of King's division was reported to me about 10 o'clock at night near Centreville. I felt sure then, and so stated, that there was no escape for Jackson. On the west of him were McDowell's corps (I did not then know that he had detached Ricketts *, Sigel's corps, and Reynolds's division, all under command of McDowell. On the east of him, and with the advance of Kearny nearly in contact with him on the Warrenton pike, were the corps of Reno and Heintzelman. Porter was supposed to be at Manassas Junction, where he ought to have been on that afternoon.

"I sent orders to McDowell (supposing him to be with his command), and also direct to General King, several times during that night and once by his own staff-officer, to hold his ground at all hazards, to prevent the retreat of Jackson toward Lee, and that at daylight our whole force from Centreville and Manassas would assail him from the east, and he would be crushed between us. I sent orders also to General Kearny at Centreville to move forward cautiously that night along the Warrenton pike; to drive in the pickets of the enemy, and to keep as closely as possible in contact with him during the night, resting his left on the Warrenton pike and throwing his right to the north, if practicable, as far as the Little River pike, and at daylight next morning to assault vigorously with his right advance, and that Hooker and Reno would certainly be with him shortly after daylight. I sent orders to General Porter, who I supposed was at Manassas Junction, to move upon Centreville at dawn, stating to him the position of our forces, and that a severe battle would be fought that morning (the 29th).

With Jackson at or near Groveton, with McDowell on the west, and the rest of the army on the east of him, while Lee, with the mass of his army, was still west of Thoroughfare Gap, the situation for us was certainly as favorable as the most sanguine person could desire, and the prospect of crushing Jackson, sandwiched between such forces, were certainly excellent. There is no doubt, had General McDowell been with his command when King's division of his corps became engaged with the enemy, he would have brought forward to its support both Sigel and Reynolds, and the result would have been to hold the ground west of Jackson at least until morning brought against him also the forces moving from the direction of Centreville.

To my great disappointment and surprise, however, I learned toward daylight the next morning (the 29th) that King's division had fallen back toward Manassas Junction, and that neither Sigel nor Reynolds had been engaged or had gone to the support of King. The route toward Thoroughfare Gap had thus been left open by the wholly unexpected retreat of King's division, due to the fact that he was not supported by Sigel and Reynolds, and an immediate change was necessary in the disposition of the troops under my command."

However, as Longstreet noted in his memoirs, Pope actually had it backwards. Longstreet's wing of the army was already on its way through Thoroughfare Gap after pushing aside relatively light resistance, and Jackson's men could actually see the musket smoke and hear the artillery produced by Longstreet's soldiers in the Gap. Longstreet wrote, "During the night the Federal commander reported to his subordinates that McDowell had 'intercepted the retreat of Jackson, and ordered concentration of the army against him,' whereas it was, of course, Jackson who had intercepted McDowell's march. He seems to have been under the impression that he was about to capture Jackson, and inclined to lead his subordinates to the same opinion."

Sure enough, Pope was operating under the mistaken assumption that Jackson's men had engaged King's division as it was retreating from Centreville, clearly unaware that Jackson had taken up that position the night before and was biding his time until Longstreet joined him. That night, Pope told Phil Kearny, who commanded a division in the Army of the Potomac, "General McDowell has intercepted the retreat of the enemy and is now in his front ... Unless he can escape by by-paths leading to the north to-night, he must be captured." In actuality, when King's division extricated itself from the fighting at Brawner's farm and continued east to meet up with the rest of Pope's army, there were no longer any Union forces between Jackson and Longstreet.

Chapter 6: August 29

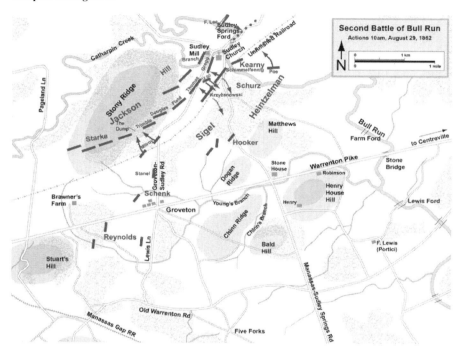

The battle lines on the morning of August 29

Pope would begin operations on August 29 laboring under an entirely faulty premise, and his various orders to different subordinates would result in a completely uncoordinated general attack on Jackson's defensive line.

"About daylight, therefore, on the 29th of August, almost immediately after I received information of the withdrawal of King's division toward Manassas Junction, I sent orders to General Sigel, in the vicinity of Groveton, to attack the enemy vigorously at daylight and bring him to a stand if possible. He was to be supported by Reynolds's division. I instructed Heintzelman to push forward from Centreville toward Gainesville on the Warrenton pike at the earliest dawn with the divisions of Kearny and Hooker, and gave orders also to Reno with his corps to follow closely in their rear. They were directed to use all speed, and as soon as they came up with the enemy to establish communication with Sigel, and to attack vigorously and promptly. I also sent orders to General Porter at Manassas Junction to move forward rapidly with his own corps and King's division of McDowell's corps, which was there also, upon Gainesville by the direct route from Manassas Junction to that place. I urged him to make all possible speed, with the purpose that he should come up with the enemy or connect himself with the left of our line near where the Warrenton pike is crossed by the road from Manassas Junction to Gainesville.

Shortly after sending this order I received a note from General McDowell, whom I had not been able to find during the night of the 28th, dated Manassas Junction, requesting that King's division be not taken from his command. I immediately sent a joint order, addressed to Generals McDowell and Porter, repeating the instructions to move forward with their commands toward Gainesville, and informing them of the position and movements of Sigel and Heintzelman."

Heintzelman

Thus, with Longstreet marching his 26,000 soldiers toward Jackson at dawn that morning, it would fall upon Jackson and his nearly 20,000 men to hold out for at least the entire morning against potentially all of Pope's army.

Luckily for the Confederates, Pope's unfamiliarity with the Confederate dispositions and his convoluted attack orders would ruin his plans. Pope intended to strike both of Jackson's flanks that morning, and Sigel began the fighting around 7:00 a.m. on Jackson's left with Robert Schenck's division, Carl Schurz's division, and Robert Milroy's brigade. His line also had John Reynolds's division from Heintzelman's corps in reserve, and he anticipated being supported by Kearny's division as well.

Sigel advanced his men without knowing exactly where Jackson's flank was, and as it turned out A.P. Hill had extended Jackson's left until it was nearly touching Bull Run creek, and Stuart's cavalry was posted on the other side of the creek crossing to provide artillery support. While Stuart's horse artillery was engaged, the cavalrymen fastened logs and dragged them on the dirt road behind their horses, kicking up a cloud of dust that was meant to confuse Union commanders into thinking Jackson had more men than he actually did.

Franz Sigel

For the next three hours, Sigel threw his corps at A.P. Hill's Light Division in a series of attacks that were not properly coordinated with the supporting elements from the other corps of the army. At the same time, even though Jackson was essentially fighting a delaying action intended to buy time for Longstreet, Hill's men couldn't help but charge forward and counterattack Sigel's men after repulsing each attack. In addition to Sigel's divisions fighting piecemeal, those divisions had their brigades fighting piecemeal. Making matters worse, Sigel made one last assault around 10:00 a.m. in the belief that Phil Kearny's division was making the attack with them. To Sigel's horror, Kearny's division didn't move as he had expected. Historians have attributed Kearny's failure to move for his disdain for Sigel, but Kearny insisted in his post-battle report, "On the 29th, on my arrival, I was assigned to the holding of the right wing, my left on Leesburg road. I posted Colonel Poe, with Berry's brigade, in first line, General Robinson, First Brigade, on his right, partly in line and partly in support, and kept Birney's most disciplined regiments reserved and ready for emergencies. Toward noon I was obliged to occupy a quarter of a mile additional on left of said road, from Schurz' troops being taken elsewhere."

Despite being repulsed, Pope wasn't done attacking Jackson's left. Hooker's division (from Heintzelman's corps) now came up, as did a brigade from Burnside's IX Corps led by Isaac Stevens. Kearny's division was also still ready to make an assault on the left. Pope arrived at the scene around noon, just in time to watch this next wave of attacks on Jackson's left.

As those attacks were starting, the first elements of Longstreet's wing were coming up on Jackson's right, as were some of Stuart's cavalry, which had been employed in guiding Longstreet's men to Jackson's line. As Longstreet's men began arriving, Longstreet recounted an exchange between he and Lee over whether to conduct an attack on Pope's left flank, which was at that time was concentrating its efforts on Jackson: "When I reported my troops in order for battle, General Lee was inclined to engage as soon as practicable, but did not order. All troops that he could hope to have were up except R. H. Anderson's division, which was near enough to come in when the battle was in progress. I asked him to be allowed to make a reconnoissance of the enemy's ground, and along his left. After an hour's work, mounted and afoot, under the August sun, I returned and reported adversely as to attack, especially in view of the easy approach of the troops reported at Manassas against my right in the event of severe contention. We knew of Ricketts's division in that quarter, and of a considerable force at Manassas Junction, which indicated one corps." Lee acquiesced to Longstreet's advice, which some Lost Cause advocates would later claim gave Longstreet the confidence to go against Lee's wishes. Considering Longstreet's disobedience of General Lee's wishes to be nearly insubordination, Lee's most famous biographer, Douglas Southall Freeman, later wrote: "The seeds of much of the disaster on July 2, 1863, at the Battle of Gettysburg were sown in that instant—when Lee yielded to Longstreet and Longstreet discovered that he would." However, Longstreet's men had marched about 30 miles and briefly fought at Thoroughfare Gap the day before, so Longstreet was well aware that his men were anything but fresh.

One of the sources of Longstreet's apprehension that day was Fitz-John Porter's corps, one of the few commands from the Army of the Potomac that would engage in substantial fighting during the battle. Porter, along with McDowell's corps, were on the left of the Union line and were advancing northwest toward what they thought would be Jackson's right when they encountered Stuart's cavalry. In fact, Stuart's cavalry had just escorted Longstreet's men to the field, and as they engaged in skirmishing, orders from Pope for Porter and McDowell arrived.

Porter

The orders, now known as the "Joint Order", essentially ordered Porter to perform the impossible. The order suggested that Porter and McDowell move along the Manassas-Gainesville Road (as they had been doing) toward Gainesville while also maintaining contact with the rest of the Union line, which at the time had John Reynolds's division on the left flank. At the same time, the order stated "as soon as communication is established [with the other divisions] the whole command shall halt. It may be necessary to fall back behind Bull Run to Centreville tonight." Finally, Pope's order added a caveat: "If any considerable advantages are to be gained from departing from this order it will not be strictly carried out."

Historian John J. Hennessy, who wrote a history on the campaign, has since labeled Pope's order "masterpiece of contradiction and obfuscation that would become the focal point of decades of wrangling." To start, it was not possible for this column to continue marching toward Gainesville and maintain contact with the left of the Union line at the same time. And in addition to the incredibly murky and contradictory suggestions, Pope gave the men on his left this order without realizing that Longstreet's wing of the army had arrived on the battlefield to Jackson's left, a deployment that induced Porter to widely choose not to make an attack on the 29th. Despite the wisdom of the decision, it was one that would lead to Porter being court-martialed and effectively ending his military career.

Somehow, even in the years after the Civil War, Pope remained mistaken about Longstreet's dispositions on the afternoon of the 29th, and he continued to direct his vitriol at Porter, who he believed had disobeyed his orders out of loyalty to McClellan, writing:

"From 1:30 to 4 o'clock P. M. very severe conflicts occurred repeatedly all along the line, and there was a continuous roar of artillery and small-arms, with scarcely an intermission. About two o'clock in the afternoon three discharges of artillery were heard on the extreme left of our line or right of the enemy's, and I for the moment, and naturally, believed that Porter and McDowell had reached their positions and were engaged with the enemy. I heard only three shots, and as nothing followed I was at a loss to know what had become of these corps, or what was delaying them, as before this hour they should have been, even With ordinary marching, well up on our left. Shortly afterward I received information that McDowell's corps was advancing to join the left of our line by the Sudley Springs road, and would probably be up within two hours. At 4:30 o'clock I sent a peremptory order to General Porter, who was at or near Dawkins's Branch, about four or five miles distant from my headquarters, to push forward at once into action on the enemy's right, and if possible on his rear, stating to him generally the condition of things on the field in front of me. At 5:30 o'clock, when General Porter should have been going into action in compliance with this order, I directed Heintzelman and Reno to attack the enemy's left. The attack was made promptly and with vigor and persistence, and the left of the enemy was doubled back toward his center. After a severe and bloody action of an hour Kearny forced the position on the left of the enemy and occupied the field of battle there."

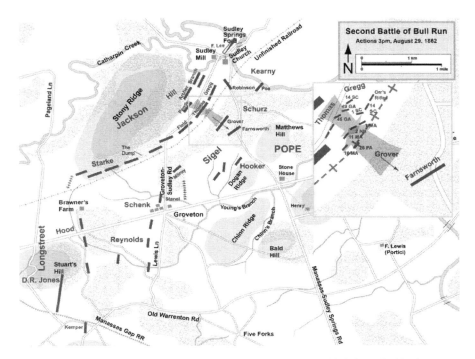

As Pope's account indicates, his failure to understand the situation on his left resulted in the mistaken belief that the afternoon would include attacks on both of Jackson's flanks instead of just one desperate assault on Jackson's left yet again. The highlight of that attack came when a brigade led by Brig. Gen. Cuvier Grover successfully marched into a gap in the Confederate line, only to be repulsed because Kearny's division did not support it. Furthermore, Pope had expected the attack to be a diversionary tactic while his left surprised Jackson's right, still unaware of Longstreet's position. Eventually Brig. Gen. Dorsey Pender's brigade sealed the gap in A.P. Hill's line.

While this was going on, Pope ordered John Reynolds to advance on the left, during which Reynolds ran into Longstreet's wing and immediately called off the advance. When Reynolds reported this to Pope, Pope refused to believe it could be Longstreet and somehow thought Reynolds had mistaken Porter's corps for Confederates. The next attack was made by Jesse Reno's division of Burnside's IX Corps, which saw one brigade attack the very center of Jackson's line without support. Once again, that attack was eventually repulsed.

With every attack having been repulsed thus far, Pope continued to hold out hope that Porter's corps would deliver him a victory, even as he remained confused as to why he hadn't heard any fighting or accounts of fighting on his left. At 4:30 p.m., Pope sent orders to Porter to attack, but Porter did not get that message until it was dusk, and he still had Longstreet in his front, making an attack on Jackson's right impossible. But Pope ordered Kearny's division to attack Jackson's left in conjunction with his order to Porter, so Kearny's division surged forward around 5:00, crashing into A.P. Hill's division, which had already taken most of the Union attacks during the day.

Kearny reported what went wrong with this new wave:

"During the first hours of combat General Birney, on tired regiments in the center falling back, of his own accord rapidly pushed across to give them a hand to raise themselves to a renewed fight. In early after noon General Pope's order, per General Roberts, was to send a pretty strong force diagonally to the front to relieve the center in the woods from pressure. Accordingly I detached for that purpose General Robinson, with his brigade; the Sixty-third Pennsylvania Volunteers, Colonel Hays; the One hundred and fifth Pennsylvania Volunteers, Captain Craig; the Twentieth Indiana, Colonel Brown, and, additionally, the Third Michigan Marksmen, under Colonel Champlin. General Robinson drove forward for several hundred yards, but the center of the main battle being shortly after driven back and out of the woods, my detachment, thus exposed, so considerably in front of all others, both flanks in air, was obliged to cease to advance, and confine themselves to holding their own. At 5 o'clock, thinking-- though at the risk of exposing my fighting line to being enfiladed--that I might drive the enemy by an unexpected attack through the woods, I brought up additionally the most of Birney's regiments---the Fourth Maine, Colonel Walker and Lieutenant-Colonel Carver: the Fortieth New York, Colonel Egan; First New York, Major Burr, and One hundred and first New York, Lieutenant-Colonel Gesner--and changed front to the left, to sweep with a rush the first line of the enemy. This was most successful. The enemy rolled up on his own right. It presaged a victory for us all. Still our force was too light. The enemy brought up rapidly heavy reserves, so that our farther progress was impeded. General Stevens came up gallantly in action to support us, but did not have the numbers."

Despite launching a fierce attack, Kearny's division could only do so much for so long until Jackson reinforced Hill's line by pulling Early's brigade from his right and sending Lawrence Branch's brigade into the fight.

Although the Union assaults had finally come to an end, Lee was still entertaining thoughts about launching an attack with Longstreet's men. Once again, Longstreet successfully argued against it, insisting that a reconnaissance and an attack in the morning was a better option. John Bell Hood's division conducted the reconnaissance in force, but nightfall brought his skirmishing with the Union left to an end.

As August 29 was drawing to a close, Pope had clearly failed to bag Jackson's wing of the army, but the battle was not a debacle either. Moreover, two of McClellan's corps from the Army of the Potomac were now nearby at Alexandria, comprising about 25,000 men. Although Pope clearly couldn't count on McClellan to actually order them forward as reinforcements anymore, he still had the option of pulling his own army back to Alexandria, uniting with McClellan's army, and then figuring out a new course of action.

Instead, Pope continued to talk himself into believing that he had Jackson on the ropes, and that Lee's army was in the process of retreating. Years later, he was still trying to justify his belief that Lee was retreating, writing:

"Every indication during the night of the 29th and up to 10 o'clock on the morning of the 30th pointed to the retreat of the enemy from our front. Paroled prisoners of our own army, taken on the evening of the 29th, who came into our lines on the morning of the 30th, reported the enemy retreating during the whole night in the direction of and along the Warrenton pike (a fact since confirmed by Longstreet's report).| Generals McDowell and Heintzelman, who reconnoitered the position held by the enemy's left on the evening of the 29th, also confirmed this statement. They reported to me the evacuation of these positions by the enemy, and that there was every indication of their retreat in the direction of Gainesville. On the morning of the 30th, as may be easily believed, our troops, who had been marching and fighting almost continuously for many days, were greatly exhausted. They had had little to eat for two days, and artillery and cavalry horses had been in harness and under the saddle for ten days, and had been almost out of forage for the last two days. It may be readily imagined how little these troops, after such severe labors and hardships, were in condition for further active marching and fighting."

Given Pope's mistaken beliefs, the one man who might have been able to extricate him from the mistake he was about to make happened to be the one man least inclined to help. For several days, George McClellan had at least 25,000 men within two days' march of Pope's army, yet he continued to insist that he couldn't move toward Manassas without the necessary cavalry and artillery. Pope might not have gotten much right in his writings about the battle after the war, but he rightly ridiculed McClellan's stance:

"On the 28th I had telegraphed General Halleck our condition, and had begged of him to have rations and forage sent forward to us from Alexandria with all speed; but about daylight on the 30th I received a note from General Franklin, written by direction of General McClellan, informing me that rations and forage would be loaded into the available wagons and cars at Alexandria as soon as I should send back a cavalry escort to guard the trains. Such a letter, when we were fighting the enemy and when

Alexandria was full of troops, needs no comment. Our cavalry was well-nigh broken down completely, and certainly we were in no condition to spare troops from the front, nor could they have gone to Alexandria and returned within the time by which we must have had provisions and forage or have fallen back toward supplies; nor am I able to understand of what use cavalry could be to guard railroad trains."

Understandably, supporters of Pope and critics of McClellan would heavily criticize the inaction and accuse McClellan of intentionally making Pope's life more difficult. It seems they were right; McClellan bragged in a private letter to his wife weeks earlier, "Pope will be badly thrashed within two days & ... they will be very glad to turn over the redemption of their affairs to me. I won't undertake it unless I have full & entire control." Even as Pope was launching a series of assaults against Jackson on August 29, McClellan suggested to Lincoln that they should "leave Pope to get out of his scrape, and at once use all our means to make the capital perfectly safe."

Chapter 7: August 30

One of the most ill-conceived attacks of the entire war would be made on August 30, and one of the best executed attacks of the entire war would follow it.

On the morning of August 30, Pope held a council of war at his headquarters, where he was unmistakably informed of Longstreet's position and that Jackson's men had not moved during the night. But as it turned out, some of Longstreet's men, a division under Richard Anderson, had arrived on the field late at night and woke up to find that they were dangerously close to the Union line. With that, they countermarched to link back up with the rest of Longstreet's wing, and when Pope heard of that movement it seemed to confirm to him that the Confederates were retreating, and he even telegraphed back to Washington that "the enemy was retreating to the mountains". Thus, even though Jackson's men were still in place and Longstreet was still posted on the Union army's left with about 25,000 men, Pope remained determined to attack what he believed was a retreating Confederate army.

Around noon, Pope ordered Porter to attack once again, this time in conjunction with Hatch's division and Reynolds's division on the Union left, up the Manassas-Gainesville turnpike. On the Union right, the divisions of Ricketts, Kearny, and Hooker, all of whom had fought hard the day before, were ordered to attack as well. Pope believed he was conducting a pincers attack on a retreating Confederate army, when in fact he was about to march Porter's corps right across Longstreet's front, all but exposing the left flank of Porter's 10,000 men to Longstreet's 25,000 Confederates. And far from retreating, Lee was going about bolstering Jackson's defenses, including posting artillery that could sweep the field in Jackson's front. Lee himself could not have drawn up a more favorable plan for the Confederates than Pope had.

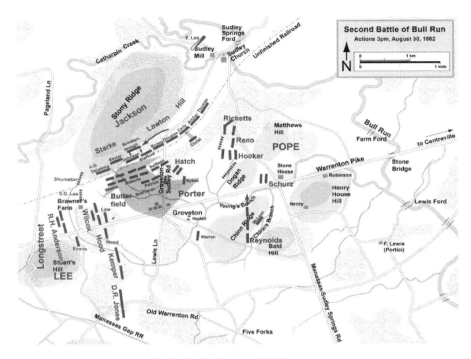

Porter's attack around 3:00 p.m.

In a campaign full of mistakes, the Union attacks managed not to be properly coordinated. Due to delays in getting his corps up, Porter would not make his assault until about an hour after the attack launched by the Union right. Jackson described how fierce the fighting was on his left in his report:

"About 2 p. m. the Federal infantry in large force advanced to the attack of our left, occupied by the division of Gen. Hill. It pressed forward, in defiance of our fatal and destructive fire, with great determination, a portion of it crossing a deep cut in the railroad track and penetrating in heavy force an interval of nearly 175 yards, which separated the right of Gregg's from the left of Thomas brigade. For a short time Gregg's brigade, on the extreme left, was isolated from the main body of the command; but the Fourteenth South Carolina Regiment, then in reserve, with the Forty-ninth Georgia, left of Col. Thomas, attacked the exultant enemy with vigor, and drove them back across the railroad track with great slaughter. Gen. McGowan reports that the opposing forces at one time delivered their volleys into each other at the distance of 10 paces. Assault after assault was made on the left, exhibiting on the part of the enemy great pertinacity and determination, but every advance was most successfully and gallantly driven back.

Gen. Hill reports that six separate and distinct assault were thus met and repulsed by his division, assisted by Hays' brigade, Col. Forno commanding.

By this time the brigade of Gen. Gregg, which from its position on the extreme left was most exposed to the enemy's attack, had nearly expended its ammunition. It had suffered severely in its men, and all its field officers except two were killed or wounded."

Porter's attack would be made under even more trying circumstances, since the division on his far left under Daniel Butterfield would have to cross about 600 yards in an open field in front of Jackson's men, who were posted behind a natural fortification in an unfinished railroad cut. On Butterfield's right was Hatch's division, which would have to march across land exposed to the batteries Lee had dutifully directed earlier in the day, not to mention Jackson's infantry. Even still, Hatch's division created a breach in Jackson's line, forcing the Stonewall Brigade to reinforce the line. The fighting was so heavy that some Confederates ran out of ammunition and began throwing rocks at the nearest Union soldiers, members of the 24th New York, which induced the Union men to throw some back.

Seeing no breakthroughs and still wary of Longstreet on his left, Porter kept his other division in reserve, but his entire command was now north of the Warrenton Turnpike and so far out in front of Longstreet that Porter's cautious alignment was still in no position to defend against the now impending flank attack. To top it off, McDowell ordered Reynolds to move his division up to support Porter's right, pulling even more Union soldiers from south of the Warrenton Turnpike and bringing them north of the Turnpike. That decision would only make it that much easier for Longstreet's assault to roll up the entire Union line, and by having only about 2,000 men still south of the Turnpike in front of Longstreet, Pope's army had inadvertently placed itself in serious danger of being trapped along Bull Run with the only roads of retreat being covered by Jackson near Sudley Springs Ford and Longstreet advancing east across the Warrenton Turnpike.

The start of Longstreet's assault at 4:00 p.m.

Around 4:00, Longstreet's assault started with the objective of reaching Henry Hill, the exact same spot McDowell's Union army had desperately sought to reach in the First Battle of Bull Run. As Longstreet explained, the advantageous positioning for his flank attack was so apparent to the men under his command that they were all but able to start the assault perfectly without even being commanded:

"Porter's masses were in almost direct line from the point at which I stood, and in enfilade fire. It was evident that they could not stand fifteen minutes under the fire of batteries planted at that point, while a division marching back and across the field to aid Jackson could not reach him in an hour, more time probably than he could stand under the heavy weights then bearing down upon him. Boldness was prudence! Prompt work by the wing and batteries could relieve the battle. Reinforcements might not be in time, so I called for my nearest batteries. Ready, anticipating call, they sprang to their places and drove at speed, saw the opportunity before it could be pointed out, and went into action. The first fire was by Chapman's battery, followed in rolling practice by Boyce's and Reilly's. Almost immediately the wounded began to drop off from Porter's ranks; the number seemed to increase with every shot; the masses began to waver, swinging back and forth, showing signs of discomfiture along the left and left centre.

In ten or fifteen minutes it crumbled into disorder and turned towards the rear. Although the batteries seemed to hasten the movements of the discomfited, the fire was less effective upon broken ranks, which gave them courage, and they made brave efforts to rally; but as the new lines formed they had to breast against Jackson's standing line, and make a new and favorable target for the batteries, which again drove them to disruption and retreat. Not satisfied, they made a third effort to rally and fight the battle through, but by that time they had fallen back far enough to open the field to the fire of S. D. Lee's artillery battalion. As the line began to take shape, this fearful fire was added to that under which they had tried so ineffectually to fight. The combination tore the line to pieces, and as it broke the third time the charge was ordered. The heavy fumes of gunpowder hanging about our ranks, as stimulating as sparkling wine, charged the atmosphere with the light and splendor of battle. Time was culminating under a flowing tide. The noble horses took the spirit of the riders sitting lightly in their saddles. As orders were given, the staff, their limbs already closed to the horses' flanks, pressed their spurs, but the electric current overleaped their speedy strides, and twenty-five thousand braves moved in line as by a single impulse. My old horse, appreciating the importance of corps headquarters, envious of the spread of his comrades as they measured the green, yet anxious to maintain his role, moved up and down his limited space in lofty bounds, resolved to cover in the air the space allotted his more fortunate comrades on the plain.

Leaving the broken ranks for Jackson, our fight was made against the lines near my front. As the plain along Hood's front was more favorable for the tread of soldiers, he was ordered, as the column of direction, to push for the plateau at the Henry House, in order to cut off retreat at the crossings by Young's Branch. Wilcox was called to support and cover Hood's left, but he lost sight of two of his brigades,--Featherston's and Pryor's, --and only gave the aid of his single brigade. Kemper and Jones were pushed on with Hood's right, Evans in Hood's direct support. The batteries were advanced as rapidly as fields were opened to them, Stribling's, J. B. Richardson's, Eshleman's, and Rogers's having fairest field for progress."

As Longstreet came crashing down from the west and south, sweeping the field before him in just 15 minutes, it became clear to Pope how tenuous his position was. Like the Confederates at First Bull Run, Pope ordered all available reinforcements to take up a defensive line on Henry Hill, and he wrote about the desperate resistance put up by some of the men under his command:

"The main attack of the enemy was made against our left, but was met with stubborn resistance by the divisions of Schenck and Reynolds, and the brigade of Milroy, who were soon reënforced on the left by Ricketts's division. The action was severe for several hours, the enemy bringing up heavy reserves and pouring mass after mass of his troops on our left. He was able also to present at least an equal force all along our line of battle. Porter's corps was halted and reformed, and as soon as it was in condition it was pushed forward to the support of our left, where it rendered distinguished service, especially the brigade of regulars under Colonel (then Lieutenant-Colonel) Buchanan.

McLean's brigade of Schenck's division, which was posted in observation on our left flank, and in support of Reynolds, became exposed to the attack of the enemy on our left when Reynolds's division was drawn back to form line to support Porter's corps, then retiring from their attack, and it was fiercely assailed by Hood and Evans, in greatly superior force. This brigade was commanded in person by General Schenck, the division commander, and fought with supreme gallantry and tenacity. The enemy's attack was repulsed several times with severe loss, but he returned again and again to the assault.

It is needless for me to describe the appearance of a man so well known to the country as General R. C. Schenck. I have only to say that a more gallant and devoted soldier never lived, and to his presence and the fearless exposure of his person during these attacks is largely due the protracted resistance made by this brigade. He fell, badly wounded, in the front of his command, and his loss was deeply felt and had a marked effect on the final result in that part of the field."

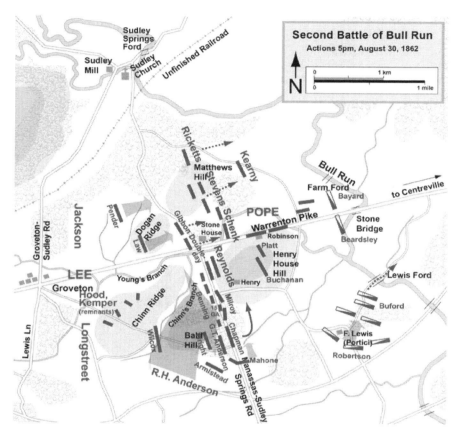

As Pope marshaled more forces into the vacuum around Henry Hill, nightfall became his best friend. By holding out on Henry Hill long enough, Pope kept the Warrenton Turnpike open so that he could retreat east across Bull Run. He was aided in this by the fact that Jackson's wing of the army was too slow to cut off that avenue of retreat, certainly a byproduct of the fact that they had been submitted to the heaviest marching and fighting of the past week. Still, Jackson has been criticized for having the slows, just like during the Seven Days' Battles; John Hennessy considered Jackson's action (or lack of it) "one of the battle's great puzzles" and "one of the most significant Confederate failures".

Though Pope's army didn't scramble back toward Washington in as much disorder as McDowell's army had during the First Battle of Bull Run, the result was ultimately the same.

And as if to antagonize Pope even more, around the same time he began retreating across the Warrenton Turnpike toward Centreville, Franklin's corps from McClellan's Army of the Potomac was marching into Centreville, about 5 miles east of Bull Run. Had Franklin been allowed to march even a day earlier, there's no telling how differently the battle might have gone.

Darkness granted Pope the respite Longstreet would not, as Longstreet noted in his memoirs: "When the last guns were fired the thickening twilight concealed the lines of friend and foe, so that the danger of friend firing against friend became imminent. The hill of the Henry House was reached in good time, but darkness coming on earlier because of thickening clouds hovering over us, and a gentle fall of rain closely following, the plateau was shut off from view, and its ascent only found by groping through the darkening rainfall. As long as the enemy held the plateau, he covered the line of retreat by the turnpike and the bridge at Young's Branch. As he retired, heavy darkness gave safe-conduct to such of his columns as could find their way through the weird mists."

The losses at the Second Battle of Bull Run were staggering, especially since the battle took place before Antietam and Gettysburg. About 10,000 soldiers, or nearly 16% of Pope's army, was killed, wounded, or captured, while Lee's army lost nearly 8,500, almost the same percentage of his forces.

Chapter 8: The Aftermath of the Battle

Lee had decisively defeated Pope, but in the immediate wake of the battle, Lee continued to hold out hope of bagging Pope's army, which he intended to accomplish by interposing his army between Pope and Washington D.C. Of course, this was made virtually impossible by elements of the Army of the Potomac, and the only major fighting after the battle came on September 1. Known as the Battle of Chantilly, Jackson's men fought some of Pope's army during a violent storm complete with lightning and pouring rain. The battle is best remembered for the death of the widely respected Phil Kearny. During the battle, Kearny, who had already lost an arm in battle, decided to investigate a gap in the Union line. When he was warned of the danger he shouted, "The Rebel bullet that can kill me has not yet been molded." Subsequently riding into Confederate troops, Kearny ignored a demand to surrender and instead attempted to escape, only to have a Rebel bullet hit him in the spine and kill him instantly. As one of the most famous soldiers of his era, Kearny was quickly recognized by A.P. Hill, who ran up to his body and yelled, "You've killed Phil Kearny, he deserved a better fate than to die in the mud."

Kearny

After two days' fighting, Lee had achieved another major victory, and he now stood unopposed in the field 12 miles away from Washington D.C. While Joseph Johnston and P.G.T. Beauregard had stayed in this position in the months after the First Battle of Bull Run, Lee determined upon a more aggressive course: taking the fight to the North. In early September, convinced that the best way to defend Richmond was to divert attention to Washington, Lee had decided to invade Maryland after obtaining Jefferson Davis's permission. In conjunction with giving Lee his approval, Davis wrote a public proclamation to the Southern people and, ostensibly, the Europeans whose recognition he hoped to gain. Recognizing the political sensitivity of appearing to invade the North instead of simply defending the home front, Davis cast the decision as one of self-defense, and that there was "no design of conquest", asserting, "We are driven to protect our own country by transferring the seat of war to that of an enemy who pursues us with a relentless and apparently aimless hostility."

Lee had also no doubt taken stock of the North's morale, both among its people and the soldiers of Pope's army and McClellan's army. In the summer of 1862, the Union had suffered more than 20,000 casualties, and Northern Democrats, who had been split into pro-war and anti-war factions from the beginning, increasingly began to question the war. As of September 1862, no progress had been made on Richmond; in fact, a Confederate army was now about to enter Maryland. And with the election of 1862 approaching, Lincoln feared the Republicans might suffer losses in the Congressional midterms that would harm the war effort.

Taking all that into account, on September 3, Lee would cross the Potomac into Maryland with his army, invading the North for the first time. Meanwhile, Lincoln restored General McClellan and removed General Pope after the second disaster at Bull Run. McClellan was still immensely popular among the Army of the Potomac, and with a mixture of men from his Army of the Potomac and Pope's Army of Virginia, he began a cautious pursuit of Lee into Maryland.

Although McClellan had largely stayed out of the political fray through 1862, McClellan's most ardent supporters could not deny that he actively worked to delay reinforcing Pope during the most recent campaign once the Army of the Potomac was evacuated from the Peninsula. Nevertheless, McClellan ultimately got what he wanted out of Pope's misfortune. Though there is some debate on the order of events that led to McClellan taking command, Lincoln ultimately restored McClellan to command, likely because McClellan was the only administrator who could reform the army quickly and efficiently.

Naturally, McClellan's ascension to command of the armies around Washington outraged the Republicans in Congress and the Lincoln Administration, some of whom had all but branded him a traitor for his inactivity in early 1862 and his poor performance on the Peninsula. This would make it all the more ironic that McClellan's campaign into Maryland during the next few weeks would bring about the release of the Emancipation Proclamation.

Of all the men who fought and died in August 1862, nobody's reputation suffered worse than John Pope, who was transferred to Minnesota to deal with the Dakota Indians, about as far away from the Civil War front as possible. Pope would spend the final 30 years of his life bitterly refighting the battle in print, as well as trying to correct the widely held opinion that he was too brash and arrogant. As he quipped in an article that appeared in the popular *Battles & Leaders of the Civil War* series, "A good deal of cheap wit has been expended upon a fanciful story that I published an order or wrote a letter or made a remark that my 'headquarters would be in the saddle.' It is an expression harmless and innocent enough, but it is even stated that it furnished General Lee with the basis for the only joke of his life. I think it due to army tradition, and to the comfort of those who have so often repeated this ancient joke in the days long before the civil war, that these later wits should not be allowed with impunity to poach on this well-tilled manor."

Not surprisingly, John Pope would continue to insist until the day he died that his detractors were mistaken, and that the Second Battle of Bull Run was greatly misunderstood:

"The battle treated of, as well as the campaign which preceded it, have been, and no doubt still are, greatly misunderstood. Probably they will remain during this generation a matter of controversy, into which personal feeling and prejudice so largely enter that dispassionate judgment cannot now be looked for. I submit this article to the public judgment with all confidence that it will be fairly considered, and as just a judgment passed upon it as is possible at this time. I well understood, as does every military man, how difficult and how thankless was the task imposed on me, and I do not hesitate to say that I would gladly have avoided it if I could have done so consistent with duty.

To confront with a small army greatly superior forces, to fight battles without the hope of victory, but only to gain time by delaying the forward movement of the enemy, is a duty the most hazardous and the most difficult that can be imposed upon any general or any army. While such operations require the highest courage and endurance on the part of the troops, they are unlikely to be understood or appreciated, and the results, however successful in view of the object aimed at, have little in them to attract public commendation or applause.

At no time could I have hoped to fight a successful battle with the superior forces of the enemy which confronted me, and which were able at any time to outflank and bear my small army to the dust. It was only by constant movement, incessant watchfulness, and hazardous skirmishes and battles, that the forces under my command were saved from destruction, and that the enemy was embarrassed and delayed in his advance until the army of General McClellan was at length assembled for the defense of Washington.

I did hope that in the course of these operations the enemy might commit some imprudence, or leave some opening of which I could take such advantage as to gain at least a partial success. This opportunity was presented by the advance of Jackson on Manassas Junction; but although the best dispositions possible in my view were made, the object was frustrated by causes which could not have been foreseen, and which perhaps are not yet completely known to the country."

Of course, it had been Pope who misunderstood the situation all along in August 1862, and it would be Pope who continued to misunderstand the campaign for the rest of his life.

Bibliography

Dawes, Rufus R. A Full Blown Yankee of the Iron Brigade: Service with the Sixth Wisconsin Volunteers. Lincoln: University of Nebraska Press, 1999.

Greene, A. Wilson. The Second Battle of Manassas. National Park Service Civil War Series. Fort Washington, PA: U.S. National Park Service and Eastern National, 2006.

Hennessy, John J. Return to Bull Run: The Campaign and Battle of Second Manassas. Norman: University of Oklahoma Press, 1993.

Herdegen, Lance J. The Men Stood Like Iron: How the Iron Brigade Won Its Name. Bloomington: Indiana University Press, 1997.

Langellier, John. Second Manassas 1862: Robert E. Lee's Greatest Victory. Oxford: Osprey

Publishing, 2002.

Longstreet, James. From Manassas to Appomattox: Memoirs of the Civil War in America. New York: Da Capo Press, 1992.

Martin, David G. The Second Bull Run Campaign: July–August 1862. New York: Da Capo Press, 1997.

The Battle of Antietam

Chapter 1: Lee Decides to Invade Maryland

After Robert E. Lee was installed as the commander of the Army of Northern Virginia during the Peninsula Campaign in June 1862, he quickly rallied the Confederate forces around Richmond and beat back George McClellan's Army of the Potomac later that month in a series of battles known as the Seven Days' Battles. As McClellan retreated up the peninsula, Lee reorganized the Army of Northern Virginia into the structure it is best remembered by. Stonewall Jackson now took command of a force consisting of his own division (now commanded by Brig. General Charles S. Winder) and those of Maj. General Richard S. Ewell, Brig. General William H. C. Whiting, and Maj. General D. H. Hill. The other wing of Lee's army was commanded by James Longstreet. On July 25, 1862, after the conclusion of the Seven Days Battles had brought the Peninsula Campaign to an end, JEB Stuart was promoted to Major General, his command upgraded to Cavalry Division.

Lee during the war

Stonewall Jackson

James Longstreet

JEB Stuart

Even before McClellan had completely withdrawn his troops, Lee sent Jackson's forces northward to intercept the new army Abraham Lincoln had placed under Maj. General John Pope, formed out of the scattered troops in the Virginia area. Pope had found success in the Western theater, and he was uncommonly brash, instructing the previously defeated men now under his command that his soldiers in the West were accustomed to seeing the backs of the enemy. Pope's arrogance turned off his own men, and it also caught the notice of Lee.

Once certain McClellan was in full retreat, Lee joined Jackson, planning to strike Pope before McClellan's troops could arrive as reinforcements. In late August 1862, in a "daring and unorthodox" move, Lee divided his forces and sent Jackson northward to flank them, ultimately bringing Jackson directly behind Pope's army and supply base. This forced Pope to fall back to Manassas to protect his flank and maintain his lines of communication. Recognizing Lee's genius for military strategy, General Jackson quickly became Lee's most trusted commander, and he would later say that he so trusted Lee's military instincts that he would even follow him into battle blindfolded.

When Pope's army fell back to Manassas to confront Jackson, his wing of Lee's army dug in along a railroad trench and took a defensive stance. The Second Battle of Manassas or Bull Run was fought August 28-30, beginning with the Union army throwing itself at Jackson the first two days. While Jackson's men defended themselves the first two days, Lee used Longstreet's wing on August 30 to deliver a devastating flank attack before reinforcements from the retreating Army of the Potomac could reach the field. Longstreet's attack swept Pope's army off the field. Fought on the same ground as the First Battle of Manassas nearly a year earlier, the result was the same: a decisive Confederate victory that sent Union soldiers scrambling back to the safety of Washington.

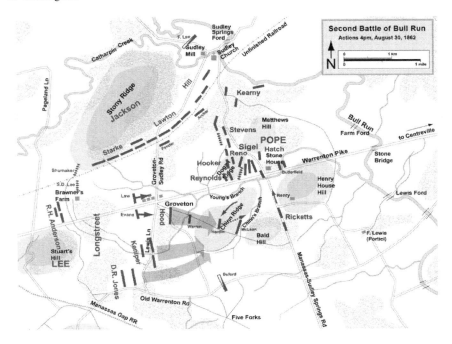

After two days' fighting, Lee had achieved another major victory, and he now stood unopposed in the field 12 miles away from Washington D.C. While Joseph Johnston and P.G.T. Beauregard had stayed in this position in the months after the First Battle of Bull Run, Lee determined upon a more aggressive course: taking the fight to the North.

In early September, convinced that the best way to defend Richmond was to divert attention to Washington, Lee had decided to invade Maryland after obtaining Jefferson Davis's permission. On September 3, the famous general reported to the Confederate president:

HEADQUARTERS ALEXANDRIA AND LEESBURG ROAD,

Near Dranesville, September 3, 1862.

His Excellency President DAVIS,

Richmond, Va.:

Mr. PRESIDENT: The present seems to be the most propitious time since the commencement of the war for the Confederate Army to enter Maryland. The two grand armies of the United States that have been operating in Virginia, though now united, are much weakened and demoralized. Their new levies, of which I understand 60,000 men have already been posted in Washington, are not yet organized, and will take some time to prepare for the field. If it is ever desired to give material aid to Maryland and afford her an opportunity of throwing off the oppression to which she is now subject, this would seem the most favorable.

After the enemy had disappeared from the vicinity of Fairfax Court House, and taken the road to Alexandria and Washington, I did not think it would be advantageous to follow him farther. I had no intention of attacking him in his fortifications, and am not prepared to invest them. If I possessed the necessary munitions, I should be unable to supply provisions for the troops. I therefore determined, while threatening the approaches to Washington, to draw the troops into Loudoun, where forage and some provisions can be obtained, menace their possession of the Shenandoah Valley, and, if found practicable, to cross into Maryland. The purpose, if discovered, will have the effect of carrying the enemy north of the Potomac, and, if prevented, will not result in much evil.

The army is not properly equipped for an invasion of an enemy's territory. It lacks much of the material of war, is feeble in transportation, the animals being much reduced, and the men are poorly provided with clothes, and in thousands of instances are destitute of shoes. Still, we cannot afford to be idle, and though weaker than our opponents in men and military equipments, must endeavor to harass if we cannot destroy them. I am aware that the movement is attended with much risk, yet I do not consider success impossible, and shall endeavor to guard it from loss. As long as the army of the enemy are employed on this frontier I have no fears for the safety of Richmond, yet I earnestly recommend that advantage be taken of this period of comparative safety to place its defense, both by land and water, in the most perfect condition. A respectable force can be collected to defend its approaches by land, and the steamer Richmond, I hope, is now ready to clear the river of hostile vessels.

Should General Bragg find it impracticable to operate to advantage on his present frontier, his army, after leaving sufficient garrisons, could be advantageously employed in opposing the overwhelming numbers which it seems to be the intention of the enemy now to concentrate in Virginia.

I have already been told by prisoners that some of Buell's cavalry have been joined to General Pope's army, and have reason to believe that the whole of McClellan's, the larger portion of Burnside's and Cox's, and a portion of Hunter's, are united to it.

What occasions me most concern is the fear of getting out of ammunition. I beg you will instruct the Ordnance Department to spare no pains in manufacturing a sufficient amount of the best kind, and to be particular, in preparing that for the artillery, to provide three times as much of the long-range ammunition as of that for smooth-bore or short-range guns. The points to which I desire the ammunition to be forwarded will be made known to the Department in time. If the Quartermaster's Department can furnish any shoes, it would be the greatest relief. We have entered upon September, and the nights are becoming cool.

I have the honor to be, with high respect, your obedient servant,

R. E. LEE, General.

A few days later, Jefferson Davis responded to Lee's suggestion by approving an invasion of Maryland subject to a number of conditions:

General R. E. LEE, Commanding, &c.:

SIR: It is deemed proper that you should, in accordance with established usage, announce, by proclamation to the people of Maryland, the motives and purposes of your presence among them at the head of an invading army, and you are instructed in such proclamation to make known--

1st. That the Confederate Government is waging this war solely for self-defense; that it has no design of conquest, or any other purpose than to secure peace and the abandonment by the United States of their pretensions to govern a people who have never been their subjects, and who prefer self-government to a union with them.

2d. That this Government, at the very moment of its inauguration, sent commissioners to Washington to treat for a peaceful adjustment of all differences, but that these commissioners were not received, nor even allowed to communicate the object of their mission; and that, on a subsequent occasion, a communication from the President of the Confederacy to President Lincoln remained without answer, although a reply was promised by General Scott, into whose hands the communication was delivered.

3d. That among the pretexts urged for continuance of the war, is the assertion that the Confederate Government desires to deprive the United States of the free navigation of the Western rivers, although the truth is that the Confederate Congress, by public act, prior to the commencement of the war, enacted that "the peaceful navigation of the

Mississippi River is hereby declared free to the citizens of any of the States upon its boundaries, or upon the borders of its navigable tributaries," a declaration to which this Government has always been, and is still, ready to adhere.

4th. That now, at a juncture when our arms have been successful, we restrict ourselves to the same just and moderate demand that we made at the darkest period of our reverses, the simple demand that the people of the United States should cease to war upon us, and permit us to pursue our own path to happiness, while they in peace pursue theirs.

5th. That we are debarred from the renewal of formal proposals for peace by having no reason to expect that they would be received with the respect mutually due by nations in their intercourse, whether in peace or in war.

6th. That, under these circumstances, we are driven to protect our own country by transferring the seat of war to that of an enemy, who pursues us with a relentless and, apparently, aimless hostility; that our fields have been laid waste, our people killed, many homes made desolate, and that rapine and murder have ravaged our frontiers; that the sacred right of self-defense demands that, if such a war is to continue, its consequences shall fall on those who persist in their refusal to make peace.

7th. That the Confederate army, therefore, comes to occupy the territory of their enemies, and to make it the theater of hostilities; that with the people themselves rests the power to put an end to this invasion of their homes, for, if unable to prevail on the Government of the United States to conclude a general peace, their own State government, in the exercise of its sovereignty, can secure immunity from the desolating effects of warfare on the soil of the State by a separate treaty of peace, which this Government will ever be ready to conclude on the most just and liberal basis.

8th. That the responsibility thus rests on the people of ------- continuing an unjust and oppressive warfare upon the Confederate States--a warfare which can never end in any other manner than that now proposed. With them is the option of preserving the blessings of peace by the simple abandonment of the design of subjugating a people over whom no right of dominion has ever been conferred, either by God or man.

In conjunction with giving Lee his approval, Davis wrote a public proclamation to the Southern people and, ostensibly, the Europeans whose recognition he hoped to gain. Recognizing the political sensitivity of appearing to invade the North instead of simply defending the home front, Davis cast the decision as one of self-defense, and that there was "no design of conquest", asserting, "We are driven to protect our own country by transferring the seat of war to that of an enemy who pursues us with a relentless and apparently aimless hostility."

Once he had his president's approval, Lee actually issued orders to be proclaimed before citizens of Maryland, acutely aware that the border state had plenty of Confederate sympathizers who might not look kindly toward having their state invaded by the Confederate army:

TO THE PEOPLE OF MARYLAND:

It is right that you should know the purpose that has brought the army under my command within the limits of your State, so far as that purpose concerns yourselves.

The people of the Confederate States have long watched with the deepest sympathy the wrongs and outrages that have been inflicted upon the citizens of a Commonwealth allied to the States of the South by the strongest social, political, and commercial ties.

They have seen with profound indignation their sister-State deprived of every right and reduced to the condition of a conquered province.

Under the pretense of supporting the Constitution, but in violation of its most valuable provisions, your citizens have been arrested and imprisoned upon no charge and contrary to all forms of law; the faithful and manly protest against this outrage made by the venerable and illustrious Marylander to whom in better days no citizen appealed for right in vain was treated with scorn and contempt; the government of your chief city has been usurped by armed strangers; your legislature has been dissolved by the unlawful arrest of its members; freedom of the press and of speech has been suppressed; words have been declared offences by an arbitrary decree of the Federal executive, and citizens ordered to be tried by a military commission for what they may dare to speak.

Believing that the people of Maryland possessed a spirit too lofty to submit to such a government, the people of the South have long wished to aid you in throwing off this foreign yoke, to enable you again to enjoy the inalienable rights of freemen and restore independence and sovereignty to your State.

In obedience to this wish our army has come among you, and is prepared to assist you with the power of its arms in regaining the rights of which you have been despoiled.

This, citizens of Maryland, is our mission, so far as you are concerned. No constraint upon your free will is intended ; no intimidation will be allowed. Within the limits of this army at least, Marylanders shall once more enjoy their ancient freedom of thought and speech. We know no enemies among you, and will protect all, of every opinion. It is for you to decide your destiny freely and without constraint.

This army will respect your choice, whatever it may be; and, while the Southern people will rejoice to welcome you to your natural position among them, they will only welcome you when you come of your own free will.

Today the decision to invade Maryland is remembered through the prism of Lee hoping to win a major battle in the North that would bring about European recognition of the Confederacy, potential intervention, and possible capitulation by the North, whose anti-war Democrats were picking up political momentum. However, Lee also hoped that the fighting in Maryland would relieve Virginia's resources, especially the Shenandoah Valley, which served as the state's "breadbasket". And though largely forgotten today, Lee's move was controversial among his own men. Confederate soldiers, including Lee, took up arms to defend their homes, but now they were being asked to invade a Northern state. An untold number of Confederate soldiers refused to cross the Potomac River into Maryland.

Lee hinted at all of this in his report after the campaign while justifying his decision to make the invasion:

"Although not properly equipped for invasion, lacking much of the material of war, and feeble in transportation, the troops poorly provided with clothing, and thousands of them destitute of shoes, it was yet believed to be strong enough to detain the enemy upon the northern frontier until the approach of winter should render his advance into Virginia difficult, if not impracticable. The condition of Maryland encouraged the belief that the presence of our army, however inferior to that of the enemy, would induce the Washington Government to retain all its available force to provide against contingencies, which its course toward the people of that State gave it reason to apprehend. At the same time it was hoped that military success might afford us an opportunity to aid the citizens of Maryland in any efforts they might be disposed to make to recover their liberties. The difficulties that surrounded them were fully appreciated, and we expected to derive more assistance in the attainment of our object from the just fears of the Washington."

For his part, General Longstreet also held the same view as Lee, believing an invasion of Maryland had plenty of advantages. He wrote of the decision in his memoirs, "The Army of Northern Virginia was afield without a foe. Its once grand adversary, discomfited under two commanders, had crept into cover of the bulwarks about the national capital. The commercial, social, and blood ties of Maryland inclined her people to the Southern cause. A little way north of the Potomac were inviting fields of food and supplies more plentiful than on the southern side; and the fields for march and manoeuvre, strategy and tactics, were even more inviting than the broad fields of grain and comfortable pasture-lands. Propitious also was the prospect of swelling our ranks by Maryland recruits."

Lee had also no doubt taken stock of the North's morale, both among its people and the soldiers of Pope's army and McClellan's army. In the summer of 1862, the Union had suffered more than 20,000 casualties, and Northern Democrats, who had been split into pro-war and anti-war factions from the beginning, increasingly began to question the war. As of September 1862, no progress had been made on Richmond; in fact, a Confederate army was now about to enter Maryland. And with the election of 1862 was approaching, Lincoln feared the Republicans might suffer losses in the Congressional midterms that would harm the war effort.

With all of that in mind, he restored General McClellan and removed General Pope after the second disaster at Bull Run. McClellan was still immensely popular among the Army of the Potomac, and with a mixture of men from his Army of the Potomac and Pope's Army of Virginia, he began a cautious pursuit of Lee into Maryland.

Although McClellan had largely stayed out of the political fray through 1862, McClellan's most ardent supporters could not deny that he actively worked to delay reinforcing Pope during the Second Manassas campaign once the Army of the Potomac was evacuated from the Peninsula. Nevertheless, McClellan ultimately got what he wanted out of Pope's misfortune. Though there is some debate on the order of events that led to McClellan taking command, Lincoln ultimately restored McClellan to command, likely because McClellan was the only administrator who could reform the army quickly and efficiently.

McClellan

Naturally, McClellan's ascension to command of the armies around Washington outraged the Republicans in Congress and the Lincoln Administration, some of whom had all but branded him a traitor for his inactivity in early 1862 and his poor performance on the Peninsula. This would make it all the more ironic that McClellan's campaign into Maryland during the next few weeks would bring about the release of the Emancipation Proclamation.

Chapter 2: Initial Movements

The most fateful decision of the Maryland Campaign was made almost immediately, when early on Lee decided to divide his army into four parts across Maryland. Lee ordered Longstreet's men to Boonsboro and then to Hagerstown, Stonewall Jackson's forces to Harpers Ferry, and Stuart's cavalry and D.H. Hill's division to screen the Army of Northern Virginia's movements and cover its rear.

D.H. Hill

Why Lee chose to divide his army is still heavily debated among historians, who have pointed to factors like the importance of maintaining his supply lines through the Shenandoah Valley. Lee was also unaware what kind of resistance he might face at places like Frederick and Harpers Ferry, and it's also possible that he simply assumed McClellan's caution would allow him to take and keep the initiative and dictate the course of the campaign. With McClellan now assuming command of the Northern forces, Lee probably expected to have plenty of time to assemble his troops and bring his battle plan to fruition.

This time, however, McClellan was better prepared to face Lee. He had beaten Lee in a campaign through western Virginia in 1861 and had clearly underestimated Lee as a result during the Peninsula Campaign, but now he realized that Lee was not the timid, indecisive general McClellan initially thought.

Though it was clear in early September that Lee had crossed the Potomac, the Army of Northern Virginia decided to use ridges, mountains and cavalry to screen their movements. McClellan believed the most realistic goal was to drive the Confederates out of Maryland and aimed to do so, but his 85,000 strong Army of the Potomac moved conservatively into Maryland during the early portion of the campaign while still dealing with logistics. A report from the infamous intelligence chief Allan Pleasanton reached McClellan and estimated the Rebel force at 100,000, while other reports couldn't ascertain the nature of the that army's movements or motives. McClellan told the Administration on September 10 that the estimates of the Army of Northern Virginia put it somewhere between 80,000-150,000 men, which obviously had a huge effect on the campaign.

With the benefit of hindsight, historians now believe that Lee's entire Army of Northern Virginia had perhaps 50,000 men at most and possibly closer to 30,000 during the Maryland campaign. It's unclear how Lee's army, which numbered 55,000 before the Maryland Campaign, suffered such a steep drop in manpower, but historians have cited a number of factors, including disease and soldiers' refusal to invade the North. Lee clearly felt the pinch too, ordering his officers to keep straggling to a minimum and calling stragglers "unworthy members of an army that has immortalized itself". And far from Longstreet's hope that an invasion of Maryland would swell the Confederate ranks with sympathizers, it's estimated that only a few dozen at most latched on with the invading army in Maryland. Union general John Gibbon, who commanded the famed Iron Brigade, also admitted his surprise with the people of Maryland, later writing, "I did not believe before coming here that there was so much Union feeling in the state... The whole population [of Frederick] seemed to turn out to welcome us. When Genl McClellan came thro the ladies nearly eat him up, they kissed his clothing, threw their arms around his horse's neck and committed all sorts of extravagances."

Gibbon

In his post-campaign report, Lee summarized the initial movements of his army leading up to September 12:

"It was decided to cross the Potomac east of the Blue Ridge, in order, by threatening Washington and Baltimore, to cause the enemy to withdraw from the south bank, where his presence endangered our communications and the safety of those engaged in the removal of our wounded and the captured property from the late battlefields. Having accomplished this result, it was proposed to move the army into Western Maryland, establish our communications with Richmond through the Valley of the Shenandoah, and, by threatening Pennsylvania, induce the enemy to follow, and thus draw him from his base of supplies.

It had been supposed that the advance upon Fredericktown would lead to the evacuation of Martinsburg and Harper's Ferry, thus opening the line of communication through the Valley. This not having occurred, it became necessary to dislodge the enemy from those positions before concentrating the army west of the mountains. To accomplish this with the least delay, General Jackson was directed to proceed with his command to Martinsburg, and, after driving the enemy from that place, to move down the south side of the Potomac upon Harper's Ferry. General McLaws, with his own and R. H. Anderson's division, was ordered to seize Maryland Heights, on the north side of the Potomac, opposite Harper's Ferry, and Brigadier-General Walker to take possession of Loudoun Heights, on the east side of the Shenandoa, where it unites with the Potomac. These several commands were directed, after reducing Harper's Ferry and clearing the Valley of the enemy, to join the rest of the army at Boonsborough or Hagerstown.

The march of these troops began on the 10th, and at the same time the remainder of Longstreet's command and the division of D. H. Hill crossed the South Mountain and moved toward Boonsborough. General Stuart, with the cavalry, remained east of the mountains, to observe the enemy and retard his advance.

A report having been received that a Federal force was approaching Hagerstown from the direction of Chambersburg, Longstreet continued his march to the former place, in order to secure the road leading thence to Williamsport, and also to prevent the removal of stores which were said to be in Hagerstown. He arrived at that place on the 11th, General Hill halting near Boonsborough to prevent the enemy at Harper's Ferry from escaping through Pleasant Valley, and at the same time to support the cavalry. The advance of the Federal Army was so slow at the time we left Fredericktown as to justify the belief that the reduction of Harper's Ferry would be accomplished and our troops concentrated before they would be called upon to meet it. In that event, it had not been intended to oppose its passage through the South Mountains, as it was desired to engage it as far as possible from its base.

General Jackson marched very rapidly, and, crossing the Potomac near Williamsport on the 11th, sent A. P. Hill's division directly to Martinsburg, and disposed the rest of his command to cut off the retreat of the enemy westward. On his approach, the Federal troops evacuated Martinsburg, retiring to Harper's Ferry on the night of the 11th, and Jackson entered the former place on the 12th, capturing some prisoners and abandoned stores."

Chapter 3: The Lost Order

On September 12, Stonewall Jackson's men were making their way to the outskirts of Harpers Ferry, whose garrison McClellan had unsuccessfully requested to have evacuated and added to his army. Meanwhile, the Union army was on the verge of entering Frederick, still unaware of Lee's dispositions but less than 20 miles behind the fragmented Confederate army.

It was around Frederick that the North was about to have one of the greatest strokes of luck during the Civil War. For reasons that are still unclear, Union troops in camp at Frederick came across a copy of Special Order 191, wrapped up among three cigars. The order contained Lee's entire marching plans for Maryland, making it clear that the Army of Northern Virginia had been divided into multiple parts, which, if faced by overpowering strength, could be entirely defeated in detail and bagged separately before they could regather into one fighting force. The Lost

Order had been issued on September 9, and it read:

HDQRS. ARMY OF NORTHERN VIRGINIA,

September 9, 1862.

I. The citizens of Fredericktown being unwilling, while overrun by members of his army, to open their stores, in order to give them confidence, and to secure to officers and men purchasing supplies for benefit of this command, all officers and men of this army are strictly prohibited from visiting Fredericktown except on business, in which case they will bear evidence of this in writing from division commanders. The provost-marshal in Fredericktown will see that his guard rigidly enforces this order.

II. Major Taylor will proceed to Leesburg, Va., and arrange for transportation of the sick and those unable to walk to Winchester, securing the transportation of the country for this purpose. The route between this and Culpeper Court-House east of the mountains being unsafe will no longer be traveled. Those on the way to this army already across the river will move up promptly; all others will proceed to Winchester collectively and under command of officers, at which point, being the general depot of this army, its movements will be known and instructions given by commanding officer regulating further movements.

III. The army will resume its march tomorrow, taking the Hagerstown road. General Jackson's command will form the advance, and, after passing Middletown, with such portion as he may select, take the route toward Sharpsburg, cross the Potomac at the most convenient point, and by Friday morning take possession of the Baltimore and Ohio Railroad, capture such of them as may be at Martinsburg, and intercept such as may attempt to escape from Harper's Ferry.

IV. General Longstreet's command will pursue the main road as far as Boonsborough, where it will halt, with reserve, supply, and baggage trains of the army.

V. General McLaws, with his own division and that of General R. H. Anderson, will follow General Longstreet. On reaching Middletown will take the route to Harper's Ferry, and by Friday morning possess himself of the Maryland Heights and endeavor to capture the enemy at Harper's Ferry and vicinity.

VI. General Walker, with his division, after accomplishing the object in which he is now engaged, will cross the Potomac at Cheek's Ford, ascend its right bank to Lovettsville, take possession of Loudoun Heights, if practicable, by Friday morning, Keys' Ford on his left, and the road between the end of the mountain and the Potomac on his right. He will, as far as practicable, co-operate with Generals McLaws and Jackson, and intercept retreat of the enemy.

VII. General D. H. Hill's division will form the rear guard of the army, pursuing the road taken by the main body. The reserve artillery, ordnance, and supply trains, &c., will precede General

Hill.

VIII. General Stuart will detach a squadron of cavalry to accompany the commands of Generals Longstreet, Jackson, and McLaws, and, with the main body of the cavalry, will cover the route of the army, bringing up all stragglers that may have been left behind.

IX. The commands of Generals Jackson, McLaws, and Walker, after accomplishing the objects for which they have been detached, will join the main body of the army at Boonsborough or Hagerstown.

X. Each regiment on the march will habitually carry its axes in the regimental ordnance wagons, for use of the men at their encampments, to procure wood, &c.

By command of General R. E. Lee:

R. H. CHILTON,

Assistant Adjutant-General.

The "Lost Order" quickly made its way to General McClellan, who took several hours to debate whether or not it was intentional misinformation or actually real. McClellan is usually faulted for not acting quickly enough on these orders, but much of the instructions are vague and seemingly contradicted recent Rebel movements. Moreover, McClellan was rightly concerned that the orders could be false misinformation meant to deceive the Union, since the manner in which the orders were lost was bizarre and could not be accounted for. After about 18 hours, McClellan was confident enough that they were accurate and famously boasted to General Gibbon, "Here is a paper with which if I cannot whip *Bobby Lee,* I will be willing to go home." McClellan also wired Lincoln, "I have the whole rebel force in front of me, but I am confident, and no time shall be lost. I think Lee has made a gross mistake, and that he will be severely punished for it. I have all the plans of the rebels, and will catch them in their own trap if my men are equal to the emergency... Will send you trophies."

Though having Lee's marching plans offered McClellan an incredible advantage, the Lost Order may also have reinforced McClellan's belief that Lee's army had a significant advantage in manpower through its vague wording of "commands."

Chapter 4: Harpers Ferry

Harpers Ferry in the 1860s

The Confederates were completely unaware of the North's luck as they began to carry out Lee's plans. To Jackson's advantage, Col. Dixon S. Miles, Union commander at Harpers Ferry, had insisted on keeping most of his troops near the town instead of taking up commanding positions on the most important position, Maryland Heights. On September 12, Confederate forces engaged the Union's marginal defenses on the heights, but only a brief skirmish ensued. Then on September 13, two Confederate brigades arrived and easily drove the Union troops from the heights--but the critical positions to the west and south of town remained heavily defended.

By September 14, Jackson had methodically positioned his artillery around Harpers Ferry and ordered Maj. Gen. A. P. Hill to move down the west bank of the Shenandoah River in preparation for a flank attack on the Union left the next morning. By the following morning, Jackson had positioned nearly fifty guns on Maryland Heights and at the base of Loudoun Heights. Then he began a fierce artillery barrage from all sides, followed by a full-out infantry assault. Realizing the hopelessness of the situation, Col. Miles raised the white flag of surrender.

Chapter 5: Dispositions Before the Battle

It's unclear when Lee realized that McClellan had found a copy of his marching orders, and it's even possible that he knew almost right away. But that still gave Lee, who only had about 18,000 men at his disposal in the vicinity, little time to regroup. On the night of September 13 McClellan's army began moving at an uncharacteristically quick pace, and the following day, the advancing Union army began pushing in on the Confederate forces at several mountain passes at South Mountain: Crampton's Gap, Turner's Gap, and Fox's Gap. If McClellan's men could successfully push their way through these gaps, they would have an even greater chance of falling upon the different pieces of Lee's army.

Despite being significantly outnumbered, Lee's army had the advantage of fighting defensively on higher terrain, and they were able to delay McClellan's advance an entire day. While Jackson's wing was forcing the Harpers Ferry garrison to surrender, Lee regathered his other scattered units around Sharpsburg near Antietam Creek. Lee braced himself for renewed hostilities on September 15, but McClellan remained cautious and did not attack the Confederates that day, allowing Jackson to finish off the garrison at Harpers Ferry and make his way back to Lee on September 16. By that point, Lee had already decided to pull back his army to Sharpsburg, with its back to the Potomac River and its front along Antietam Creek, affording his army at least one natural obstacle separating his army from McClellan's.

McClellan's lead elements arrived around Sharpsburg on the night of September 15, and the rest of the army came up on September 16, but McClellan did not order a general attack that day out of fear that he was still heavily outnumbered. Had he done so, he would not only have had an overwhelming advantage but would not have had to deal with A.P. Hill's Light Division, which was still busy at Harpers Ferry.

With McClellan's men all in position on the night of the 16th, McClellan decided to give general battle on the 17th. Longstreet described the scene before the battle commenced: "The blue uniforms of the federals appeared among the trees that crowned the heights on the eastern bank of the Antietam. The number increased, and larger and larger grew the field of blue until is seemed to stretch as far as the eye could see, and from the tops of the mountains down to the edge of the stream gathered the great army of McClellan."[4]

Still operating under the belief that he was outnumbered, McClellan's plan was to break Lee's left flank in the northern sector, because the crosses that he knew about over Antietam Creek (Burnside's Bridge and the bridge leading to Boonsboro) were held on the other side by Confederates who could operate along the high ground. McClellan's cavalry had not scouted other passes along Antietam Creek, and he and his officers seemed to be unaware that the Antietam Creek was so shallow in places around those bridges that the men could have waded across without trying to squeeze across bridges.

---

[4]   Gaffney, P., and D. Gaffney. *The Civil War: Exploring History One Week at a Time.* Page 179.

Worried about being outnumbered, McClellan's plan called for an assault with only half his army, starting with two corps along the Confederate left, and the support of perhaps a third or fourth corps. Meanwhile, he initially planned to launch diversionary attacks in the center and the Confederate right. However, the late night skirmishing and probing conducted by men of Hooker's I Corps on the night of the 16th suggested to Lee that they would attack there in force on the morning of the 17th, and before the battle he bolstered his left flank. He also sent word to A.P. Hill and Lafayette McLaws to force march with all haste to Sharpsburg.

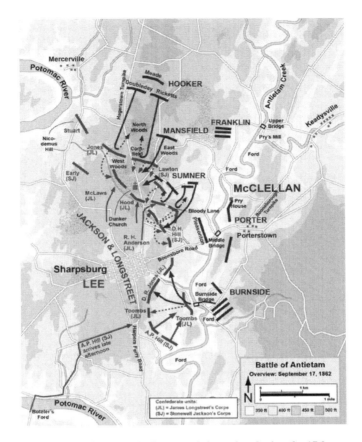

The dispositions at Antietam and the action during the 17th

Chapter 6: The Beginning of the Battle

As Lee had guessed, and as McClellan intended, the Battle of Antietam began near dawn on the morning of the 17th, with the advance of Hooker's I Corps down the Hagerstown Turnpike toward the small white Dunker Church, a small one room building that served as a church for a small group of German Baptists. Initially opposing Hooker's 8,500 man Corps were Stonewall Jackson's men, which numbered just under 8,000. Jackson's defenders were deployed across the Turnpike in the West Woods on the left, and a cornfield on the right.

The Dunker Church in the background

Hooker decided to start the fighting with an artillery bombardment due to the fact that the nature of the terrain made it unclear what his corps would be facing in the cornfield and the West Woods. Hooker's men could see the Confederates' bayonets shining in the cornfield, but the corn was high enough to conceal their number. During the artillery duel, infantry pushed forward until there was a fierce pitched battle in the cornfield, including hand-to-hand fighting. Colonel Benjamin Cook of the 12th Massachusetts later recalled his experience in the cornfield as "the most deadly fire of the war. Rifles are shot to pieces in the hands of the soldiers, canteens and haversacks are riddled with bullets, the dead and wounded go down in scores."

Battle of Antietam
6 am, September 17, 1862

Jackson discussed his men's fighting in his post-battle report:

"About sunrise the Federal infantry advanced in heavy force to the edge of the wood on the eastern side of the turnpike, driving in our skirmishers. Batteries were opened in front from the the wood with shell and canister, and our troops became exposed for near an hour to a terrific storm of shell, canister, and musketry. Gen. Jones having been compelled to leave the field, the command of Jackson's division devolved upon Gen. Starke. With heroic spirit our lines advanced to the conflict, and maintained their position, in the face of superior numbers, with stubborn resolution, sometimes driving the enemy before them and sometimes compelled to fall back before their well-sustained and destructive fire. Fresh troops from time to time relieved the enemy's ranks, and the carnage on both sides was terrific.

At this early hour Gen. Starke was killed. Col. Douglass, commanding Lawton's brigade, was also killed. Gen. Lawton, commanding division, and Col. Walker, commanding brigade, were severely wounded. More than half of the brigades of Lawton and Hays were either killed or wounded, and more than a third of Trimble's, and all the regimental commanders in those brigades, except two, were killed or wounded. Thinned in their ranks and exhausted of their ammunition, Jackson's division and the brigades of Lawton, Hays, and Trimble retired to the rear, and Hood, of Longstreet's command, again took the position from which he had been before relieved.

In the mean time Gen. Stuart moved his artillery to a position nearer to the main command, and more in our rear. Early, being now directed, in consequence of the disability of Gen. Lawton, to take command of Ewell's division, returned with his brigade (with the exception of the Thirteenth Virginia Regiment, which remained with Gen. Stuart) to the piece of wood where he had left the other brigades of his division when he was separated from them. Here he found that the enemy had advanced his infantry near the wood in which was the Dunkard church, and had planted a battery across the turnpike near the edge of the wood and an open field, and that the brigades of Lawton, Hays, and Trimble had fallen back some distance to the rear. Finding here Cols. Grigsby and Stafford, with a portion of Jackson's division, which formed on his left, he determined to maintain his position there if re-enforcements could be sent to his support, of which he was promptly assured. Col. Grigsby, with his small command, kept in check the advance of the enemy on the left flank, while Gen. Early attacked with great vigor and gallantry the column on his right and front."

Abner Doubleday, though wrongly credited for inventing baseball, led the division making the attack on the Confederates' far left. He would later report about the fierce fighting in the vicinity of the West Woods:

"The general order of battle was for two regiments of Patrick's brigade to precede the main body, deployed as skirmishers, and supported by Patrick's two remaining regiments; these to be followed by Phelps' brigade, 200 paces in the rear, and this in turn by Doubleday's brigade, with the same interval. In accordance with this disposition, General Patrick deployed the Twenty-first New York, under Colonel Rogers, as skirmishers on the right, and the Thirty-fifth New York, under Colonel Lord, on the left, supporting the former with the Twentieth New York Militia, Lieutenant-Colonel Gates, and the latter with the Twenty-third New York, Colonel Hoffman.

By General Hatch's order, Phelps' brigade advanced in column of divisions at half distance, preserving the intervals of deployment. My brigade advanced in the same order. On reaching a road part way up the mountain, and parallel to its summit, each brigade deployed in turn and advanced in line of battle. Colonel Phelps' brigade, owing to an accidental opening, preceded for a while our line of skirmishers, but soon halted, and advanced in line some 30 paces in their rear. General Patrick rode to the front with his skirmishers, drew the fire of the enemy, and developed their position. They lay behind a fence on the summit running north and south, fronted by a woods and backed by a corn-field, full of rocky ledges. Colonel Phelps now ordered his men to advance, and General Hatch rode through the lines, pressing them forward. They went in with a cheer, poured in a deadly fire, and drove the enemy from his position behind the fence, after a short and desperate conflict, and took post some yards beyond.

Here General Hatch was wounded and turned over the command to me, and as during the action Colonel Wainwright, Seventy-sixth New York Volunteers, was also wounded, the command of my brigade subsequently devolved upon Lieutenant-Colonel Hermann, Fifty-sixth Pennsylvania Volunteers. Phelps' brigade being few in number, and having suffered severely, I relieved them just at dusk with my brigade, reduced by former engagements to about 1,000 men, who took position beyond the fence referred to, the enemy being in heavy force some 30 or 40 paces in our front. They pressed heavily upon us, attempting to charge at the least cessation of our fire. At last I ordered the troops to cease firing, lie down behind the fence, and allowed the enemy to charge to within about 15 paces, apparently under the impression that we had given way. Then, at the word, my men sprang to their feet and poured in a deadly volley, from which the enemy fled in disorder, leaving their dead within 30 feet of our line.

I learned from a wounded prisoner that we were engaged with 4,000 to 5,000, under the immediate command of General Pickett, with heavy masses in their vicinity. He stated also that Longstreet in vain tried to rally the men, calling them his pets, and using every effort to induce them to renew the attack. The firing on both sides still continued, my men aiming at the flashes of the enemy's muskets, as it was too dark to see objects distinctly, until our cartridges were reduced to two or three rounds.

General Ricketts now came from the right and voluntarily relieved my men at the fence, who fell back some 10 paces and lay down on their arms. A few volleys from Ricketts ended the contest in about thirty minutes, and the enemy withdrew from the field--not, however, until an attempt to flank us on our left, which was gallantly met by a partial change of front of the Seventy-sixth New York Volunteers, under Colonel Wainwright, and the Seventh Indiana, under Major Grover. In this attempt the enemy lost heavily, and were compelled to retreat in disorder.

While the main attack was going on at the fence referred to, Colonel Rogers, with his own and Lieutenant-Colonel Gates' regiments (the Twentieth New York State Militia and Twenty-first New York Volunteers, of Patrick's brigade), rendered most essential service by advancing his right and holding a fence bounding the northeast side of the same corn-field, anticipating the enemy, who made a furious rush to seize this fence, but were driven back. Colonel Rogers was thus enabled to take the enemy in flank, and also to pick off their cannoneers and silence a battery which was at the right and behind their main body."

Despite Jackson's valiant defense, the Union advance kept pushing forward along the West Woods and the Turnpike, and Jackson's line was on the verge of collapse by 7:00 a.m. In one of the most legendary parts of the battle, John Bell Hood's Texans had come up to the field and had not eaten breakfast, so they were held in reserve and allowed to start preparing a meal. Just before they could eat, however, they were called into action, infuriating his men. Thankfully for the Confederates, it would be the Union who felt the brunt of their fury. Hood explained:

"The extreme suffering of my troops for want of food induced me to ride back to General Lee, and request him to send two or more brigades to our relief, at least for the night, in order that the soldiers might have a chance to cook their meagre rations. He said that he would cheerfully do so, but he knew of no command which could be spared for the purpose; he, however, suggested I should see General Jackson and endeavor to obtain assistance from him. After riding a long time in search of the latter, I finally discovered him alone, lying upon the ground, asleep by the root of a tree. I aroused him and made known the half-starved condition of my troops; he immediately ordered Lawton's, Trimble's and Hays's brigades to our relief. He exacted of me, however, a promise that I would come to the support of these forces the moment I was called upon. I quickly rode off in search of my wagons, that the men might prepare and cook their flour, as we were still without meat; unfortunately the night was then far advanced, and, although every effort was made amid the darkness to get the wagons forward, dawn of the morning of the 17th broke upon us before many of the men had had time to do more than prepare the dough. Soon thereafter an officer of Lawton's staff dashed up to me, saying, "General Lawton sends his compliments with the request that you come at once to his support." "To arms" was instantly sounded and quite a large number of my brave soldiers were again obliged to march to the front, leaving their uncooked rations in camp.

Still, indomitable amid every trial, they moved off by the right flank to occupy the same position we had left the night previous. As we passed, about sunrise, across the pike and through the gap in the fence just in front of Dunkard Church, General Lawton, who had been wounded, was borne to the rear upon a litter, and the only Confederate troops, left on that part of the field, were some forty men who had rallied round the gallant Harry Hays. I rode up to the latter, and, finding that his soldiers had expended all their ammunition, I suggested to him to retire, to replenish his cartridge boxes, and reassemble his command.

My command remained near the church, with empty cartridge boxes, holding aloft their colors whilst Frobel's batteries rendered most effective service in position further to the right, where nearly all the guns of the battalion were disabled. Upon the arrival of McLaws's Division, we marched to the rear, renewed our supply of ammunition, and returned to our position in the wood, near the church, which ground we held till a late hour in the afternoon, when we moved somewhat further to the right and bivouacked for the night."

Hood's division had helped the Confederates stave off the first major assault in the West Woods, and Hooker's attack fizzled out in part because Hooker was seriously injured during the fighting. Hooker had been seemingly everywhere during the fighting, and many of his comrades believed that Antietam would have turned out differently had he not been injured. Before his injury, Hooker said of the cornfield, "every stalk of corn in the northern and greater part of the field was cut as closely as could have been done with a knife, and the slain lay in rows precisely as they had stood in their ranks a few moments before."

Hooker was replaced by George Meade, who would ironically also replace Hooker as commander of the Army of the Potomac before Gettysburg, and Meade explained to his wife after the battle:

"Yesterday and the day before my division commenced the battle, and was in the thickest of it.

I was hit by a spent grape-shot, giving me a severe contusion on the right thigh, but not breaking the skin. Baldy [Meade's horse] was shot through the neck, but will get over it. A cavalry horse I mounted afterwards was shot in the flank. When General Hooker was wounded, General McClellan placed me in command of the army corps, over General Ricketts's head, who ranked me. This selection is a great compliment, and answers all my wishes in regard to my desire to have my services appreciated. I cannot ask for more, and am truly grateful for the merciful manner I have been protected, and for the good fortune that has attended me. I go into the action to-day as the commander of an army corps. If I survive, my two stars are secure, and if I fall, you will have my reputation to live on. God bless you all! I cannot write more. I am well and in fine spirits. Your brother Willie is up here, but was not in action yesterday."

As the I Corps' attack fizzled out, Jackson explained what happened next:

The force in front was giving way under this attack when another heavy column of Federal troops were seen moving across the plateau on his left flank. By this time the expected re-enforcements (consisting of Semmes' and Anderson's brigades and a part of Barksdale's, of McLaws' division) arrived, and the whole, including Grigsby's command, now united, charged upon the enemy, checking his advance, then driving him back with great slaughter entirely from and beyond the wood, and gaining possession of our original position. No further advance, beyond demonstrations, was made by the enemy on the left."

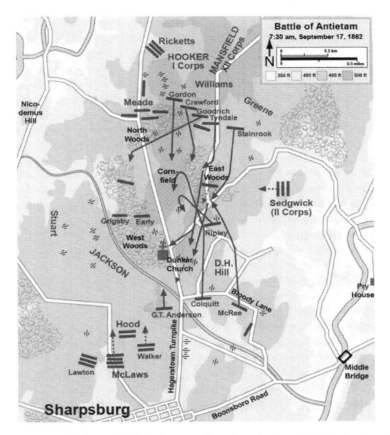

Battle of Antietam
7:30 am, September 17, 1862

Jackson was referring to the Union's uncoordinated attacks from the East Woods, east of the cornfield. Hooker's I Corps was relieved by the XII Corps under Joseph Mansfield, who had been promoted to Corps command just a few days earlier and was so new to command and unfamiliar with the terrain that he advanced his men in a file that was 10 ranks deep instead of the normal 2-rank-deep battle line. On top of that, Mansfield got confused by Confederate fire from the cornfield, mistakenly believing that it was friendly fire. And once he got all the necessary information and the delays sorted out, he was mortally wounded, with one of his men explaining, "The general, tottering in his saddle, goaded the bleeding horse north along the Smoketown Road, away from the 10th Maine, until he came upon the right company of the 125th Pennsylvania. Captain Gardner (K Co.), who noticed that the general seemed ill, immediately called for some men to help the general dismount. Sergeant John Caho (K Co.)

and Privates Sam Edmunson (K Co.) and E.S. Rudy (H Co.), with two stragglers, gently eased the bleeding officer from his horse. Forming a chair with their muskets, the five men picked up Mansfield and carried him to a lone tree in the rear of their line, where they left him to await the arrival of a surgeon."

Mansfield

As the XII Corps struggled, Edwin Sumner's II Corps began an unsupported and uncoordinated attack from the east, entering the East Woods in confusion. Like Mansfield, Sumner's battle line was comprised unusually and made an inviting target for Confederate artillery. The Corps suffered over 2,000 casualties in half an hour, with division commander John Sedgwick suffering a serious injury. Sumner has long been criticized for the lack of coordination and the unusual battle formation.

By 10:00 a.m., over 13,000 men had become casualties in just 4 hours, and two Union corps commanders were out of the fight.

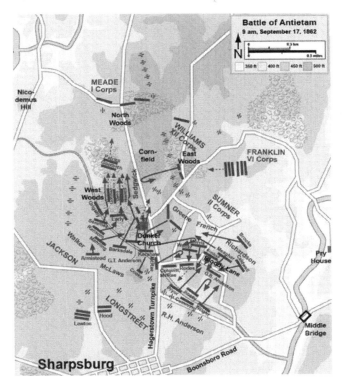

As if the fighting in the north wasn't fierce enough, the fighting at midday would turn one sunken road into "Bloody Lane". Having been repulsed in the north, the next Union attacks focused on the center of the Confederate line, beginning ironically with a division of Sumner's II Corps which had gotten lost in the East Woods during the attack in the north and ventured south. With Sumner's II Corps advancing in a disorderly fashion and being badly repulsed, Sumner initially asked French's lost division to make a diversionary attack on the center.

There French's men found D.H. Hill's division, which after South Mountain was reduced to only about 2,500 men itself. On top of that, some of Hill's brigades had reinforced Jackson's men during the morning, meaning French had veered right into the most lightly defended part of the Confederate line. However, Hill's men were protected by the features of the "sunken road", a dirt road that had been worn down over the years by wagons and thus formed a sort of trench that made defensive warfare much safer.

General Longstreet reported after the battle:

"Hood was not strong enough to resist the masses thrown against him. Several of Maj. Gen. D. H. Hill's brigades re-enforced the position; but even with these our forces seemed but a handful when compared with the hosts thrown against us. The commands engaged the enemy, however, with great courage and determination, and, retiring very slowly, delayed him until the forces of Generals Jackson and Walker came to our relief. D.R. Jones' brigade, under Col. G. T. Anderson, came up about the same moment; soon after this the divisions of Major-Generals McLaws and R. H. Anderson. Col. S. D. Lee's reserve artillery was with General Hood, and took a distinguished part in the attack on the evening of the 16th, and in delaying that of the 17th. General Jackson soon moved off to our left for the purpose of turning the enemy's right flank, and the other divisions, except Walker's, were distributed at other points of the line. As these movements were made, the enemy again threw forward his masses against my left. This attack was met by Walker's division, two pieces of Captain Miller's battery, of the Washington Artillery, and two pieces of Captain Boyce's battery, and was driven back in some confusion. An effort was made to pursue, but our line was too weak. Colonel Cooke, of the Twenty-seventh North Carolina, very gallantly charged with his own regiment, but, his supply of ammunition being exhausted and he being unsupported, he was obliged to return to his original position in the line.

From this moment our center was extremely weak, being defended by but part of Walker's division and four pieces of artillery; Cooke's regiment, of that division, being without a cartridge. In this condition, again the enemy's masses moved forward against us. Cooke stood with his empty guns, and waved his colors to show that his troops were in position. The artillery played upon their ranks, with canister. Their lines began to hesitate."

The dead in the Bloody Lane

Longstreet was referencing Anderson's division, which arrived at 10:30 a.m. and represented the last reserve Lee currently had at his disposal. But as Anderson's men fortified the line, 4,000 Union soldiers from Maj. Gen. Israel B. Richardson's division of Sumner's II Corps took up the fight on French's left. He was soon joined by another attack against the center of the line by Thomas F. Meagher's famous Irish Brigade, easily recognizable thanks to their emerald green flags. Although the Confederate line had a strong vantage point, one Union soldier noted of their predicament, "We were shooting them like sheep in a pen. If a bullet missed the mark at first it was liable to strike the further bank, angle back, and take them secondarily."

As the fighting in the center raged, Col. Francis C. Barlow and 350 men from two New York regiments took a commanding position that oversaw the sunken road and allowed them to pour in a deadly flanking fire that enfiladed the Confederate line. Miscommunication by the Confederates over how to face this threat inadvertently resulted in an entire brigade marching toward the rear back toward Sharpsburg, breaking the Confederate line.

At this point, it was about 1:00 p.m., and in the middle another 5,500 casualties had been incurred. As the broken Confederate line started retreating, Franklin's VI Corps, comprised of 12,000 men, were ready to advance on the center. In the field, Franklin's request to advance was denied by Edwin Sumner, who in addition to commanding the II Corps was in command of the "grand division", making him responsible for that wing of the army thanks to the unwieldy structure of the Army of the Potomac's leadership. Franklin thus had to attempt to make the request to McClellan himself, whose headquarters were over a mile to the rear, costing precious time. McClellan personally rode to the area, listened to both men's arguments, and decided to hold Franklin's men in place, still clearly concerned that he was outnumbered.

Chapter 8: Burnside's Attack

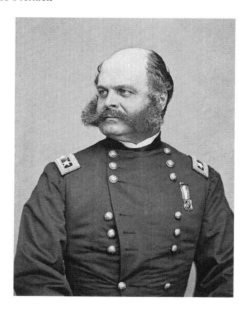

Burnside

Lee's army may ultimately have been saved by the Northern army's inability to cross the creek near "Burnside's Bridge". Ambrose Burnside had been given command of the "Right Wing" of the Army of the Potomac (the I Corps and IX Corps) at the start of the Maryland Campaign for the Battle of South Mountain, but McClellan separated the two corps at the Battle of Antietam, placing them on opposite ends of the Union battle line. However, Burnside continued to act as though he was a wing commander instead of a corps commander, so instead of directly commanding his IX corps, he funneled orders through General Jacob D. Cox. This poor organization contributed to the corps's hours-long delay in attacking and crossing what is now called "Burnside's Bridge" on the right flank of the Confederate line.

Making matters worse, Burnside did not perform adequate reconnaissance of the area, which afforded several easy fording sites of the creek out of range of the Army of Northern Virginia. Instead of unopposed crossings, his troops were forced into repeated assaults across the narrow bridge which was dominated by Confederate sharpshooters on high ground across the bridge. On top of that, Burnside's failure to have his men wade across meant that they were easily repulsed a couple of times trying to force their way across the bridge. McClellan got so fed up that he began sending couriers, and at one point he ordered an aide, "Tell him if it costs 10,000 men he must go now." Burnside reacted angrily, "McClellan appears to think I am not trying my best to carry this bridge; you are the third or fourth one who has been to me this morning with similar orders." As Confederate staff officer Henry Kyd Douglas later pointed out, "Go and look at [Burnside's Bridge], and tell me if you don't think Burnside and his corps might have executed a hop, skip, and jump and landed on the other side. One thing is certain, they might have waded it that day without getting their waist belts wet in any place."

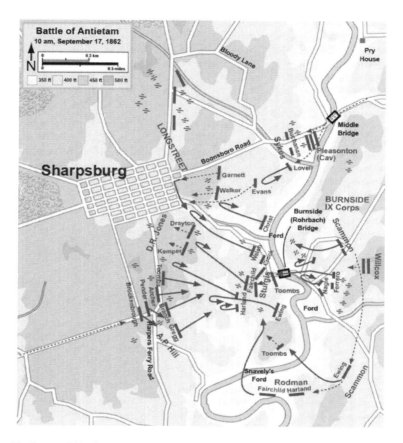

Battle of Antietam
10 am, September 17, 1862

Burnside discussed his dispositions in his post-battle report, as well as describing the now famous "Burnside's Bridge" and the terrain near where he was ordered to attack:

General Cox was still retained in temporary command of the Ninth Army Corps, which was the only portion of my command then with me, and my orders were to a great extent given directly to him, and I would respectfully refer the general commanding to his very excellent and minute report. The distribution of the forces was as follows: On the crest of the hill immediately in front of the bridge was Benjamin's battery of six 20-pounders, with the remaining batteries in rear of the crest under partial cover; in rear of Benjamin's battery on the extreme right, joining on to General Sykes' division, was General Crook's brigade, with General Sturgis' division in his rear; on the left, and in rear of Benjamin's battery, was Rodman's division, with Scammon's brigade in support; General Willcox's division was held in reserve. The whole command bivouacked in these positions in three lines on the night of the 16th.

On the morning of the 17th the enemy opened a heavy artillery fire on our lines, but did us little harm. Our batteries were soon brought to bear on their batteries, which were soon silenced and two of his caissons blown up.

About this time I received an order from the general commanding to make my dispositions to carry the stone bridge over the Antietam nearly opposite our center, but to await further orders before making the attack. I accordingly threw my lines forward.

The disposition of the troops at this time was as follows: General Crook's brigade and General Sturgis' division immediately in front of the bridge and the ford, a short distance above, their front covered by the Eleventh Connecticut, Col. H. W. Kingsbury, thrown out as skirmishers; General Rodman's division, with Scammon's brigade in support, opposite the ford, some three-quarters of a mile below the bridge; General Willcox's division in the woods at the left of Benjamin's battery, in rear of the other lines. Benjamin's battery retained its original position, and the following batteries were placed in advance on his right and left, those on the left overlooking the bridge and the heights above it; Clark's and Durell's on the right; Muhlenberg's, Cook's, and McMullin's on the left, and one section of Simmonds' with Crook's brigade and one section with Benjamin's battery. The battery of Dahlgren boat howitzers, attached to the Ninth New York, covered the crossing of Rodman's division at the ford below.

At 10 o'clock I received an order from the general commanding to make the attack. I directed Colonel Kingsbury, of the Eleventh Connecticut, to move forward with his line of skirmishers, and directed General Cox to detail General Crook's brigade to make the assault. General Rodman was directed to cross over at the ford below the bridge, and join on to the left of the command, which was to be thrown over the bridge. From General Crook's position it was found to be almost impossible to carry the bridge, and General Sturgis was ordered to make a detail from his division for that purpose. He immediately sent forward the Second Maryland (Lieutenant-Colonel Duryea) and the Sixth New Hampshire (Colonel Griffin), which regiments made several successive attacks in the most gallant style, but were driven back by the galling fire of the enemy. I then directed the batteries on the left to concentrate their fire on the woods above the bridge, and sent word to General Sturgis to detail the Fifty-first Pennsylvania (Colonel Hartranft) and the Fifty-first New York (Colonel Potter) to assault the bridge and carry it at all hazards. In the mean time Colonel Crook had brought a section of his battery to bear upon the heights just above the bridge. General Sturgis, by a judicious posting of these two regiments in rear of a spur which fronted the bridge, succeeded in protecting them from the enemy's fire until they reached the crest of the spur, at which point they commenced their charge and carried the bridge at the point of the bayonet at about 1 o'clock, the whole division following immediately.

The regiments separated at the head of the bridge to the right and left, and moved up the steep bank crowning the heights immediately beyond. Our loss at this place was fearful, the enemy being posted in rifle-pits and behind barricades, within easy musket range of our men, and almost entirely concealed and covered from our shots. We lost at this point some of our most valuable officers. Among them was Col. H. W. Kingsbury, of the Eleventh Connecticut, and Lieutenant-Colonel Bell, of the Fifty-first Pennsylvania.

Colonel Crook's brigade crossed immediately after Sturgis' division, and took its position in support in rear. General Rodman's division succeeded in crossing the fords below, after a sharp fight of musketry and artillery, and joined on to the left of Sturgis, Scammon's brigade crossing after him and taking his position in rear and in support. General Willcox's division was ordered across to take position on the right of General Sturgis. In describing the ground here and the bridge, I cannot do better than to copy that contained in the excellent report of General Cox:

> 'The bridge itself is a stone structure of three arches, with stone parapet above, this parapet to some extent flanking the approach to the bridge at either end. The valley in which the stream runs is quite narrow, the steep slope on the right bank approaching quite to the water's edge. On this slope the roadway is scarped, running both ways from the bridge end, and, passing to the higher lands above by ascending through ravines above and below, the other ravine being some 600 yards above the bridge was a strong stone fence, running parallel to the stream; the turns of the roadway were covered by rifle-pits and breastworks made of rails and stone, all of which defenses, as well as the woods which covered the slope, were filled with the enemy's infantry and sharpshooters. Besides the infantry defenses, batteries were placed to enfilade the bridge and all its approaches. The crest of the first hill above the bridge is curved toward the stream at the extremes, forming a sort of natural tete-de-pont. The next ridge beyond rises somewhat higher, though with less regularity, the depression between the two being but slight, and the distance varying in places from 300 to 700 yards.'

The dispositions being completed, about 3 o'clock, in accordance with instructions received from the general commanding, I directed General Cox to move forward with the whole command, except Sturgis' division, which was left in reserve, in the order in which they were formed, and attack the town of Sharpsburg and the heights on the left.

Eventually, after about three hours and several attempts, the Union men pushed their way across, but once they were on the other side of the Antietam they delayed yet again to regroup. After two hours attempting to get ammunition across the bridge, Burnside's men began another general advance against the Confederate right, which by now had been reinforced by every conceivable unit Lee could muster. Meanwhile, A.P. Hill's men were on the march and nearing the vicinity. They had intended to be brought up to the Confederate left, but Lee ordered him to come up on the Confederate right instead.

As Hill's men neared Boteler's Ford, the best available route across the Potomac for the Confederates, Burnside began shifting his men around the Confederate right even though he heavily outnumbered them, in the hopes that a move on Boteler's Ford would cut Lee's army off and trap it along the Potomac. Around 3:00 p.m., Burnside ordered nearly 8,000 fresh soldiers to push west, and meanwhile the streets of Sharpsburg were filled with retreating Confederates. Lee's army was disorganized and on the verge of being broken.

As Burnside's men pushed in on his right flank, Lee turned to see dust from a unit marching from the southwest. Had they been Union men, his entire army may have been bagged at Sharpsburg, and when Lee asked whose troops they were, one of his aides assured him, "They are flying the Virginia flags." Lee excitedly announced, "It is A.P. Hill from Harpers Ferry!" One of Jackson's aides recalled Hill's arrival just in the nick of time:

"But then, just then, A.P. Hill, picturesque in his red battleshirt, with 3 of his brigades, 2500 men, who had marched 17 miles from Harpers Ferry and had waded the Potomac, appeared upon the scene. Tired and footsore, the men forgot their woes in that supreme moment, and with no breathing time braced themselves to meet the coming shock. They met it and stayed it. The blue line staggered and hesitated, and hesitating, was lost. At the critical moment A.P. Hill was always at his strongest. ... Again A.P. Hill, as at Manassas, Harper's Ferry, and elsewhere had struck with the right hand of Mars. No wonder both Lee and Jackson, when, in the delirium of their last moments on earth, they stood again to battle saw the form of A.P. Hill leading his columns on; but it is a wonder and a shame that the grave of this valiant Virginian has not a stone to mark it and keep it from oblivion."

Writer William Allan would note of Hill's performance:

"It was at this critical moment that A. P. Hill, who had marched seventeen miles from Harper's Ferry that morning, and had waded the Potomac, reached the field upon the flank of Burnside's victorious column. With a skill, vigor and promptness, which cannot be too highly praised, A. P. Hill formed his men in line, and threw them upon Burnside's flank. Toombs, and the other brigades of D. R, Jones's division, gave such aid as they were able. The Confederate artillery was used with the greatest courage and determination to check the enemy, but it was mainly A. P. Hill's attack which decided the day at this point, and drove Burnside in confusion and dismay back to the bridge. There is no part of General James Longstreet's article more unworthy than the single line in which he obscurely refers to the splendid achievement of a dead comrade, whose battles, like Ney's, were all for his country, and none against it, and who crowned a brilliant career by shedding his life's blood to avert the crowning disaster. A.P. Hill's march was a splendid one. He left Harper's Ferry sixteen hours after McLaws, but reached the battle-field only five hours behind him. McLaws had, however, the night to contend with. The vigor of Hill's attack, with hungry and march worn men, is shown by the fact that he completely overthrew forces twice as numerous as his own. Though his force of from two thousand to three thousand five hundred men was too small to permit of an extended aggressive, his arrival was not less opportune to Lee than was that of Blucher to Wellington at Waterloo, nor was his action when on the field in any way inferior to that of the Prussian field-marshal."

With Hill crashing down on his left flank, Burnside lost his nerve, even though the IX Corps still heavily outnumbered Hill's Light Division even after incurring 20% casualties during the day already. Burnside would write in his post-battle report:

"This order was obeyed in the most cheerful and gallant manner, the officers and soldiers moving forward with the greatest enthusiasm, driving everything before them. General Willcox, with General Crook in support, moved up on both sides of the Sharpsburg road, and succeeded in reaching the outskirts of the village. General Rodman succeeded in carrying the main heights on the left of the town, one of his regiments (the Ninth New York) capturing one of the most formidable of the enemy's batteries; but at this juncture the enemy was largely re-enforced by General A. P. Hill's light division, which had just arrived from Harper's Ferry, and by numerous batteries from their extreme left. During the attack General Rodman was forced to bear more to the left than was intended when the advance was ordered, and General Cox was forced to move him more to the right with a view to strengthening the line, during which movement General Rodman was mortally wounded while gallantly leading his command to the assault.

At this time Colonel Harland's brigade was driven back, leaving the battery which they had captured. Colonel Scammon's brigade changed its front to the rear on its right, thus protecting our left flank. It was now nearly sundown. I at once ordered General Sturgis' division forward in support, and, notwithstanding the hard work in the early part of the day and a lack of ammunition, they moved with the greatest alacrity and enthusiasm, holding the enemy at bay and fighting him at close quarters till long after dark.

It being apparent that the enemy was strongly re-enforced, and that we could not be re-enforced, the command was ordered to fall back to the crests above the bridge, which movement was performed in the most perfect order under cover of the batteries on the height, the same formation being adopted that was made before the attack."

Thus, Burnside ordered a general retreat back to Antietam Creek and waited there while requesting more reinforcements from McClellan, who informed him, "I can do nothing more. I have no infantry." When told he had repulsed men under the command of Burnside, his West Point friend, Hill was reportedly asked if he knew his old classmate, to which he responded, "Ought to! He owes me eight thousand dollars!" Hill had allegedly loaned the money to Burnside during their friendlier antebellum days.

Of course, McClellan's assertion that he had no infantry was not entirely true. By the end of the afternoon, Union attacks on the flanks and the center of the line had been violent but eventually unsuccessful. Aware that his army was badly bloodied but fearing Lee had many more men than he did, McClellan refused to commit fresh reserves from Franklin's VI Corps or Fitz-John Porter's V Corps. McClellan's decision was probably sealed by Fitz John Porter telling him, "Remember, General, I command the last reserve of the last Army of the Republic." Thus, the day ended in a tactical stalemate, with the Union suffering nearly 12,500 casualties (including over 2,000 dead) and the Confederates suffering over 10,000 casualties (including over 1,500 dead). Nearly 1/4th of the Army of the Potomac had been injured, captured or killed, and the same could be said for nearly 1/3rd of Lee's Army of Northern Virginia. It was the deadliest and bloodiest day in American history.

After the battle, McClellan wrote to his wife, "Those in whose judgment I rely tell me that I fought the battle splendidly and that it was a masterpiece of art. ... I feel I have done all that can be asked in twice saving the country. ... I feel some little pride in having, with a beaten & demoralized army, defeated Lee so utterly. ... Well, one of these days history will I trust do me justice." Historians have generally been far less kind with their praise, criticizing McClellan for not sharing his battle plans with his corps commanders, which prevented them from using initiative outside of their sectors. McClellan also failed to use cavalry in the battle; had cavalry been used for reconnaissance, other fording options might have prevented the debacle at Burnside's Bridge. As historian Stephen Sears would point out in his seminal book about the Maryland Campaign, "In making his battle against great odds to save the Republic, General McClellan had committed barely 50,000 infantry and artillerymen to the contest. A third of his army did not fire a shot. Even at that, his men repeatedly drove the Army of Northern Virginia to the brink of disaster, feats of valor entirely lost on a commander thinking of little beyond staving off his own defeat."

Chapter 9: Lee's Retreat and the Aftermath

On the morning of September 18, Lee's army prepared to defend against a Union assault that ultimately never came. Finally, an improvised truce was declared to allow both sides to exchange their wounded. That evening, Lee's forces began withdrawing across the Potomac to return to Virginia.

McClellan made one push against Lee's army at nearby Shepherdstown. Shortly before dusk on September 19, Union Brig. General Charles Griffin sent 2,000 infantry and sharpshooters from Maj. General Fitz-John Porter's V Corps across the Potomac River at Boteler's Ford (also known as Shepardstown Ford) in pursuit, only to pull them back the following day when Stonewall Jackson's men entered the fray. However, Union General Adelbert Ames had mistakenly received orders to advance across the Potomac into Virginia, so he sent the 20th Maine regiment wading into the water, which actually encountered retreating Union troops as they did, and they were promptly fired upon by a barrage of Confederate artillery.

The 20th Maine would become famous at Gettysburg, but here they had no fighting chance. Just as soon as Joshua Lawrence Chamberlain's 20th had crossed, their bugles sounded retreat. Remaining calm atop his horse, Chamberlain redirected his men back across the river, "steadying his men through a deep place in the river where several of the Fifth New York were drowned in his presence." And although Lieutenant Colonel Chamberlain had his horse shot out from under him, he succeeded in returning his regiment safely back to shore with only three casualties suffering minor wounds, his ability to remain calm under pressure now apparent.

As the Battle of Shepherdstown indicated, Lee's rear guard was formidable enough that officers throughout the Army of the Potomac concurred with McClellan's actions not to go after the Army of Northern Virginia. Lee's army then moved toward the Shenandoah Valley while the Army of the Potomac hovered around Sharpsburg.

Although Antietam ended as a tactical draw, the Maryland Campaign is now widely considered a turning point in the Civil War. It resulted in forcing Lee's army out of Maryland and back into Virginia, making it a strategic victory for the North and an opportune time for President Abraham Lincoln to issue the Emancipation Proclamation. James McPherson would summarize the critical importance of the Maryland Campaign: "No other campaign and battle in the war had such momentous, multiple consequences as Antietam. In July 1863 the dual Union triumphs at Gettysburg and Vicksburg struck another blow that blunted a renewed Confederate offensive in the East and cut off the western third of the Confederacy from the rest. In September 1864 Sherman's capture of Atlanta reversed another decline in Northern morale and set the stage for the final drive to Union victory. These also were pivotal moments. But they would never have happened if the triple Confederate offensives in Mississippi, Kentucky, and most of all Maryland had not been defeated in the fall of 1862."

Although McClellan is often criticized for the way he conducted the fighting at Antietam, Lee has not gone without criticism either. Longstreet's artillery chief, Porter Alexander, who would be tasked with conducting the artillery bombardment before Pickett's Charge at Gettysburg, was extremely critical of Lee for the Maryland Campaign, writing in his memoirs:

"Lee's hopes were by no means so exaggerated as McClellan's fears. He counted upon no hope from Maryland, until his own army should have demonstrated its ability to maintain itself within the state. He hardly hoped for more than 'to detain the enemy upon the northern frontier until the approach of winter should render his advance into Virginia difficult, if not impracticable.' But he did entertain hopes of a decisive victory here on a field more remote from a safe place of refuge for the enemy than his victories of the Seven Days and of 2d Manassas had been. The hope would have been reasonable had his army been larger and his armament better, but under all the circumstances and conditions it was as improbable of realization as the chance of an earthquake would have been. He did, indeed, win a complete victory over all the infantry which the enemy engaged, but their position was more favorable to prevent his making a counter-stroke than was his to resist their attack. Their heavy guns across the Antietam gave him protection, just as at Fredericksburg the Federal artillery on the Stafford heights, afterward in two battles, safely covered the Federal infantry on the opposite shore.

Briefly, Lee took a great risk for no chance of gain except the killing of some thousands of his enemy with the loss of, perhaps, two-thirds as many of his own men. That was a losing game for the Confederacy. Its supply of men was limited; that of the enemy was not. That was not war! Yet now, who would have it otherwise? History must be history and could not afford to lose this battle from its records. For the nation is immortal and will forever prize and cherish the record made that day by both sides, as actors in the boldest and the bloodiest battle ever fought upon this continent."

Lincoln and McClellan meeting after Antietam

McClellan had successfully removed Lee's army from Maryland, but he had failed to knock Lee's army out while it was on the ropes. When Lee escaped back to Virginia without pursuit, the Lincoln Administration was greatly frustrated.

Despite heavily outnumbering the Southern army and badly damaging it during the battle of Antietam, McClellan never did pursue Lee across the Potomac, citing shortages of equipment and the fear of overextending his forces. General-in-Chief Henry W. Halleck wrote in his official report, "The long inactivity of so large an army in the face of a defeated foe, and during the most favorable season for rapid movements and a vigorous campaign, was a matter of great disappointment and regret." Lincoln sardonically referred to the Army of the Potomac as General McClellan's bodyguard, and in one October message to McClellan, Lincoln didn't bother trying to conceal his disgust, writing, "I have just read your dispatch about sore-tongued and fatigued horses, Will you pardon me for asking what the horses of your army have done since the Battle of Antietam that fatigues anything?"

Some of Lincoln's assertions make clear his lack of familiarity with military matters.

McClellan still had to deal with the logistical reorganization of his army and the rehabilitation after having suffered about 10,000 casualties in one day. And as Lincoln grew more disenchanted with McClellan, specifically the state of inertia along the Potomac, JEB Stuart rode around McClellan's army for the second time in early October, displaying just how unable the Union forces were to cover the Potomac crossings.

McClellan also faced growing public pressure and pressure from the Administration to advance before the midterm elections. McClellan wished to wait until Spring of 1863 to resume active campaigning, hoping once again to use the Peninsula, but he was compelled to move by mid-October. McClellan saw the campaign as merely a temporary way of placating the Administration before positioning his army around Fredericksburg to plan for the following Spring.

Lincoln had finally had enough of McClellan's "slows", and his constant excuses for not taking forward action. Lincoln relieved McClellan of his command of the Army of the Potomac on November 7, 1862, effectively ending the general's military career. Once again using the media to deflect his inadequacies, McClellan blamed Washington for having not sent more men and equipment before mounting the Antietam offensive. Lincoln reportedly responded, "Sending reinforcements to McClellan is like shoveling flies across a barn."[5] McClellan's military career was essentially over, having ended in disgrace.

Ironically, when McClellan was removed, the army was at a highpoint in terms of morale, and McClellan was starting to understand that if the Administration wouldn't allow a transfer of his army onto the Peninsula, he would have to continue sliding east along the overland route using available railroads, which is similar in scope to Ulysses S. Grant's 1864 Overland Campaign.

But it was not to be for another 2 years. On November 7, 1862, McClellan was replaced by Ambrose Burnside, one of the subordinates most responsible for the shortcomings of the Maryland campaign.

Bibliography

Freeman, Douglas Southall. *R.E. Lee: A Biography*, 1934-5.

Blount, Jr., Roy. *Robert E. Lee*. New York: Penguin Books, 2003.

Connelly, Thomas L. *The Marble Man: Robert E. Lee and His Image in American Society*. New York: Alfred A. Knopf, 1977.

---

[5]   Lanning, Michael Lee. *The Civil War 100*. Page 189. Pages 189--190.

Dowdey, Clifford (editor). *The Wartime Papers of R. E. Lee.* New York: Bramhall House, 1961.

Van Doren Stern, Philip. *Robert E. Lee: The Man and the Soldier.* New York: Bonanza Books, 1963.

Robertson, James I., Jr. *General A.P. Hill: The Story of a Confederate Warrior.* New York: Vintage Publishing, 1992.

Alexander, Edward P. *Fighting for the Confederacy: The Personal Recollections of General Edward Porter Alexander.* (Gary W. Gallagher, ed.). Chapel Hill: University of North Carolina Press, 1989.

Alexander, E. P. *Military Memoirs of a Confederate: A Critical Narrative.* New York: Charles Scribner's Sons, 1907. Accessed via GoogleBooks:
http://books.google.com/books?id=wvB2AAAAMAAJ&printsec=frontcover&dq=military+mem oirs+of+a+confederate&hl=en&ei=810eTc-
VB8H8Ab6qKzSDQ&sa=X&oi=book_result&ct=result&resnum=1&ved=0CC8Q6AEwAA#v= onepage&q&f=false

The Battle of Fredericksburg

Chapter 1: The Aftermath of Antietam

When Lincoln fired McClellan after Antietam, the president appointed one of the men principally responsible for the Union's failure to score a decisive victory at the battle. To his credit, Burnside didn't believe he was competent to command the entire army, a very honest (and accurate) judgment. However, Burnside also didn't want the command to go to Fighting Joe Hooker, who had been injured while aggressively fighting with his I Corps at Antietam in the morning. Thus, he accepted. Porter Alexander, the Confederate artillery chief for James Longstreet's corps, summed up what the Confederates thought of Burnside in his memoirs: "The designation of Burnside to succeed McClellan was a great surprise to old army circles, both in the Federal and Confederate armies; and was, perhaps, an unpleasant one to Burnside himself. He was popular, but not greatly esteemed as a general. He had commanded a brigade at the first battle of Bull Run, but had in no way risen above, even if he reached, the average of the brigade commanders. He had later had the luck to command the expedition to the N. C. Sounds, where his overwhelming force easily overcame the slight resistance that it met. This gained him the prestige, in newspapers and political circles, of successful independent command. As commander of a corps, he was one of the four next in line for promotion —Burnside, Hooker, Sumner, and Franklin."

Chapter 2: Moving Toward Fredericksburg

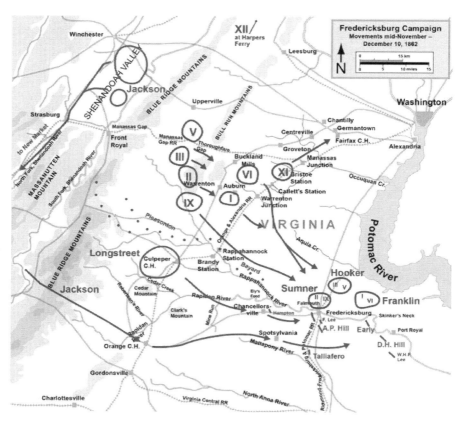

The armies move toward Fredericksburg

Given the way McClellan was sacked, Burnside understood he was under pressure from the Lincoln Administration to be aggressive, but instead of going for Lee's army, which was split with Stonewall Jackson's men covering their supply lines in the Shenandoah, Burnside made his objective Richmond. After deliberating for a few days, Burnside relayed to the Administration that he would try to keep Lee in place by feigning movements in the Army of Northern Virginia's vicinity before shifting his army southeast and crossing the Rappahannock River to

Fredericksburg. Burnside preferred this movement because it protected his flank from Stonewall Jackson's corps, in no small part due to the havoc Jackson had wreaked in his Valley Campaign earlier that year.

Stonewall Jackson

Thus, instead of striking out at Lee's nearby army, Burnside began moving the Army of the Potomac southeast on November 15 toward the Rappahannock River. But even as he was moving his army, problems with his army's logistics cropped up, specifically with pontoon bridges. The bridges were needed to cross the Rappahannock River, and had they been there on time, the Army of the Potomac would have beaten Lee's Army of Northern Virginia to Fredericksburg, forcing the Confederates to take up a defensive line closer to Richmond and allowing Burnside's men an unopposed crossing. Instead, the Administration had failed to provide the bridges on time at Falmouth, a few miles west and across river from Fredericksburg, on November 17. Instead of sending Edwin "Bull" Sumner's corps across as an advance, Burnside cautiously kept his army together out of concern rising waters from rains might make it impossible for the rest of the army to ford the river.

The Army of the Potomac's failure to cross the Rappahannock in mid-November allowed Lee to reach Fredericksburg with General James Longstreet's corps on November 23, where they were posted to the west of the town on the imposing Marye's Heights. By the end of November, Stonewall Jackson's corps had arrived in the vicinity, and Lee posted him to Longstreet's right to defend against crossing sites downstream from Fredericksburg.

Longstreet described the terrain in his memoirs:

"At the west end of the ridge where the river cuts through is Taylor's Hill (the Confederate left), which stands at its highest on a level with Stafford Heights. From that point the heights on the south side spread, unfolding a valley about a mile in width, affording a fine view of the city, of the arable fields, and the heights as they recede to the vanishing limits of sight. Next below Taylor's is Marye's Hill, rising to half the elevation of the neighboring heights and dropping back, leaving a plateau of half a mile, and then swelling to the usual altitude of the range. On the plateau is the Marye mansion. Along its base is a sunken road, with retaining walls on either side. That on the east is just breast-high for a man, and just the height convenient for infantry defence and fire. From the top of the breast-work the ground recedes gradually till near the canal, when it drops off three or four feet, leaving space near the canal of a rod or two of level ground. The north end of the sunken road cuts into the plank or Gordonsville road, which is an extension of Hanover Street from near the heart of the town. At the south end it enters the Telegraph road, extending out from the town limits and up over the third, or Telegraph Hill, called, in its bloody baptismal, "Lee's Hill." An unfinished railroad lies along the Telegraph road as far as the highlands. The Fredericksburg and Potomac Railroad lies nearly parallel with the river four miles, and then turns south through the highlands. The old stage road from the city runs about half-way between the river and the railroad four miles, when it turns southwest and crosses the railroad at Hamilton's Crossing. The hamlet of Falmouth, on the north side of the river, was in front of the right centre of the Federal position, half a mile from Fredericksburg."

Longstreet

Longstreet's artillery chief, Porter Alexander, explained just how strong a defensive position Marye's Heights afforded:

"There was, however, one natural feature which proved of great value. The Confederate line occupied a range of low hills nearly parallel to the river and a few hundred yards back from the town. The Telegraph road, sunken from three to five feet below the surface, skirted the bottom of these hills for about 800 yards, until it reached the valley of Hazel Run, into which it turned. This sunken road was made part of the line of battle for McLaws's infantry. It not only formed a parapet invisible to the enemy until its defenders rose to fire over it, but it afforded ample space for several ranks to load and fire, and still have room behind them for free communication along the line. In easy canister range, nine guns on the hills above could fire over the heads of the infantry."

While Longstreet's men started to approach Fredericksburg, the town itself received a surrender request from Edwin Sumner on November 21, citing the fact that Confederates had been shooting at them from locations inside the town. Longstreet's chief artillerist, Porter Alexander, explained how this led to the evacuation of many of the town's citizens:

"On the 21st Sumner sent a formal demand for the surrender of the town, basing it upon the statement that his troops had been fired upon from under cover of the houses, and that mills and manufactories in the town were furnishing provisions and clothing to the enemy. He demanded an answer by 5 P. M., and said that if the surrender was not immediate at nine next morning, he would shell the town, the intermediate 16 hours being allowed for the removal of women and children.

This note, only received by the Mayor at 4.40 P. M., was referred to Longstreet, who authorized a reply to be made that the city would not be used for the purposes complained of, but that the Federals could only occupy the town by force of arms. Mayor Slaughter pointed out that the civil authorities had not been responsible for the firing which had been done, and, further, that during the night it would be impossible to remove the noncombatants. During the night Sumner sent word that in consideration of the pledges made, and, in view of the short time remaining for the removal of women and children, the batteries would not open as had been proposed.

But the letter left it to be inferred that the purpose to shell was only postponed, and Lee, who had now arrived, advised the citizens to vacate the town. This advice was followed by the greater part of the population. It was pitiable to see the refugees endeavoring to remove their possessions and encamping in the woods and fields, for miles around, during the unusually cold weather which soon followed."

By the time Burnside had all the bridges he needed, Longstreet's corps had been on the high ground outside of Fredericksburg for days, and Stonewall Jackson's corps had arrived. At this point, there was a lull in action on both sides for several days, leaving Lee to wonder what Burnside intended to do with his nearly 115,000 man army. On December 6, Lee wrote a dispatch to President Jefferson Davis back in Richmond:

"The enemy still maintain his position north of the Rappahannock. I can discover no indications of his advancing, or of transferring his troops to other positions. Scouts on both of his flanks north of the Rappahannock report no movement, nor have those stationed on the Potomac discovered the collection of transport or the passage of troops down that river.

Gen. Burnside's whole army appears to be encamped between the Rappahannock and Potomac. His apparent inaction suggests the probability that he is waiting for expected operations elsewhere, and I fear troops may be collecting south of James River. Yet I get no reliable information of organized or tried troops being sent to that quarter, nor am I aware of any of their general officers in whom confidence is placed being there in command. There is an evident concentration of troops hitherto disposed in other parts of Virginia, but whether for the purpose of augmenting Gen. Burnside's army or any other I cannot tell…

I have heard that, on the 30th ultimo, ten regiments from Virginia had reached the Baltimore depot, in Washington, their destination unknown. Should Gen. Cox have withdrawn from the Kanawha Valley, I should think the State troops, under Gen. Floyd, could protect that country, and would recommend that the Confederate troops be brought at once to Staunton, to operate in the Shenandoah Valley, if necessary, or south of James River. I think the strength of the enemy south of James River is greatly exaggerated, but have no means of ascertaining the fact.

From the reports forwarded to me by Gen. G. W. Smith, the officers serving there seem to be impressed with its magnitude. If I felt sure of our ability to resist the advance of the enemy south of that river, it would relieve me of great embarrassment, and I should feel better able to oppose the operations which may be contemplated by Gen. Burnside. I presume that the operations in the Department of the West and South will require all the troops in each, but, should there be a lull of the war in these departments, it might be advantageous to leave a sufficient covering force to conceal the movement, and draw an active, when the exigency arrives, to the vicinity of Richmond. Provisions and forage in the mean time could be collected in Richmond. When the crisis shall have passed, these troops could be returned to their departments with re-enforcements.

I need not state to you the advantages of a combination of our troops for a battle, if it can be accomplished, and, unless it can be done, we must make up our minds to fight with great odds against us.

I hope Your Excellency will cause me to be advised when, in your judgment, it may become necessary for this army to move nearer Richmond. It was never in better health or in better condition for battle than now. Some shoes, blankets, arms, and accouterments are still wanting, but we are occasionally receiving small supplies, and I hope all will be provided in time.

There was quite a fall of snow yesterday, which will produce some temporary discomfort.

I have the honor to be, with great respect, your obedient servant,

R. E. LEE"

One of the reasons Burnside hadn't moved is because Burnside himself wasn't sure if Lee knew of his strategy. Burnside had intended to cross the Army of the Potomac east of Fredericksburg downriver, but Lee had positioned Jackson's men to prevent just such a crossing.

When Union gunboats were attacked by men under Jackson's command, including Jubal Early's division and D.H. Hill's division, Burnside believed that Lee had correctly anticipated where he intended to move. At the same time, it also made him assume that Lee's right was strengthened to the east of Fredericksburg, and that the Army of Northern Virginia's center and/or left would be weakened as a result. That assumption ultimately induced Burnside to attempt the crossing of the Rappahannock directly in front of Fredericksburg itself, as he explained in a December 9 dispatch to Union general-in-chief Henry Halleck, "I think now the enemy will be more surprised by a crossing immediately in our front than any other part of the river. ... I'm convinced that a large force of the enemy is now concentrated at Port Royal, its left resting on Fredericksburg, which we hope to turn."

Burnside would explain what he hoped to accomplish in his official report after the campaign:

"During my preparations for crossing at the place I had at first selected, I discovered that the enemy had thrown a large portion of his force down the river and elsewhere, thus weakening his defenses in front; and also thought I discovered that he did not anticipate the crossing of our whole force at Fredericksburg; and I hoped, by rapidly throwing the whole command over at that place, to separate, by a vigorous attack, the forces of the enemy on the river below from the forces behind and on the crests in tile rear of the town, in which case we should fight him with great advantages in our favor. To do this we had to gain a height on the extreme right of the crest, which height commanded a new road, lately built by the enemy for purposes of more rapid communication along his lines; which point gained, his positions along the crest would have been scarcely tenable, and he could have been driven from them easily by an attack on his front, in connection with a movement in rear of the crest."

Chapter 3: Crossing the Rappahannock

The pontoon bridges used by William Franklin's "Grand Division" to cross the Rappahannock

In the early morning hours of December 11, with all of the necessary supplies on hand and his artillery situated on the commanding Stafford Heights in his rear, Burnside ordered the Union's engineers to begin building half a dozen pontoon bridges at several points along the Rappahannock, with two of them near the center of the town, one on the southern part of the town, and three more downriver. The orders would bring about some of the most unique fighting of the Civil War.

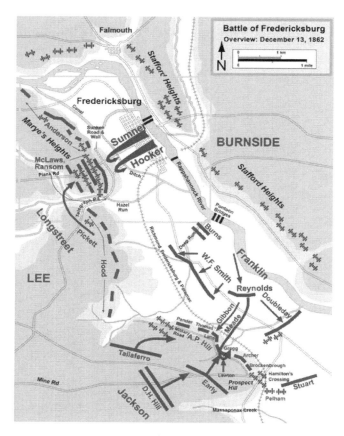

The locations of the pontoon bridges are marked as black lines across the river

Fully aware that the Army of the Potomac would have to cross the river somewhere at some time, Lafayette McLaws's division, representing the left of the Army of Northern Virginia's line, had men posted all along the front in a way that would allow the Confederate defenders to contest a crossing. That included several regiments along the river bank and some in the town of Fredericksburg itself. As soon as Confederates in these advanced positions noted the Union movements, a Confederate battery sounded a signal alert by firing twice around 4:00 a.m. The Army of Northern Virginia was already aware of Burnside's attempts to cross the river before they'd barely begun.

One of the engineers, Wesley Brainerd of the 50th New York Engineers, recalled, "A long line of arms moving rapidly up and down was all I saw, for a moment later they were again obscured by the fog. But I knew too well that line of arms was ramming cartridges and that the crisis was near." Sure enough, the engineers were met by a strong volley that Brainerd described, "The bullets of the enemy rained upon my bridge. They went whizzing and zipping by and around me, pattering on the bridge, splashing into the water and thugging through the boats."

McLaws explained his dispositions as the Union engineers began building pontoon bridges in his front:

> "One brigade was constantly on duty in the city to guard the town and defend the river crossings as far down as a quarter of a mile below Deep Run Creek. Two regiments from General Anderson's division picketed the river bank above the town, reporting to the brigadier-general in charge of the brigade on duty in the city. The orders were that two guns should be fired from one of my batteries in a central position, which would be the signal that the enemy were attempting to cross. These were the positions of my command and the orders governing them up to the 10th instant. On that day the brigade of General Barksdale, composed of the Mississippi troops, were on duty in the city.

> About 2 a.m. on the 11th, General Barksdale sent me word that the movements of the enemy indicated they were preparing to lay down their pontoon bridges, and his men were getting into position to defend the crossing. About 4.30 o'clock he notified me that the bridges were being placed, and he would open fire so soon as the working parties came in good range of his rifles. I gave the order, and the signal guns were fired about 5 a.m.

> I had been notified from your headquarters the evening previous (the 10th instant) to have all the batteries harnessed up at daylight on the 11th, and I had given orders that my whole command should be under arms at the same time.

> General Barksdale kept his men quiet and concealed until the bridges were so advanced that the working parties were in easy range, when he opened fire with such effect the bridges were abandoned at once. Nine separate and desperate attempts were made to complete the bridges under fire of their sharpshooters and guns on the opposite banks, but every attempt being attended with such severe loss from our men--posted in rifle-pits, in the cellars of the houses along the banks, and from behind whatever offered concealment--that the enemy abandoned their attempts for the time and opened a terrific fire from their numerous batteries concentrated along the hills just above the river."

Barksdale

As McLaws indicated, the defenseless Union engineers were more than a little skittish about being exposed to Confederate fire as they defenselessly tried to construct pontoon bridges across the river. In response, the Army of the Potomac's artillery opened up on the town with about 150 guns, trying to force the Confederate defenders out of the town and thus out of range of the pontoon bridges, but the Confederate defenders were able to hide in cellars and maintain their positions. One of Brainerd's comrades in the 50th New York Engineers, surgeon Clark Raum, described the bombardment, "When the artillery fairly opened the roar was terrific – dreadful – I know of no words to express it. The screeching of the shells thru the air the whiz of the solid shot, the boom, boom, boom of the cannon, the sharp ring of the rifles and rattle of the musketry all commingles made one's ears tingle.

Despite the artillery fire, Barksdale's brigade continued to employ sharpshooters from buildings in town, completely frustrating the attempts to construct the pontoon bridges near the town. Around 2:00, a completely flustered Burnside complained, "The army is held by the throat by a few sharpshooters!" Eventually, Henry Hunt concocted a new plan to help the crossings. Hunt suggested to Burnside that infantry should be ferried across the river and then spread out to establish a line on the western bank of the river, pushing forward to fight the Confederate defenders in town while the engineers completed the pontoon bridges. Burnside initially hesitated, believing that it would result in "death to most of those who should undertake the voyage", but the men of Colonel Norman Hall's brigade let off three cheers in response to Hall's suggestion that his men be given the assignment. With that, the order was given, and by now the

Confederates' use of the town had so enraged the Union officers that the men now set to ferry across were ordered to give no quarter and take no prisoners among the Confederates they found in the town.

Around 3:00 p.m., now nearly 12 hours since the attempt to cross had started, about 130 men from the 7th Michigan and 19th Massachusetts were ferried across the river in small boats, but this was no pleasure cruise. One Union soldier looking on at the scene watching it unfold explained, "An oarsman would be seen relinquishing his oar and falling down dead or wounded in the bottom of his boat or overboard into the river. Then another would drop while not a few of their partners with rifles in hand were suffering a similar fate by their side...It may have been the saddest sight during my life in the army."

Once they made it, they formed a skirmish line for the purposes of fighting the Confederates in town. As they engaged in running street battles to clear Fredericksburg one street at a time, the engineers were able to complete the pontoon bridges less than 90 minutes later. To help secure the landing zones, the Army of the Potomac fired thousands of artillery shells at the city and the Confederates positioned on the ridges to the west of Fredericksburg. One Confederate officer described the scene as a "line of angry blazing guns firing through white clouds of smoke & almost shaking the earth with their roar. Over & in the town the white winkings of the bursting shells reminded one of a countless swarm of fire-flies. Several buildings were set on fire, & their black smoke rose in remarkably slender, straight, & tall columns for two hundred feet, perhaps, before they began to spread horizontally & unite in a great black canopy." One of Barksdale's men from the 17th Mississippi described the kind of fighting going on all throughout Fredericksburg, "There were six men in the basement of [a] two-story house, and any one of them now living will testify to the fact that the house was tom to pieces, the chimney falling down in the basement among us; .... A few moments after the batteries opened, several regiments of Union infantry came yelling down the hill toward the river, laying hold of the boats and coming over toward where we were stationed. As they came up the bank we tried to get out at the end of the house."

From his position along the left of the Confederate line, Porter Alexander described his view of the shelling of Fredericksburg:

"The city, except its steeples, was still veiled in the mist which had settled in the valleys. Above it and in it incessantly showed the round white clouds of bursting shells, and out of its midst there soon rose three or four columns of dense black smoke from houses set on fire by the explosions. The atmosphere was so perfectly calm and still that the smoke rose vertically in great pillars for several hundred feet before spreading outward in black sheets. The opposite bank of the river, for two miles to the right and left, was crowned at frequent intervals with blazing batteries, canopied in clouds of white smoke.

Beyond these, the dark blue masses of over 100,000 infantry in compact columns, and numberless parks of white-topped wagons and ambulances massed in orderly ranks, all awaited the completion of the bridges. The earth shook with the thunder of the guns, and, high above all, a thousand feet in the air, hung two immense balloons. The scene gave impressive ideas of the disciplined power of a great army, and of the vast resources of the nation which had sent it forth."

As the 7th Michigan and 19th Massachusetts struggled in their fight in Fredericksburg, the 20th Massachusetts crossed into town and bolstered them, advancing house by house. One of the men of the 20th Massachusetts later noted the "Michigan men made a rush at the nearest houses and took quite a number of prisoners. The orders to the whole Brigade were to bayonet every armed man found firing from a house ..., but it was not of course obeyed.... In fact no prisoners were taken but the few the Michigans took and the wounded who lay about struck by our shells. The 7th Michigan were deployed on the left and a short distance up the street at the foot of which we landed, and the 19th on the right, both holding houses, fences, etc., and exchanging shots with the Rebels who were a little farther back .... When a good many troops had got over, we were advanced up the street."

The Confederates had taken up such strong positions in houses that many of the Union soldiers in town found themselves being fired upon by an invisible enemy, often seeing nothing but a muzzle flash. One soldier in the 20th Massachusetts explained, "Here we cleared the houses near us, but shot came from far and near – we could see no one and were simply murdered...every shot of the enemy took effect. How I escaped I cannot say, as more than a dozen actually fell on me."

With the pontoon bridges completed, the first to cross were advanced elements of Edwin Sumner's Grand Division. Burnside had organized the Army of the Potomac into three "Grand Divisions", which gave the Grand Division commanders control over several corps. McClellan had used a similar organization during the Maryland Campaign, and it caused him serious problems at Antietam when Burnside continued acting like a Grand Division commander instead of simply a corps commander, needlessly causing delays in orders being passed down the chain of command. Sumner's Grand Division consisted of Darius Couch's II Corps (which included divisions led by Winfield S. Hancock, Oliver O. Howard, and William H. French), Orlando B. Willcox's IX Corps (which included divisions led by William W. Burns, Samuel D. Sturgis, and George W. Getty), and a cavalry division led by Alfred Pleasonton.

Sumner

Barksdale's brigade retreated by fighting a delaying defense in depth that prevented the Union from fully taking Fredericksburg until night began to fall. In the process of crossing and clearing the town, the Army of the Potomac had suffered more than 350 casualties, inflicting about 240 on the Confederates themselves. The crossing and fighting in Fredericksburg that day were unprecedented. It was the first time the U.S. Army had intentionally bombarded an American city, the first time American soldiers crossed a body of water under enemy fire, and the first major urban combat of the Civil War.

When the Union soldiers had taken complete control of the town, they exacted their vengeance with a fury by looting buildings throughout the town. Lee would later liken their activities at Fredericksburg to the Vandals, but it's no surprise that the Union soldiers were enraged by the tactics of the Confederate sharpshooters, who had hidden in private homes to take potshots at them and make December 11 a miserable day. The Union soldiers wreaked such havoc that one news correspondent in Fredericksburg wrote, "In some cases the whole side of a house has been shot away, roofs and chimneys have tumbled in, window frames smashed to atoms, and doors jarred from the hinges." One Union soldier noted, "Furniture of all sorts is strewn along the streets.... Every namable household utensil or article of furniture, stoves, crockery and glass-ware, pots, kettles and tins, are scattered, and smashed and thrown everywhere, indoors and out, as if there had fallen a shower of them in the midst of a mighty whirlwind."

The Market House at the edge of Fredericksburg was Barksdale's headquarters on December 11

The construction of pontoon bridges to the south went much more smoothly, thanks to the protection of artillery. Of course, that didn't mean there were no delays. Despite the fact the bridges south of town were completed by 11:00 a.m. and William Franklin's Grand Division was ordered to cross at 4:00 p.m., only one brigade made the crossing that day, and the rest wouldn't be across until 1:00 p.m. on December 12. As a result, Stonewall Jackson was able to recall Early's division and D.H. Hill's division, both of which were posted further downriver, in the early morning hours of December 13 without suffering any consequences.

Franklin

Franklin's Grand Division was the rule rather than the exception. The Army of the Potomac spent most of December 12 crossing the river and planning to align for battle on December 13. But despite having all of December 12 to concoct a battle plan, Burnside managed to do no more than pass on vague instructions to his officers. Burnside conducted a personal reconnaissance south of Fredericksburg on the afternoon of December 12, but when Franklin asked him for orders, he held off on issuing any concrete orders during the day. Franklin's 60,000 man Grand Division, responsible for the entire left wing of Burnside's army, would not be given a battle plan for December 13 until after 7:00 a.m. on the 13th itself.

Chapter 4: Fighting South of Fredericksburg

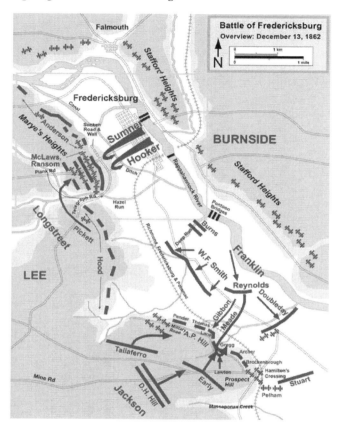

"My God, General Reynolds, did they think my division could whip Lee's whole army?" – George Meade

The Battle of Fredericksburg has long been remembered as a Union debacle, and a decisive Confederate victory, based almost entirely on the fighting that took place in the late afternoon of December 13. Before the assaults on Marye's Heights, however, Burnside hoped to turn the Confederates' position by pushing Stonewall Jackson's corps back on the Confederate right and thus flanking Longstreet's well-defended position on Marye's Heights outside of town. Given that the Army of the Potomac vastly outnumbered the Confederates, by upwards of 50,000 soldiers, the plan had a decent chance of success if executed properly.

The problem is the plan was never executed properly because it was unclear just what Burnside's plan was. On December 12, Burnside had told Franklin that he was envisioning that Franklin's Grand Division would attack Jackson's corps while being supported by Hooker's Grand Division, but the orders Franklin received on the morning of December 13 instructed Franklin to hold his position while sending "a division at least" to seize Prospect Hill, the highest ground in the area. Naturally, Sumner expected that the attack would consist of his entire Grand Division, but apparently Burnside thought a demonstration by one division of one corps would convince Lee to withdraw toward Richmond.

Given the confusing orders, Franklin decided to follow the letter of the orders. On the morning of December 13, a dense fog hung in the valley Fredericksburg is located in, keeping the armies hidden from each other, and while the armies bided their time Franklin instructed I Corps commander John Reynolds to choose one of his divisions to make the attack. Reynolds tapped George Meade's 4,500 man division, to be supported by John Gibbon's division. Abner Doubleday's division was to cover the advance's left flank by facing south and combating JEB Stuart's cavalry, which had situated itself at a nearly 90 degree angle on the Confederates' right flank to offer enfilading fire.

Meade

Meade's men began their advance forward in heavy fog around 8:30 a.m. with Gibbon's division in back of them, and as they reached Richmond Road, they began receiving enfilading fire from JEB Stuart's artillery, being manned by the young "gallant" Major John Pelham, who opened on them with 2 guns. As Union artillery tried to silence Pelham's guns from their dangerous position, Stuart told Pelham he could withdraw, to which Pelham responded, "Tell the General I can hold my ground." The 24th Michigan Infantry, a brand new regiment full of raw recruits, was ordered to deal with Pelham, but they were unable to stop Pelham's battery until it began to run low on ammunition after about an hour. Lee would later praise the young Major, stating, "It is glorious to see such courage in one so young."

"Gallant John Pelham"

Once the fog started to lift around 10:30, Jackson's artillery began raining down on the advancing Union soldiers from Prospect Hill, stopping Meade's division in its tracks about 600 yards from the hill around 11:00 a.m. Meade described the fighting to his wife, "On the 13th it was determined to make an attack from both positions, and the honor of leading this attack was assigned to my division. I cannot give you all the details of the fight, but will simply say my men went in beautifully, carried everything before them, and drove the enemy for nearly half a mile, but finding themselves unsupported on either right or left, and encountering an overwhelming force of the enemy, they were checked and finally driven back. As an evidence of the work they had to do, it is only necessary to state that out of four thousand five hundred men taken into action, we know the names of eighteen hundred killed and wounded. There are besides some four hundred missing, many of whom are wounded."

Meade was more detailed in his official report:

"Early on the morning of the 13th, I accompanied the general commanding the First Corps to the headquarters of the left grand division, where the commanding general indicated the point he was instructed to attack, and I was informed my division had been selected to make the attack.

The point indicated was on the ridge, or rather range of heights, extending from the Rappahannock, in the rear of Fredericksburg, to the Massaponax, and was situated near the left of this ridge, where it terminated in the Massaponax Valley. Between the heights to be attacked and the plateau on which the left grand division was posted, there was a depression or hollow of several hundred yards in width, through which, and close to the foot of the heights, the Richmond railroad ran. The heights along the crest were wooded. The slope to the railroad from the extreme left for the space of 300 or 400 yards was clear; beyond this it was wooded, the woods extending across the hollow and in front of the railroad. The plateau on our side was level and cultivated ground up to the crest of the hollow, where there was quite a fall to the railroad. The enemy occupied the wooded heights, the line of railroad, and the wood in front. Owing to the wood, nothing could be seen of them, while all our movements on the cleared ground were exposed to their view. Immediately on receiving orders, the division was moved forward across the Smithfield ravine, advancing down the river some 700 or 800 yards, when it turned sharp to the right and crossed the Bowling Green road, which here runs in a parallel direction with the railroad. Some time was consumed in removing the hedge fences on this road, and bridging the drains on each side for the passage of the artillery.

Between 9 and 10 o'clock the column of attack was formed as follows: The First Brigade in line of battle on the crest of the hollow, and facing the railroad, with the Sixth Regiment deployed as skirmishers; the Second Brigade in rear of the First 300 paces; the Third Brigade by the flank, its right flank being a few rods to the rear of the First Brigade, having the Ninth Regiment deployed on its flank as skirmishers and flankers, and the batteries between the First and Second Brigades. This disposition had scarcely been made when the enemy opened a brisk fire from a battery posted on the Bowling Green road, the shot from which took the command from the left and rear.

Apprehending an attack from this quarter, the Third Brigade was faced to the left, thus forming, with the First, two sides of a square. Simpson's battery was advanced to the front and left of the Third Brigade, and Cooper's and Ransom's batteries moved to a knoll on the left of the First Brigade. These batteries immediately opened on the enemy's battery, and, in conjunction with some of General Doubleday's batteries in our rear, on the other side of the Bowling Green road, after twenty minutes' firing, silenced and compelled the withdrawal of the guns. During this artillery duel the enemy advanced a body of sharpshooters along the Bowling Green road, and under cover of the hedges and trees on the roadside."

As Meade's men stayed in place under heavy fire from Jackson's corps on Prospect Hill, Meade got ever more desperate about finding someone, anyone, to support his division in the attack. He explained the action in his report:

"As soon as the enemy's guns were silenced, the line of infantry was ordered to the attack. The First Brigade, on the right, advanced several hundred yards over cleared ground, driving the enemy's skirmishers before them, till they reached the woods previously described as being in front of the railroad, which they entered, driving the enemy out of them to the railroad, where they were found strongly posted in ditches and behind temporary defenses. The brigade (First) drove them from there and up the heights in their front, though, owing to a heavy fire being received on their right flank, they obliqued over to that side, but continued forcing the enemy back till they had crossed the crest of the hill; crossed a main road which runs along the crest, and reached open ground on the other side, where they were assailed by a severe fire from a large force in their front, and, at the same time, the enemy opened a battery which completely enfiladed them from the right flank. After holding their ground for some time, no support arriving, they were compelled to fall back to the railroad. The Second Brigade, which advanced in rear of the First, after reaching the railroad, was assailed with so severe a fire on their right flank that the Fourth Regiment halted and formed, faced to the right, to repel this attack. The ether regiments, in passing through the woods, being assailed from the left, inclined in that direction and ascended the heights, the Third going up as the One hundred and twenty-first of the brigade was retiring. The Third continued to advance, and reached nearly the same point as the First Brigade, but was compelled to withdraw for the same reason. The Seventh engaged the enemy to the left, capturing many prisoners and a stand of colors, driving them from their rifle-pits and temporary defenses, and continuing the pursuit till, encountering the enemy's re-enforcements, they were in turn driven back. The Third Brigade had not advanced over 100 yards, when the battery on the height on its left was remanned, and poured a destructive fire into its ranks. Perceiving this, I dispatched my aide-de-camp, Lieutenant Dehon, with orders for General Jackson to move by the right flank till he could clear the open ground in front of the battery, and then, ascending the height through the woods, swing around to the left and take the battery. Unfortunately Lieutenant Dehon fell just as he reached General Jackson, and a short time afterward the latter officer was killed. The regiments, however, did partially execute the movement by obliquing to the right, and advancing across the railroad, a portion ascending the heights in their front. The loss of their commander, and the severity of the fire from both artillery and infantry to which they were subjected, compelled them to withdraw, when those on their right withdrew."

One of the reasons Meade was so desperate for help is because a Confederate mistake had given the Union an opening right in his front, so long as enough soldiers were pushed forward.

Despite the fact Jackson's men had been in the area for two weeks, Jackson's line had only been formed the day before when all of his divisions were recalled from the various crossing points downriver of Fredericksburg. When they formed a line, A.P. Hill's Light Division had a 600 yard gap in it near a small, swampy patch of woods. If the Confederates thought Union men would not hit the gap, they were unpleasantly surprised when Meade's 1st brigade poured into the gap and hit one of the brigades in A.P. Hill's division right on its flank. Confederate brigadier Maxcy Gregg was so taken by surprise that he initially thought Meade's men were Confederate comrades and ordered his men not to fire. When he rode to the front of his own line, his mistake cost him his life when one of the advancing Union soldiers shot him through the spine.

Fortunately for the Confederates, they were able to plug their gap by sending forth Jubal Early's division and William Taliaferro's division at just the right time. Early described the action:

"Shortly after noon we heard in our front a very heavy musketry fire, and soon a courier from General Archer came to the rear in search of General A. P. Hill, stating that General Archer was very heavily pressed and wanted reinforcements. Just at that moment, a staff officer rode up with an order to me from General Jackson, to hold my division in readiness to move to the right promptly, as the enemy was making a demonstration in that direction. This caused me to hesitate about sending a brigade to Archer's assistance, but to be prepared to send it if necessary, I ordered Colonel Atkinson to get his brigade ready to advance, and the order had been hardly given, before the adjutant of Walker's battalion of artillery came galloping to the rear with the information that the interval on Archer's left (an awful gulf as he designated it) had been penetrated by heavy columns of the enemy, and that Archer's brigade and all our batteries on the right would inevitably be captured unless there was instant relief. This was so serious an emergency that I determined to act upon it at once notwithstanding the previous directions from General Jackson to hold my division in readiness for another purpose, and I accordingly ordered Atkinson to advance with his brigade.

I was then entirely unacquainted with the ground in front, having been able when I first got up to take only a hasty glance at the country to our right, and I asked Lieutenant Chamberlain, Walker's adjutant, to show the brigade the direction to advance. In reply he stated that the column of the enemy which had penetrated our line was immediately in front of the brigade I had ordered forward, and that by going right ahead there could be no mistake. The brigade, with the exception of one regiment, the 13th Georgia, which did not hear the order, accordingly moved off in handsome style through the woods, but as it did so Lieutenant Chamberlain informed me that it would not be sufficient to cover the entire gap in our line, and I ordered Colonel Walker to advance immediately with my own brigade on the left of Atkinson.

The enemy's column in penetrating the interval mentioned had turned Archer's left and Lane's right, while they were attacked in front, causing Archer's left and Lane's entire brigade to give way, and one column had encountered Gregg's brigade, which, being taken somewhat by surprise, was thrown into partial confusion, resulting in the death of General Gregg, but the brigade was rallied and maintained its ground. Lawton's brigade advancing rapidly and gallantly under Colonel Atkinson, encountered that column of the enemy which had turned Archer's left, in the woods on the hill in rear of the line, and by a brilliant charge drove it back down the hill, across the railroad, and out into the open plains beyond, advancing so far as to cause a portion of one of the enemy's batteries to be abandoned. The brigade, however, on getting out into the open plain came under the fire of the enemy's heavy guns, and the approach of a fresh and heavy column on its right rendered it necessary that it should retire, which it did under orders from Colonel Evans, who had succeeded to the command by reason of Atkinson's being severely wounded.

Two of Brockenborough's regiments from the right participated in the repulse of the enemy. Colonel Walker advanced, at a double quick, further to the left, encountering one of the columns which had penetrated the interval, and by a gallant and resolute charge he drove it back out of the woods across the railroad into the open plains beyond, when, seeing another column of the enemy crossing the railroad on his left, he fell back to the line of the road, and then deployed the 13th Virginia Regiment to the left, and ordered it to advance under cover of the timbers to attack the advancing column on its flank. This attack was promptly made and Thomas' brigade, attacking in front at the same time, the enemy was driven back with heavy loss.

As soon as Atkinson and Walker had been ordered forward, Hoke was ordered to move his brigade to the left of Hays, but before he got into position, I received a message stating that Archer's brigade was giving way and I ordered Hoke to move forward at once to Archer's support, obliquing to the right as he moved. Just as Hoke started, I received an order from General Jackson, by a member of his staff, to advance to the front with the whole division, and Hays' brigade was at once ordered forward in support of Hoke. The 13th Georgia Regiment which had been left behind on the advance of Lawton's brigade was ordered to follow Hoke's brigade and unite with it.

Hoke found a body of the enemy in the woods in rear of Archer's line on the left, where the regiments on that flank, which had been attacked in rear, had given way, but Archer still held the right with great resolution, though his ammunition was exhausted. Upon a gallant charge, by the brigade under Hoke, the enemy was driven out of the woods upon his reserves posted on the railroad in front, and then by another charge, in which General Archer participated, the railroad was cleared and the enemy was pursued to a fence some distance beyond, leaving in our hands a number of prisoners, and a large number of small arms on the field.

The movements of the three brigades engaged have been described separately from the necessity of the case, but they were all engaged at the same time, though they went into action separately and in the order in which they have been mentioned, and Lawton's brigade had advanced further out into the plains than either of the others.

On riding to the front, I directed Lawton's brigade, which was retiring, to be re-formed in the woods-Colonel Atkinson had been left in front severely wounded and he fell into the enemy's hands. Captain E. P. Lawton, Assistant Adjutant General of the brigade, a most gallant and efficient officer, had also been left in front at the extreme point to which the brigade advanced, mortally wounded, and he likewise fell into the enemy's hands.

I discovered that Hoke had got too far to the front where he was exposed to the enemy's artillery, and also to a flank movement on his right, and I sent an order for him to retire to the original line, which he did, anticipating the order by commencing to retire before it reached him. Two of his regiments and a small battalion were left to occupy the line of the railroad where there was cover for them and his other two regiments, along with the 13th Georgia, which had not been engaged, were put in the slight trenches previously occupied by Archer's brigade. Walker continued to hold the position on the railroad which he had taken after repulsing the enemy. Lawton's brigade was sent to the rear for the purpose of resting and replenishing its ammunition. Hays' brigade, which had advanced in rear of Hoke, had not become engaged, but in advancing to the front it had been exposed to a severe shelling which the enemy began, as his attacking columns were retiring in confusion before my advancing brigades. Hays was posted in rear of Hoke for the purpose of strengthening the right in the event of another advance. When I had discovered Lawton's brigade retiring, I sent to General D. H. Hill for reinforcements for fear that the enemy might again pass through the unprotected interval, and he sent me two brigades, but before they arrived Brigadier General Paxton, who occupied the right of Taliaferro's line, had covered the interval by promptly moving his brigade into it.

The enemy was very severely punished for this attack, which was made by Franklin's grand division, and he made no further attack on our right. During this engagement and subsequently there were demonstrations against A. P. Hill's left and Hood's right which were repulsed without difficulty.."

As Meade's men fought desperately to exploit the Confederate mistake and keep a gap open, officers in the rear vacillated over how to proceed. Gibbon refused to let any of his brigades support Meade's assault, operating under the belief that he was supposed to maintain a support position. One of his brigades would not move forward to Meade's help until 1:30 p.m., more than 2 hours after Meade's men had started the assault. 2 more brigades followed, but all three of these were sharply repulsed. Yet another supporting brigade was thrown into the fray, but the Confederates drove them back in fierce hand-to-hand fighting that drove the disorganized Union soldiers back. Simply put, the supporting brigades had made their attacks too late to help Meade's breakthrough in Jackson's line. An enraged Meade complained to his corps commander, "My God, General Reynolds, did they think my division could whip Lee's whole army?"

As the Union soldiers were pushed back, Early had trouble controlling his own men, and some of them led a counterattack without orders, continuing forward in a chase after the retreating Union men. This brought them through an open field, allowing Union artillery to unleash grapeshot canister blasts on them. Early's counterattack also coincided with an advance by General David Birney's division of the Union III Corps, which finally began moving forward after Meade singlehandedly ordered them forward with profanity that one staffer said "almost makes the stones creep." Birney's men were far too late to help Meade's attack, but they stopped the Confederate advance. Stonewall Jackson's men withdrew back to their defensive positions on the high ground, bringing the fighting south of Fredericksburg to an end. Franklin had lost 5,000 casualties, and Stonewall Jackson had lost nearly 3,500 casualties.

With the fighting ending around the middle of the afternoon, Burnside had already concentrated on trying to dislodge Longstreet from Marye's Heights, and when he learned that his men had failed to force Stonewall Jackson's withdrawal, he apparently did not have contingency plans or decide on a new plan. When he ordered Franklin to "advance his right and front," the kind of general attack that very well could have been successful hours earlier, Franklin refused on the grounds that all of his men had already been engaged and were battered. In reality, Franklin still had about 20,000 men at his disposal, comprised of the VI Corps and Doubleday's division, who had not fought in the infantry battle at all.

Meade was bitter for weeks, and he described the effect the fighting had on his division:

"It will be seen from the foregoing that the attack was for a time perfectly successful.' The enemy was driven from the railroad, his rifle-pits, and breastworks, for over half a mile. Over 300 prisoners were taken and several standards, when the advancing line encountered the heavy re-enforcements of the enemy, who, recovering from the effects of our assault, and perceiving both our flanks unprotected, poured in such a destructive fire from all three directions as to compel the line to fall back, which was executed without confusion. Perceiving the danger of the too great penetration of my line, without support, I dispatched several staff officers both to General Gibbon's command and General Birney's (whose division had replaced mine at the batteries from whence we advanced), urging an advance to my support, the one on my right, the other on my left. A brigade of Birney's advanced to our relief just as my men were withdrawn from the wood, and Gibbon's division advanced into the wood on our right in time to assist materially in the safe withdrawal of my broken line.

An unsuccessful effort was made to reform the division in the hollow in front of the batteries. Failing in this, the command was reformed beyond the Bowling Green road and marched to the ground occupied the night before, where it was held in reserve till the night of the 15th, when we recrossed the river.

Accompanying this report is a list giving the names of the killed, wounded, and missing, amounting in the aggregate to 179 killed, 1,082 wounded, and 509 missing. When I report that 4,500 men is a liberal estimate of the strength of the division taken into action, this large loss, being 40 per cent., will fully bear me out in the expression of my satisfaction at the good conduct of both officers and men. While I deeply regret the inability of the division, after having successfully penetrated the enemy's lines, to remain and hold what had been secured, at the same time I deem their withdrawal a matter of necessity. With one brigade commander killed, another wounded, nearly half their number hors du combat, with regiments separated from brigades, and companies from regiments, and all the confusion and disorder incidental to the advance of an extended line through wood and other obstructions, assailed by a heavy fire, not only of infantry but of artillery--not only in front but on both flanks--the best troops would be justified in withdrawing without loss of honor."

The fighting conducted by Meade's division was one of the most talked-about aspects of the battle among Civil War veterans after the war, so much so that Longstreet went out of his way in his memoirs to discuss the fact that it had been compared to Pickett's Charge:

"The charge of Meade's division has been compared with that of Pickett's, Pettigrew's, and Trimble's at Gettysburg, giving credit of better conduct to the former. The circumstances do not justify the comparison.

When the fog lifted over Meade's advance he was within musket-range of A. P. Hill's division, closely supported on his right by Gibbon's, and guarded on his left by Doubleday's division. On Hill's right was a fourteen-gun battery, on his left eight guns. Meade broke through Hill's division, and with the support of Gibbon forced his way till he encountered part of Ewell's division, when he was forced back in some confusion. Two fresh divisions of the Third Corps came to their relief, and there were as many as fifty thousand men at hand who could have been thrown into the fight. Meade's march to meet his adversary was half a mile,--the troops of both sides fresh and vigorous.

Of the assaulting columns of Pickett, Pettigrew, and Trimble, only four thousand seven hundred under Pickett were fresh; the entire force of these divisions was only fifteen thousand strong. They had a mile to march over open field before reaching the enemy's line, strengthened by field-works and manned by thrice their numbers. The Confederates at Gettysburg had been fought to exhaustion of men and munitions. They lost about sixty per cent. of the assaulting forces,--Meade about forty. The latter had fresh troops behind him, and more than two hundred guns to cover his rallying lines. The Confederates had nothing behind them but field batteries almost exhausted of ammunition. That Meade made a brave, good fight is beyond question, but he had superior numbers and appointments. At Gettysburg the Confederate assault was made against intrenched lines of artillery and infantry, where stood fifty thousand men."

Chapter 5: It Is Well That War Is So Terrible

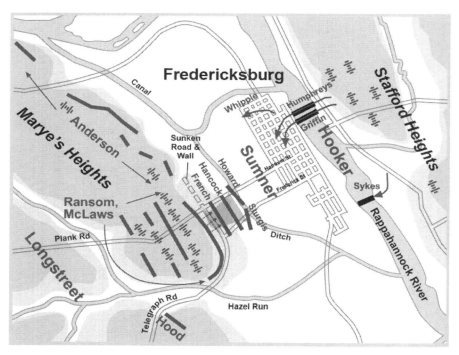

Although the Union almost broke the Confederate lines in the South, they were ultimately repulsed, and the battle is mostly remembered for the piecemeal attacks the Union army made on heavily fortified positions Longstreet's men took up on Marye's Heights. With the massacre at Antietam still fresh in his mind (partially caused by the Confederates having not constructed defensive works), Longstreet ordered trenches, abatis (obstacles formed by felled trees with sharpened branches), and fieldworks to be constructed, which to Longstreet's credit helped set a precedent for all future defensive battles of the Army of Northern Virginia. To his thinking, if the artillery didn't keep Union forces at bay, the 2500 Confederates lined up four-deep behind a quarter-mile long four-foot stone wall would deter even the most foolhardy.

Colonel Alexander kept busy re-positioning Longstreet's artillery. Captain Sam Johnston, Lee's engineer in charge of the Army of Northern Virginia, accompanied Alexander on his reconnoitering to supervise the positioning of Lee's gun pits: Lee said the guns were to be placed on the brow or reverse slope of the heights so they might square-off with Union artillery on Stafford Heights. Alexander, however, had a much different strategy in mind. Expecting the Union attack to fall on their far-left flank, Alexander positioned the gun pits to fire directly into the advancing Union infantry and sweep the battlefield, essentially disagreeing with General Lee's assessment that the Confederate ordnance could not duel effectively with the enemy's guns at such a distance. After some verbal disagreement, Lee walked away, leaving the gun pits' positioning unchanged. Upon General Longstreet's inspection of the artillery, Alexander reported proudly, "General, we cover that ground now so well that we will comb it as with a fine-tooth comb. A chicken could not live on that field when we open on it!"

During the time the two armies jockeyed for optimal position, Colonel Alexander received the nickname "the cuss with the spy glass" from Union troops, the result of his precise shelling of Union sharpshooters with a 24-pound howitzer, said to be his favorite gun. In one case, Alexander was able to target a building hidden from view by low hills and trees containing Union sharpshooters, lobbing a shell containing 175 mini-balls that nearly brushed the grass as it curved the hill but still hit the building dead center. Confederates along the line shouted, "That got 'em! That got 'em! You can hear 'em just a hollerin' and a groanin' in there!"

As the fog lifted across Fredericksburg around 10:30, Burnside's first attack against Marye's Heights was getting ready to move forward. Operating under the mistaken belief that Franklin's division would be the decisive attack that forced Lee to withdraw to a new defensive line, Burnside ordered Edwin Sumner to send "a division or more" to take the Confederate left, essentially giving him the same kind of vague instructions Franklin had received. In an army composed of over 100,000 men, Burnside had effectively given his two subordinates discretionary orders to push forward as few as 10,000 men against Lee's nearly 70,000 strong Army of Northern Virginia.

Thus, William H. French's division of Darius Couch's II Corps began moving forward through town, dodging Confederate shells while passing obstacles like houses, fences, and gardens that broke up the line in places and forced them to reform under fire. Couch explained what his men had to go through just to approach the Heights in his official report: In rear of the town the ground is a broken plain, traversed about midway by a canal or ditch, running from right to left. Across this plain, some 600 yards from the outer edge of town, commences the first rise of hills on which the enemy had erected his batteries. Two roads cut the plain nearly at right angles with the canal--the one a plank road, leading to Culpeper, to the right; the other, to the left, the Telegraph road leading to Richmond." Longstreet's guns had that whole space covered, and any Union soldier "lucky enough to survive the artillery would have to meet 2,000 of McLaws's men at the front of the Heights near the sunken road and 7,000 men situated on the crest of the Heights.

The wall along the sunken road offered the Confederate defenders invaluable protection.

On top of having to push one of his divisions forward, Couch also received orders to help General Willcox link up with the right of Franklin's Grand Division, necessarily keeping some of his men out of the assault: "The major-general commanding directs me to say to you that General Willcox has been ordered to extend to the left, so as to connect with Franklin's right. You will extend your right so far as to prevent the possibility of the enemy occupying the upper part of the town. You will then form a column of a division for the purpose of pushing in the direction of the Plank and Telegraph roads, for the purpose, of seizing the height in rear of the town. This column will advance in three lines, with such intervals as you may Judge proper, this movement to be covered by a heavy line of skirmishers in front and on both flanks. You will hold another division in readiness to advance in support of this movement, to be formed in the same manner as the leading division. Particular care and precaution must be taken to prevent collision with our own troops in the fog. The movement will not commence until you receive orders. The watchword will be 'Scott.'"

French's division began pushing toward the Heights, with Winfield Scott Hancock's division about 200 yards behind him to support the assault, and French's men were cut down en masse. Moreover, French's men stopped to fire their own volleys at the Confederate defenders, which made them sitting targets and delayed their advance. Most of the division was stopped about 125 yards from the wall of the sunken road. Those that got closer found that their only protection was to stay completely down on the ground and/or hide behind their comrades' corpses. 50% of French's division was wounded, killed or captured in the assault. Those who were still alive and hugging the ground actually grabbed at the legs and feet of their advancing comrades, urging and begging them to withdraw instead of get themselves killed.

Longstreet described what his men did to Hancock's advancing division in his memoirs: "Hancock, coming speedily with his division, was better organized and in time to take up the fight as French was obliged to retire. This advance was handsomely maintained, but the galling fire they encountered forced them to open fire. Under this delay their ranks were cut up as rapidly as they had collected at the canal, and when within a hundred yards of the stone wall they were so thinned that they could do nothing but surrender, even if they could leap to the road-bed. But they turned, and the fire naturally slackened, as their hurried steps took them away to their partial cover. The troops behind the stone wall were reinforced during this engagement by two of Cooke's regiments from the hill-top, ordered by General Ransom, and General McLaws ordered part of Kershaw's brigade in on their right."

Having seen hundreds of his men cut down in the first hour, French realized the strategy was hopeless, so he used his last division to try a flank attack: "Seeing shortly that this could not be done, the men falling by hundreds, Howard was directed to move his division to the right of the Telegraph road, and turn the enemy's left, the ground presenting some favorable features for such an attack." Furthermore, Sumner sent in one of the IX Corps' divisions, led by Samuel Sturgis.

Howard described the fate of his men in his post-battle report:

"At about 12.55 p.m. I was ordered to move to the right of Hancock and attack the works there, debouching on the right of the Plank road, where I had already located a company of sharpshooters, of General Sully's command, to pick off the enemy's cannoneers within range. This order was immediately countermanded by General Couch, and I was sent to support General Hancock. My command was moved out, Colonel Owen's brigade in front. He was ordered by me cross the bridge over the mill-race, which is just outside of the town, moving on Hanover street by the flank, left in front. As soon as he reached a plowed field on the left of the road, he was to deploy and move forward in line of battle. This he did in fine style. He moved, without breaking his line, to the vicinity of a small brick house, where he halted, because unsupported, and, fearing he should lose ground, caused the men to lie down. He was now within 100 yards of the enemy's first line. I sent him word to hold what he had got, and to push forward the first opportunity, and not to fire, except when he had something to fire at. Colonel Hall, meanwhile, following Colonel Owen by the flank, was ordered by General Couch, both directly and through me, to deploy to the right of Hanover street, which he did. He made several bold attempts to storm the enemy's rifle-pits, but the concentrated fire of artillery and infantry was too much to carry men through. He kept what ground he got. I held General Sully in the outskirts of the town, ready to support or relieve either brigade. Colonel Hall sent for re-enforcements, stating that his ammunition was getting low. General Sully sent him two regiments, which prolonged his line to the right. Another of General Sully's was deployed on the left of the road, and afterward endeavored to re-enforce Colonel Owen.

This, then, was the condition of things at 4 p.m.: Owen extending from the road which prolonged Hanover street to General Willcox's command; Hall extending from the same road to the right. Now a brigade of General Humphreys' division formed in my rear. Hazard's battery (Company B, Rhode Island Artillery) was sent forward across the mill-race, took position just in rear of Owen's line, and fired briskly. Captain Hazard's conduct was equal to anything I ever saw on a field of battle. With the loss of 16 men hors de combat, he drove up cowardly reluctance to help him move and serve his guns. General Humphreys desired him to cease firing, when the general gallantly led forward his men. They reached my line, a portion passed it a little, met a tremendous volley of musketry and grape, and fell back. One of my regiments, the One hundred and twenty-seventh Pennsylvania, went with him. All were rallied at the millrace ravine. As soon as the battery ceased it was withdrawn, as also was Captain Frank's New York Battery, which had followed Hazard's, and did good service near the same advanced ground."

Neither Howard nor Sturgis could make any headway. In the span of a few hours, Couch's II Corps had lost over 4,000 men, and Sturgis had lost over 1,000. Longstreet, one of the most grizzled generals on either side of the war, was amazed by what he was seeing on the Heights. As Union soldiers threw themselves at his heavily fortified position along the high ground, they were mowed down again and again. General Longstreet compared the near continuous fall of soldiers on the battlefield to "the steady dripping of rain from the eaves of a house." At one point, Lee raised concerns to Longstreet about his line being broken, to which Longstreet replied, "General, if you put every man on the other side of the Potomac on that field to approach me over the same line, and give me plenty of ammunition, I will kill them all before they reach my line."

By the middle of the afternoon, 4 divisions had failed to make any headway against Marye's Heights, but Burnside stubbornly decided to stick with the plan, and he next ordered Hooker's entire Grand Division to cross the Rappahannock and attack the Heights. After performing his own reconnaissance in the front, Hooker returned across the river to urge Burnside not to make the attack. Burnside, who remained behind the river throughout the day and never conducted his own reconnaissance on the 13th, refused Hooker's advice. Given the fact that Burnside despised Hooker, the rejection probably came as no surprise to the disgusted commander of the Central Division.

Adding to the Army of the Potomac's problem, the lull in the charges against the Heights allowed some of Longstreet's men to arrive as reinforcements, including George Pickett's division and John Bell Hood's division. Inexplicably, the movement of these Confederates led some of the Federals to mistakenly (and optimistically) believe that the Confederates were retreating, inducing the V Corps division led by Andrew A. Humphreys to "exploit" the situation. Aware of what had happened before, Humphreys ordered his men to empty their muskets so that they would not stop to shoot, but as his men moved forward, the line was broken by Confederate fire and the fact that injured soldiers on the field started grabbing at their legs and pleading with them not to push forward. Humphreys's men made it to within 50 yards of the wall before hitting the ground, and they were followed by another V Corps division, this one led by George Sykes, which added to Humphreys's problems by stopping and firing at the Confederates, leaving Humphreys's men to dodge the crossfire coming from both sides.

Hooker returned from the meeting with Burnside around 4:00 p.m. and ordered forward Getty's division of the IX Corps. Getty was to attempt a flank attack on the far left of Marye's Heights, and they tried to do so undetected even as night started to fall. When they were discovered, however, they were sharply repulsed.

In the end, a recorded 14 assaults were made on Marye's Heights by elements of 7 Union divisions, resulting in upwards of 8,000 soldiers killed, wounded, or missing, all despite the fact Burnside originally intended for a diversionary attack on the Heights while Franklin made the main attack south of town. Despite all their efforts, not one Union soldier got within 100 feet of the wall at Marye's Heights before being shot or forced to withdraw or drop to the ground. The Confederates had suffered just 1,200 casualties near the heights. Watching the assaults against the Heights at one point during the battle, Lee turned to Longstreet and made one of his most famous remarks of the war: "It is well that war is so terrible, otherwise we should grow too fond of it."

With night falling, the Union assaults stopped, and as Longstreet put it, "The charges had been desperate and bloody, but utterly hopeless." Still, that didn't bring an end to the misery. After all, it was the dead of winter, and those who had survived the assaults were now forced to freeze on the battlefield still hugging the ground, knowing full well that even the slightest move might result in Confederates firing at them. On top of that, the cries of the wounded, and the inability of the soldiers to help for fear of getting shot, added to the misery.

One of the most popular legends of the battle is that one Confederate soldier, Richard Rowland Kirkland, risked his life to bring water to the wounded strewn across the field in front of Marye's Heights. When his commanding officer, Joseph B. Kershaw, denied his request to use a white handkerchief to avoid being shot, Kirkland allegedly replied, "All right, sir, I'll take my chances." With that, Kirkland is said to have gathered canteens, filled them with water, and walked around the battlefield offering aid to the wounded, and soldiers on both sides watched and let him do it unharmed for more than 90 minutes. Kershaw later wrote that when it became clear what Kirkland was doing, wounded soldiers across the battlefield cried for water, and Kirkland stopped to help every single one. For his actions, Kirkland was branded the "Angel of Marye's Heights", and a monument at Fredericksburg commemorates the story.

"The Angel of Marye's Heights"

If the story sounds too good to be true, that's because it almost certainly is. While Kershaw wrote about it well after the war, no official report makes mention of Kirkland's actions, not even the commander of his own regiment. There are no accounts by Union soldiers in the field that night substantiating the legend either. Casting even more doubt on the story, one of the men in Kershaw's brigade tells a similar story in his history of the brigade without mentioning Kirkland:

"In one of the first charges made during the day a Federal had fallen, and to protect himself as much as possible from the bullets of his enemies, he had by sheer force of will pulled his body along until he had neared the wall. Then he failed through pure exhaustion. From loss of blood and the exposure of the sun's rays, he called loudly for water.... To go to his rescue was to court certain death... But one brave soldier from Georgia dared all, and during the lull in the firing leaped the walls, rushed to the wounded soldier, and raising his head in his arms, gave him a drink of water, then made his way back and over the wall amid a hail of bullets knocking the dirt up all around him."

One thing that did make an appearance that night was the Northern Lights, a rare phenomenon that at the time had no scientific explanation. Southern soldiers took it as a divine omen and wrote about it frequently in their diaries. The Union soldiers saw less divine inspiration in the Northern Lights and mentioned it less in their own.

Chapter 6: The Aftermath of the Battle of Fredericksburg

"A stunning defeat to the invader, a splendid victory to the defender of the sacred soil." – *Richmond Examiner*

During the night of December 13, Burnside continued to insist on assaulting Marye's Heights, even vowing to lead the IX Corps himself, which had been his old command at Antietam. His subordinates vigorously argued against that or any other assault, even as the commanding general made the wild claim that the failure to take the Heights had been the fault of poorly executed orders on the behalf of his officers.

Meanwhile, there was still the issue of the men stuck on the field. As one Union soldier from Sykes' division, Lt. Colonel Robert C. Buchanan, noted, "At daylight firing commenced between the pickets, and it was soon found that my position was completely commanded, so that if an individual showed his head above the crest of the hill he was picked off by the enemy's sharpshooters immediately…" Buchanan also accused Confederates of shooting at Union hospital attendants trying to reach and help the wounded, writing, "The enemy shot my men after they were wounded, and also the hospital attendants as they were conveying the wounded off the ground, in violation of every law of civilized warfare." Another Union soldier wrote, "Our line was now about 80 yards in front of a stone wall, behind which the enemy was posted in great numbers… To move even was sure to draw the fire of the enemy's sharpshooters, who were posted in the adjacent houses and in tree-tops, and whose fire we were unable to return. Thus the troops remained for twelve long hours, unable to eat, drink, or attend to the calls of nature, for so relentless were the enemy that not even a wounded man or our stretcher-carriers were exempted from their fire."

Finally, on the afternoon of December 14, Burnside and Lee agreed to a temporary truce that would allow each side to tend to their wounded. With the armies still in position throughout that day, Burnside finally withdrew back across the Rappahannock River on December 15. Although Lee had accomplished a decisive victory over Burnside's forces, the Union general had positioned his reserves and supply line so strategically that he could easily fall back without breaking lines of communication--while Lee had no such reserves or supplies. And since Lee didn't have the men to pursue and completely wipe out Burnside's army, Lee chose not to give chase. Some have contended that this was a military blunder, but given the positioning of the Union artillery on Stafford Heights across the river, a Confederate advance might have met the kind of fate those unfortunate enough to charge Marye's Heights did on December 13.

Either way, the fighting in 1862 was done, and the decisive Confederate victory buoyed the Confederacy's hopes. Lee was described by the *Charleston Mercury* as "jubilant, almost off-balance, and seemingly desirous of embracing everyone who calls on him." The results of the Maryland Campaign from 3 months earlier were apparently old news or forgotten by the *Mercury*, which boasted, "General Lee knows his business and the army has yet known no such word as fail."

Naturally, Fredericksburg represented one of the low points of the Civil War for the North, with the Army of the Potomac having suffered an almost unheard of 8:1 ratio in losses compared to Lee's army. Lincoln reacted to the news by writing, "If there is a worse place than hell, I am in it." It showed too, as noted by Pennsylvania Governor Andrew Curtin, who told Lincoln after touring the battlefield, "It was not a battle, it was a butchery". Curtin noted the president was "heart-broken at the recital, and soon reached a state of nervous excitement bordering on insanity." Radical Republicans frustrated at the prosecution of the war took it out on the generals and the Lincoln Administration; Michigan Senator Zachariah Chandler claimed, "The President is a weak man, too weak for the occasion, and those fool or traitor generals are wasting time and yet more precious blood in indecisive battles and delays." Perhaps the *Cincinnati Commercial* summed up the battle best in reporting, "It can hardly be in human nature for men to show more valor or generals to manifest less judgment, than were perceptible on our side that day."

Although there was jubilant talk in the South of the North giving up the fight imminently after Fredericksburg, it was clearly premature. Lee had concluded an incredibly successful year for the Confederates in the East, but the South was still struggling. The Confederate forces in the West had failed to win a major battle, suffering defeat at places like Shiloh in Tennessee and across the Mississippi River. As the war continued into 1863, the southern economy continued to deteriorate. Southern armies were suffering serious deficiencies of nearly all supplies as the Union blockade continued to be effective as stopping most international commerce with the Confederacy. Moreover, the prospect of Great Britain or France recognizing the Confederacy had been all but eliminated by the Emancipation Proclamation.

Given the unlikelihood of forcing the North's capitulation, the Confederacy's main hope for victory was to win some decisive victory or hope that Abraham Lincoln would lose his reelection bid in 1864, and that the new president would want to negotiate peace with the Confederacy. Understandably, this colored Confederate war strategy, and unquestionably Lee's, in 1863, which goes a long way toward explaining what happened at Chancellorsville and Gettysburg.

As for those battles, Burnside would not be with the Army of the Potomac during them. In January, a month removed from Fredericksburg, Lincoln fired the man who believed he was not up to the job of commanding the Army of the Potomac but took it anyway to prevent Joe Hooker from becoming the commanding general. As fate would have it, Burnside was replaced by Joe Hooker.

Bibliography

Alexander, Edward P. Military Memoirs of a Confederate: A Critical Narrative. New York: Da Capo Press, 1993.

Center of Military History. Fredericksburg Staff Ride: Briefing Book. Washington, DC: United States Army Center of Military History, 2002.

Eicher, David J. The Longest Night: A Military History of the Civil War. New York: Simon & Schuster, 2001.

Esposito, Vincent J. West Point Atlas of American Wars. New York: Frederick A. Praeger, 1959. OCLC 5890637.

Foote, Shelby. The Civil War: A Narrative. Vol. 2, Fredericksburg to Meridian. New York: Random House, 1958.

Freeman, Douglas S. R. E. Lee, A Biography. 4 vols. New York: Charles Scribner's Sons, 1934–35.

Gallagher, Gary W., ed. The Fredericksburg Campaign: Decision on the Rappahannock. Chapel Hill: University of North Carolina Press, 1995.

Rable, George C. Fredericksburg! Fredericksburg! Chapel Hill: University Of North Carolina Press, 2002.

Tucker, Spencer C. "First Battle of Fredericksburg." In Encyclopedia of the American Civil War: A Political, Social, and Military History, edited by David S. Heidler and Jeanne T. Heidler. New York: W. W. Norton & Company, 2000.

U.S. War Department, The War of the Rebellion: a Compilation of the Official Records of the Union and Confederate Armies. Series 1, Vol. XXI, Part 1. Washington, DC: U.S. Government Printing Office, 1880–1901.

Welcher, Frank J. The Union Army, 1861–1865 Organization and Operations. Vol. 1, The

Eastern Theater. Bloomington: Indiana University Press, 1989.

The Battle of Stones River

Chapter 1: Middle Tennessee

The most famous battle in the West during the Civil War may have been the Battle of Shiloh, where General Ulysses S. Grant's army barely survived an onslaught against Albert Sidney Johnston's Confederates near the border between Tennessee and Georgia, but the location and result of that battle have often obscured the fact that the Confederates and Federals were desperately contesting the state of Tennessee and Kentucky to the north and east throughout the year.

Johnston's push against Grant had been at the directive of President Jefferson Davis, who wanted his commanders in the West to be aggressive, and in October 1862 Braxton Bragg's Army of Mississippi marched into Kentucky in an attempt to capture that all important border state. At the Battle of Perryville on October 8, Bragg's army defeated a corps from Union commander Don Carlos Buell's Army of the Ohio, but after the battle Bragg retreated back into Tennessee, meeting up with Kirby Smith's 10,000 Confederates and merging forces around Murfreesboro. After some of his men were sent to help garrison Vicksburg on the Mississippi River, Bragg's newly christened Army of Tennessee was about 35,000 strong.

Don Carlos Buell had received much of the credit for the victory at Shiloh in April, and probably undeservedly so, but he has been fiercely criticized for his performance at Perryville after leaving two of his army's corps idle during the battle. In *All for the Regiment*, historian Gerald J. Prokopowicz asserted, "The two other corps of Buell's army were each as large as the entire Confederate force engaged. Had they both advanced boldly once the battle was underway, they could have seized the town of Perryville, cut off the attackers from their supply depots in central Kentucky, and very possibly achieved a decisive battlefield victory on the model of Austerlitz or Waterloo."

When Buell failed to vigorously pursue Bragg's retreating army and decided to stay around Nashville, the impatient Lincoln Administration reorganized the command in that vicinity, creating the Department of the Cumberland under William Rosecrans. With that, Buell's Army of the Ohio became part of a new army led by Rosecrans, the Army of the Cumberland, in late October. Lincoln wanted Rosecrans to quickly lead an offensive against the nearby Confederates and thrust into eastern Tennessee, but Rosecrans had other ideas and insisted in his post-battle report that he needed to reorganize and outfit the army for two months instead:

"Assuming command of the army at Louisville on October 27, it was found concentrated at Bowling Green and Glasgow, distant about 113 miles from Louisville, from whence, after replenishing with ammunition, supplies, and clothing, they moved on to Nashville, the advance corps reaching that place on the morning of November 7, a distance of 183 miles from Louisville.

At this distance from my base of supplies, the first thing to be done was to provide for the subsistence of the troops and open the Louisville and Nashville Railroad. The cars commenced running through on November 26, previous to which time our supplies had been brought by rail to Mitchellsville, 35 miles north of Nashville, and from thence, by constant labor, we had been able to haul enough to replenish the exhausted stores for the garrison at Nashville and subsist the troops of the moving army.

From November 26 to December 26 every effort was bent to complete the clothing of the army; to provide it with ammunition, and replenish the depot at Nashville with needful supplies; to insure us against want from the largest possible detention likely to occur by the breaking of the Louisville and Nashville Railroad, and to insure this work the road was guarded by a heavy force posted at Gallatin. The enormous superiority in numbers of the rebel cavalry kept our little cavalry force almost within the infantry lines, and gave the enemy control of the entire country around us. It was obvious from the beginning that we should be confronted by Bragg's army, recruited by an inexorable conscription, and aided by clans of mounted men, formed into a guerrilla-like cavalry, to avoid the hardships of conscription and infantry service. The evident difficulties and labors of an advance into this country, and against such a force, and at such distance from our base of operations, with which we were connected but by a single precarious thread, made it manifest that our policy was to induce the enemy to travel over as much as possible of the space that separated us, thus avoiding for us the wear and tear and diminution of our forces, and subjecting the enemy to all this inconvenience, besides increasing for him and diminishing for us the dangerous consequences of a defeat. The means taken to obtain this end were eminently successful. The enemy, expecting us to go into winter quarters at Nashville, had prepared his own winter quarters at Murfreesborough, with the hope of possibly making them at Nashville, and had sent a large cavalry force into West Tennessee to annoy Grant, and another large force into Kentucky to break up the railroad."

As Rosecrans's account suggests, he was reluctant to push forward with an offensive until he was certain his army was ready, and even then he started overestimating the size of Bragg's army near Murfreesboro. For his part, Bragg's post-battle report would claim Rosecrans had 60,000 effectives, when in fact Rosecrans only had about 66% of that. Meanwhile, as Rosecrans was getting everything he felt was necessary around Nashville, Confederate cavalry led by Col. John Hunt Morgan harassed Rosecrans's lines of communication and supply lines around the area, scoring a win at the Battle of Hartsville that only further demoralized the Union.

Rosecrans's hesitation is sometimes viewed as needless dawdling, but his concerns were also understandable given the timing. It was rare for 19th century armies to campaign during the winter months, which made traveling harder, illnesses more likely, and lowered morale due to additional hardships associated with cold weather. Despite that, the Lincoln Administration had to deal with politics, most notably midterm election losses that November, and after feeling like a golden opportunity had been lost at Antietam, Lincoln and his War Department were all that more anxious for a grand push. It would have disastrous results for Ambrose Burnside and the Army of the Potomac against Lee's Army of Northern Virginia in mid-December at the Battle of Fredericksburg, and Rosecrans likely would have waited until spring of 1863 himself if his job wasn't on the line.

Rosecrans and Bragg

As a result, Rosecrans would put his army in motion on the day after Christmas. Of all the commanders who led armies during major battles of the Civil War, historians have by and large agreed that the most inept generals to face each other were Rosecrans and Bragg, and the Stones River campaign would be the first major reason for those harsh assessments.

Chapter 2: Moving to Murfreesboro

Bragg's estimate that Rosecrans had 60,000 effectives may have been accurate had it not failed to account for the fact that Rosecrans would have to leave men around Nashville, and by the time he put his Army of the Cumberland in motion toward Murfreesboro and Bragg's army, he had only about 40,000 men on the move.

On December 26, the three "wings" of the Union army began heading southeast, encountering Joseph Wheeler's Confederate cavalry from nearly the beginning. With Union cavalry screening the movements, Major General Thomas Crittenden's left wing, which included divisions led by Generals Thomas Wood, John Palmer, and Horatio Van Cleve, began marching along the Nashville and Chattanooga Railroad. Major General Alexander McCook, which included divisions led by Jefferson Davis, Richard Johnson, and Little Phil Sheridan, marched south along the Nolensville Turnpike before swinging to the east and marching toward Murfreesboro. Finally, George H. Thomas's center wing, which included divisions led by Lovell Rousseau, James Negley, Speed Fry and Robert Mitchell, moved via the Wilson Turnpike along the Nashville and Decatur Railroad before swinging eastward and using the same route of Crittenden's wing along the Nashville and Chattanooga Railroad.

Thomas

Rosecrans would prove time and again over the next year that fighting pitched battles was hardly his strong suit, but at least when he faced Bragg, his grand movements were typically successful. While separating his three wings left each one vulnerable if they could be attacked and defeated in detail, Bragg simply didn't have enough men to do the job, and by marching in three columns, Bragg had to pull back William Hardee's men toward Murfreesboro to avoid having them turned, and he resolved to stand his ground there, leading Hardee to later complain, "The field of battle offered no particular advantages for defense."

Despite the fact Murfreesboro was only about 20 miles away from Nashville, Rosecrans's army did not reach the outskirts until December 29, a whole 3 days of marching, thanks in part to Wheeler's cavalry and the commander's caution. And despite that caution or perhaps because of it, Confederate cavalry had their way with the Union army before the battle, and Wheeler captured 1,000 prisoners and burned supplies riding completely around the Army of the Cumberland.

Wheeler

Meanwhile, the left wing of Rosecrans's army nearly suffered a disaster on December 29 due to the mistaken belief that they could occupy Murfreesboro itself. In addition to being a Confederate hotbed, General Crittenden failed to realize that the Confederate army had been firmly camped there for nearly a month. Rosecrans reported what happened that afternoon:

"About 3 p.m. a signal message coming from the front, from General Palmer, that he was in sight of Murfreesborough, and that the enemy were running, an order was sent to General Crittenden to send a division to occupy Murfreesborough. This led General Crittenden, on reaching the enemy's front, to order Harker's brigade to cross the river at a ford on his left, where he surprised a regiment of Breckinridge's division and drove it back on its main line, not more than 500 yards distant, in considerable confusion; and he held this position until General Crittenden was advised, by prisoners captured by Harker's brigade, that Breckinridge was in force on his front, when, it being dark, he ordered the brigade back across the river, and reported the circumstances to the commanding general on his arrival, to whom he apologized for not having carried out the order to occupy Murfreesborough. The general approved of his action, of course, the order to occupy Murfreesborough having been based on the information received from General Crittenden's advance division that the enemy were retreating from Murfreesborough."

On Monday, December 29, Rosecrans began forming his battle line north and west of Stones River, leading Bragg to believe that Rosecrans was going to try to turn his left flank. As a result, Bragg pulled one of Hardee's divisions from his right flank and marched them to the left flank, . Bragg explained:

"Late on Monday it became apparent the enemy was extending his right, so as to flank us on the left. McCown's division, in reserve, was promptly thrown to that flank and added to the command of Lieutenant-General Polk. The enemy not meeting our expectations of making an attack on Tuesday, which was consumed in artillery firing and heavy skirmishing, with the exception of a dash late in the evening on the left of Withers' division, which was repulsed and severely punished, it was determined to assail him on Wednesday morning, the 31st. For this purpose, Cleburne's division, Hardee's corps, was moved from the second line on the right to the corresponding position on the left, and Lieuten-ant-General Hardee was ordered to that point and assigned to the command of that and McCown's division. This disposition, the result of necessity, left me no reserve, but Breckinridge's command on the right, now not threatened, was regarded as a source of supply for any re enforcements absolutely necessary to other parts of the field. Stone's River, at its then stage, was fordable at almost any point for infantry, and at short intervals perfectly practicable for artillery.

These dispositions completed, Lieutenant-General Hardee was ordered to assail the enemy at daylight on Wednesday, the 31st, the attack to be taken up by Lieutenant-General Polk's command in succession to the right flank, the move to be made by a constant wheel to the right, on Polk's right flank as a pivot, the object being to force the enemy back on Stone's River, and, if practicable, by the aid of the cavalry, cut him off from his base of operations and supplies by the Nashville pike. The lines were now bivouacked at a distance in places of not more than 500 yards, the camp-fires of the two being within distinct view. Wharton's cavalry brigade had been held on our left to watch and check the movements of the enemy in that direction, and to prevent his cavalry from gaining the railroad in our rear, the preservation of which was of vital importance. In this he was aided by Brig. Gen. A. Buford, who had a small command of about 600 new cavalry. The duty was most ably, gallantly, and successfully performed."

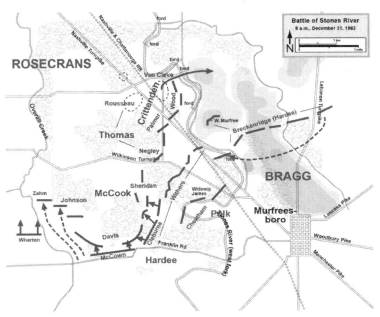

The movements on December 30 and early December 31

As Bragg was planning to use the men on his left flank to attack the Union's right flank in the morning of the 31st, Rosecrans was planning to use Crittenden's left wing to attack the Confederates' right flank around the same time:

"A meeting of the corps commanders was called at the headquarters of the commanding general for this evening. General Thomas arrived early, received his instructions, and retired. General Crittenden, with whom the commanding general had talked freely during the afternoon, was sent for, but was excused at the request of his chief of staff, who sent word that he was very much fatigued and was asleep. Generals McCook and Stanley arrived about 9 o'clock, to whom was explained the following plan of battle.

McCook was to occupy the most advantageous position, refusing his right as much as practicable and necessary to secure it, to receive the attack of the enemy; or, if that did not come, to attack himself, sufficient to hold all the force on his front; Thomas and Palmer to open with skirmishing, and engage the enemy's center and left as far as the river; Crittenden to cross Van Cleve's division at the lower ford, covered and supported by the sappers and miners, and to advance on Breckinridge; Wood's division to follow by brigades, crossing at the upper ford and moving on Van Cleve's right, to carry everything before them into Murfreesborough. This would have given us two divisions against one, and, as soon as Breckinridge had been dislodged from his position, the batteries of Wood's division, taking position on the heights east of Stone's River, in advance, would see the enemy's works in reverse, would dislodge them, and enable Palmer's division to press them back, and drive them westward across the river or through the woods, while Thomas, sustaining the movement on the center, would advance on the right of Palmer, crushing their right, and Crittenden's corps, advancing, would take Murfreesborough, and then, moving westward on the Franklin road, get in their flank and rear and drive them into the country toward Salem, with the prospect of cutting off their retreat and probably destroying their army.

It was explained to them that this combination, insuring us a vast superiority on our left, required for its success that General McCook should be able to hold his position for three hours; that, if necessary to recede at all, he should recede, as he had advanced on the preceding day, slowly and steadily, refusing his right, thereby rendering our success certain.

Having thus explained the plan, the general commanding addressed General McCook as follows: "You know the ground; you have fought over it; you know its difficulties. Can you hold your present position for three hours? To which General McCook responded, "Yes, I think I can." The general commanding then said, 6, I don't like the facing so much to the east, but must confide that to you, who know the ground. If you don't think your present the best position, change it. It is only necessary for you to make things sure." And the officers then returned to their commands.

At daylight on the morning of the 31st the troops breakfasted and stood to their arms, and by 7 o'clock were preparing for the battle."

Essentially, both armies were attacking with their left and hoping their right could hold on long enough for their own attack to have time to work. Both sides were confident, and Phil Sheridan later noted in his memoirs, "The precision that had characterized every manoeuvre of the past three days, and the exactness with which each corps and division fell into its allotted place on the evening of the 30th, indicated that at the outset of the campaign a well-digested plan of operations had been prepared for us; and although the scheme of the expected battle was not known to subordinates of my grade, yet all the movements up to this time had been so successfully and accurately made as to give much promise for the morrow, and when night fell there was general anticipation of the best results to the Union army."

Little Phil Sheridan

The night before the battle began in earnest, the two sides were bivouacked so close to each other that the armies' respective bands played music to each other across the battlefield, with the Union bands playing Yankee Doodle and dueling it out with Confederate renditions of Dixie and the Bonnie Blue Flag. When one of the bands switched to Home Sweet Home, other bands started playing the song, and men on both sides sang together.

Unfortunately for them, the harmonies of that night would be replaced by the thunderous volleys of artillery and musketry a few hours later.

Chapter 3: December 31

Rosecrans's report suggests that McCook was anticipating an attack on the Union right and would attempt to hold out for 3 hours, but Sheridan noted that his wing commander McCook seemed overly optimistic despite reports of Confederate movements in the early morning of the 31st:

"At 2 o'clock on the morning of the 31st General Sill came back to me to report that on his front a continuous movement of infantry and artillery had been going on all night within the Confederate lines, and that he was convinced that Bragg was massing on our right with the purpose of making an attack from that direction early in the morning. After discussing for a few minutes the probabilities of such a course on the part of the enemy, I thought McCook should be made acquainted with what was going on, so Sill and I went back to see him at his headquarters, not far from the Griscom House, where we found him sleeping on some straw in the angle of a worm-fence. I waked him up and communicated the intelligence, and our consequent impressions. He talked the matter over with us for some little time, but in view of the offensive-defensive part he was to play in the coming battle, did not seem to think that there was a necessity for any further dispositions than had already been taken. He said that he thought Johnson's division would be able to take care of the right, and seemed confident that the early assault which was to be made from Rosecrans's left would anticipate and check the designs which we presaged."

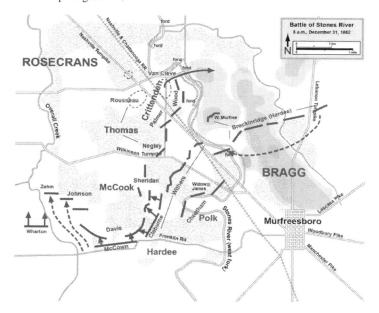

Action on the morning of December 31

One problem with Rosecrans's plan and McCook's optimism was that Bragg's army was ready to attack before Crittenden's wing crossed the Stones River on the other side of the field to attack the Confederates' right flank, but perhaps the most inexplicable problem was that some of McCook's men were not ready to defend when one of Hardee's divisions led by John McCown began the attack at dawn. Despite Sheridan's report to McCook, and Rosecrans's battle plan being discussed the night before, for some reason the Union soldiers in Richard Johnson's division were caught completely by surprise while eating breakfast when the Confederates struck.

Not surprisingly, Johnson's division was routed and sent into a panicked retreat, with the Confederates in dogged pursuit. As McCown and Hardee lost control of the pursuing Confederates, they began drifting to the left, creating a gap in the Confederate line that was then filled by Patrick Cleburne's division on their right. Cleburne, known as the "Stonewall Jackson of the West", was perhaps the most able division commander in the West, and his men began sweeping away the Union defenders on their right. The Confederates ran right past the campfires that were cooking Union soldiers' breakfasts and started capturing Union artillery batteries before they had even fired off a round. Johnson's division suffered over 50% casualties, a number of them simply being captured.

Bragg reported the effects of McCown's attack and the problem that developed as a result of the Confederates' pursuit of the fleeing Federals:

"The failure of Major-General McCown to execute during the night an order for a slight change in the line of his division, and which had to be done the next morning, caused some delay in the general and vigorous assault by Lieutenant-General Hardee. But about 7 o'clock the rattle of musketry and roar of artillery announced the beginning of the conflict. The enemy was taken completely by surprise. General and staff officers were not mounted, artillery horses not hitched, and infantry not formed. A hot and inviting breakfast of coffee and other luxuries, to which our gallant and hardy men had long been strangers, was found upon the fire unserved, and was left while we pushed on to the enjoyment of a more inviting feast, that of captured artillery, fleeing battalions, and hosts of craven prisoners begging for the lives they had forfeited by their acts of brutality and atrocity.

While thus routing and pushing the enemy in his front, Lieutenant-General [W. J.] Hardee announced to me by a messenger that the movement was not being as promptly executed by Major-General Cheatham's command on his right (the left of Lieutenant-General Polk's corps) as he expected, and that his line was, consequently, exposed to an enfilade fire from the enemy's artillery in that front."

As Johnson's division disintegrated, Jefferson Davis's division tried to quickly put up a defense, only to be routed by Cleburne's attack quickly. David would later report:

"The night passed off quietly until about daylight, when the enemy's forces were observed by our pickets to be in motion. Their object could not, however, with certainty, be determined until near sunrise, when a vigorous attack was made upon

Willich's and Kirk's brigades. These troops seemed not to have been fully prepared for the assault, and, with little or no resistance, retreated from their position, leaving their artillery in the hands of the enemy. This left my right brigade exposed to a flank movement, which the enemy was now rapidly executing, and compelled me to order Post's brigade to fall back and partially change its front. Simultaneous with this movement the enemy commenced a heavy and very determined attack on both Carlin's and Woodruff's brigades. These brigades were fully prepared for the attack, and received it with veteran courage. The conflict was fierce in the extreme on both sides. Our loss was heavy and that of the enemy no less. It was, according to my observations, the best contested point of the day, and would have been held, but for the overwhelming force moving so persistently against my right. Carlin, finding his right flank being so severely pressed, and threatened with being turned, ordered his troops to retire."

Despite the fact that two entire Union divisions on the right had quickly left the line, news of just how bad the situation was on the Union right was not initially reported to Rosecrans, who explained, "Within an hour from the time of the opening of the battle, a staff officer from General McCook arrived, announcing to me that the right wing was heavily pressed and needed assistance; but I was not advised of the rout of Willich's and Kirk's brigades, nor of the rapid withdrawal of Davis' division, necessitated thereby--moreover, having supposed his wing posted more compactly, and his right more refused than it really was, the direction of the noise of battle did not indicate to me the true state of affairs. I consequently directed him to return and direct General McCook to dispose his troops to the best advantage, and to hold his ground obstinately. Soon after, a second officer from General McCook arrived, and stated that the right wing was being driven--a fact that was but too manifest by the rapid movement of the noise of battle toward the north."

Once it became clearer that the right wing was facing disaster, Rosecrans pulled back Crittenden's wing and aborted that attack so that he could start shifting men to shore up his right flank. It would take Johnson nearly three hours to rally his broken division several miles in the rear, leaving others to try to deal with the emergency. At one point, Rosecrans was in the thick of shuffling his line around when his chief of staff, Col. Julius Garesché, was beheaded by a cannonball right next to him and covered him in Garesché's blood. Rosecrans explained how he reformed his line:

"General Thomas was immediately dispatched to order Rousseau, then in reserve, into the cedar brakes to the right and rear of Sheridan. General Crittenden was ordered to suspend Van Cleve's movement across the river, on the left, and to cover the crossing with one brigade, and move the other two brigades westward across the fields toward the railroad for a reserve. Wood was also directed to suspend his preparations for crossing, and to hold Hascall in reserve. At this moment fugitives and stragglers from

McCook's corps began to make their appearance through the cedar-brakes in such numbers that I became satisfied that McCook's corps was routed. I, therefore, directed General Crittenden to send Van Cleve in to the right of Rousseau; Wood to send Colonel Harker's brigade farther down the Murfreesborough pike, to go in and attack the enemy on the right of Van Cleve's, the Pioneer Brigade meanwhile occupying the knoll of ground west of Murfreesborough pike, and about 400 or 500 yards in rear of Palmer's center, supporting Stokes' battery (see accompanying drawing). Sheridan, after sustaining four successive attacks, gradually swung his right from a southeasterly to a northwesterly direction, repulsing the enemy four times, losing the gallant General Sill, of his right, and Colonel Roberts, of his left brigade, when, having exhausted his ammunition, Negley's division being in the same predicament, and heavily pressed, after desperate fighting, they fell back from the position held at the commencement, through the cedar woods, in which Rousseau's division, with a portion of Negley's and Sheridan's, met the advancing enemy and checked his movements."

As men from Thomas's center began shifting to the Union right, Sheridan was taking extreme measures to protect his own division's flank, which he explained in his memoirs:

"Both Johnson's and Davis's divisions were now practically gone from our line, having retired with a loss of all formation, and they were being closely pursued by the enemy, whose columns were following the arc of a circle that would ultimately carry him in on my rear. In consequence of the fact that this state of things would soon subject me to a fire in reverse, I hastily withdrew Sill's brigade and the reserve regiments supporting it, and ordered Roberts's brigade, which at the close of the enemy's second repulse had changed front toward the south and formed in column of regiments, to cover the withdrawal by a charge on the Confederates as they came into the timber where my right had originally rested. Roberts made the charge at the proper time, and was successful in checking the enemy's advance, thus giving us a breathingspell, during which I was able to take up a new position with Schaefer's and Sill's brigades on the commanding ground to the rear, where Hescock's and Houghtaling's batteries had been posted all the morning.

The general course of this new position was at right angles with my original line, and it took the shape of an obtuse angle, with my three batteries at the apex. Davis, and Carlin of his division, endeavored to rally their men here on my right, but their efforts were practically unavailing, though the calm and cool appearance of Carlin, who at the time was smoking a stumpy pipe, had some effect, and was in strong contrast to the excited manner of Davis, who seemed overpowered by the disaster that had befallen his command. But few could be rallied, however, as the men were badly demoralized, and most of them fell back beyond the Wilkinson pike, where they reorganized behind the troops of General Thomas."

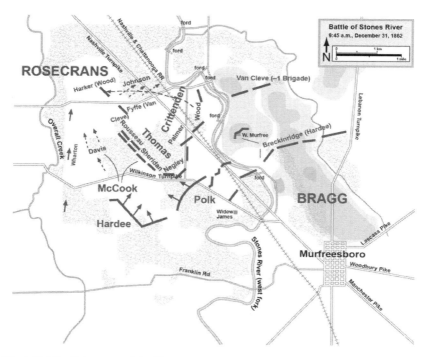

The initial Confederate attack had been so successful that it was actually making it all but impossible for Bragg to make a coordinated push with both Hardee's men and Polk's men immediately on their right. As previously noted, there was a delay in an attack by Benjamin Cheatham's division, and when Cheatham's division and Jones Withers's division made their concerted attack in the late morning, it was more of a second assault than anything else. Withers was repulsed by Sheridan's heavily pressed division, while Cheatham's assault was made piecemeal in such a haphazard way that he was later accused of being drunk. Even still, Sheridan's brigadiers were all mortally wounded on the field, and his division lost nearly a third of its men in just a few hours. Before noon, Sheridan's division was so depleted and short on ammunition that he had to pull it out of the line and reform behind George H. Thomas's reinforcements. Sheridan explained:

> "As the enemy was recoiling from his first attack, I received a message from Rosecrans telling me that he was making new dispositions, and directing me to hold on where I was until they were completed. From this I judged that the existing conditions of the battle would probably require a sacrifice of my command, so I informed Roberts and Schaefer that we must be prepared to meet the demand on us by withstanding the

assault of the enemy, no matter what the outcome. Every energy was therefore bent to the simple holding of our ground, and as ammunition was getting scarce, instructions were given throughout the command to have it reserve its fire till the most effective moment. In a little while came a second and a third assault, and although they were as daring and furious as the first, yet in each case the Confederates were repulsed, driven back in confusion, but not without deadly loss to us, for the noble Roberts was killed, and Colonel Harrington, of the Twenty-Seventh Illinois, who succeeded to his brigade, was mortally wounded a few minutes later. I had now on the death-roll three brigade commanders, and the loss of subordinate officers and men was appalling, but their sacrifice had accomplished the desired result; they had not fallen in vain. Indeed, the bravery and tenacity of my division gave to Rosecrans the time required to make new dispositions, and exacted from our foes the highest commendations."

By 10:00 a.m., Rosecrans's army was holding on for dear life. Nearly 30 guns and 3,000 Union soldiers had been captured, and the right flank was a complete mess. Their saving grace was the topography; Crittenden's left wing was behind the Stones River while the Confederates opposite them were on the eastern side across the river, making it more difficult to attack that side and start pressing both Union flanks simultaneously. As a result, when the Union's defensive line was being driven back, it was being driven back into a tighter line, shaped like a U, making it that much easier to reinforce their own lines even as the Confederate line began to spread further and further apart. As Bragg's biographer Grady McWhiny explained, "Unless the Union army collapsed at the first onslaught, it would be pushed back into a tighter and stronger defensive position as the battle continued, while the Confederate forces would gradually lose momentum, become disorganized, and grow weaker. Like a snowball, the Federals would pick up strength from the debris of battle if they retreated in good order. But the Confederates would inevitably unwind like a ball of string as they advanced."

Any hopes Bragg had of driving the Union's left flank were undone by John Breckinridge, whose division of Hardee's corps was on the far right. Breckinridge had been one of the Democratic presidential candidates along with "The Little Giant" Stephen Douglas in 1860, and both of them lost to Lincoln that November, but his political importance had all but assured he would receive an important military command at the outbreak of the war. Unfortunately for both the North and South, political generals were typically inept, and that was definitely the case with Breckinridge. Breckinridge was too slow to notice Crittenden's attack had been aborted, so he refused to send some of his brigades to the Confederate left to reinforce the attack and also refused to move forward himself. Making matters worse, Bragg received bad intelligence about Union movements that made him believe a new threat to his right flank was imminent. Not only did Bragg countermand the orders for Breckinridge to send two brigades, he also began reinforcing Breckinridge's flank:

"As early as 10 a.m. Major-General Breckinridge was called on for one brigade, and soon after for a second, to re-enforce, or act as a reserve to, Lieutenant-General Hardee. His reply to the first call represented the enemy crossing Stone's River in heavy force in his immediate front, and on receiving the second order he informed me they had already crossed in heavy force and were advancing on him in two lines. He was immediately ordered not to await attack, but to advance and meet them. About this same time a report reached me that a heavy force of the enemy's infantry was advancing on the Lebanon road, about 5 miles in Breckinridge's front. Brigadier-General Pegram, who had been sent to that road to cover the flank of the infantry with his cavalry brigade (save two regiments detached with Wheeler and Wharton), was ordered forward immediately to develop any such movement. The orders for the two brigades from Breckinridge were countermanded, while dispositions were made, at his request, to re-enforce him."

In essence, while the Confederates on the left were in a dogfight trying to break the Union's right flank, Bragg began mistakenly bolstering his own right despite the fact there were no major Union forces in Breckinridge's front. It was not until 11:00 a.m. that Breckinridge actually moved some of his men forward only to find nothing in his front; Bragg would later accuse him of drunkenness.

Breckinridge

Breckinridge dithered so much that it would not be until the middle of the afternoon that his men were used in an assault, and as fate would have it they would be part of the most famous fighting of the entire battle. As the Federals kept reinforcing and defending the western side of the Nashville Turnpike, Confederates from Breckinridge's division and Leonidas Polk's corps began advancing and smashed into the center and left of the Union line, where it was sharply repulsed by Col. William B. Hazen's brigade in a rocky wooded area that would become known as "Hell's Half-Acre". With Sheridan having been forced to form his division at a right angle, Hazen's brigade had become the salient in the U-shaped line, and if it was routed, the Confederates would have split the Army of the Cumberland in two, separating Crittenden from McCook and George H. Thomas, and would have been in the rear of both isolated parts of the Union army. Hazen and his regimental commanders barely held on in the small 4 acre part of their line, determined to stand "even if it cost the last man we had." Hazen would be wounded in the shoulder but almost immediately be promoted for gallantry that day, and veterans of his brigade would actually erect a monument on the spot while the Civil War was still ongoing, making it the oldest Civil War monument.

Hazen

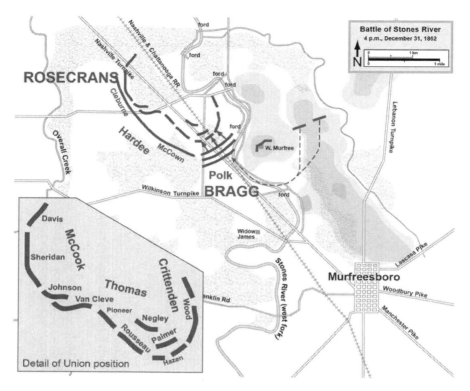

The Confederate assault in the afternoon

When Breckinridge's piecemeal attacks were repulsed by Hazen's brigade, and a second concerted attack with Polk's men were repulsed, the fighting had all but finished for the day. Polk's post-battle report detailed some of the confusion in the Confederate command that afternoon resulting from Breckinridge's delay:

My last reserve having been exhausted, the brigades of Major-General Breckinridge's division, and a small brigade of [Brigadier-]General J. K. Jackson, posted to guard our right flank, were the only troops left that had not been engaged. Four of these were ordered to report to me. They came in detachments of two brigades each, the first arriving nearly two hours after Donelson's attack, the other about an hour after the first. The commanders of these detachments, the first composed of the brigades of Generals [D. W.] Adams and Jackson, the second under General Breckinridge in person, consisting of the brigades of General [William] Preston and

Colonel [J. B.] Palmer, had pointed out to them the particular object to be accomplished, to wit, to drive in the enemy's left, and, especially, to dislodge him from his position in the Round Forest. Unfortunately, the opportune moment for putting in these detachments had passed. Could they have been thrown upon the enemy's left immediately following Chalmers' and Donelson's assault in quick succession, the extraordinary strength of his position would have availed him nothing. That point would have been carried, and his left, driven back on his panic-stricken right, would have completed his confusion and insured an utter rout. It was, however, otherwise, and the time lost between Donelson's attack and the coming up of these detachments in succession enabled the enemy to recover his self-possession, to mass a number of heavy batteries, and concentrate a strong infantry force on the positions, and thus make a successful attack very difficult. Nevertheless, the brigades of Adams and Jackson assailed the enemy's line with energy, and, after a severe contest, were compelled to yield and fall back. They were promptly rallied by General Breckinridge, who, having preceded his other brigades, reached the ground at that moment, but as they were very much cut up, they were not required to renew the attack. The brigades of Preston and Palmer, on arriving, renewed the assault with the same undaunted determination, but as another battery had been added since the previous attack, to a position already strong and difficult of access, this assault was alike ineffectual. The enemy, though not driven from his position, was severely punished, and, as the day was far spent, it was not deemed advisable to renew the attack that evening, and the troops held the line they occupied for the night."

That night, Rosecrans and his senior officers had to decide whether to retreat or stay and fight more. Rosecrans was pressed by some to retreat, but he was determined to stay and fight, and he was supported by George H. Thomas, who famously stated at the council of war, "This army does not retreat." Rosecrans would later write of December 31:

"We had lost heavily in killed and wounded, and a considerable number in stragglers and prisoners; also twenty-eight pieces of artillery, the horses having been slain, and our troops being unable to with draw them by hand over the rough ground; but the enemy had been thoroughly handled and badly damaged at all points, having had no success where we had open ground and our troops were properly posted: none which did not depend on the original crushing in of our right and the superior masses which were in consequence brought to bear upon the narrow front of Sheridan's and Negley's divisions, and a part of Palmer's, coupled with the scarcity of ammunition, caused by the circuitous road which the train had taken, and the inconvenience of getting it from a remote distance through the cedars. Orders were given for the issue of all the spare ammunition, and we found that we had enough for another battle, the only question being where that battle was to be fought.

It was decided, in order to complete our present lines, that the left should be retired some 250 yards to a more advantageous ground, the extreme left resting on Stone's River, above the lower ford, and extending to Stokes' battery. Starkweather's and Walker's brigades arriving near the close of the evening, the former bivouacked in close column, in reserve, in rear of McCook's left, and the latter was posted on the left of Sheridan, near the Murfreesborough pike, and next morning relieved Van Cleve, who returned to his position in the left wing."

Rosecrans didn't believe his army was defeated, but Bragg certainly did, sending a telegram to Richmond that night claiming, "The enemy has yielded his strong position and is falling back. We occupy whole field and shall follow him...God has granted us a happy New Year."

Chapter 4: January 1-3

Bragg may have believed Rosecrans was defeated, but he had also lost 9,000 men himself on December 31, a staggering 25% of his men, and he had failed to deliver the finishing stroke. Both armies mostly decided to lick their wounds on New Year's Day, with Bragg only sending forth a couple of reconnaissances-in-force to ascertain whether Rosecrans was reorganizing his line, or, as Bragg figured, preparing to retreat:

"At dawn on Thursday morning, January 1, orders were sent to the several commanders to press forward their skirmishers, feel the enemy, and report any change in his position. Major-General Breckinridge had been transferred to the right of Stone's River, to resume the command of that position, now held by two of his brigades. It was soon reported that no change had occurred, except the withdrawal of the enemy from the advanced position occupied by his left flank. Finding, upon further examination, that this was the case, the right flank of Lieutenant-General Polk's corps was thrown forward to occupy the ground for which we had so obstinately contended the evening before. This shortened our line considerably, and gave us possession of the entire battle-field, from which we gleaned the spoils and trophies throughout the day and transferred them rapidly to the rear. A careful reconnaissance of the enemy's position was ordered, and the most of the cavalry was put in motion for the roads in his rear, to cut off his trains and develop any movement. It was soon ascertained that he was still in very heavy force all along our front, occupying a position strong by nature and improved by such work as could be done at night and by his reserves. In a short time reports from the cavalry informed me heavy trains were moving toward Nashville, some of the wagons loaded and all the ambulances filled with wounded. These were attacked at different places; many wagons were destroyed and hundreds of prisoners paroled. No doubt this induced the enemy to send large escorts of artillery, infantry, and cavalry with later trains, and thus the impression was made on our ablest cavalry commanders that a retrograde movement was going on. Our forces, greatly wearied and much reduced by heavy losses, were held ready to avail themselves of any change in the enemy's position, but it was deemed unadvisable to assail him as then established. The whole day, after these dispositions, was passed without an important movement on either side, and was consumed by us in gleaning the battlefield, burying the dead, and replenishing ammunition."

As Bragg was laboring under the impression that Rosecrans was retreating, Rosecrans was actually going about trying to bolster his defensive line. To do so, he ordered Van Cleve's division from Crittenden's wing to cross the Stones River and take the high ground, allowing him to post batteries there. Although this meant that Rosecrans was effectively splitting his army, with Crittenden's wing on the east side of the Stones River and Thomas and McCook on the west, the river itself would cover the gap, and the Union soldiers still controlled the road that would allow their wings to link back together.

On the morning of January 2, Bragg was still anticipating a Union retreat, but now he put together plans to assault the Army of the Cumberland, using Breckinridge's men on their right flank:

> "At daylight on Friday, the 2d, the orders to feel the enemy and ascertain his position were repeated with the same results. The cavalry brigades of Wheeler and Wharton had returned during the night greatly exhausted from long-continued service with but little rest or food to either men or horses. Both commanders reported the indications from the enemy's movements the same. Allowing them only a few hours to feed and rest, and sending the two detached regiments back to Pegram's brigade, Wharton was ordered to the right flank across Stone's River, to assume command in that quarter and keep me advised of any change. Wheeler with his brigade was ordered to gain the enemy's rear again, and remain until he could definitely report whether any retrograde movement was being made. Before Wharton had taken his position, observation excited my suspicions in regard to a movement having been made by the enemy across Stone's River immediately in Breckinridge's front. Reconnaissances by several staff officers soon developed the fact that a division had quietly crossed unopposed and established themselves on and under cover of an eminence, marked B on map No. 2, from which Lieutenant-General Polk's line was both commanded and enfiladed. The dislodgment of this force or the withdrawal of Polk's line was an evident necessity. The latter involved consequences not to be entertained. Orders were accordingly given for the concentration of the whole of Major-General Breckinridge's division in front of the position to be taken, the addition to his command of ten 12-pounder Napoleon guns, under Capt. F. H. Robertson, an able and accomplished artillery officer, and for the cavalry forces of Wharton and Pegram, about 2,000 men, to join in the attack on his right. Major-General Breckinridge was sent for and advised of the movement and its objects, the securing and holding of the position which protected Polk's flank and gave us command of the enemy's by which to enfilade him. He was informed of the forces placed at his disposal, and instructed with them to drive the enemy back, crown the his, intrench his artillery, and hold the position.

To distract their attention from our real object, a heavy artillery fire was ordered to be opened from Polk's front at the exact hour at which the' movement was to begin. At other points throughout both lines all was quiet. General Breckinridge at 3.30 p.m. reported he would advance at 4 o'clock."

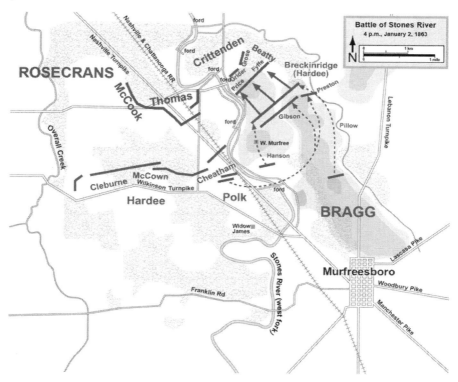

The beginning of the attack

It's unclear why Bragg would rely on Breckinridge to make a massive attack after his performance on December 31, and on top of that Breckinridge thought the attack was suicidal, given that the Union defenders had all of the previous day to fortify their spot and post their artillery. Despite initial protestations, Breckinridge's men pushed forward as ordered and were able to steadily advance, but it only had the effect of pushing the Union defenders across McFadden Ford and safely into the rest of the Union defensive line held by Thomas and McCook. While Breckinridge's men kept moving forward, they were met by artillery fire from batteries safely posted across the Stones River.

The Confederate attack stalled around McFadden Ford, suffering enfilading battery fire that helped inflict nearly 2,000 casualties in the first hour, but Bragg still intended to try to press the attack, as he explained in his report:

"Polk's batteries promptly opened fire and were soon answered by the enemy. A heavy cannonade of some fifteen minutes was succeeded by the fire of musketry, which soon became general. The contest was short and severe; the enemy was driven back and the eminence gained, but the movement as a whole was a failure, and the position was again yielded. Our forces were moved, unfortunately, so far to the left as to throw a portion of them into and over Stone's River, where they encountered heavy masses of the enemy, while those against whom they were intended to operate on our side of the river had a destructive enfilade on our whole line. Our second line was so close to the front as to receive the enemy's fire, and, returning it, took their friends in rear. The cavalry force was left entirely out of the action. Learning from my own staff officers, sent to the scene, of the disorderly retreat being made by General Breckinridge's division, Brigadier-General Patton Anderson's fine brigade of Mississippians (the nearest body of troops) was promptly ordered to his relief."

Bragg was so ignorant of the situation in that sector that while he was trying to reinforce Breckinridge's men, Negley's division of Thomas's wing began its own counterattack, pushing Breckinridge's division into full retreat. Breckinridge was so shaken by the repulse of his attack that he rode around part of his line, comprised of a brigade of Kentucky troops known as the Orphan Brigade due to the fact Kentucky was occupied by Union armies, and cried out, "My poor Orphans! My poor Orphans!"

By the time Breckinridge's attack was finished, night was falling, and Bragg went about reorganizing Breckinridge's division and reforming his line. By the beginning of January 3, both armies were virtually in the same lines as the last few days.

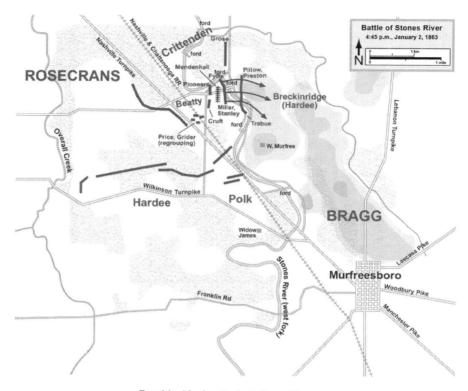

Breckinridge's attack stalls. 4:45 p.m.

On January 1, Bragg woke up certain of victory and confident that Rosecrans would retreat. On January 3, Bragg woke up certain that he had to retreat himself:

> On Saturday morning, the 3d, our forces had been in line of battle for five days and nights, with but little rest, having no reserves; their baggage and tents had been loaded and the wagons were 4 miles off; their provisions, if cooked at all, were most imperfectly prepared, with scanty means; the weather had been severe from cold and almost constant rain, and we had no change of clothing, and in many places could not have fires. The necessary consequence was great exhaustion of officers and men, many having to be sent to the hospitals in the rear, and more still were beginning to straggle from their commands, an evil from which we had so far suffered but little. During the whole of this day the rain continued to fall with little intermission, and the rapid rise in Stone's River indicated it would soon be unfordable. Late on Friday night I had

received the captured papers of Major-General [A. McD.] McCook, commanding one corps d'armée of the enemy, showing their effective strength to have been very near, if not quite, 70,000 men. Before noon, reports from Brigadier-General Wheeler satisfied me the enemy, instead of retiring, was receiving re-enforcements. Common prudence and the safety of my army, upon which even the safety of our cause depended, left no doubt on my mind as to the necessity of my withdrawal from so unequal a contest. My orders were accordingly given about noon for the movement of the trains, and for the necessary preparation of the troops.

Chapter 5: The Aftermath of the Battle of Stones River

"Just as at Perryville, Bragg seemed to change under stress from a bold and aggressive attacker to a hesitant and cautious retreater. He had, of course, sound reasons for withdrawing from Murfreesboro. His principal subordinates advised him to retreat. He had lost nearly 30% of his men in the recent battles; if forced to fight again without some rest, his army might disintegrate. But his decision to retreat allowed his enemies to charge that once again Bragg had lost his nerve." – Grady McWhiny

Rosecrans would barely give chase as Bragg retreated, in part because it was raining heavily on January 3, making the use of artillery impossible. By the following day, Rosecrans learned that Bragg had retreated. Like Bragg, who claimed it was necessary to retreat due to his army being outnumbered, Rosecrans incorrectly claimed in his report to Washington that his men had defeated a superior army, writing, "On the whole, it is evident that we fought superior numbers on unknown ground; inflicted much more injury than we suffered; were always superior on equal ground with equal numbers, and failed of a most crushing victory on Wednesday by the extension and direction of our right wing."

On January 5, the Union army occupied Murfreesboro, and Rosecrans was all too happy to stop there, confident that he had just scored an important campaign victory. While it's true that Rosecrans held possession of the field after the battle and occupied Murfreesboro, the fighting itself was a total stalemate, and almost a disaster for the Army of the Cumberland. All told, there were nearly 25,000 casualties in the battle, most on December 31, with a total of nearly 13,000 Federals and 12,000 Confederates killed, wounded or captured. It was the costliest battle of the Civil War to date and the 6th costliest battle of the entire war.

Sheridan described the ghastly scene on the battlefield after the fighting was done:

"As soon as possible after the Confederate retreat I went over the battle-field to collect such of my wounded as had not been carried off to the South and to bury my dead. In the cedars and on the ground where I had been so fiercely assaulted when the battle opened on the morning of the 31st, evidences of the bloody struggle appeared on every hand in the form of broken fire-arms, fragments of accoutrements, and splintered trees. The dead had nearly all been left unburied, but as there was likelihood of their mutilation by roving swine, the bodies had mostly been collected in piles at different points and inclosed by rail fences. The sad duties of interment and of caring for the wounded were completed by the 5th."

Rosecrans's belief that he had scored a big victory was echoed by the Lincoln Administration, which was only too happy to credit him and call the battle a victory after the debacle at Fredericksburg less than three weeks earlier. But while it certainly succeeded in permanently stopping Bragg from threatening Kentucky, Rosecrans has been criticized for his management of the battle by some historians, particularly for his handling of the dispositions on the night of the 30th. Henry M. Cist, a member of Rosecrans's staff, wrote in his history *The Army Of The Cumberland*:

"Why did Rosecrans's plan of battle miscarry so fatally and Bragg's come so near absolute success? The fault was not in the plan as conceived by the former. The near success of the latter proved a vindication of that. The originator of the plan was not at fault personally, for at no time during the battle did he falter or prove unequal to his command. When called on to give up his plan of the offensive and assume the defensive to save his army, the wonderful power of Rosecrans as a general over troops was never displayed to a greater advantage. With the blood from a slight wound on his check, in a light blue army overcoat, through the mud and rain of the battle-field, he rode along the line inspiring his troops with the confidence he felt as to the final result. To Rosecrans there was but one outcome to the battle at Stone's River, and that was victory. When some of his general officers advised retreat to Nashville, not for an instant did he falter in his determination to 'fight or die right here.' The demoralization of one of his division commanders was so great, that on Thursday afternoon, when the rebels were massing on Rosecrans's right, this general, commanding a division, announced to his brigade commanders that in the event of the anticipated assault resulting disastrously, he proposed to take his division and cut his way through to Nashville. To his troops--the greater part of whom had never seen Rosecrans under the enemy's fire--when on their return from the cedars, they formed anew in front of the Nashville pike--seeing the Commanding General of the army riding fearlessly on the extreme front, in the heat of battle, cool and collected, giving orders and encouraging his men--his mere presence was an inspiration. His personal bravery was never more fully shown than when he rode down to the 'Round Forest' with his staff, under fire, at the time Garesché was killed by a shell that only missed the chief by a few inches. In this ride Rosecrans had three mounted orderlies shot dead while following him. When the entire extent of McCook's disaster in its crushing force was revealed to him, he felt the full burden of his responsibility, and rising to the demands of the hour he was superb. Dashing from one point to another, quick to discern danger and ready to meet it, shrinking from no personal exposure, dispatching his staff on the gallop, hurrying troops into position, massing the artillery and forming his new lines on grounds of his own choosing, confident of ultimate success, and showing his troops that he had all confidence in them, it was worth months of an ordinary life-time to have been with Rosecrans when by his own unconquered spirit he plucked victory from defeat and glory from disaster.

But if the plan was not at fault, what was? Rosecrans started from Nashville for an offensive campaign, and before his plan of battle had met the test, he was compelled to abandon it, and assume the defensive. Where was the fault and who was to blame? The fault was McCook's defective line, and in part Rosecrans was responsible for it. He ought never to have trusted the formation of a line of battle so important to the safety of his whole army to McCook alone, and he certainly knew this. Rosecrans gave his personal attention to the left, but he should at least have ordered the change his quick eye detected as necessary in McCook's line, and not trusted to chance and McCook's ability to withstand the attack with his faulty line. No one who saw him at Stone's River the 31st of December will say aught against the personal bravery and courage of McCook under fire. All that he could do to aid in repairing the great disaster of that day he did to the best of his ability. He stayed with Davis's division under fire as long as it held together, and then gave personal directions to Sheridan's troops, in the gallant fight they made against overwhelming odds. As Rosecrans himself says in his official report of McCook, 'a tried, faithful, and loyal soldier, who bravely breasted the battle at Shiloh and Perryville, and as bravely on the bloody field of Stone's River.' But there is something more than mere physical bravery required in a general officer in command of as large a body of troops as a corps d'armee. As an instructor at West Point, McCook maintained a high rank. As a brigade and division commander under Buell, there was none his superior in the care and attention he gave his troops on the march, in camp, or on the drill-ground. His division at Shiloh as it marched to the front on the second day did him full credit, and in his handling of it on that field he did credit to it and to himself. What McCook lacked was the ability to handle large bodies of troops independently of a superior officer to give him commands. This was his experience at Perryville, and it was repeated at Stone's River. With the known results of Perryville, McCook ought never to have been placed in command of the 'right wing.' Rosecrans at Stone's River, of necessity was on the left, and being there he should have had a general in command of the right with greater military capacity than McCook. Rosecrans's confidence was so slight in his commander of the left that he felt his own presence was needed there in the movement of the troops in that part of the plan of battle.

Rosecrans in his report repeatedly speaks of 'the faulty line of McCook's formation on the right.' But he knew of this on the 30th, and told McCook that it was improperly placed. McCook did not think so. Rosecrans told him that it faced too much to the cast and not enough to the south, that it was too weak and long, and was liable to be flanked.

Knowing all this and knowing McCook's pride of opinion, for McCook told him he 'did not see how he could make a better line,' or a 'better disposition of my troops,' it was the plain duty of Rosecrans to reform the line, to conform to what it should be in his judgment. The order to McCook to build camp fires for a mile beyond his right, was another factor that brought about the combination that broke the line on the right. Rosecrans was correct in the conception of this, in order to mislead Bragg and cause him to strengthen his left at the expense of his right. Had Bragg awaited Rosecrans's attack, this building of fires was correct--if it took troops away from the right to reinforce the left; but this it did not do. Bragg moved McCown and Cleburne's divisions from his right to his left on Tuesday, but after this Bragg brought none of his forces across the river until Wednesday afternoon. The building of the fires caused Bragg to prolong his lines, lengthening them to the extent that before Hardee struck Kirk's and Willich's brigades, he thought our line extended a division front to their right. Finding this not to be the case, he whirled his left with all the force of double numbers on to the right of McCook. The rebels then swinging around threw themselves in the rear of Johnson's division before they struck any troops on their front. Of course it is mere guess-work to say just what the outcome might have been of any other formation of the line, but it is safe to say that had the left instead of the centre of Hardee struck the right of McCook, there would have been a better chance for the troops on the extreme right of his line to have shown the spirit that was in them, before they were overpowered by mere superiority of numbers."

Perhaps the most surprising byproduct of the Battle of Stones River is that Rosecrans and Bragg would both be in position to command armies against each other the following year at the Battle of Chickamauga. Bragg's unsuccessful campaigns, culminating in the Battle of Perryville and the Battle of Stones River, led to harsh criticism from some of the men under his command, including the equally incompetent Lt. Gen. Leonidas Polk, as well as William Hardee and Simon Bolivar Buckner. Hardee would actually demand to be transferred out of Bragg's army before Chickamauga.

Bragg was a classmate of Jefferson Davis's at West Point, and it has long been asserted that Davis's friendship with Bragg kept the incompetent commander in a position too far above his station for too long. Bragg would not be relieved of command of the Army of Tennessee until nearly the end of 1863, by which time he had alienated most of his senior officers. General James Longstreet, who fought under Bragg at Chickamauga, later stated to Jefferson Davis, "Nothing but the hand of God can help as long as we have our present commander." General Joseph E. Johnston may have put it best when he quipped, "I know Mr. Davis thinks he can do a great many things other men would hesitate to attempt. For instance, he tried to do what God failed to do. He tried to make a soldier of Braxton Bragg."

Bragg would actually stay in command longer than Rosecrans, who was relieved after his disastrous performance at Chickamauga. Though he had been conspicuously gallant at the front during the near disaster at Stones River on December 31, he actually retreated from the field during the climactic fighting at Chickamauga and rode back to Chattanooga, where he was later allegedly found weeping and seeking solace from a staff priest. It would fall on his principal subordinate, George H. Thomas, to rally the remnants of the Army of the Cumberland at Chickamauga, make an impromptu defense, and save the army from potential destruction, all of which earned Thomas the famous nickname "The Rock of Chickamauga".

Rosecrans would be relieved soon after during the Confederate siege of Chattanooga, fittingly replaced in command of the Army of the Cumberland by George H. Thomas himself.

Bibliography

Connelly, Thomas L. Autumn of Glory: The Army of Tennessee 1862–1865. Baton Rouge: Louisiana State University Press, 1971.

Cozzens, Peter. No Better Place to Die: The Battle of Stones River. Urbana: University of Illinois Press, 1990.

Crittenden, Thomas L. "The Union Left at Stone's River." In Battles and Leaders of the Civil War, vol. 3, edited by Robert Underwood Johnson and Clarence C. Buel. New York: Century Co., 1884-1888.

Daniel, Larry J. Days of Glory: The Army of the Cumberland, 1861–1865. Baton Rouge: Louisiana State University Press, 2004.

Hess, Earl J. Banners to the Breeze: The Kentucky Campaign, Corinth, and Stones River. Lincoln: University of Nebraska Press, 2000.

Horn, Stanley F. The Army of Tennessee: A Military History. Indianapolis: Bobbs-Merrill, 1941.

McDonough, James Lee. "Battle of Stones River." In Battle Chronicles of the Civil War: 1862, edited by James M. McPherson. Connecticut: Grey Castle Press, 1989.

McWhiney, Grady. Braxton Bragg and Confederate Defeat. Vol. 1. New York: Columbia University Press, 1969 (additional material, Tuscaloosa: University of Alabama Press, 1991).

The Battle of Chancellorsville

Chapter 1: Preparing for the Chancellorsville Campaign

"My plans are perfect. May God have mercy on General Lee for I will have none." – Joseph Hooker

After the Union debacle at the Battle of Fredericksburg, the fighting in the Eastern theater of the Civil War during 1862 was done, and the decisive Confederate victory buoyed the Confederacy's hopes. Confederate commander Robert E. Lee was described by the *Charleston Mercury* as "jubilant, almost off-balance, and seemingly desirous of embracing everyone who calls on him." The results of Antietam and the Maryland Campaign from 3 months earlier were apparently old news or forgotten by the *Mercury*, which boasted, "General Lee knows his business and the army has yet known no such word as fail."

Naturally, Fredericksburg represented one of the low points of the Civil War for the North, with the Army of the Potomac having suffered an almost unheard of 8:1 ratio in losses compared to Lee's army. Lincoln reacted to the news by writing, "If there is a worse place than hell, I am in it." It showed too, as noted by Pennsylvania Governor Andrew Curtin, who told Lincoln after touring the battlefield, "It was not a battle, it was a butchery". Curtin noted the president was "heart-broken at the recital, and soon reached a state of nervous excitement bordering on insanity." Radical Republicans frustrated at the prosecution of the war took it out on the generals and the Lincoln Administration; Michigan Senator Zachariah Chandler claimed, "The President is a weak man, too weak for the occasion, and those fool or traitor generals are wasting time and yet more precious blood in indecisive battles and delays." Perhaps the *Cincinnati Commercial* summed up the battle best in reporting, "It can hardly be in human nature for men to show more valor or generals to manifest less judgment, than were perceptible on our side that day."

Although there was jubilant talk in the South of the North giving up the fight imminently after Fredericksburg, it was clearly premature. Lee had concluded an incredibly successful year for the Confederates in the East, but the South was still struggling. The Confederate forces in the West had failed to win a major battle, suffering defeat at places like Shiloh in Tennessee and across the Mississippi River. As the war continued into 1863, the southern economy continued to deteriorate. Southern armies were suffering serious deficiencies of nearly all supplies as the Union blockade continued to be effective as stopping most international commerce with the Confederacy. Moreover, the prospect of Great Britain or France recognizing the Confederacy had been all but eliminated by the Emancipation Proclamation.

Given the unlikelihood of forcing the North's capitulation, the Confederacy's main hope for victory was to win some decisive victory or hope that Abraham Lincoln would lose his reelection bid in 1864, and that the new president would want to negotiate peace with the Confederacy. Understandably, this colored Confederate war strategy, and unquestionably Lee's, in 1863, which goes a long way toward explaining what happened at Chancellorsville and Gettysburg.

As for those battles, Burnside would not be with the Army of the Potomac during them. In January, a month removed from Fredericksburg, Lincoln fired the man who believed he was not up to the job of commanding the Army of the Potomac but took it anyway to prevent Joe Hooker from becoming the commanding general. As fate would have it, Burnside was replaced by Joe Hooker.

Darius N. Couch, who was in command of the II Corps during the Chancellorsville campaign, described some of the measures Hooker took to whip his demoralized army back into a strong fighting force:

"For some days there had been a rumor that Hooker had been fixed upon for the place, and on the 26th of January it was confirmed. This appointment, undoubtedly, gave very general satisfaction to the army, except perhaps to a few, mostly superior officers, who had grown up with it, and had had abundant opportunities to study Hooker's military character; these believed that Mr. Lincoln had committed a grave error in his selection. The army, from its former reverses, had become quite disheartened and almost sulky; but the quick, vigorous measures now adopted and carried out with a firm hand had a magical effect in toning up where there had been demoralization and inspiring confidence where there had been mistrust. Few changes were made in the heads of the general staff departments, but for his chief-of-staff Hooker applied for Brigadier-General Charles P. Stone, who, through some untoward influence at Washington, was not given to him. This was a mistake of the war dignitaries, although the officer finally appointed to the office, Major-General Daniel Butterfield, proved himself very efficient. Burnside's system of dividing the army into three grand divisions was set aside, and the novelty was introduced of giving to each army corps a distinct badge, an idea which was very popular with officers and men."

Couch

One noteworthy change Hooker also made in his command structure that Couch did not mention is that he organized all of his cavalry into one corps under George Stoneman, instead of continuing to attach separate brigades of cavalry to the individual corps in the army. This had led to uncoordinated uses of the cavalry, diluting the Union cavalry's ability to conduct reconnaissance and also weakening their impact in battle. Hooker was following Lee's lead in placing the cavalry under one command, but he committed what's considered one of the greatest blunders of the Chancellorsville campaign by thereafter sending the entire cavalry on a raid behind enemy lines instead of using them in their traditional roles of screening the army and conducting reconnaissance.

Joe Hooker

As Hooker was adding to his army and reorganizing it, Lee was actually detaching some of his army due to a shortage of supplies. In late March 1863, Lee reported, 'The men are cheerful, and I receive but few complaints, still I do not consider it enough to maintain them in health and vigor, and I fear they will be unable to endure the hardships of the approaching campaign. Symptoms of scurvy are appearing among them, and, to supply the place of vegetables, each regiment is directed to send a daily detail to gather sassafras buds, wild onions, garlic, lamb's quarter, and poke sprouts; but for so large an army the supply obtained is very small."

In addition to that hardship, Lee had detached about 15,000 from Longstreet's corps to defend against potential Union assaults made on the Peninsula, as McClellan had done the year before.

When supplies became an issue, Lee ordered Longstreet's men to start gathering supplies around the countryside in Virginia and North Carolina, with the hope that the supplies could be gathered in time before the rest of the army had to face a major attack. As it would turn out, two of Longstreet's divisions, John Bell Hood's and George Pickett's, would be over 100 miles away and way too far away to march back in time to join a battle.

Lee

Hooker was ready to place his reorganized juggernaut in motion by mid-April, and with that in mind he devised a simple strategy that called on Stoneman's cavalry to conduct a raid deep behind enemy lines, destroying the Confederate supply lines and cutting Lee's communications with Richmond. Hooker figured this would compel Lee to abandon his line along the

Rappahannock River and Fredericksburg and withdraw closer to Richmond, at which time the Army of the Potomac would start giving chase. As it turned out, heavy rains forced a delay in the cavalry raid, but as the battle of Chancellorsville itself would suggest, Lee would not have abandoned his current defensive line anyway.

Having witnessed a host of setbacks in 1862 and Burnside's "Mud March" fiasco at the beginning of 1863, President Lincoln was understandably upset, complaining, "I greatly fear it is another failure already." But after Hooker's first plan was scrapped, he came up with an even more ambitious second plan while discussing it with the leaders in Washington in late April. Once again the cavalry would be sent on a raid far to the south of Lee's lines, but this time Hooker planned to demonstrate along Fredericksburg with much of his army in an attempt to keep Lee's attention while also stealthily marching three of his corps across the Rappahannock several miles to the west, positioning them to strike Lee's left and rear. With supply lines and communication lines cut in his rear, Hooker figured Lee would be forced to fall back, and with this plan a large chunk of Hooker's army would already be across the Rappahannock ready to pursue.

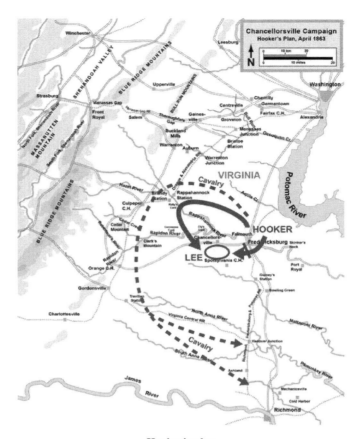

Hooker's plan

As Hooker's army prepared to march, he rightly labeled the Army of the Potomac "the finest army on the planet", and historians have largely credited him for his plan. Porter Alexander agreed, writing in his memoirs, "On the whole I think this plan was decidedly the best strategy conceived in any of the campaigns ever set foot against us. And the execution of it was, also, excellently managed, up to the morning of May 1st.

On the other hand, Hooker was taking a major risk by dividing his army, with one part of it across the river and the other part of it on the other side in no position to come to its support. Longstreet noted the predicament this strategy could cause in his memoirs, and he even went so far as to suggest his belief that Lee should've invited the movement and stood ready to fight a defensive battle:

"General Hooker had split his army in two, and was virtually in the condition which President Lincoln afterwards so graphically described in his letter addressed to him June 5 following,--viz.:

'I would not take any risk of being entangled upon the river, like an ox jumped half over a fence and liable to be torn by dogs front and rear, without a fair chance to gore one way or to kick the other.'

My impression was, and is, that General Lee, standing under his trenches, would have been stronger against Hooker than he was in December against Burnside, and that he would have grown stronger every hour of delay, while Hooker would have grown weaker in morale and in confidence of his plan and the confidence of his troops. He had interior lines for defence, while his adversary was divided by two crossings of the river, which made Lee's sixty thousand for defence about equal to the one hundred and thirteen thousand under General Hooker. By the time that the divisions of Pickett and Hood could have joined General Lee, General Hooker would have found that he must march to attack or make a retreat without battle. It seems probable that under the original plan the battle would have given fruits worthy of a general engagement. The Confederates would then have had opportunity, and have been in condition to so follow Hooker as to have compelled his retirement to Washington, and that advantage might have drawn Grant from Vicksburg; whereas General Lee was actually so crippled by his victory that he was a full month restoring his army to condition to take the field. In defensive warfare he was perfect. When the hunt was up, his combativeness was overruling."

Chapter 2: Getting the Jump on Lee

Hooker had designed a grand strategy, and during the first few days he put it in motion, it went nearly flawlessly. On April 27, the column of nearly 40,000 Union soldiers led by Henry Slocum, the XII Corps commander, began marching west to cross the Rappahannock and Rapidan rivers miles upstream and went completely undetected by Lee. In conjunction with that movement, Hooker began demonstrating near Fredericksburg with a large part of his army, as if he was about to force a crossing like Burnside had done in December. Couch explained the dispositions:

In order to confound Lee, orders were issued to assemble the Sixth, Third, and First corps under Sedgwick at Franklin's Crossing and Pollock's Mill, some three miles below Fredericksburg, on the left, before daylight of the morning of the 29th, and throw two bridges across and hold them. This was done under a severe fire of sharp-shooters. The Second Corps, two divisions, marched on the 28th for Banks's Ford, four miles to the right; the other division, Gibbon's, occupying Falmouth, near the river-bank, was directed to remain in its tents, as they were in full view of the enemy, who would readily observe their withdrawal.

Slocum

With these distractions, the plan called for the three corps (V, XI and XII) being guided by Slocum to arrive near Chancellorsville around April 30, which consisted of one mansion at a crossroads between the Orange Turnpike and Orange Plank Road. This was essential because the "Wilderness" was directly to the west of Chancellorsville, and it was so tangled that coordinated troop activity in that sector would be all but impossible, as Grant and Lee would find out a year later in May 1864. While they were concentrating there, Stoneman's cavalry set out on April 30 to harry Lee's lines in the south, Couch's II Corps was able to cross on April 30 miles west of Fredericksburg, and the III Corps under Dan Sickles was able to cross the Rappahannock the night of April 30. By the morning of May 1, Hooker had nearly 70,000 men around Chancellorsville, more than Lee's entire army, and Hooker still had John Sedgwick's VI Corps and John Reynolds's I Corps trying to cross in Lee's front a few miles south of Fredericksburg.

As the Army of the Potomac conducted these movements from April 27-30, Lee's army stayed in its defensive line near Fredericksburg, largely unaware of Hooker's intentions. Hooker's movements had worked perfectly, and he had Lee in just the position he had hoped for when concocting the plan. On April 30, Hooker issued General Orders No. 47, prematurely congratulating his army:

> "It is with heartfelt satisfaction the commanding general announces to the army that the operations of the last three days have determined that our enemy must either ingloriously fly, or come out from behind his defenses and give us battle on our own ground, where certain destruction awaits him.
>
> The operations of the Fifth, Eleventh, and Twelfth Corps have been a succession of splendid achievements."

Chapter 3: May 1

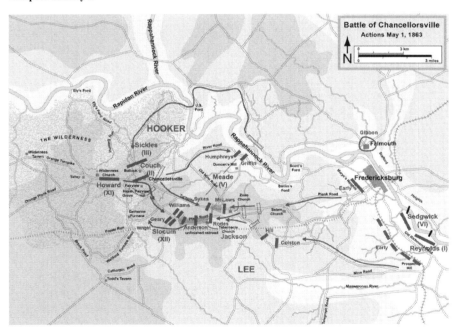

After the war, one of the most famous quotes of the battle allegedly came from Hooker, as reported in a history of the campaign published early in the 20th century. According to author and Civil War veteran John Bigelow Jr., there was a famous exchange between Hooker and division commander Abner Doubleday, in which Doubleday asked Hooker on the march toward Gettysburg, "What was wrong with you at Chancellorsville? Some say you were injured by a shell, and others that you were drunk; now tell us what it was." Hooker allegedly replied, "Doubleday, I was not hurt by a shell, and I was not drunk. For once I lost confidence in Hooker, and that is all there is to it."

Modern historians have strongly disputed that any such exchange took place, and it would certainly be out of character for Hooker, whose arrogance strongly turned off many of his comrades. But in an effort to explain why Hooker conducted such an ambitious campaign only to halt an offensive on May 1 when he had Lee where he wanted, it has often been said that Hooker lost his nerve.

While that has long been an accepted version of what happened, Hooker's General Orders on April 30 indicate that Hooker's plan was to march into a position that would force Lee to retreat or come out of his defenses to attack Hooker. In other words, Hooker's words suggest that he intended to fight a defensive battle all along if Lee would actually give battle, a possibility Hooker largely discounted.

It's also understandable why Hooker figured Lee wouldn't stand his ground and fight. To do so, Lee would have to shift at least part of his army a few miles to the west to face the Union soldiers gathering there, moving his men out of the vicinity of Fredericksburg even while two whole corps of the Army of the Potomac was in their front there. Essentially, Lee would have to split his forces and face the enemy in two fronts, while being heavily outnumbered in both.

Lee had not correctly anticipated what Hooker was doing with the column that set off on April 27 to head to Chancellorsville, but as he explained in his report after the campaign, the fact that Sedgwick and Reynolds were only demonstrating with their corps south of Fredericksburg during those days suggested to him that they were not intended to be the main thrust against his army:

"No demonstration was made opposite any other part of our lines at Fredericksburg, and the strength of the force that had crossed and its apparent indisposition to attack indicated that the principal effort of the enemy would be made in some other quarter. This impression was confirmed by intelligence received from General Stuart that a large body of infantry and artillery was passing up the river. During the forenoon of the 29th, that officer reported that the enemy had crossed in force near Kelly's Ford on the preceding evening. Later in the day he announced that a heavy column was moving from Kelly's toward Germanna Ford, on the Rapidan, and another toward Ely's Ford, on that river. The routes they were pursuing after crossing the Rapidan converge near Chancellorsville, whence several roads lead to the rear of our position at

Fredericksburg."

Lee had sent one of the two divisions of Longstreet's corps that had stayed with his army under Richard Anderson toward Chancellorsville on April 29, but that division and the few Confederate forces posted along the Rappahannock crossings in that area would clearly be no match for the several corps Hooker had near Chancellorsville on May 1. Lee had to choose whether he would withdraw as Hooker expected or whether he would stay and fight.

As Longstreet alluded to in his memoirs, Lee was aggressive when he sensed an opportunity, and on May 1 he gambled that Sedgwick and Reynolds were merely a diversionary force that would not cause him trouble if he shifted the vast majority of his army to face the rest of Hooker's men near Chancellorsville. Thus, nearly 80% of Lee's army began marching west toward Chancellorsville in the early morning, leaving about 10,000 Confederates in Marye's Heights outside of Fredericksburg to defend against the 40,000 Union soldiers in their front. The rest of Lee's army, consisting of under 50,000 men, marched to the Zoan and Tabernacle churches along the Orange Turnpike and Orange Plank Road about two miles east of Chancellorsville. With that, the Confederates were outnumbered by 30,000 on their right and about 20,000 on their left.

While the Confederates started digging in along the Turnpike and the Plank Road, Hooker directed two divisions from George Meade's V Corps to head east down the River Road toward Banks's Ford, where they would guard a crossing for the rest of the army, the other division from the V Corps to head east on the Turnpike, and the XII Corps to march down the Plank Road, which meant these divisions would march straight into Confederate positions. Hooker kept Oliver Howard's XI Corps, Couch's II Corps, and Sickles's III Corps in reserve.

Hooker had a sizable numbers advantage, but he was sending three different columns down three different roads, making a coordinated attack practically impossible. As a result, the three roads would see piecemeal actions, beginning with Sykes's division of Meade's Corps hitting Lafayette McLaws's division on the Turnpike. The two sides pushed each other back and forth, while Richard Anderson's division found itself fighting elements of the XII Corps and XI Corps along the Plank Road. While the Union fought along those two roads, Meade's other divisions marched unopposed on the River Road toward Banks's Ford.

When McLaws's division had pushed Sykes's division back along the Turnpike, they got within a mile of Chancellorsville and were able to see the environment Hooker was positioned in. Lee explained in his report:

"At 11 a.m. the troops moved forward upon the Plank and old Turnpike roads, Anderson, with the brigades of Wright and Posey, leading on the former; McLaws, with his three brigades, preceded by Mahone's, on the latter. Generals Wilcox and Perry, of Anderson's division, co-operated with McLaws. Jackson's troops followed Anderson on the Plank road. Colonel Alexander's battalion of artillery accompanied the advance. The enemy was soon encountered on both roads, and heavy skirmishing with infantry and artillery ensued, our troops pressing steadily forward. A strong attack upon General McLaws was repulsed with spirit by Semmes' brigade, and General Wright, by direction of General Anderson, diverging to the left of the Plank road, marched by way of the unfinished railroad from Fredericksburg to Gordonsville, and turned the enemy's right. His whole line thereupon retreated rapidly, vigorously pursued by our troops until they arrived within about 1 mile of Chancellorsville. Here the enemy had assumed a position of great natural strength, surrounded on all sides by a dense forest filled with a tangled undergrowth, in the midst of which breastworks of logs had been constructed, with trees felled in front, so as to form an almost impenetrable abatis. His artillery swept the few narrow roads by which his position could be approached from the front, and commanded the adjacent woods."

Jackson

While Lee's report makes clear that Hooker was in a strong defensive position, it was also in a position that would make troop movements much more difficult. On the other hand, the ground that the Union divisions were fighting over was high ground with enough openings to place and use artillery. However, instead of pushing his reserves forward, during the middle of the fighting Hooker ordered his advanced divisions to fall back to Chancellorsville, shocking the subordinates who were commanding men in the middle of the fray. As Couch explained:

"Meade was finally pushed out on the left over the Banks's Ford and turnpike roads, Slocum and Howard on the right along the Plank road, the left to be near Banks's Ford by 2 P. M., the right at the junction of its line of movement with the turnpike at 12 M. No opposition was met, excepting that the division marching over the turnpike came upon the enemy two or three miles out, when the sound of their guns was heard at Chancellorsville, and General Hooker ordered me to take Hancock's division and proceed to the support of those engaged. After marching a mile and a half or so I came upon Sykes, who commanded, engaged at the time in drawing back his advance to the position he then occupied. Shortly after Hancock's troops had got into a line in front, an order was received from the commanding general 'to withdraw both divisions to Chancellorsville.' Turning to the officers around me, Hancock, Sykes, Warren, and others, I told them what the order was, upon which they all agreed with me that the ground should not be abandoned, because of the open country in front and the commanding position. An aide, Major J. B. Burt, dispatched to General Hooker to this effect, came back in half an hour with positive orders to return. Nothing was to be done but carry out the command, though Warren suggested that I should disobey, and then he rode back to see the general. In the meantime Slocum, on the Plank road to my right, had been ordered in, and the enemy's advance was between that road and my right flank. Sykes was first to move back, then followed by Hancock's regiments over the same road. When all but two of the latter had withdrawn, a third order came to me, brought by one of the general's staff: 'Hold on until 5 o'clock.' It was then perhaps 2 P. M. Disgusted at the general's vacillation and vexed at receiving an order of such tenor, I replied with warmth unbecoming in a subordinate: 'Tell General Hooker he is too late, the enemy are already on my right and rear. I am in full retreat.'"

Hooker was thus ceding the high ground around the roads and opting to dig in near the Wilderness instead, leaving some of the corps commanders beside themselves. George Meade complained, "My God, if we can't hold the top of the hill, we certainly can't hold the bottom of it!" Couch also considered it the moment the battle was lost, writing, "Proceeding to the Chancellor House, I narrated my operations in front to Hooker, which were seemingly satisfactory, as he said: 'It is all right, Couch, I have got Lee just where I want him; he must fight me on my own ground.' The retrograde movement had prepared me for something of the kind, but to hear from his own lips that the advantages gained by the successful marches of his lieutenants were to culminate in fighting a defensive battle in that nest of thickets was too much, and I retired from his presence with the belief that my commanding general was a whipped man. The army was directed to intrench itself."

On the night of May 1, Lee still had to decide whether to pull his army back or attack Hooker. He was still hoping to destroy the entire portion of Hooker's army at Chancellorsville before Sedgwick and Reynolds began pushing back his sparse defensive line near Fredericksburg. Jackson agreed with him, and as the two met that night to discuss their options. Jackson biographer Robert Lewis Dabney described their meeting:

"When Friday night arrived, Generals Lee and Jackson met, at a spot where the road to the Catharine Iron Furnace turned southwestward from the plank-road, which was barely a mile in front of Hooker's works. Here, upon the brow of a gentle hill, grew a cluster of pine-trees, while the gound was carpeted with the clean, dry sedge and fallen leaves. They selected this spot, with their respective Staffs, to bivouac, while the army lay upon their weapons, a few yards before them, and prepared to sleep upon the ground, like their men. General Stuart had now joined them, and reported the results of his reconnoissances upon the south and west of Hooker's position. He had ascertained that the Federal commander had left a whole corps, under General Reynolds, at Ely's Ford, to guard his communications there, and that he had massed ninety thousand men around Chancellorsville, under his own eye, fortifying them upon the east, south and, southwest, as has been described. But upon the west and northwest his encampments were open, and their movements were watched by Stuart's pickets, who were secreted in the wilderness there. He had also ascertained, that almost all their cavalry had broken through the line of the Rapid Ann in one body, and had invaded the south, followed and watched by the brigade of W. H. Lee, evidently bent upon a grand raid against the Confederate communications. Generals Lee and Jackson now withdrew, and held an anxious consultation. That Hooker must be attacked, and that speedily, was clear to the judgments of both."

"The Last Meeting" between Lee and Jackson

As Lee realized, however, "It was evident that a direct attack upon the enemy would be attended with great difficulty and loss, in view of the strength of his position and his superiority of numbers." Thanks to reports from Stuart's cavalry that Hooker's left was well-defended (thanks to Meade's march on River Road) and his right was "in the air" with an open flank, Lee decided "to endeavor to turn his right flank and gain his rear, leaving a force in front to hold him in check and conceal the movement." In other words, having already split his army in two in the face of a larger army, Lee now planned to split his army into three by having some of his command march around Hooker's right, defying all military convention. Dabney explained:

"General Lee had promptly concluded, that while, on the one hand, immediate attack was proper, some more favorable place for assault must be sought, by moving farther toward Hooker's right. The attempt to rout ninety thousand well armed troops, entrenched at their leisure, by a front attack, with thirty-five thousand, would be too prodigal of patriot blood, and would offer too great a risk of repulse. He had accordingly already commanded his troops to commence a movement toward their left, and communicated his views to General Jackson, who warmly concurred in their wisdom. A report was about this time received from General Fitz Hugh Lee, of Stuart's command, describing the position of the Federal army, and the roads which he held with his cavalry leading to its rear. General Jackson now proposed to throw his command entirely into Hooker's rear, availing himself of the absence of the Federal cavalry, and the presence of the Confederate horse, and to assail him from the West, in concert with Anderson and McLaws. Stuart was there with his active horsemen to cover this movement; and he believed that it could be made with comparatively little risk, and, when accomplished, would enable him to crush the surprised enemy. He well knew that he was apparently proposing a 'grand detachment'; a measure pronounced by military science so reprehensible, in the presence of an active adversary."

With that decision, the stage was set for two of the most dramatic days of the Civil War.

Chapter 4: May 2

Having decided on the night of May 1 to try to turn Hooker's right flank, the Confederates went about getting a guide who could lead Jackson's command on the march. Charles C. Wellford, the man who owned the nearby Catherine Furnace, gave Jackson's mapmaker information about a road near Catherine Furnace that would take them to Brock Road and allow Jackson to march northwest toward Wilderness Tavern, placing them squarely in the flank and rear of Howard's XI Corps. The backwoods route was intended to hide the march from Union pickets, and the lack of Union cavalry to screen the Army of the Potomac made the stealthy march that much likelier to succeed.

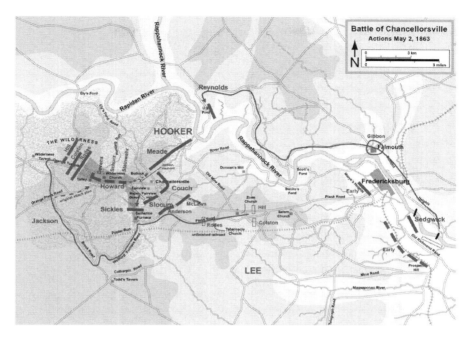

As Jackson began marching his command that morning along a 12 mile route, Lee started digging in with Anderson's division and McLaws's division in Hooker's front along the Turnpike and the Plank Road. With Jackson's 28,000 men marching around Hooker's right, Lee now had less than 15,000 soldiers holding the line in front of Hooker's 70,000. Meanwhile, Hooker was also still digging in, and to bolster his numbers he ordered Reynolds to leave the Fredericksburg front and march to Chancellorsville to join the right flank. It was a circuitous march that had no hope of reaching Chancellorsville on May 2.

One of the great myths of Stonewall Jackson's legendary flank attack on May 2 is that it came as a complete surprise to the Army of the Potomac when the Confederates came bursting out of the woods on their flank. In fact, despite Stuart's cavalry screening the march in order to hide it to the best of their ability, there were several different times during the day that Union forces spotted the Confederate column and alerted their superiors. As Darius Couch explained:

> "On the morning of May 2d our line had become strong enough to resist a front attack unless made in great force; the enemy had also been hard at work on his front, particularly that section of it between the Plank road and turnpike. Sedgwick, the previous night, had been ordered to send the First Corps (Reynolds's) to Chancellorsville. At 7 A. M. a sharp cannonade was opened on our left, followed by

infantry demonstrations of no particular earnestness. Two hours later the enemy were observed moving a mile or so to the south and front of the center, and later the same column was reported to the commander of the Eleventh Corps by General Devens, whose division was on the extreme right flank. At 9:30 A. M. a circular directed to Generals Slocum and Howard called attention to this movement and to the weakness of their flanks."

News of Jackson's flank march reached Hooker within hours of its start, and Hooker guessed that it was either a retreat or a flanking march, so at 9:30 he warned XI Corps commander Oliver Howard, "We have good reason to suppose the enemy is moving to our right. Please advance your pickets for purposes of observation as far as may be safe in order to obtain timely information of their approach." Howard claimed later that morning that his corps was "taking measures to resist an attack from the west."

While Hooker was inviting Lee to attack around Chancellorsville, he ordered Sedgwick's VI Corps to "attack the enemy in his front [if] an opportunity presents itself with a reasonable expectation of success". Despite having a 4-1 advantage in manpower, Sedgwick decided to be cautious, possibly remembering what had happened when Union soldiers tried to storm Marye's Heights during the Battle of Fredericksburg the previous December. As a result, Sedgwick decided not to attack the Confederate line, manned by Jubal Early's greatly stretched division. Sedgwick has been heavily criticized by historians ever since, but he rationalized his decision in his post-campaign report:

"The following day, Saturday, May 2, Reynolds' corps was withdrawn from my command, and ordered to proceed to headquarters of the army, at or near Chancellorsville, one division, General Wheaton's, of the Sixth Corps, being sent by General Newton to cover his crossing and take up his bridge. I was also ordered to take up all the bridges at Franklin's crossing and below before daylight. This order was received at 5.25 a.m., after daylight, and could not, of course, be executed without attracting the observation of the enemy, and leaving him free to proceed against the forces under General Hooker."

Sedgwick

Lee had divided his army once on May 1 and again on May 2 by betting on Sedgwick's inaction in front of Early, and Sedgwick played right into it. Meanwhile, as Hooker was giving Sedgwick discretionary orders to possibly advance, he decided to try to intercept Jackson's column by moving Sickles's III corps "cautiously toward the road followed by the enemy, and harass the movement as much as possible". This order took the III Corps south past the high ground at Hazel Grove and interposed it between Richard Anderson's division and Jackson's column. By the time the men of the III Corps reached their destination, however, a rearguard conducted by the 23rd Georgia Infantry kept Sickles from harassing Jackson's advance. The 23rd Georgia would lose a majority of its men defending Jackson's rear, and eventually two brigades from A.P. Hill's famous "Light Division" had to reinforce them to cover Jackson.

Around 3:00, Jackson and cavalry officer Fitzhugh Lee were able to scout the Union's lines from high ground near the Plank Road. Despite Howard having told Hooker that he was preparing for the possibility of an attack on his flank, Jackson found Howard's men idling around, completely unprepared for what was about to hit them. In addition to being unprepared, the XI Corps was composed of a bunch of raw recruits who had never seen battle, and those who had seen action performed poorly at Second Manassas. The very reason they were on the far right was because Hooker didn't intend to use them for major combat operations.

As Jackson's men reached the crossroads near Wilderness Tavern, the opening in the area allowed him to form battle lines that straddled the Orange Turnpike in the rear of the XI Corps. They would then be marching through thick underbrush that not only completely obscured them but also scratched them up and tore their clothes. Despite the inevitable noises made by 21,000 men moving forward through a forest, and the scurrying of various animals out of the forest, Howard's corps still remained unprepared, and many of them were mostly concerned with cooking their dinner.

Sometime between 5-6 p.m., Jackson's men came hurdling out of the forest and fell upon Howard's hapless corps, many of whom had stacked unloaded rifles while sitting around campfires. Almost immediately, Jackson's attack rolled up Devens's division, and though Schurz's division tried to form an emergency defensive line in Jackson's front, they were quickly swept aside after finding themselves flanked on both sides. Dabney described the initial moments of the attack:

"With a wild hurrah, the line of Rodes burst upon them from the woods, and the first volley decided their utter rout. The second line, commanded by Colston, unable to restrain their impetuosity, rushed forward at the shout, pressed upon the first, filling up their gaps, and firing over their heads, so that thenceforward the two were almost merged into one, and advanced together, a dense and impetuous mass. For three miles the Federalists were now swept back by a resistless charge. Even the works which confronted the west afforded them no protection; no sooner were they manned by the enemy, than the Confederates dashed upon them with the bayonet, and the defenders were either captured or again put to flight. The battle was but a continued onward march, with no other pause than that required for the rectification of the line, disordered by the density of the woods."

As Dabney's account suggests, the nature of the flank attack ensured that the Confederate officers began losing control of their commands almost immediately as they began rushing forward, but the XI Corps was even more out of control. Howard tried to valiantly rally his routed corps as they began fleeing in a panicked rout eastward, but he was no George H. Thomas and this was no Chickamauga. Most of his soldiers simply ran right past him until they reached Fairview, an open field near Hooker's headquarters at the Chancellor house. The vanguard of Jackson's attack, Robert Rodes's division, chased them the entire way until being brought to heel by the artillery posted there shortly after 7:00. Hooker tried to rally an emergency defensive line by pulling one of Sickles's III Corps divisions, who due to unusual sound acoustics had not heard any of the fighting despite the fact it was going on just 2.5 miles away from them, but it was the fading daylight that would ultimately blunt the Confederate attack.

The greatest resistance Jackson faced in his attack was the temptations that invited his men to stop their pursuit, including food, personal artifacts, guns, and other supplies. Jackson continued to order his subordinates, "Press forward", and he tried to urge the soldiers to keep up what had now become a disorganized pursuit. The XI Corps had lost ¼ of its strength, 2,500 men (nearly half of whom had been captured), in an hour, while its general officers suffered a substantial number of casualties trying to rally their men. By the time the flank attack had petered out,

Jackson's men were within sight of Hooker's headquarters at Chancellorsville, and Sickles's III Corps was now positioned between Jackson and the rest of Lee's force.

Lee had not been idle during Jackson's flank attack either, as explained by his nephew, cavalry officer Fitzhugh Lee, after the war: "During the flank march of his great lieutenant, Lee reminded the troops in his front of his position by frequent taps on different points of their lines, and when the sound of cannon gave notice of Jackson's attack, Lee ordered that Hooker's left be strongly pressed to prevent his sending re-enforcements to the point assailed."

Jackson's flank march permanently tarnished Oliver Howard's career and reputation, and he was well aware of it. In his post-campaign report, he took pains to try to explain what happened on the night of May 2:

"At about 6 p.m. I was at my headquarters, at Dowdall's Tavern, when the attack commenced. I sent my chief of staff to the front when firing was heard. General Schurz, who was with me, left at once to take command of his line. It was not three minutes before I followed. When I reached General Schurz's command, I saw that the enemy had enveloped my right, and that the First Division was giving way. I first tried to change the front of the deployed regiments. I next directed the artillery where to go; then formed a line by deploying some of the reserve regiments near the church. By this time the whole front on the north of the Plank road had given way. Colonel Buschbeck's brigade was faced about, and, lying on the other side of the rifle-pit embankment, held on with praiseworthy firmness. A part of General Schimmelfennig's and a part of General Krzyzanowski's brigades moved gradually back to the north of the Plank road and kept up their fire. At the center and near the Plank road there was a blind panic and great confusion. By the assistance of my staff and some other officers, one of whom was Colonel Dickinson, of General Hooker's staff, the rout was considerably checked, and all the artillery, except eight pieces, withdrawn. Some of the artillery was well served, and told effectively on the advancing enemy. Captain Dilger kept up a continuous fire until we reached General Betty's position.

Now as to the causes of this disaster to my corps:

1. Though constantly threatened and apprised of the moving of the enemy, yet the woods was so dense that he was able to mass a large force, whose exact whereabouts neither patrols, reconnaissances, nor scouts ascertained. He succeeded in forming a column opposite to and outflanking my right.

2. By the panic produced by the enemy's reverse fire, regiments and artillery were thrown suddenly upon those in position.

3. The absence of General Barlow's brigade, which I had previously located in reserve

and en echelon with Colonel von Gilsa's, so as to cover his right flank. This was the only general reserve I had. My corps was very soon reorganized near Chancellorsville, and relieved General Meade's corps, on the left of the general line. Here it remained until Wednesday morning, when it resumed its position, as ordered, at the old camp."

Although the flank attack began to lose its steam as the sun went down, Jackson remained active all along his front, and in the process of conducting his own personal reconnaissance during the night, he positioned himself between the lines. Along with some of his staff, Jackson rode so closely to the Union line that some of the horses in his party were shot during a Union musket volley:

"He had now advanced a hundred yards beyond his line of battle, evidently supposing that, in accordance with his constant orders, a line of skirmishers had been sent to the front, immediately upon the recent cessation of the advance. He probably intended to proceed to the place where he supposed this line crossed the turnpike, to ascertain from them what they could learn concerning the enemy. He was attended only by a half dozen mounted orderlies, his signal officer, Captain Wilbourne, with one of his men, and his aide, Lieutenant Morrison, who had just returned to him. General A. P. Hill, with his staff also proceeded immediately after him, to the front of the line, accompanied by Captain Boswell of the Engineers, whom General Jackson had just detached to assist him. After the General and his escort had proceeded down the road a hundred yards, they were surprised by a volley of musketry from the right, which spread toward their front, until the bullets began to whistle among them, and struck several horses."

After that close call, Jackson, Hill, and the staffers started riding back toward their own lines, only to be confused for Union soldiers by their own men, soldiers of the 18th North Carolina:

"General Jackson was now aware of their proximity, and perceived that there was no picket or skirmisher between him and his enemies. He therefore, turned to ride hurriedly back to his own troops; and, to avoid the fire, which was, thus far, limited to the south side of the road, he turned into the woods upon the north side. It so happened that General Hill, with his escort, had been directed by the same motive almost to the same spot.

As the party approached within twenty paces of the Confederate troops, these, evidently mistaking them for cavalry, stooped, and delivered a deadly fire. So sudden and stunning was this volley, and so near at hand, that every horse which was not shot down, recoiled from it in panic, and turned to rush back, bearing their riders toward the approaching enemy. Several fell dead upon the spot, among them the amiable and courageous Boswell; and more were wounded. Among the latter was General Jackson. His right hand was penetrated by a ball, his left forearm lacerated by another, and the same limb broken a little below the shoulder by a third, which not only crushed the bone, but severed the main artery. His horse also dashed, panic-stricken, toward the enemy, carrying him beneath the boughs of a tree which inflicted severe blows, lacerated his face, and almost dragged him from the saddle. His bridle hand was now powerless, but seizing the reins with the right hand, notwithstanding its wound, he arrested his career, and brought the animal back toward his own lines.

General Jackson drew up his horse, and sat for an instant gazing toward his own men, as if in astonishment at their cruel mistake, and in doubt whether he should again venture to approach them."

After personally dressing Jackson's wounds, Hill briefly took command of the Second Corps, until he was himself wounded in the legs, leaving him unable to walk or ride a horse. Hill relinquished command to Rodes, who realized he was over his head and directed JEB Stuart himself to take temporary command of the Second Infantry Corps, a decision Lee seconded when news reached him.

A.P. Hill

Jackson had been nearly hit by Union gunfire, and after he was injured, a litter started trying to carry him to the rear while coming under Union artillery fire, causing even more troubles:

"The party was now met by a litter, which someone had sent from the rear; and the General was placed upon it, and borne along by two soldiers, and Lieutenants Smith and Morrison. As they were placing him upon it, the enemy fired a volley of canister-shot up the road, which passed over their heads. But they had proceeded only a few steps before the discharge was repeated, with a more accurate aim. One of the soldiers bearing the litter was struck down, severely wounded; and had not Major Leigh, who was walking beside it, broken his fall, the General would have been precipitated to the ground. He was placed again upon the earth; and the causeway was now swept by a hurricane of projectiles of every species, before which it seemed that no living thing could survive. The bearers of the litter, and all the attendants, excepting Major Leigh and the General's two aides, left him, and fled into the woods on either hand, to escape the fatal tempest; while the sufferer lay along the road, with his feet toward the foe, exposed to all its fury.

It was now that his three faithful attendants displayed a heroic fidelity, which deserves to go down with the immortal name of Jackson to future ages. Disdaining to save their lives by deserting their chief, they lay down beside him in the causeway, and sought to protect him as far as possible with their bodies. On one side was Major Leigh, and on the other Lieutenant Smith. Again and again was the earth around them torn with volleys of canister, while shells and minie balls flew hissing over them, and the stroke of the iron hail raised sparkling flashes from the flinty gravel of the roadway. General Jackson struggled violently to rise, as though to endeavor to leave the road; but Smith threw his arm over him, and with friendly force held him to the earth, saying: "Sir, you must lie still; it will cost you your life if you rise." He speedily acquiesced, and lay quiet; but none of the four hoped to escape alive. Yet, almost by miracle, they were unharmed; and, after a few moments, the Federalists, having cleared the road of all except this little party, ceased to fire along it, and directed their aim to another quarter."

After being painfully carried back behind the Confederate lines, Jackson had his left arm amputated. When Lee heard of Jackson's injuries, he sent his religious leader Chaplain Lacy to Stonewall with the message, "Give him my affectionate regards, and tell him to make haste and get well, and come back to me as soon as he can. He has lost his left arm, but I have lost my right arm."

In a chaotic turn of events, the Confederacy's famous cavalry chief, JEB Stuart, was now in charge of the bulk of Lee's infantry. Making matters even more difficult for a general who had been leading cavalry the entire war, he had to reorganize the corps, which had gotten intermingled and disorganized in the attack. Stuart reported after the battle:

"It was already dark when I sought General Jackson, and proposed, as there appeared nothing else for me to do, to take some cavalry and infantry over and hold the Ely's Ford road. He approved the proposition, and I had already gained the heights overlooking the ford, where was a large number of camp-fires, when Captain [R. H. T.] Adams, of General A. P. Hill's staff, reached me post-haste, and informed me of the sad calamities which for the time deprived the troops of the leadership of both Jackson and Hill, and the urgent demand for me to come and take command as quickly as possible. I rode with rapidity back 5 miles, determined to press the pursuit already so gloriously begun. General Jackson had gone to the rear, but General A. P. Hill was still on the ground, and formally turned over the command to me. I sent also a staff officer to General Jackson to inform him that I would cheerfully carry out any instructions he would give, and proceeded immediately to the front, which I reached at 10 p.m.

I found, upon reaching it, A. P. Hill's division in front, under Heth, with Lane's, McGowan's, Archer's, and Heth's brigades on the right of the road, within half a mile of Chancellorsville, near the apex of the ridge, and Pender's and Thomas' on the left. I found that the enemy had made an attack on our right flank, but were repulsed. The fact, however, that the attack was made, and at night, made the apprehensive of a repetition of it, and necessitated throwing back the right wing, so as to meet it. I was also informed that there was much confusion on the right, owing to the fact that some troops mistook friends for the enemy and fired upon them. Knowing that an advance under such circumstances would be extremely hazardous, much against my inclination, I felt bound to wait for daylight. General Jackson had also sent me word to use my own discretion. The commanding general was with the right wing of the army, with which I had no communication except by a very circuitous and uncertain route. I nevertheless sent a dispatch to inform him of the state of affairs, and rode around the lines restoring order, imposing silence, and making arrangements for the attack early next day. I sent Col. E. P. Alexander, senior officer of artillery, to select and occupy with artillery positions along the line bearing upon the enemy's position, with which duty he was engaged all night."

Stuart

As if the day hadn't gone poorly enough, Hooker ordered Sickles to make an attack later in the night, only for his men to be mistaken by the XII Corps artillery near Fairview as Confederates. The lone Union assault of the day would be halted by friendly fire.

Around the same time that night, Hooker fired off an order to Sedgwick, still around Fredericksburg, and ordered him to attack with all dispatch. Hooker had now correctly assumed that the Confederates in Sedgwick's front were a skeleton force, and the order to attack was sound, but unfortunately the manner in which he directed Sedgwick to attack required a 14 mile countermarch. Sedgwick reported:

"That night at 11 o'clock I received an order, dated 10.10 p.m., directing me to cross the Rappahannock at Fredericksburg immediately upon receipt of the order, and move in the direction of Chancellorsville until I connected with the major-general commanding; to attack and destroy any force on the road, and be in the vicinity of the general at daylight.

I had been informed repeatedly by Major-General Butterfield, chief of staff, that the force in front of me was very small, and the whole tenor of his many dispatches would have created the impression that the enemy had abandoned my front and retired from the city and its defenses had there not been more tangible evidence than the dispatches in question that the chief of staff was misinformed."

Due to Sedgwick's inaction earlier on May 2 and the nature of the orders that night, Sedgwick's men spent the entire day idle in front of an enemy ¼ their size.

Chapter 5: May 3

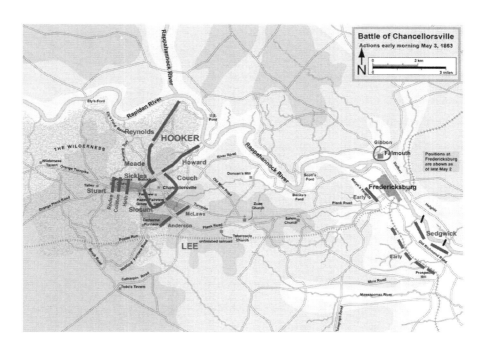

The morning of May 3

The Battle of Chancellorsville is best remembered for Stonewall Jackson's legendary flank attack on the night of May 2, but the battle would be decided on May 3. Despite the debacle suffered by the XI Corps, the Army of the Potomac still outnumbered Lee's army in the vicinity, and Jackson's corps (now commanded by Stuart) was still separated from the rest. Lee was determined to ensure Jackson's corps linked up with the rest of the army by attacking Sickles, whose III Corps stood between them along Hazel Grove.

In one of the most fateful decisions of the war, Lee's objective was actually obtained by Hooker's own orders. Early that morning, as the Confederates were preparing an attack despite being outnumbered by nearly 40,000 men, Hooker pulled the III Corps back from Hazel Grove to the Plank Road, covering his flanks and forming a horseshoe defensive line so that Sickles's corps would not be a salient in the line capable of being hit by both wings of the Confederate army around Chancellorsville. With that ground being ceded, Porter Alexander, who had been tasked by Stuart with conducting reconnaissance for placing artillery, was allowed to simply establish about 30 guns on the high ground at Hazel Grove. Alexander explained the consequences of Hooker's poor decision in his memoirs, "Altogether, I do not think there was a more brilliant thing done in the war than Stuart's extricating that command from the extremely critical position in which he found it."

As Hooker abandoned the high ground at Hazel Grove in favor of Fairview, Stuart's artillery began bombarding the Union positions from the high ground, not only forcing General Hooker's troops from Fairview but essentially decimating the Union lines while destroying Hooker's headquarters at Chancellor House. Of this turn of events, Stuart wrote, "As the sun lifted the mist that shrouded the field, it was discovered that the ridge on the extreme right was a fine position for concentrating artillery. I immediately ordered thirty pieces to that point, and, under the happy effects of the battalion system, it was done quickly. The effect of this fire upon the enemy's batteries was superb."

With Stuart's artillery now posted, the Confederates attacked all along the line at dawn, with Stuart's men advancing along the Plank Road from the west while Anderson and McLaws attacked up the Turnpike and Plank Road on the other side of Hooker's army. Stuart launched a savage attack with three divisions all advancing forward together, two of which were in support just a few hundred yards behind. Although many of them had exhausted themselves routing the XI Corps the night before, they were up to the challenge, as Stuart reported:

"At early dawn, Trimble's division composed the second line and Rodes' division the third. The latter had his rations on the spot, and, as his men were entirely without food, was extremely anxious to issue. I was disposed to wait a short time for this purpose; but when, as preliminary to an attack, I ordered the right of the first line to swing around and come perpendicular to the road, the order was misunderstood for an order to attack, and that part of the line became engaged. I ordered the whole line to advance and the second and third lines to follow. As the sun lifted the mist that shrouded the field, it was discovered that the ridge on the extreme right was a fine position for concentrating artillery. I immediately ordered thirty pieces to that point, and, under the happy effects of the battalion system, it was done quickly. The effect of this fire upon the enemy's batteries was superb.

In the meantime the enemy was pressing our left with infantry, and all the re-enforcements I could obtain were sent there. Colquitt's brigade, of Trimble's division, ordered first to the right, was directed to the left to support Pender. Iverson's brigade, of the second line, was also engaged there, and the three lines were more or less merged into one line of battle, and reported hard pressed. Urgent requests were sent for re-enforcements, and notices that the troops were out of ammunition, &c. I ordered that the ground must be held at all hazards; if necessary, with the bayonet. About this time also our right connected with Anderson's left, relieving all anxiety on that subject. I was now anxious to mass infantry on the left, to push the enemy there, and sent every available regiment to that point.

About 8 a.m. the works of the enemy directly in front of our right were stormed, but the enemy's forces retiring from the line facing Anderson, which our batteries enfiladed, caused our troops to abandon these works, the enemy coming in their rear. It was stormed a second time, when I discovered the enemy making a flank movement to the left of the road, for the purpose of dislodging our forces, and hastened to change the front of a portion of our line to meet this attack, but the shortness of the time and the deafening roar of artillery prevented the execution of this movement, and our line again retired. The third time it was taken, I made disposition of a portion of Ramseur's brigade to protect the left flank. Artillery was pushed forward to the crest, sharpshooters were posted in a house in advance, and in a few moments Chancellorsville was ours (10 a.m.). The enemy retired toward Ely's Ford, the road to United States Ford branching one-half mile west of Chancellorsville.

In this hotly contested battle the enemy had strong works on each side of the road, those on the commanding ridge being heavily defended by artillery. The night also had given him time to mass his troops to meet this attack, but the desperate valor of Jackson's corps overcame every obstacle and drove the enemy to his new line of defense, which his engineers had constructed in his rear, ready for occupation, at the intersection of the Ely's Ford and United States Ford roads."

While the Union and Confederate armies fought all along the lines, the Confederate artillery at Hazel Grove became an absolute menace, providing artillerists the opportunity to strike the heart of Hooker's positions. In his seminal history *Lee's Lieutenants*, biographer Douglas Southall Freeman described one artillery exchange during the day: "At Hazel Grove, in short, the finest artillerists of the Army of Northern Virginia were having their greatest day. They had improved guns, better ammunition and superior organization. With the fire of battle shining through his spectacles, William Pegram rejoiced. 'A glorious day, Colonel,' he said to Porter Alexander, 'a glorious day!'"

If Hooker had not regretted his decision to evacuate Hazel Grove earlier in the morning, he probably did around 9:00 a.m., when an artillery shell hit a pillar of the Chancellor house while he was standing near it. Hooker later noted that the shattered pillar struck him "violently... in an erect position from my head to my feet." It's long been speculated that Hooker suffered a concussion, but initially he refused to relinquish command to Couch or any of his staffers. Hooker's injury has long been cited as yet another reason why his generalship became more cautious after May 1.

Even before Hooker was injured, Darius Couch, Hooker's second-in-command, was bewildered not only by the lack of communications coming from Hooker but also the overly cautious timidity that Hooker was displaying:

"Upon the south porch of that mansion General Hooker stood leaning against one of its pillars, observing the fighting, looking anxious and much careworn. After the fighting had commenced I doubt if any orders were given by him to the commanders on the field, unless, perhaps, 'to retire when out of ammunition.' None were received by me, nor were there any inquiries as to how the battle was going along my front. On the right flank, where the fighting was desperate, the engaged troops were governed by the corps and division leaders. If the ear of the commanding general was, as he afterward stated, strained to catch the sound of Sedgwick's guns, it could not have heard them in the continuous uproar that filled the air around him; but as Sedgwick, who was known as a fighting officer, had not appeared at the time set - daylight - nor for some hours after, it was conclusive evidence that he had met with strong opposition, showing that all of Lee's army was not at Chancellorsville, so that the moment was favorable for Hooker to try his opponent's strength with every available man. Moreover, the left wing might at that very time be in jeopardy, therefore he was bound by every patriotic motive to strike hard for its relief. If he had remembered Mr. Lincoln's injunction ('Gentlemen, in your next fight put in all of your men'), the face of the day would have been changed and the field won for the Union arms."

In addition to injuring and likely concussing Hooker, who would spend the next hour in a daze before temporarily relinquishing command, the Confederate artillery ultimately made Fairview untenable for the Union line, the closest open high ground near Hazel Grove and the point at which Lee and Stuart were able to link their forces back together around 10:00 a.m. Stuart had made himself conspicuous during the fighting, as Couch explained:

"In the meanwhile Stuart was pressing the attack. At one time his left was so strongly resisted that his three lines were merged into one. To a notice sent him that the men were out of ammunition, he replied that they must hold their ground with the bayonet. About this time Stuart's right connected with Anderson's left, uniting thus the detached portions of General Lee's army. He then massed infantry on his left and stormed the Federal works. Twice he was repulsed, but the third time Stuart placed himself on horseback at the head of the troops, ordered the charge, carried the intrenchments, and held them, singing with ringing voice, 'Old Joe Hooker, won't you come out of the wilderness?' An eye-witness says he could not get rid of the impression that Harry of Navarre led the charge, except that Stuart's plume was black, for everywhere the men followed his feather. Anderson at the same time moved rapidly upon Chancellorsville, while McLaws made a strong demonstration in his front. At 10 A. M. the position at Chancellorsville was won, and Hooker had withdrawn to another line nearer the Rappahannock. Preparations were at once made by Lee to attack again, when further operations were arrested by intelligence received from Fredericksburg."

Lee's aide-de-camp, Charles Marshall, described the climactic scene:

"Lee's presence was the signal for one of those uncontrollable bursts of enthusiasm which none can appreciate who has not witnessed them. The fierce soldiers, with their faces blackened with the smoke of battle, the wounded crawling with feeble limbs from the fury of the devouring flames, all seemed possessed with a common impulse. One long unbroken cheer, in which the feeble cry of those who lay helpless on the earth blended with the strong voices of those who still fought, rose high above the roar of battle and hailed the presence of a victorious chief. He sat in the full realization of all that soldiers dream of—triumph; and as I looked at him in the complete fruition of the success which his genius, courage, and confidence in his army had won, I thought that it must have been from some such scene that men in ancient days ascended to the dignity of gods."

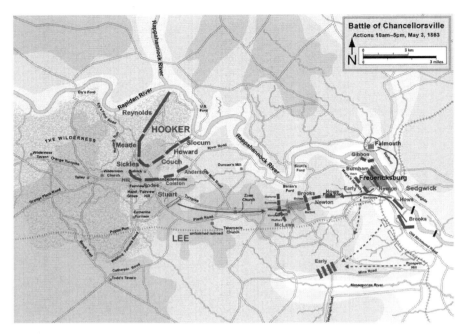

Despite this important success, whatever relief Lee felt upon linking back up with Stuart was almost immediately tempered by news that his right was collapsing against Sedgwick near Fredericksburg. Early had ordered to hold the line unless his men were attacked by "overwhelming numbers," in which case he was to withdraw his men to the south toward Richmond. But if Sedgwick seemed to be withdrawing from in front of him, Early was supposed to shift his men west and join the rest of Lee's army near Chancellorsville.

As it turned out, Early would begin to inadvertently retreat from his defensive line before Sedgwick even attacked on May 3, thanks to miscommunication. Early explained what happened in his memoirs:

"During the morning I rode to Lee's Hill for the purpose of observing the enemy's movements from that point, and I observed a considerable portion of his infantry in motion up the opposite river bank. While I was, in company with Generals Barksdale and Pendleton, observing the enemy's manoeuvre and trying to ascertain what it meant, at about 11 o'clock A. M., Colonel R. H. Chilton, of General Lee's staff, came to me with a verbal order to move up immediately towards Chancellorsville with my whole force, except a brigade of infantry and Pendleton's reserve artillery, and to leave at

Fredericksburg the brigade of infantry and a part of the reserve artillery to be selected by General Pendleton, with instructions to the commander of this force to watch the enemy's movements, and keep him in check if possible, but if he advanced with too heavy a force to retire on the road to Spottsylvania Court-House-General Pendleton being required to send the greater part of his reserve artillery to the rear at once.

This order took me very much by surprise, and I remarked to Colonel Chilton that I could not retire my troops without their being seen by the enemy, whose position on Stafford Heights not only overlooked ours, but who had one or two balloons which he was constantly sending up from the heights to make observations, and stated that he would inevitably move over and take possession of Fredericksburg and the surrounding Heights. The Colonel said he presumed General Lee understood all this, but that it was much more important for him to have troops where he was, than at Fredericksburg, and if he defeated the enemy there he could easily retake Fredericksburg; he called my attention to the fact, which was apparent to us all, that there was a very heavy force of infantry massed on the slopes near Falmouth which had moved up from below, and stated that he had no doubt the greater portion of the force on the other side was in motion to reinforce Hooker. He repeated his orders with great distinctness in the presence of General Pendleton, and in reply to questions from us, said that there could be no mistake in his orders.

This was very astounding to us, as we were satisfied that we were then keeping away from the army, opposed to General Lee, a much larger body of troops than my force could engage or neutralize if united to the army near Chancellorsville. It is true that there was the force massed near Falmouth and the indications were that it was moving above, but still there was a much larger force of infantry stationed below, which evinced no disposition to move. While we were conversing, information was brought me that the enemy had abandoned his lower crossing, and that our skirmishers had advanced tothe Pratt house, but he still, however, maintained his position at the mouth of Deep Creek with a division of infantry and a number of guns on our side of the river.

The orders as delivered to me left me no discretion, and believing that General Lee understood his own necessities better than I possibly could, I did not feel justified in acting on my own judgment, and I therefore determined to move as directed. It subsequently turned out that Colonel Chilton had misunderstood General Lee's orders, which were that I should make the movement indicated if the enemy did not have a sufficient force in my front to detain the whole of mine, and it was to be left to me to judge of that, the orders, in fact, being similar to those given me at first. It also turned out that the troops seen massed near Falmouth were the 1st corps under Reynolds, moving up to reinforce Hooker, and that the 6th corps, Sedgwick's own, remained behind. "

Early

Early was alerted to the mistake in time to form his whole defensive line again by the early morning of May 3, but he was still vastly outnumbered. Early split his forces south of Fredericksburg and west of them, contesting the south while hoping Union fears about Marye's Heights would allow him to hold that position with fewer men. As a result, Marye's Heights, which had been turned into an unassailable fortress by Longstreet's corps in December 1862, was now manned by just two brigades, led by William Barksdale and Harry Hays.

When the fighting started near Marye's Heights that morning, it probably felt like déjà vu to the Union soldiers who knew full well that nearly 8,000 men had fallen in front of the dreaded stone wall at the base of Marye's Heights. And sure enough, the initial two assaults were repulsed by the two hard-pressed Confederate brigades holding it. How much longer they might have held the position against further assaults is unclear, because a flag of truce for the purposes of collecting the dead and wounded allowed Union soldiers to literally walk up to the rifle pit and see how undermanned the Confederates truly were. With that critical information, a third Union charge at the point of bayonets drove the remnants of the two Confederate brigades out of their rifle pits on Marye's Heights in minutes. For the first time in the campaign, one of Lee's lines had been broken by the Union.

Confederate casualties behind the stone wall at Marye's Heights

With his position now becoming untenable, Early began to fight while retreating to the south; having been attacked by overwhelming numbers, he was following Lee's orders and pulling his men away from Chancellorsville. Had Lee been at the scene, he almost certainly would have ensured that Early retreated west toward the rest of the army, but instead Early's retreat south would open up Sedgwick's path to Lee's rear at Chancellorsville.

Though Early was retreating away from the rest of the army, his men successfully delayed Sedgwick for hours around Fredericksburg on May 3, helped in large measure by the brigade of Cadmus Wilcox, who explained the nature of the Early's retreat from Fredericksburg:

"Seeing a group of officers near Stansbury's house, I rode to them, and met Generals Barksdale and Hays. The former informed me that the enemy were in considerable force in and below Fredericksburg (this was the first intimation I had of the fact), and expressed some anxiety as to his right flank, and said that he should have reenforcements. I now determined not to move my command up the road until I knew definitely the intention of the enemy, and ordered them in the ravine opposite Dr.

Taylor's, where they would be near and yet out of sight. I now rode to the vicinity of the Marye house, to see and confer with General Barksdale. While near the house, I saw great numbers of the enemy in Fredericksburg, and a battery in the street running near the cemetery was firing occasional shots at a battery of ours to the left of the Plank road. I returned to my command without seeing General Barksdale, and, on my return, saw several regiments of the enemy's infantry moving out of the upper edge of the town. I had been with my command but a few minutes when one of General Barksdale's staff reported to me that the general was hard pressed, and wanted me to send him a regiment. I instantly ordered the Tenth Alabama to move in the direction of the Marye house, and rode rapidly in that direction myself, and when in the open field and high ground between Stansbury's and the Plank road, saw Hays' brigade moving over in the direction of the Plank road. This I supposed to be for the support of General Barksdale, but upon inquiry from one of Hays' regiments learned that the enemy had taken Marye's Hill end a portion of two of Barksdale's regiments, and that Hays' brigade was falling back to the Telegraph road. Soon a courier from General Barksdale confirmed this report, and with a suggestion from General Barksdale that I also had better fall back to the Telegraph road. On the left of the Plank road the ground in rear of Marye's Hill is higher, and overlooks and commands well that hill. Believing that my own and Hays' brigade could form in line, extending from near Stansbury's house along the crests of the hills toward the Plank road, and contest the field at least for a time successfully, with the enemy, I asked General Hays not to cross the Plank road, but to remain with me. This he declined doing, having been ordered to fall back to the Telegraph road, and was soon out of sight."

Wilcox

As a result of Lee's orders, and much to Wilcox's confusion and chagrin, instead of reforming a defensive line west of Fredericksburg, Hays and Barksdale retreated south and fell back with the rest of Early's division. Thankfully for the Confederates, Wilcox opted to continue fighting a delayed retreat west, buying time for Lee to hurry men east from Chancellorsville to try to stop Sedgwick's advance. Wilcox reported his initial stand:

"Finding myself alone on the left of the Plank road, with the enemy in full view on the crests of the first range of hills in rear of Fredericksburg, and with three times my own force clearly seen and in line, I felt it a duty to delay the enemy as much as possible in his advance, and to endeavor to check him all that I could should he move forward on the Plank road. With this view, I formed my brigade promptly in line along the crests of the hills running near Stansbury's house, at right angles to the Plank road. Two rifled pieces of Lewis' battery were placed in position to the rear of the left of my line, and two slightly in front of my right, which rested some 500 or 600 yards in front of Guest's house. Skirmishers were thrown forward, covering my entire front. As soon as the four pieces of artillery were in position, they opened fire upon the enemy's lines, some 800 or 900 yards to the front. This held the enemy in check for some time. At length they deployed skirmishers to the front and began to advance. This was slow, and, delayed by frequent halts, they seemed reluctant to advance. The enemy now brought a six-gun battery to the front on the left of the Plank road, not far from Marye's house, and opened with a fire of shells upon my line. The enemy's skirmishers now advanced and engaged ours, not nearer, however, than 350 or 400 yards, their solid lines remaining some distance behind the skirmishers. The enemy's battery having fired for some time, both the skirmishers and lines in rear advanced. They had also moved by a flank across the Plank road, and it was reported to me that they were moving up on the far side of the road, and were on a line with my right flank. The artillery was now directed to withdraw; then the skirmishers rejoined their regiments, and all moved to the rear on the River road, half a mile in rear of Dr. Taylor's, where they were halted for a few minutes."

Sedgwick continued pushing west down the Turnpike while Wilcox waited for reinforcements, and around 5:00 p.m., the two lines found themselves just 5 miles away from Lee's rear around Salem Church. Finally, Wilcox was joined by 4 brigades, pulled from McLaws and Anderson, bringing the Confederate forces up to 10,000 men. Wilcox described the climactic finale of the fighting in the east in his post-war report:

The enemy's artillery ceased to fire near 5 p.m. Their skirmishers then advanced; a spirited fire ensued between the skirmishers for some fifteen or twenty minutes. Ours then retired, firing as they fell back. The enemy's skirmishers pursued, followed by their solid lines of infantry and still a third line in rear. On either side of the road, as they advanced from the toll-gate, were open fields, and the ground slightly ascending. These fields continued to within about 250 yards of the church, and then woods, thick, but of small growth. When the front line of the enemy reached this wood, they made a slight halt; then, giving three cheers, they came with a rush, driving our skirmishers rapidly before them. Our men held their fire till their men came within less than 80 yards, and then delivered a close and terrible fire upon them, killing and wounding many and causing many of them to waver and give way. The enemy still press on, surround the school-house, and capture the entire company of the Ninth Alabama stationed in it, and, pressing hard upon the regiment in rear of the school-house, throw it in confusion and disorder, and force it to yield ground. The Ninth Alabama, in rear of this regiment, spring forward as one man, and, with the rapidity of lightning, restore the continuity of our line, breaking the lines of the enemy by its deadly fire and forcing him to give way, and, following him so that he could not rally, retake the school-house, free the captured company, and in turn take their captors. The entire line of the enemy on the right of the road is repulsed, and our men follow in rapid pursuit. The regiment that had given way to the first onset of the enemy now returned to the attack and joined in the pursuit. The enemy did not assail with the same spirit on the left of the road, and were more easily repulsed, and now are followed on either side of the road, which is crowded with a confused mass of the discomfited enemy. With a good battery to play upon this retreating mass, the carnage would have been terrific. There was no rallying or reforming of this line. Another line came up the Plank road at a double-quick, and, filing to the right and left, formed line in front of my brigade. This line was scarcely formed before they were broken by the fire of my men, and fled to the rear.

The pursuit continued as far as the toll-gate. Semmes' brigade and my own were the only troops that followed the retreating enemy. In rear of the gate were heavy reserves of the enemy. Our men were now halted and reformed, it being quite dark, and retired, not pursued by the enemy, leaving pickets far to the front in the open field. The vigor of the enemy's attack at the church was doubtless due to the fact that they believed there was only one brigade to resist them, and that they anticipated an easy affair of it, while the number of dead and wounded left on the field attests the obstinacy of the resistance of our men--200 of the former and more than 150 of the latter, and largely over 200 prisoners not wounded and 1 Federal flag captured.

Thus ended this spirited conflict at Salem Church; a bloody repulse to the enemy, rendering entirely useless to him his little success of the morning at Fredericksburg. The rear of our army at Chancellorsville was now secure and free from danger, and the Sixth Army Corps of the enemy and a part of the Second were now content to remain on the defensive.

Although Wilcox exuberantly described the result as a "bloody repulse", the truth is that Sedgwick was running out of daylight to continue his advance. As a result, Lee's rear was saved. Hooker would later complain that Sedgwick had not advanced as promptly as he should've, no doubt annoyed by what he considered Sedgwick's second straight day of failure: "My object in ordering General Sedgwick forward ...was to relieve me from the position in which I found myself at Chancellorsville...In my judgment General Sedgwick did not obey the spirit of my order, and made no sufficient effort to obey it...When he did move it was not with sufficient confidence or ability on his part to manoeuvre his troops."

Chancellorsville is not the most famous battle of the war, and it's best remembered for the events of May 2, but the action on May 3 may have been the most tactically complex of the war. Lee's army had made assaults on two parts of the Union line at Chancellorsville to ensure that his army linked back up, while still managing to maintain a defensive line and halt Sedgwick's advance on the right, thus conducting a successful offensive on his left and a successful defense on his right. The casualty count attests to the fact that the fighting was just as fierce as it was complex. Over 21,000 men were killed, wounded, or captured on May 3, 1863, making it the second bloodiest day in American history, barely behind the Battle of Antietam.

Chapter 6: Hooker Withdraws

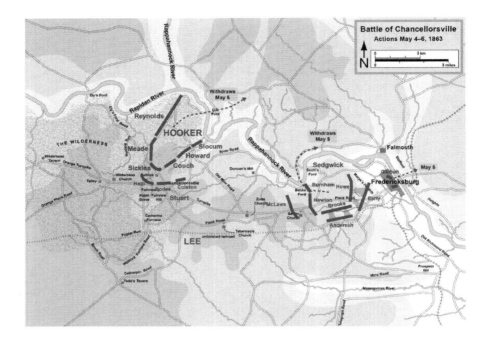

"As to the charge that the battle was lost because [Hooker] was intoxicated, I have always stated that he probably abstained from the use of ardent spirits when it would have been far better for him to have continued in his usual habit in that respect. The shock from being violently thrown to the ground, together with the physical exhaustion resulting from loss of sleep and the anxiety of mind incident to the last six days of the campaign, would tell on any man." – Darius Couch

Lee had managed to win every gamble he took from May 1-3, and he had masterfully defended his right while simultaneously striking at Hooker on his left, but the armies woke up on the morning of May 4 with the Army of the Potomac still heavily outnumbering the Army of Northern Virginia near Chancellorsville and near Salem Church just west of Fredericksburg. Hooker's flanks and Sedgwick's flanks rested on the Rapidan and Rappahannock rivers respectively, which meant they were secure, but with their forces divided and Lee's army between them, Hooker was worried that the advantage of interior lines gave Lee a chance to destroy one of the two separated armies.

Throughout May 4, Hooker dug in, and the lack of offensive activity convinced Lee that he could detach more of Anderson's division to confront Sedgwick to the right. Lee was also able to recall Early's division, which now marched back north and reoccupied Marye's Heights on Sedgwick's left flank, linking up with the men from McLaws's division and Anderson's division opposite Sedgwick. Lee hoped to attack Sedgwick, now slightly outnumbering him, but delays in Anderson's march and hesitation by McLaws resulted in the attack not starting until 6:00 p.m. Sedgwick had spent all day drawing up defensive lines to protect his retreat back across the Rappahannock, so he was able to repulse the half-hearted offensive that night.

After the Confederate attack stopped and night fell, Sedgwick began extricating his command at Banks's Ford, recrossing the Rappahannock during the night of May 4-5. Hooker had taken a defensive stance and had idled all day near Chancellorsville, yet he now used Sedgwick's withdrawal as the pretext for a withdrawal of his own. Before doing so, however, he called a council of war on the night of May 4 and discussed the matter with his principal subordinates. Couch recounted that night's council of war:

> "At 12 o'clock on the night of the 4th - 5th General Hooker assembled his corps commanders in council. Meade, Sickles, Howard, Reynolds, and myself were present; General Slocum, on account of the long distance from his post, did not arrive until after the meeting was broken up. Hooker stated that his instructions compelled him to cover Washington, not to jeopardize the army, etc. It was seen by the most casual observer that he had made up his mind to retreat. We were left by ourselves to consult, upon which Sickles made an elaborate argument, sustaining the views of the commanding general. Meade was in favor of fighting, stating that he doubted if we could get off our guns. Howard was in favor of fighting, qualifying his views by the remark that our present situation was due to the bad conduct of his corps, or words to that effect. Reynolds, who was lying on the ground very much fatigued, was in favor of an advance. I had similar views to those of Meade as to getting off the guns, but said I 'would favor an advance if I could designate the point of attack.' Upon collecting the suffrages, Meade, Reynolds, and Howard voted squarely for an advance, Sickles and myself squarely no; upon which Hooker informed the council that he should take upon himself the responsibility of retiring the army to the other side of the river. As I stepped out of the tent Reynolds, just behind me, broke out, 'What was the use of calling us together at this time of night when he intended to retreat anyhow?'

Thus, during the next day, Hooker began the process of pulling his command back across the river, a delicate process that started with removing the artillery and clearing the roads so that the infantry would not get bottled up. In the early morning hours of May 6, the rest of the corps began crossing the river, with Meade's V Corps protecting the retreat on the south bank. Even still, Couch, who was in command on the south bank of the Rapidan because Hooker was already across, claimed he was tempted to try to fight:

"Near midnight I got a note from Meade informing me that General Hooker was on the other side of the river, which had risen over the bridges, and that communication was cut off from him. I immediately rode over to Hooker's headquarters and found that I was in command of the army, if it had any commander. General Hunt, of the artillery, had brought the information as to the condition of the bridges, and from the reports there seemed to be danger of losing them entirely. After a short conference with Meade I told him that the recrossing would be suspended, and that 'we would stay where we were and fight it out,' returning to my tent with the intention of enjoying what I had not had since the night of the 30th ultimo - a good sleep; but at 2 A. M., communication having been reestablished, I received a sharp message from Hooker, to order the recrossing of the army as he had directed, and everything was safely transferred to the north bank of the Rappahannock."

As a result, the Army of the Potomac was safely back on the other side of the river by May 6, greatly surprising Lee, who was still making plans to attack Hooker in hopes of destroying his command against the Rapidan. Incredibly, upon withdrawing back across the river and retreating, Hooker issued General Orders No. 49, which actually congratulated his army on their recent achievements:

"The major-general commanding tenders to this army his congratulations on its achievements of the last seven days. If it has not accomplished all that was expected, the reasons are well known to the army. It is sufficient to say they were of a character not to be foreseen or prevented by human sagacity or resource.

In withdrawing from the south bank of the Rappahannock before delivering a general battle to our adversaries, the army has given renewed evidence of its confidence in itself and its fidelity to the principles it represents. In fighting at a disadvantage, we would have been recreant to our trust, to ourselves, our cause, and our country.

Profoundly loyal, and conscious of its strength, the Army of the Potomac will give or decline battle whenever its interest or honor may demand. It will also be the guardian of its own history and its own fame.

By our celerity and secrecy of movement, our advance and passage of the rivers were undisputed, and on our withdrawal not a rebel ventured to follow.

The events of the last week may swell with pride the heart of every officer and soldier of this army. We have added new luster to its former renown. We have made long marches, crossed rivers, surprised the enemy in his intrenchments, and whenever we have fought have inflicted heavier blows than we have received.

We have taken from the enemy 5,000 prisoners; captured and brought off seven pieces of artillery, fifteen colors; placed hors de combat 18,000 of his chosen troops; destroyed his depots filled with vast amounts of stores; deranged his communications; captured prisoners within the fortifications of his capital, and filled his country with fear and consternation.

We have no other regret than that caused by the loss of our brave companions, and in this we are consoled by the conviction that they have fallen in the holiest cause ever submitted to the arbitrament of battle."

Whether Hooker truly believed the contents of his orders or not, the rest of his officers and the rank-and-file were well aware of what their retreat meant.

The following day, on May 7, Stoneman's cavalry reentered Union lines east of Richmond on the Peninsula. Hooker's poor use of Stoneman's cavalry had deprived him of necessary reconnaissance on May 2 and made it that much easier for Stuart's cavalry to determine the XI Corps had its right flank in the air. For his part, Stoneman had accomplished nothing of importance, failing to destroy any of the supply lines or communication lines Hooker anticipated he would.

Chapter 7: The Aftermath of Chancellorsville

The Chancellorsville campaign officially came to an end with Hooker's withdrawal on May 6, but the most important casualty of the campaign would not come until 4 days later.

After being wounded and carried behind the lines on the night of May 2, Stonewall Jackson had his arm amputated, after which he was transported to Thomas C. Chandler's plantation well behind the battle lines to convalesce. He seemed to be recovering, and his wife and newborn daughter joined him at the plantation, but his doctors were unaware Jackson was exhibiting common symptoms that indicated oncoming pneumonia. Jackson lay dying in the Chandler plantation outbuilding on Sunday, May 10, 1863 with his wife Anna at his side. He comforted his wife, telling her, "It is the Lord's Day…my wish is fulfilled. I always wanted to die on Sunday." Near the end, a delirious Jackson seemed to have his mind on war, blurting out, "Tell A. P. Hill to prepare for actions! Pass the infantry to the front! Tell Major Hawks…" His final words were "Let us cross over the river, and rest under the shade of the trees."

The loss of Jackson was a crushing one for the Confederacy and Lee's army. In his post-campaign report, Lee wrote of his fallen subordinate, "The movement by which the enemy's position was turned and the fortune of the day decided was conducted by the lamented Lieutenant-General Jackson, who, as has already been stated, was severely wounded near the close of the engagement on Saturday evening. I do not propose here to speak of the character of this illustrious man, since removed from the scene of his eminent usefulness by the hand of an inscrutable but all-wise Providence. I nevertheless desire to pay the tribute of my admiration to the matchless energy and skill that marked this last act of his life, forming, as it did, a worthy conclusion of that long series of splendid achievements which won for him the lasting love and gratitude of his country."

The Battle of Chancellorsville is widely remembered as Lee's greatest victory. Historian Robert Krick, who wrote a history of the campaign and titled his book *Lee's Greatest Victory*, notes, "Lee's Chancellorsville consisted of a pastiche of unbelievably risky gambits that led to a great triumph. Hooker's campaign, after the brilliant opening movements, degenerated into a tale of opportunities missed and troops underutilized." And from a tactical standpoint, there's no question that Chancellorsville was Lee's masterpiece. Every gamble paid off, every decision he made ended up being the right one, and he was assisted by skilled subordinates like Stuart and Jackson. He seamlessly switched between taking the offensive and skillfully defending on two separate fronts over the course of several days, and he ultimately forced an army more than twice the size of his to withdraw and abort the campaign.

However, as Longstreet noted in his memoirs, the context of the Chancellorsville campaign cannot be forgotten. Lee had gained a complete strategic and tactical victory, but it was more a result of Hooker becoming cautious. The casualties among the two sides were 17,000 Union soldiers killed, captured or wounded, with about 13,000 Confederates killed, captured, or wounded. In other words, Lee lost nearly 25% of his army, and though he inflicted 4,000 more casualties on Hooker's army, the Army of the Potomac lost about 15% of its manpower. The Confederates were undermanned and lacked the resources of the Union throughout the war, and while Lee had blunted the latest offensive by the Army of the Potomac, the campaign all but ended with the two armies in the same positions they had been in 10 days earlier. No matter how many times Lee won a battle like Chancellorsville, the Confederacy would still lose the war. As Longstreet would put it in his memoirs, "The battle as pitched and as an independent affair was brilliant, and if the war was for glory could be called successful, but, besides putting the cause upon the hazard of a die, it was crippling in resources and of future progress, while the wait of a few days would have given time for concentration and opportunities against Hooker more effective than we experienced with Burnside at Fredericksburg. This was one of the occasions where success was not a just criterion."

Naturally, an analysis of Chancellorsville far different today given the hindsight of knowing the Civil War's final result than it was in May 1863. At the time, Chancellorsville was one of the most stunning battles of the Civil War, and Lincoln was shook to the core, exclaiming after the battle, "My God! My God! What will the country say?" At the same time, the South's joy at hearing of the victory was completely dampened by the loss of Jackson, and Longstreet recalled that when he rejoined the army, "I found [Lee] in sadness, notwithstanding that he was contemplating his great achievement and brilliant victory of Chancellorsville, for he had met with great loss as well as great gains. The battle had cost heavily of his army, but his grief was over the severe wounding of his great lieutenant, General Thomas Jonathan Jackson, the head of the Second Corps of the Army of Northern Virginia; cut off, too, at a moment so much needed to finish his work in the battle so handsomely begun."

Ultimately, Chancellorsville's most decisive impact and legacy can be found in the many ways it shaped Lee's subsequent Pennsylvania Campaign. At the beginning of 1863, Lee felt the Confederate cause needed the kind of decisive victory and master stroke that could win the war with one grand battle. It's why Lee constantly felt compelled to attack an army twice his army's size multiple times at Chancellorsville, and his failure to knockout Hooker made him that much more anxious to win a crushing victory at Gettysburg.

Lee's impatience with the status quo after Chancellorsville also induced him to invade Pennsylvania in the first place. Knowing that victories on Virginia soil meant little to an enemy that could simply retreat, regroup, and then return with more men and more advanced equipment, Lee would next set his sights on a Northern invasion, aiming to turn Northern opinion against the war and against President Lincoln. With his men already half-starved from dwindling provisions, Lee intended to confiscate food, horses, and equipment as they pushed north, and he also hoped to influence Northern politicians into giving up their support of the war by penetrating into Harrisburg or even Philadelphia. Given the right circumstances, Lee's army might even be able to capture either Baltimore or Philadelphia and use the city as leverage in peace negotiations.

Before Lee even made that invasion, the results at Chancellorsville led to major reorganizations of both armies that directly influenced how Gettysburg was fought. Not surprisingly, there were some serious shakeups in Chancellorsville's aftermath as Union generals pointed the fingers at each other. Hooker had a list of scapegoats, including XI Corps commander Oliver O. Howard, cavalry leader George Stoneman, and VI Corps commander John Sedgwick. Of course, just as many blamed Hooker, pointing out that a sizable amount of the Army of the Potomac had barely fought at all during the Chancellorsville campaign. The strongest critic was II Corps commander Darius N. Couch, who vowed never to serve under Hooker again and subsequently transferred out of the Army of the Potomac back to Pennsylvania to lead the state militia. He would be succeeded by Winfield Scott Hancock as the new commander of the II Corps, and Hancock would be the most conspicuous Union hero during the last two days of Gettysburg, including during Pickett's Charge.

Hancock

George Meade would later privately claim in a letter to his wife, "Hooker never lost his head, nor did he ever allow himself to be influenced by me or my advice. The objection I have to Hooker is that he did not and would not listen to those around him; that he acted deliberately on his own judgment, and in doing so, committed, as I think, fatal errors. If he had lost his head, and I had been placed in command, you may rest assured a very different result would have been arrived at, whether better or worse for us cannot be told now."

On May 10, 1863, as Stonewall Jackson lay dying, Meade wrote to his wife, "There is a great deal of talking in the camp, and I see the press is beginning to attack Hooker. I think these last operations have shaken the confidence of the army in Hooker's judgment, particularly among the superior officers. I have been much gratified at the frequent expression of opinion that I ought to be placed in command. Three of my seniors (Couch, Slocum and Sedgwick) have sent me word that they were willing to serve under me. Couch, I hear, told the President he would not serve any longer under Hooker, and recommended my assignment to the command. I mention all this confidentially. I do not attach any importance to it, and do not believe there is the slightest probability of my being placed in command."

Meade would get his private wish. Lincoln would relieve Hooker of command just a few days before the Battle of Gettysburg and name Meade the new commander of the Army of the Potomac. Meade would hold his ground during the battle and become the first Union general to inflict a decisive defeat upon Lee and his Army of Northern Virginia.

In the wake of Stonewall Jackson's death, Lee reorganized his army, creating three Corps out of the previous two, with A.P. Hill and Richard S. Ewell "replacing" Jackson. Hill had been a successful division commander, but he was constantly battling bouts of sickness that left him disabled, which would occur at Gettysburg. Ewell had distinguished himself during the Peninsula Campaign, but he suffered a serious injury during Second Manassas that historians often credit as making him more cautious in command upon his return. Ewell is often blamed for the Confederate loss at Gettysburg because of his inaction on Day 1 of the battle. Late in the afternoon of the battle's first day, Lee sent discretionary orders to Ewell that Cemetery Hill be taken "if practicable", but ultimately Ewell chose not to attempt the assault. Lee's order has been criticized because it left too much discretion to Ewell, leaving historians to speculate on how the more aggressive Stonewall Jackson would have acted on this order if he had lived to command this wing of Lee's army, and how differently the second day of battle would have proceeded with Confederate possession of Culp's Hill or Cemetery Hill. Discretionary orders were customary for General Lee because Jackson and Longstreet, his other principal subordinate, usually reacted to them aggressively and used their initiative to act quickly and forcefully. Ewell's decision not to attack, whether justified or not, may have ultimately cost the Confederates the battle. Edwin Coddington, widely considered the historian who wrote the greatest history of the battle, concluded, "Responsibility for the failure of the Confederates to make an all-out assault on Cemetery Hill on July 1 must rest with Lee. If Ewell had been a Jackson he might have been able to regroup his forces quickly enough to attack within an hour after the Yankees had started to retreat through the town. The likelihood of success decreased rapidly after that time unless Lee were willing to risk everything."

General Ewell

The second day of the fighting at Gettysburg may have also been dramatically shaped by the experiences at Chancellorsville. On Day 2 of the battle, Union III Corps commander Dan Sickles disobeyed Meade's orders and took it upon himself to advance his entire corps one half mile forward to a peach orchard, poising himself to take control of higher ground. Some historians assert that Sickles had held a grudge against Meade for taking command from his friend Joseph Hooker and intentionally disregarded orders, but it has also been speculated by some historians that Sickles moved forward to occupy high ground in his front due to the devastation unleashed against the III Corps at Chancellorsville once Confederates took high ground and operated their artillery on Hazel Grove. Sickles's decision at Gettysburg created a gap in the Union line that shaped hours of fighting and resulted in Sickles having the III Corps nearly annihilated in the process.

Given the unorthodox and controversial generalship at the battle, the mortal wounding of Stonewall Jackson at the pinnacle of his brilliant career, and the decisive impact it had on the men that fought it and the battle that came after it, it's no wonder that Chancellorsville continues to fascinate Americans nearly 150 years after it was fought.

Bibliography

Alexander, Edward P. Fighting for the Confederacy: The Personal Recollections of General Edward Porter Alexander. Edited by Gary W. Gallagher.

Catton, Bruce. Glory Road. Garden City, NY: Doubleday and Company, 1952.

Cullen, Joseph P. "Battle of Chancellorsville." In Battle Chronicles of the Civil War: 1863, edited by James M. McPherson. Connecticut: Grey Castle Press, 1989.

Freeman, Douglas S. Lee's Lieutenants: A Study in Command. 3 vols. New York: Scribner, 1946.

Furgurson, Ernest B. Chancellorsville 1863: The Souls of the Brave. New York: Knopf, 1992.

Gallagher, Gary W. The Battle of Chancellorsville. National Park Service Civil War series. Conshohocken, PA: U.S. National Park Service and Eastern National, 1995.

Hebert, Walter H. Fighting Joe Hooker. Lincoln: University of Nebraska Press, 1999.

Krick, Robert K. Chancellorsville—Lee's Greatest Victory. New York: American Heritage Publishing Co., 1990.

Sears, Stephen W. Chancellorsville. Boston: Houghton Mifflin, 1996.

The Battle of Gettysburg

Chapter 1: The Battle of Brandy Station

In the spring of 1863, General Lee discovered that McClellan had known of his plans and was able to force a battle at Antietam before all of General Lee's forces had arrived. General Lee now believed that he could successfully invade the North again, and that his defeat before was due in great measure to a stroke of bad luck. In addition, General Lee hoped to supply his army on the unscathed fields and towns of the North, while giving war ravaged northern Virginia a rest. After Chancellorsville, Longstreet and Lee met to discuss options for the Confederate Army's summer campaign. Longstreet advocated detachment of all or part of his corps to be sent to Tennessee, citing Union Maj. General Ulysses S. Grant's advance on Vicksburg, the critical Confederate stronghold on the Mississippi River. Longstreet argued that a reinforced army under Bragg could defeat Rosecrans and drive toward the Ohio River, compelling Grant to release his hold on Vicksburg. Lee, however, was opposed to a division of his army and instead advocated a large-scale offensive (and raid) into Pennsylvania. In addition, General Lee hoped to supply his army on the unscathed fields and towns of the North, while giving war ravaged northern Virginia a rest.

Knowing that victories on Virginia soil meant little to an enemy that could simply retreat, regroup, and then return with more men and more advanced equipment, Lee set his sights on a Northern invasion, aiming to turn Northern opinion against the war and against President Lincoln. With his men already half-starved from dwindling provisions, Lee intended to confiscate food, horses, and equipment as they pushed north--and hopefully influence Northern politicians into giving up their support of the war by penetrating into Harrisburg or even Philadelphia. Given the right circumstances, Lee's army might even be able to capture either Baltimore or Philadelphia and use the city as leverage in peace negotiations.

In the wake of Jackson's death, Lee reorganized his army, creating three Corps out of the previous two, with A.P. Hill and Richard S. Ewell "replacing" Stonewall. Hill had been a successful division commander, but he was constantly battling bouts of sickness that left him disabled, which would occur at Gettysburg. Ewell had distinguished himself during the Peninsula Campaign, suffering a serious injury that historians often credit as making him more cautious in command upon his return.

In early June, the Army of Northern Virginia occupied Culpeper, Virginia. After their victories at Fredericksburg and Chancellorsville against armies twice their size, Confederate troops felt invincible and anxious to carry the war north into Pennsylvania. Assuming his role as Lee's "Eyes of the Army" for the Pennsylvania Campaign, Stuart bivouacked his men near the Rappahannock River, screening the Confederate Army against surprise Union attacks. Taken with his recent successes, Stuart requested a full field review of his units by General Lee, and on

June 8, paraded his nearly 9,000 mounted troops and four batteries of horse artillery for review, also charging in simulated battle at Inlet Station about two miles southwest of Brandy Station. While Lee himself was unavailable to attend the review, some of the cavalrymen and newspaper reporters at the scene complained that all Stuart was doing was "feeding his ego and exhausting the horses." He began to be referred to as a "headline-hunting show-off."

Despite the critics, Stuart basked in the glory. Renowned Civil War historian Stephen Sears described the scene, "The grand review of June 5 was surely the proudest day of Jeb Stuart's thirty years. As he led a cavalcade of resplendent staff officers to the reviewing stand, trumpeters heralded his coming and women and girls strewed his path with flowers. Before all of the spectators the assembled cavalry brigade stretched a mile and a half. After Stuart and his entourage galloped past the line in review, the troopers in their turn saluted the reviewing stand in columns of squadrons. In performing a second "march past," the squadrons started off at a trot, then spurred to a gallop. Drawing sabers and breaking into the Rebel yell, the troopers rush toward the horse artillery drawn up in battery. The gunners responded defiantly, firing blank charges. Amidst this tumult of cannon fire and thundering hooves, a number of ladies swooned in their escorts' arms."[6]

However much Stuart enjoyed "horsing around", there was serious work to be done. The following day, Lee ordered Stuart to cross the Rappahannock and raid Union forward positions, shielding the Confederate Army from observation or interference as it moved north. Already anticipating this imminent offensive move, Stuart had ordered his troops back into formation around Brandy Station. Here, Stuart would endure the first of two low points in his military career: the Battle of Brandy Station, the largest predominantly cavalry engagement of the Civil War.

Union Maj. General Joseph Hooker interpreted Stuart's presence around Culpeper as a precursor to a raid on his army's supply lines. In response, he ordered his cavalry commander, Maj. General Alfred Pleasonton, to take a combined force of 8,000 cavalry and 3,000 infantry on a raid to "disperse and destroy" the 9,500 Confederates. Crossing the Rappahannock River in two columns on June 9,1863 at Beverly's Ford and Kelly's Ford, the first infantry unit caught Stuart completely off-guard, and the second surprised him yet again. Suddenly the Confederates were being battered both front and rear by mounted Union troops.

In addition to being the largest cavalry battle of the war, the chaos and confusion that ensued across the battlefield also made Brandy Station unique in that most of the fighting was done while mounted and using sabers. One account of the battle noted, "Of the bodies that littered the field that day, the vast majority were found to have perished by the sword."

---

6   Sears, Stephen W. *Gettysburg*. Page 64.

After 10 hours of charges and countercharges that swept back and forth across Fleetwood Hill (where Stuart had headquartered the night before) involving drawn sabers and revolvers, Pleasonton decided to withdraw his exhausted men across the Rappahannock River. Stuart immediately claimed a Confederate victory because his men had managed to hold the field and inflicted more casualties on the enemy while forcing Pleasonton to withdraw before locating Lee's infantry. But Stuart was trying to save face, and nobody else, including Lee, took his view of the battle. The fact was, the Southern cavalry under Stuart had not detected the movement of two large columns of Union cavalry and had fallen prey to not one but *two* surprise attacks. Two days later the Richmond *Enquirer* reported, "If Gen. Stuart is to be the eyes and ears of the army we advise him to see more, and be seen less. Gen. Stuart has suffered no little in public estimation by the late enterprises of the enemy."[7]

Lee was now painfully aware of the increased competency of the Union cavalry, as well as the decline of the seemingly once-invincible Southern mounted armed forces under Stuart. Moreover, Stuart was now smarting from the negative publicity and the hit his reputation had taken at Brandy Station. The prideful, vainglorious cavalry leader hoped to bring glory to himself.

Chapter 2: Lee Invades Pennsylvania

During the first weeks of summer of 1863, as Stuart screened the army and completed several well-executed offenses against Union cavalry, many historians think it likely that he had already planned to remove the negative effect of Brandy Station by duplicating one of his now famous circumnavigating rides around the enemy army. But as Lee began his march north through the Shenandoah Valley in western Virginia, it is highly unlikely that is what he wanted or expected.

Before setting out on June 22, the methodical Lee gave Stuart specific instructions as to the role he was to play in the Pennsylvania offensive: as the "Eyes of the Army" he was to guard the mountain passes with part of his force while the Army of Northern Virginia was still south of the Potomac River, and then cross the river with the remainder of his army and screen the right flank of Confederate general Richard Stoddert Ewell's Second Corps as it moved down the Shenandoah Valley, maintaining contact with Ewell's army as it advanced towards Harrisburg.

But instead of taking the most direct route north near the Blue Ridge Mountains, Stuart chose a much more ambitious course of action.

Stuart decided to march his three best brigades (under Generals Hampton and Fitzhugh Lee, and Col. John R. Chambliss) between the Union army and Washington, north through Rockville to Westminster, and then into Pennsylvania--a route that would allow them to capture supplies along the way and wreak havoc as they skirted Washington. In the aftermath, the *Washington*

---

[7]   Wert, Jeffry D. *Cavalryman of the Lost Cause: A Biography of J.E.B. Stuart.* Page 251.

Star would write: "The cavalry chief [Stuart] interpreted his marching orders in a way that best suited his nature, and detached his 9000 troopers from their task of screening the main army and keeping tabs on the Federals. When Lee was in Pennsylvania anxiously looking for him, Stuart crossed the Potomac above Washington and captured a fine prize of Federal supply wagons . . . ."[8]

But to complicate matters even more, as Stuart set out on June 25 on what was probably a glory-seeking mission, he was unaware that his intended path was blocked by columns of Union infantry that would invariably force him to veer farther east than he or Lee had anticipated. Ultimately, his decision would prevent him from linking up with Ewell as ordered and deprive Lee of his primary cavalry force as he advanced deeper and deeper into unfamiliar enemy territory. According to Halsey Wigfall (son of Confederate States Senator Louis Wigfall) who was in Stuart's infantry, "Stuart and his cavalry left [Lee's] army on June 24 and did not contact [his] army again until the afternoon of July 2, the second day of the [Gettysburg] battle."[9]

According to Stuart's own account, on June 29 his men clashed briefly with two companies of Union cavalry in Westminster, Maryland, overwhelming and chasing them "a long distance on the Baltimore road," causing a "great panic" in the city of Baltimore. On June 30, the head of Stuart's column then encountered Union Brig. General Judson Kilpatrick's cavalry as it passed through Hanover--reportedly capturing a wagon train and scattering the Union army--after which Kilpatrick's men were able to regroup and drive Stuart and his men out of town. Then after a twenty-mile trek in the dark, Stuart's exhausted men reached Dover, Pennsylvania, on the morning of July 1 (which they briefly occupied).

Late on the second day of the battle, Stuart finally arrived, bringing with him the caravan of captured Union supply wagons, and he was immediately reprimanded by Lee. One account describes Lee as "visibly angry" raising his hand "as if to strike the tardy cavalry commander."[10] While that does not sound like Lee's style, Stuart has been heavily criticized ever since, and it has been speculated Lee took him to task harshly enough that Stuart offered his resignation. Lee didn't accept it, but he would later note in his after battle report that the cavalry had not updated him as to the Army of the Potomac's movements.

Given great discretion in his cavalry operations before the battle, Stuart's cavalry was too far removed from the Army of Northern Virginia to warn Lee of the Army of the Potomac's movements. As it would turn out, Lee's army inadvertently stumbled into Union cavalry and then the Union army at Gettysburg on the morning of July 1, 1863, walking blindly into what

[8]   Stepp, John W. & Hill, William I. (editors), *Mirror of War, the Washington Star reports the Civil War*. Page 199.
[9]   Eaton, Clement. *Jefferson Davis*. Page 178.
[10]   Philips, David. *Crucial Land Battles*. Page 75.

became the largest battle of the war.

Meade Takes Command

Though he had privately confided to his wife that he desired command of the Army of the Potomac, Meade never publicly expressed his wishes to those in charge, thus avoiding the political squabbling among generals. On June 28, however, he got his wish.

Before sunrise on that morning, a messenger entered Major General George Meade's field headquarters, shook the sleeping general and said, "I'm afraid I've come to give you some trouble, General."[11] Jumping to his feet, Meade's first thought was that he was being arrested-- probably for arguing with Hooker on the battlefield. Informed that he had replaced Maj. General Joseph Hooker as commander of the Army of the Potomac (Lincoln had passed over his friend, the more qualified John F. Reynolds), Meade at first protested, stating that he didn't want the job. Informed that his promotion was not a "request," Meade hitched up his sagging long underwear, ran his fingers through his thinning hair and said, "Well, I've been tried and condemned without a hearing, and I suppose I shall have to go to the execution."[12] Historians have also speculated that it may well have been Mead's foreign birth that got him selected over Reynolds. As such, he was excluded from running for the U. S. Presidency and therefore posed no future threat to Lincoln, as Reynolds may have if successful. Of course, that doesn't square with reports that Reynolds turned the offer down.

In addition to being informed by Hooker that he was in command, Meade received a telegram from general-in-chief Henry Halleck:

"General:
You will receive with this the order of the President placing you in command of the Army of the Potomac. Considering the circumstances, no one ever received a more important command; and I cannot doubt that you will fully justify the confidence which the Government has reposed in you.
You will not be hampered by any minute instructions from these headquarters. Your army is free to act as you may deem proper under the circumstances as they arise. You will, however, keep in view the important fact that the Army of the Potomac is the covering army of Washington, as well as the army of operation against the invading forces of the rebels. You will therefore manoeuvre and fight in such a manner as to cover the Capital and also Baltimore, as far as circumstances will admit. Should General Lee move upon either of these places, it is expected that you will either anticipate him or arrive with him, so as to give him battle.
All forces within the sphere of your operations will be held subject to your orders.

---

[11]   Stevens, Joseph E. *1863: The Rebirth of a Nation*. Page 230.
[12]   Stevens, Joseph E. *1863: The Rebirth of a Nation*. Page 231.

Harper's Ferry and its garrison are under your direct orders.

You are authorized to remove from command and send from your army any officer or other person you may deem proper; and to appoint to command as you may deem expedient.

In fine, General, you are intrusted with all the power and authority which the President, the Secretary of War, or the General-in-Chief can confer on you, and you may rely on our full support.

You will keep me fully informed of all your movements and the positions of your own troops and those of the enemy, so far as known.

I shall always be ready to advise and assist you to the utmost of my ability.

Very respectfully,

Your obedient servant,

H. W. Halleck, General-in-Chief."

Meade then issued General Orders No. 67:

By direction of the President of the United States, I hereby assume command of the Army of the Potomac.

As a soldier, in obeying this order—an order totally unexpected and unsolicited—I have no promises or pledges to make.

The country looks to this army to relieve it from the devastation and disgrace of a foreign invasion. Whatever fatigues and sacrifices we may be called upon to undergo, let us have in view, constantly, the magnitude of the interests involved, and let each man determine to do his duty, leaving to an all-controlling Providence the decision of the contest.

It is with great diffidence that I relieve in the command of this army an eminent and accomplished soldier, whose name must ever appear conspicuous in the history of its achievements; but I rely upon the hearty support of my companions in arms to assist me in the discharge of the duties of the important trust which has been confided to me.

George G. Meade, Major General, commanding.

When word of Meade's promotion spread around camp, it certainly surprised many men. After all, Meade lacked charisma, did not exude confidence, and did not arouse enthusiasm among his men by his presence. In fact, considering the many times he'd been wounded (or nearly wounded), many considered him a danger to his men and to himself. Even his trusty horse "Old Baldy" had been wounded under him at Second Bull Run and again at Antietam. Ultimately, the best thing his men could say about him was that at least he had never made any ruinous mistakes.

Assuming command of the Army of the Potomac on June 28 at Prospect Hall in Frederick,

Maryland, (with his second son, George, now part of his staff), Meade had his work cut out for him, though few apparently considered his position. Having to first locate his forces, he then had to review Hooker's strategy, study the most recent intelligence reports, and then determine the appropriate course of action, all the while keeping an eye fixed on Lee. Ultimately disregarding Hooker's plans to strike into the Cumberland Valley, Meade opted to march on Harrisburg, Pennsylvania to move toward the Susquehanna River, keeping his troops between Lee's army and Washinton.

Upon taking command, Meade began drawing up defensive positions around northern Maryland about a dozen miles south of Gettysburg. His proposed line would be referred to as the Pipe Creek Circular, but it would never be implemented due to actions outside of Meade's control.

It is believed that one of the first notices Lee got about the Army of the Potomac's movements actually came from a spy named "Harrison", a man who apparently worked undercover for Longstreet but of whom little is known. Harrison reported that General George G. Meade was now in command of the Union Army and was at that very moment marching north to meet Lee's army. According to Longstreet, he and Lee were supposedly on the same page at the beginning of the campaign. "His plan or wishes announced, it became useless and improper to offer suggestions leading to a different course. All that I could ask was that the policy of the campaign should be one of defensive tactics; that we should work so as to force the enemy to attack us, in such good position as we might find in our own country, so well adapted to that purpose—which might assure us of a grand triumph. To this he readily assented as an important and material adjunct to his general plan." Lee later claimed he "had never made any such promise, and had never thought of doing any such thing," but in his official report after the battle, Lee also noted, "It had not been intended to fight a general battle at such a distance from our base, unless attacked by the enemy.

Chapter 3: July 1, 1863

Without question, the most famous battle of the Civil War took place outside of the small town of Gettysburg, Pennsylvania, which happened to be a transporation hub, serving as the center of a wheel with several roads leading out to other Pennsylvanian towns. Lee was unaware of Meade's position when an advanced division of Hill's Corps marched toward Gettysburg on the morning of July 1.

The battle began with John Buford's Union cavalry forces skirmishing against the advancing division of Heth's just outside of town. Buford intentionally fought a delaying action that was meant to allow John Reynolds' I Corps to reach Gettysburg and engage the Confederates, which eventually set the stage for a general battle.

Buford

The I Corps was led by Pennsylvanian General John F. Reynolds, an effective general that had been considered for command of the entire army in place of Hooker and was considered by many the best general in the army. Since Lee had invaded Pennsylvania, many believe that Reynolds was even more active and aggressive than he might have otherwise been. In any event, Reynolds was personally at the front positioning two brigades, exhorting his men, "Forward men! Forward for God's sake, and drive those fellows out of the woods."

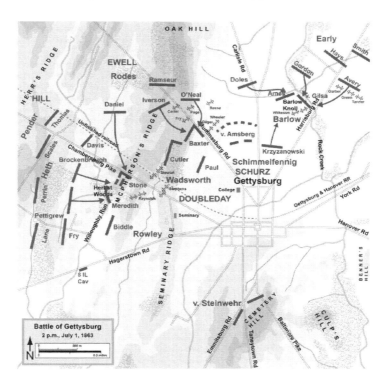

Battle of Gettysburg
2 p.m., July 1, 1863

    As he was at the front positioning his men, Reynolds fell from his horse, having been hit by a bullet behind the ear that killed him almost instantly. With his death, command of the I Corps fell upon Maj. Gen. Abner Doubleday, the Civil War veteran wrongly credited for inventing baseball. Despite the death of the corps commander, the I Corps successfully managed to drive the Confederates in their sector back, highlighted by sharp fighting from the Iron Brigade, a brigade comprised of Wisconsin, Indiana, and Michigan soldiers from the "West". In an unfinished railroad cut, the 6th Wisconsin captured the 2nd Mississippi, and regimental commander Rufus Dawes reported, "The officer replied not a word, but promptly handed me his sword, and his men, who still held them, threw down their muskets. The coolness, self possession, and discipline which held back our men from pouring a general volley saved a hundred lives of the enemy, and as my mind goes back to the fearful excitement of the moment, I marvel at it."

Reynolds

Around noon, the battle hit a lull, in part because Confederate division commander Henry Heth was under orders to avoid a general battle in the absence of the rest of the Army of Northern Virginia. At that point, however, the Union had gotten the better of the fighting, and the Confederate army was concentrating on the area, with more soldiers in Hill's corps in the immediate vicinity and Ewell's corps marching from the north toward the town.

As the Union's I Corps held the line, General Oliver O. Howard and his XI Corps came up on the right of the I Corps, eager to replace the stain the XI Corps had suffered at Chancellorsville thanks to Stonewall Jackson. As a general battle began to form northwest of town, news was making its way back to Meade several miles away that Reynolds had been killed, and that a battle was developing.

Meade had been drawing up a proposed defensive line several miles away from Gettysburg near Emmitsburg, Maryland, but when news of the morning's fighting reached him, Meade sent II Corps commander Winfield Scott Hancock ahead to take command in the field, putting him in temporary command of the "left wing" of the army consisting of the I, II, III and XI Corps. Meade also charged Hancock with determining whether to fight the general battle near Gettysburg or to pull back to the line Meade had been drawing up. Hancock would not be the senior officer on the field (Oliver Howard outranked him), so the fact that he was ordered to take command of the field demonstrates how much Meade trusted him.

As Hancock headed toward the fighting, and while the Army of the Potomac's I and XI Corps engaged in heavy fighting, they were eventually flanked from the north by Ewell's Confederate Corps, which was returning toward Gettysburg from its previous objective. For the XI Corps, it was certainly reminiscent of their retreat at Chancellorsville, and they began a disorderly retreat through the streets of the small town. Fighting broke out in various places throughout the town, while some Union soldiers hid in and around houses for the duration of the battle. Gettysburg's citizens also fled in the chaos and fighting.

After a disorderly retreat through the town itself, the Union men began to dig in on high ground to the southeast of the town. When Hancock met up with Howard, the two briefly argued over the leadership arrangement, until Howard finally acquiesced. Hancock told the XI Corps commander, "I think this the strongest position by nature upon which to fight a battle that I ever saw." When Howard agreed, Hancock replied, "Very well, sir, I select this as the battle-field."

As the Confederates sent the Union corps retreating, Lee arrived on the field and saw the importance of the defensive positions the Union men were taking up along Cemetery Hill and Culp's Hill. Late in the afternoon, Lee sent discretionary orders to Ewell that Cemetery Hill be taken "if practicable", but ultimately Ewell chose not to attempt the assault. Lee's order has been criticized because it left too much discretion to Ewell, leaving historians to speculate on how the more aggressive Stonewall Jackson would have acted on this order if he had lived to command this wing of Lee's army, and how differently the second day of battle would have proceeded with Confederate possession of Culp's Hill or Cemetery Hill. Discretionary orders were customary for General Lee because Jackson and Longstreet, his other principal subordinate, usually reacted to them aggressively and used their initiative to act quickly and forcefully. Ewell's decision not to attack, whether justified or not, may have ultimately cost the Confederates the battle. Edwin Coddington, widely considered the historian who wrote the greatest history of the battle, concluded, "Responsibility for the failure of the Confederates to make an all-out assault on Cemetery Hill on July 1 must rest with Lee. If Ewell had been a Jackson he might have been able to regroup his forces quickly enough to attack within an hour after the Yankees had started to retreat through the town. The likelihood of success decreased rapidly after that time unless Lee were willing to risk everything."

With so many men engaged and now taking refuge on the high ground, Meade, who was an engineer like Lee, abandoned his previous plan to draw up a defensive line around Emmittsburg a few miles to the south. After a council of war, the Army of the Potomac decided to defend at Gettysburg.

Day 1 by itself would have been one of the 25 biggest battles of the Civil War, and it was a tactical Confederate victory. Union casualties were almost 9,000, and the Confederates suffered slightly more than 6,000. But the battle had just started, and thanks to the actions of Meade and Hancock, the largest battle on the North American continent would take place on the ground of their choosing.

Chapter 4: July 2, 1863

By the morning of July 2, Major General Meade had put in place what he thought to be the optimal battle strategy. Positioning his now massive Army of the Potomac in what would become known as the "fish hook", he'd established a line configuration that was much more compact and maneuverable than Lee's, which allowed Meade to shift his troops quickly from inactive parts of the line to those under attack without creating new points of vulnerability. Moreover, Meade's army was taking a defensive stance on the high ground anchored by Culp's Hill, Cemetery Hill, and Cemetery Ridge. Meade also personally moved the III Corps under Maj. General Daniel Sickles into position on the left of the line.

On the morning of July 2, Meade was determined to make a stand at Gettysburg, and Lee was determined to strike at him. That morning, Lee decided to make strong attacks on both Union flanks while feinting in the middle, ordering Ewell's corps to attack Culp's Hill on the Union right while Longstreet's corps would attack on the Union left. Lee hoped to seize Cemetery Hill, which would give the Confederates the high ground to harass the Union supply lines and command the road to Washington, D.C. Lee also believed that the best way to do so would be to use Longstreet's corps to launch an attack up the Emmitsburg Road, which he figured would roll up the Union's left flank, presumed to be on Cemetery Hill. Lee was mistaken, due in part to the fact Stuart and his cavalry couldn't perform reconnaissance. In fact, the Union line extended farther south than Cemetery Hill, with the II Corps positioned on Cemetery Ridge and the III Corps nearly as far south as the base of Little Round Top and Round Top. Moreover, Ewell protested that this battle plan would demoralize his men, since they'd be forced to give up the ground they had captured the day before.

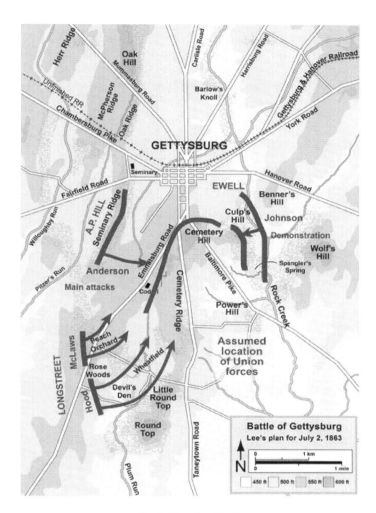

Lee's Plan for July 2

Longstreet's Assault

As it turned out, both attacks ordered by Lee would come too late. Though there was a controversy over when Lee ordered Longstreet's attack, Longstreet's march got tangled up and caused several hours of delay. Lost Cause advocates attacking Longstreet would later claim his attack was supposed to take place as early as possible, although no official Confederate orders gave a time for the attack. Lee gave the order for the attack around 11:00 a.m., and it is known that Longstreet was reluctant about making it; he still wanted to slide around the Union flank, interpose the Confederate army between Washington D.C. and the Army of the Potomac, and force Meade to attack them. Between Longstreet's delays and the mixup in the march that forced parts of his corps to double back and make a winding march, Longstreet's men weren't ready to attack until about 4:00 p.m.

Longstreet's biographer, Jeffrey Wert, wrote, "Longstreet deserves censure for his performance on the morning of July 2. He allowed his disagreement with Lee's decision to affect his conduct. Once the commanding general determined to assail the enemy, duty required Longstreet to comply with the vigor and thoroughness that had previously characterized his generalship. The concern for detail, the regard for timely information, and the need for preparation were absent." Edwin Coddington, whose history of the Gettysburg Campaign still continues to be considered the best ever written, described Longstreet's march as "a comedy of errors such as one might expect of inexperienced commanders and raw militia, but not of Lee's ' War Horse' and his veteran troops." Coddington considered it "a dark moment in Longstreet's career as a general."

Writing about July 2, Longstreet criticized Lee, insisting once again that the right move was to move around the Union flank. "The opportunity for our right was in the air. General Halleck saw it from Washington. General Meade saw and was apprehensive of it. Even General Pendleton refers to it in favorable mention in his official report. Failing to adopt it, General Lee should have gone with us to his right. He had seen and carefully examined the left of his line, and only gave us a guide to show the way to the right, leaving the battle to be adjusted to formidable and difficult grounds without his assistance. If he had been with us, General Hood's messengers could have been referred to general Headquarters, but to delay and send messengers five miles in favor of a move that he had rejected would have been contumacious. The opportunity was with the Confederates from the assembling on Cemetery Hill. It was inviting of their preconceived plans. It was the object of and excuse for the invasion as a substitute for more direct efforts for the relief of Vicksburg. Confederate writers and talkers claim that General Meade could have escaped without making aggressive battle, but that is equivalent to confession of the inertia that failed to grasp the opportunity."

As Longstreet's men began their circuitous march, Union III Corps commander Dan Sickles took it upon himself to advance his entire corps one half mile forward to a peach orchard, poising himself to take control of higher ground. Some historians assert that Sickles had held a grudge against Meade for taking command from his friend Joseph Hooker and intentionally disregarded orders. It has also been speculated by some historians that Sickles moved forward to occupy high ground in his front due to the devastation unleashed against the III Corps at Chancellorsville once Confederates took high ground and operated their artillery on Hazel Grove. Sickles and

Meade would feud over the actions on Day 2 in the years after the war, after Sickles (who lost a leg that day) took credit for the victory by disrupting Lee's attack plans. Historians have almost universally sided with Meade, pointing out that Sickles nearly had his III Corps annihilated during Longstreet's attack.

Sickles

Whatever the reasoning for Sickles' move, this unauthorized action completely undermined Meade's overall strategy by effectively isolating Sickles' corps from the rest of the Union line and exposing the Union left flank in the process. By the early afternoon of July 2, nothing but the fog of war was preventing the Confederates from turning and crushing Sickles' forces, then moving to outflank the entire Union Army.

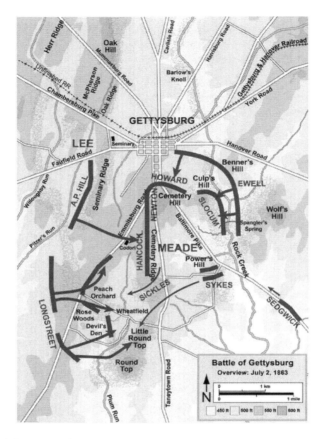

With General George Meade once again in command, General Hancock and the II Corps was positioned on Cemetery Ridge, roughly in the center of the Union line. Since Lee intended to strike at both Union flanks, theoretically Hancock's men should very well not have been engaged at all on the second day of the battle. But as a result of the fact Sickles had moved his men so far out of position, it created a major gap in the Union line and brought the III Corps directly into Longstreet's path. It was 4:00 p.m. by the time Longstreet's two divisions were in position for the attack, and they were taken completely by surprise whent hey found the III Corps in front of them on the Emmitsburg Road. Division commander John Bell Hood lobbied Longstreet to change up the plan of attack, but at this late time in the day Longstreet refused to modify Lee's orders.

Thus, in the late afternoon, the fighting on Day 2 began in earnest, and Longstreet's assault commenced by smashing into Sickles III Corps, engaging them in a peach orchard, wheat field, and Devil's Den, an outcropping of boulders that provided the Confederates prime cover.

When it became obvious that Sickles' III Corps was in dire straits, the chaos in that sector acted like a vacuum that induced both sides to pour more men into the vicinity. Moreover, when Sickles was injured by a cannonball that nearly blew off his leg, command of the III Corps fell upon II Corps commander Hancock as well. As Meade tried to shuffle reinforcements to his left, Hancock sent in his II Corps' First Division (under Brig. General John C. Caldwell) to reinforce the III Corps in the wheat field. The fighting in the wheat field was so intense that Caldwell's division would be all but annihilated during the afternoon.

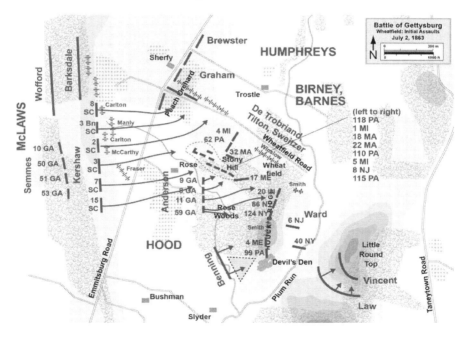

At the same time, men from Confederate General A. P. Hill's corps made their advance toward the Union center, forcing the Army of the Potomac to rally defenses and rushed unit to critical spots to patch the holes. With Hill in his front and Longstreet's attack to his left, Hancock was in the unenviable position of having to attempt to resist Confederate advances spread out over a few miles, at least until more and more reserves could be rushed over from the other side of the Union line to the army's left flank. At one point, Hancock ordered a regiment to make what was essentially a suicidal bayonet charge into the face of Hill's Confederates on Cemetery Ridge. Hancock sent the First Minnesota to charge a Confederate brigade four times its size. One of the Minnesota volunteers, one William Lochren later said, "Every man realized in an instant what the order meant -- death or wounds to us all; the sacrifice of the regiment to gain a few minutes time and save the position, and probably the battlefield -- and every man saw and accepted the necessity of the sacrifice."[13] While extremely costly to the regiment (the Minnesotans suffered 87% casualties, the worst of any regiment at Gettysburg), this heroic sacrifice bought time to organize the defensive line and kept the battle from turning in favor of the Confederates. Hancock would write of them, "I cannot speak too highly of this regiment and its commander in its attack, as well as in its subsequent advance against the enemy, in which it lost three-fourths of the officers and men engaged."

As Longstreet's assault on the Union left continued, his line naturally got more and more entangled as well. As Longstreet's men kept moving to their right, they reached the base of Little Round Top and Round Top, two rocky hills south of Gettysburg proper, at the far left. When Meade's chief engineer, Brig. General Gouverneur Warren, spotted the sun shining off the bayonets of Longstreet's men as they moved toward the Union left, it alerted the Army of the Potomac of the need to occupy Little Round Top, high ground that commanded much of the field.

With Warren having alerted his superiors to the importance of Little Round Top, Strong Vincent's brigade moved into position, under orders from Warren to "hold this ground at any costs," As part of Strong Vincent's brigade, Chamberlain's 20th Maine was on the left of the line, and thus Chamberlain's unit represented the extreme left of the Army of the Potomac's line.

In front of Vincent's brigade was General Evander Law's advancing Alabama Brigade (of Hood's Division). Law ordered 5 regiments to take Little Round Top, the 4th, 15th, and 47th Alabama, and the 4th and 5th Texas, but they had already marched more than 20 miles just to reach that point. They were now being asked to charge up high ground on a muggy, hot day.

Nevertheless, the Confederates made desperate assaults against Little Round Top, even after being repulsed by the Union defenders several times. In the middle of the fighting, after he saw Confederates trying to push around his flank, Chamberlain stretched his line until his regiment was merely a single-file line, and he then had to order his left (southernmost) half to swing back, thus forming an angle in their line in an effort to prevent a flank attack. Despite suffering heavy losses, the 20th Maine held through two subsequent charges by the 15th Alabama and other Confederate regiments for nearly 2 hours.

---

[13]   Davis, Kenneth C. *The Civil War: Everything You Need to Know About America's Greatest Conflict but Never Learned.* Page 301.

Chamberlain

Even after repulsing the Confederates several times, Chamberlain and his regiment faced a serious dilemma. With casualties mounting and ammunition running low, in desperation, Chamberlain *claimed* to have ordered his left wing to initiate an all-out, pivoting bayonet charge. With the 20th Maine charging ahead, the left wing wheeling continually to make the charging line swing like a hinge, thus creating a simultaneous frontal assault and flanking maneuver, they ultimately succeeded in not only taking the hill, but capturing 100 Confederate soldiers in the process. Chamberlain suffered two slight wounds in the battle, one when a shot ricocheted off his sword scabbard and bruised his thigh, another when his right foot was struck by a piece of shrapnel. With this success, Chamberlain was credited with preventing the Union flank from being penetrated and keeping the Confederates from pouring in behind Union lines.

Ultimately, it was the occupation and defense of Little Round Top that saved the rest of the Union line at Gettysburg. Had the Confederates commanded that high ground, it would have been able to position artillery that could have swept the Union lines along Cemetery Ridge and Cemetery Hill, which would have certainly forced the Army of the Potomac to withdraw from their lines. Chamberlain would be awarded the coveted Congressional Medal of Honor for "daring heroism and great tenacity in holding his position on the Little Round Top against repeated assaults, and carrying the advance position on the Great Round Top", and the 20th Maine's actions that day became one of the most famous attacks of the Battle of Gettysburg and the Civil War as a whole.

But did it really happen that way? Though historians have mostly given Chamberlain the credit for the order to affix bayonets and make the charge down Little Round Top, and Chamberlain received the credit from Sharaa's *The Killer Angels* and the movie *Gettysburg*, some recent researchers have claimed that Lt. Holman S. Melcher initiated the charge. According to

Chamberlain however, Melcher had requested permission to make an advance to help some of his wounded men, only to be told by Chamberlain that a charge was about to be ordered anyway.

While Chamberlain's men held the extreme left, the rest of Vincent's brigade struggled desperately to the right, and Vincent himself would be mortally wounded in the fighting. The Confederates had advanced as far as Devil's Den, but Warren continued to bring reinforcements to Little Round Top to hold off Confederate attempts on the high ground. For the rest of the battle, even after the Confederates were repulsed from Little Round Top, their snipers in Devil's Den made the defenders of Little Round Top miserable. Confederate sharpshooters stationed around Devil's Den mortally wounded General Stephen Weed, whose New York brigade had arrived as reinforcements, and when his friend, artilleryman Lt. Charles Hazlett leaned over to comfort Weed or hear what he was trying to say, snipers shot Hazlett dead as well.

The fighting on the Union left finally ended as night fell. George Sykes, the commander of the V Corps, later described Day 2 in his official report, "Night closed the fight. The key of the battle-field was in our possession intact. Vincent, Weed, and Hazlett, chiefs lamented throughout the corps and army, sealed with their lives the spot intrusted to their keeping, and on which so much depended.... General Weed and Colonel Vincent, officers of rare promise, gave their lives to their country."

Ewell's Attack

Ewell's orders from Lee had been to launch a demonstration on the Union right flank during Longstreet's attack, which started at about 4:00 p.m. as well, and in support of the demonstration by Hill's corps in the center. For that reason, Ewell would not launch his general assault on Culp's Hill and Cemetery Hill until 7:00 p.m.

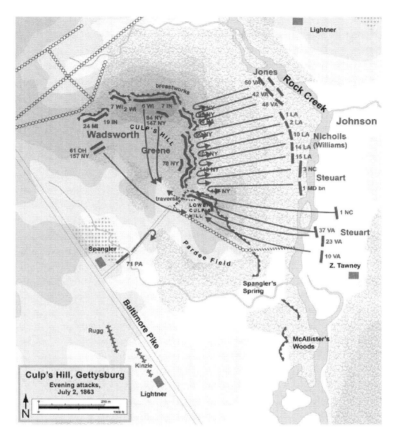

Culp's Hill, Gettysburg
Evening attacks,
July 2, 1863

While the Army of the Potomac managed to desperately hold on the left, Ewell's attack against Culp's Hill on the other end of the field met with some success in pushing the Army of the Potomac back. However, the attack started so late in the day that nightfall made it impossible for the Confederates to capitalize on their success. Due to darkness, a Confederate brigade led by George H. Steuart was unaware that they were firmly beside the Army of the Potomac's right flank, which would have given them almost unlimited access to the Union army's rear and its supply lines and line of communication, just 600 yards away. the main line of communication for the Union army, the Baltimore Pike, only 600 yards to their front. Col. David Ireland and the 137th New York desperately fought to preserve the Union army's flank, much the same way Chamberlain and the 20th Maine had on the other side, and in the process the 137th lost a third of their men.

Ewell's men would spend the night at the base of Culp's Hill and partially up the hill, in positions that had been evacuated by Union soldiers after Meade moved some of them to the left to deal with Longstreet's attack. It would fall upon the Confederates to pick up the attack the next morning.

That night, Meade held another council of war. Having been attacked on both flanks, Meade and his top officers correctly surmised that Lee would attempt an attack on the center of the line the next day. Moreover, captured Confederates and the fighting and intelligence of Day 2 let it be known that the only Confederate unit that had not yet seen action during the fighting was George Pickett's division of Longstreet's corps.

Chapter 5: July 3, 1863

Lee's Plan

If July 2 was Longstreet's worst day of the Civil War, July 3 was almost certainly Robert E. Lee's. After the attack on July 2, Longstreet spent the night continuing to plot potential movements around Little Round Top and Big Round Top, thinking that would again get the Confederate army around the Union's flank. Longstreet himself did not realize that a reserve corps of the Union army was poised to block that maneuver.

Longstreet did not meet with Lee on the night of July 2, so when Lee met with him the following morning he found Longstreet's men were not ready to conduct an early morning attack, which Lee had wanted to attempt just as he was on the other side of the lines against Culp's Hill. With Pickett's men not up, however, Longstreet's corps couldn't make such an attack. Lee later wrote that Longstreet's "dispositions were not completed as early as was expected."

On the morning of July 3, the Confederate attack against Culp's Hill fizzled out, but by then Lee had already planned a massive attack on the Union center, combined with having Stuart's cavalry attack the Union army's lines in the rear. A successful attack would split the Army of the Potomac at the same time its communication and supply lines were severed by Stuart, which would make it possible to capture the entire army in detail.

There was just one problem with the plan, as Longstreet told Lee that morning: no 15,000 men who ever existed could successfully execute the attack. The charge required marching across an open field for about a mile, with the Union artillery holding high ground on all sides of the incoming Confederates. Longstreet ardently opposed the attack, but, already two days into the battle, Lee explained that because the Army of the Potomac was here on the field, he must strike at it. Longstreet later wrote that he said, "General Lee, I have been a soldier all my life. It is my opinion that no fifteen thousand men ever arrayed for battle can take that position."[14] Longstreet proposed instead that their men should slip around the Union forces and occupy the high ground, forcing Northern commanders to attack them, rather than vice versa.

Realizing the insanity of sending 15,000 men hurtling into all the Union artillery, Lee planned to use the Confederate artillery to try to knock out the Union artillery ahead of time. Although old friend William Pendleton was the artillery chief, the artillery cannonade would be supervised by Porter Alexander, Longstreet's chief artillerist, who would have to give the go-ahead to the charging infantry because they were falling under Longstreet's command.

Longstreet was certain of failure, but Pickett and the men preparing to make the charge were confident in their commanders and themselves. As Stuart was in the process of being repulsed, just after 1:00 p.m. 150 Confederate guns began to fire from Seminary Ridge, hoping to incapacitate the Union center before launching an infantry attack. Confederate brigadier Evander Law said of the artillery bombardment, "The cannonade in the center ... presented one of the most magnificent battle-scenes witnessed during the war. Looking up the valley towards Gettysburg, the hills on either side were capped with crowns of flame and smoke, as 300 guns, about equally divided between the two ridges, vomited their iron hail upon each other."

Alexander discussed the early part of the cannonading, including some that he had not ordered:

"A little before noon there sprung up upon our left a violent cannonade which was prolonged for fully a half-hour, and has often been supposed to be a part of that ordered to precede Pickett's charge. It began between skirmishers in front of Hill's corps over the occupation of a house. Hill's artillery first took part in it, it was said, by his order. It was most unwise, as it consumed uselessly a large amount of his ammunition, the lack of which was much felt in the subsequent fighting. Not a single gun of our corps fired a shot, nor did the enemy in our front.

When the firing died out, entire quiet settled upon the field, extending even to the skirmishers in front, and also to the enemy's rear; whence behind their lines opposing us we had heard all the morning the noise of Johnson's combats.

My 75 guns had all been carefully located and made ready for an hour, while the infantry brigades were still not yet in their proper positions, and I was waiting for the signal to come from Longstreet, when it occurred to me to send for the nine howitzers under Richardson, that they might lead in the advance for a few hundred yards before coming into action. Only after the cannonade had opened did I learn that the guns had been removed and could not be found. It afterward appeared that Pendleton had

[14]   Gaffney, P. and D. Gaffney. *The Civil War: Exploring History One Week at a Time*. Page 282.

withdrawn four of the guns, and that Richardson with the other five, finding himself in the line of the Federal fire during Hill's cannonade, had moved off to find cover. I made no complaint, believing that had these guns gone forward with the infantry they must have been left upon the field and perhaps have attracted a counter-stroke after the repulse of Pickett's charge.

Meanwhile, some half-hour or more before the cannonade began, I was startled by the receipt of a note from Longstreet as follows: —

'Colonel: If the artillery fire does not have the effect to drive off the enemy or greatly demoralize him, so as to make our effort pretty certain, I would prefer that you should not advise Pickett to make the charge. I shall rely a great deal upon your judgment to determine the matter and shall expect you to let Gen. Pickett know when the moment offers.'

Until that moment, though I fully recognized the strength of the enemy's position, I had not doubted that we would carry it, in my confidence that Lee was ordering it. But here was a proposition that I should decide the question. Overwhelming reasons against the assault at once seemed to stare me in the face. Gen. Wright of Anderson's division was standing with me. I showed him the letter and expressed my views. He advised me to write them to Longstreet, which I did as follows:—

'General: I will only be able to judge of the effect of our fire on the enemy by his return fire, as his infantry is little exposed to view and the smoke will obscure the field. If, as I infer from your note, there is any alternative to this attack, it should be carefully considered before opening our fire, for it will take all the artillery ammunition we have left to test this one, and if result is unfavorable we will have none left for another effort. And even if this is entirely successful, it can only be so at a very bloody cost.'

To this note, Longstreet soon replied as follows: —

'Colonel: The intention is to advance the infantry if the artillery has the desired effect of driving the enemy's off, or having other effect such as to warrant us in making the attack. When that moment arrives advise Gen. Pickett and of course advance such artillery as you can use in aiding the attack.'"

At daylight Pickett had advanced his division to a spot "into a field near a branch," a few hundred yards behind the main Confederate line on Seminary Ridge. Forming battlelines, his men advanced east a few hundred yards before being ordered to lie down and wait. Advancing again through Spangler's Woods, they were again directed to lay down—this time behind the crest on which the Confederate artillery batteries were perched. Jocking for position to form the right wing of the afternoon's assault, Pickett then had his men form two lines, with Brigadier

Generals James Kemper and Richard Garnett in the first line, right to left, and Brigadier General Lewis Armistead to the rear. As a result, Pickett's men were forced to lay down during a ferocious artillery bombardment from both sides that certainly had to unnerve his men, but Pickett continued a dangerous ride along the lines as Union shells burst all around him, shouting to his men, "Up, men, and to your posts! Don't forget today that you are from Old Virginia."[15] One of the men in Kemper's brigade of Pickett's division recalled, "The first shot or two flew harmlessly over our heads; but soon they began to get the range, and then came--well, what General Gibbon, on the other side, called "pandemonium." First there was an explosion in the top of our friendly tree, sending a shower of limbs upon us. In a second there was another, followed by a piercing shriek, which caused Patton to spring up and run to see what was the matter. Two killed outright and three frightfully wounded, he said on his return."

East Cavalry Field

As Longstreet had predicted, from the beginning the plan was an abject failure. As Stuart's cavalry met its Union counterparts near East Cavalry Field, a young cavalry officer named George Custer convinced division commander Brig. General David McMurtrie Gregg to allow his brigade to stay and fight, even while Custer's own division was stationed to the south out of the action.

---

[15] Vectorsite.net, "July 1863 (3): Don't Forget Today That You Are From Old Virginia."

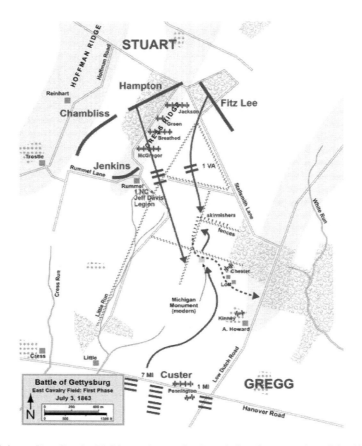

The fighting at East Cavalry Field turned out to be Custer's best known action of the Civil War, and it was his brigade that bore the brunt of the casualties in repulsing Stuart's cavalry. Right as the Confederates were starting the artillery bombardment ahead of Pickett's Charge, Stuart's men met Gregg's on the field.

After Stuart's men sent Union skirmishers scurrying, Gregg ordered Custer to counterattack with the 7th Michigan Cavalry Regiment. Custer led the charge personally, exhorting his men with the rallying cry, "Come on you Wolverines!" In the ensuing melee, which featured sabers and close range shooting, Custer had his horse shot out from under him, at which point he took a bugler's horse and continued fighting. Ultimately, his men sent Stuart's cavalry retreating, forcing Stuart to order in reinforcements.

Custer

Stuart's reinforcements sent the 7th Michigan in retreat, but now Custer rallied the 1st Michigan regiment to charge in yet another counterattack, with the same rallying cry, ""Come on you Wolverines!" Both sides galloped toward each other and crashed head on, engaging in more fierce hand-to-hand combat. Eventually, the Union held the field and forced Stuart's men to retreat.

Custer's brigade lost over 200 men in the attack, the highest loss of any Union cavalry brigade at Gettysburg, but he had just valiantly performed one of the most successful cavalry charges of the war. Custer wasn't exactly humble about his performance, writing in his official report after the battle, "I challenge the annals of warfare to produce a more brilliant or successful charge of cavalry."

Pickett's Charge

As Stuart was in the process of being repulsed, just after 1:00 p.m. 150 Confederate guns began to fire from Seminary Ridge, hoping to incapacitate the Union center before launching an infantry attack, but they mostly overshot their mark. The artillery duel could be heard from dozens of miles away, and all the smoke led to Confederate artillery constantly overshooting their targets. Realizing that the artillery was meant for them as a way of softening them up for an infantry charge, Hancock calmly rode his horse up and down the line of the II Corps, both inspiring and assuring his men with his own courage and resolve. During the massive Confederate artillery bombardment that preceded the infantry assault, Hancock was so conspicuous on horseback reviewing and encouraging his troops that one of his subordinates pleaded with him that "the corps commander ought not to risk his life that way." Hancock reportedly replied, "There are times when a corps commander's life does not count."

At some point before the charge, Pickett apparently managed to somehow hastily write a letter to his wife Sallie:

"At early dawn, darkened by the threatening rain, Armistead, Garnett, Kemper and your Soldier held a heart-to-heart powwow.

All three sent regards to you, and Old Lewis pulled a ring from his little finger and making me take it, said, "Give this little token, George, please, to her of the sunset eyes, with my love, and tell her the 'old man' says since he could not be the lucky dog he's mighty glad that you are."

Dear old Lewis—dear old "Lo," as Magruder always called him, being short for Lothario. Well, my Sally, I'll keep the ring for you, and some day I'll take it to John Tyler and have it made into a breastpin and set around with rubies and diamonds and emeralds. You will be the pearl, the other jewel. Dear old Lewis!

Just as we three separated to go our different ways after silently clasping hands, our fears and prayers voiced in the "Good luck, old man," a summons came from Old Peter, and I immediately rode to the top of the ridge where he and Marse Robert were making a reconnaissance of Meade's position. "Great God!" said Old Peter as I came up. "Look, General Lee, at the insurmountable difficulties between our line and that of the Yankees—the steep hills, the tiers of artillery, the fences, the heavy skirmish line—and then we'll have to fight our infantry against their batteries. Look at the ground we'll have to charge over, nearly a mile of that open ground there under the rain of their canister and shrapnel."

"The enemy is there, General Longstreet, and I am going to strike him," said Marse Robert in his firm, quiet, determined voice.

About 8 o'clock I rode with them along our line of prostrate infantry. They had been told to lie down to prevent attracting attention, and though they had been forbidden to cheer they voluntarily arose and lifted in reverential adoration their caps to our beloved commander as we rode slowly along. Oh, the responsibility for the lives of such men as these! Well, my darling, their fate and that of our beloved Southland will be settled ere your glorious brown eyes rest on these scraps of penciled paper—your Soldier's last letter, perhaps.

Our line of battle faces Cemetery Ridge. Our detachments have been thrown forward to support our artillery which stretches over a mile along the crests of Oak Ridge and Seminary Ridge. The men are lying in the rear, my darling, and the hot July sun pours its scorching rays almost vertically down upon them. The suffering and waiting are almost unbearable.

. . . .

Well, my sweetheart, at one o'clock the awful silence was broken by a cannon-shot and then another, and then more than a hundred guns shook the hills from crest to base, answered by more than another hundred—the whole world a blazing volcano, the whole of heaven a thunderbolt—then darkness and absolute silence—then the grim and gruesome, low-spoken commands—then the forming of the attacking columns. My brave Virginians are to attack in front. Oh, may God in mercy help me as He never helped before!

I have ridden up to report to Old Peter. I shall give him this letter to mail to you and a package to give you if—Oh, my darling, do you feel the love of my heart, the prayer, as I write that fatal word?

Now, I go; but remember always that I love you with all my heart and soul, with every fiber of my being; that now and forever I am yours—yours, my beloved. It is almost three o'clock. My soul reaches out to yours—my prayers. I'll keep up a skookum tumtum for Virginia and for you, my darling."

Eventually, Union artillery chief Henry Hunt cleverly figured that if the Union cannons stopped firing back, the Confederates might think they successfully knocked out the Union batteries. On top of that, the Union would be preserving its ammunition for the impending charge that everyone now knew was coming. When they stopped, Lee, Alexander, and others mistakenly concluded that they'd knocked out the Union artillery.

A short time later, the Confederates were prepared to step out for the charge that bears Pickett's name, even though he commanded only about a third of the force and was officially under Longstreet's direction. Today historians typically refer to the charge as the Pickett-Pettigrew-Trimble Assault or Longstreet's Assault to be more technically correct. Since A.P. Hill was sidelined with illness, Pettigrew's and Trimble's divisions were delegated to Longstreet's authority as well. To make matters worse, Hill's sickness resulted in organizational snafus. Without Hill to assign or lead troops, some of his battle-weary soldiers of the previous two days were tapped to make the charge while fresh soldiers in his corps stayed behind.

Porter Alexander described the drama-filled moments during which he advised Pickett to begin the charge:

"It was just 1 P. M. by my watch when the signal guns were fired and the cannonade opened. The enemy replied rather slowly at first, though soon with increasing rapidity. Having determined that Pickett should charge, I felt impatient to launch him as soon as I could see that our fire was accomplishing anything. I guessed that a half-hour would elapse between my sending him the order and his column reaching close quarters. I dared not presume on using more ammunition than one hour's firing would consume, for we were far from supplies and had already fought for two days. So I determined to send Pickett the order at the very first favorable sign and not later than after 30 minutes firing.

At the end of 20 minutes no favorable development had occurred. More guns had been added to the Federal line than at the beginning, and its whole length, about two miles, was blazing like a volcano. It seemed madness to order a column in the middle of a hot July day to undertake an advance of three-fourths of a mile over open ground against the centre of that line.

But something had to be done. I wrote the following note and despatched it to Pickett at 1.25:—

'General: If you are to advance at all, you must come at once or we will not be able to support you as we ought. But the enemy's fire has not slackened materially and there are still 18 guns firing from the cemetery.'

I had hardly sent this note when there was a decided falling off in the enemy's fire, and as I watched I saw other guns limbered up and withdrawn. We frequently withdrew from fighting Federal guns in order to save our ammunition for their infantry. The enemy had never heretofore practised such economy. After waiting a few minutes and seeing that no fresh guns replaced those withdrawn, I felt sure that the enemy was feeling the punishment, and at 1.40 I sent a note to Pickett as follows:—

'For God's sake come quick. The 18 guns have gone. Come quick or my ammunition will not let me support you properly.'

This was followed by two verbal messages to the same effect by an officer and sergeant from the nearest guns. The 18 guns had occupied the point at which our charge was to be directed. I had been incorrectly told it was the cemetery. Soon only a few scattered Federal guns were in action, and still Pickett's line had not come forward, though scarcely 300 yards behind my guns.

I afterward learned what had followed the sending of my first note. It reached Pickett in Longstreet's presence. He read it and handed it to Longstreet. Longstreet read and stood silent. Pickett said, 'General, shall I advance?' Longstreet knew that it must be done, but was unwilling to speak the words. He turned in his saddle and looked away. Pickett saluted and said, 'I am going to move forward, sir,' and galloped off.

Longstreet, leaving his staff, rode out alone and joined me on the left flank of the guns. It was doubtless 1.50 or later, but I did not look at my watch again. I had grown very impatient to see Pickett, fearing ammunition would run short, when Longstreet joined me. I explained the situation. He spoke sharply,— 'Go and stop Pickett where he is and replenish your ammunition.' I answered: 'We can't do that, sir. The train has but little. It would take an hour to distribute it, and meanwhile the enemy would improve the time.'

Longstreet seemed to stand irresolute (we were both dismounted) and then spoke slowly and with great emotion: 'I do not want to make this charge. I do not see how it can succeed. I would not make it now but that Gen. Lee has ordered it and is expecting it.'

I felt that he was inviting a word of acquiescence on my part and that if given he would again order, 'Stop Pickett where he is.' But I was too conscious of my own youth and inexperience to express any opinion not directly asked. So I remained silent while Longstreet fought his battle out alone and obeyed his orders."

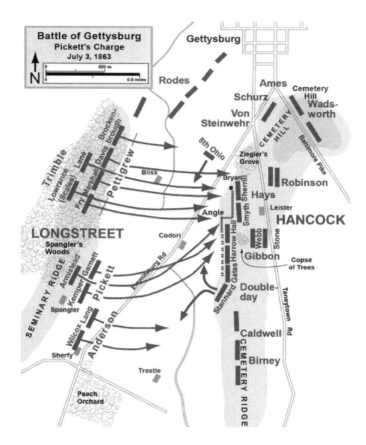

Thus, about 15,000 Confederates stepped out in sight and began their charge with an orderly march starting about a mile away, no doubt an inspiring sight to Hancock and the Union men directly across from the oncoming assault. Pickett launched his attack as ordered, but within five minutes the men came to the top of a low rise where his line came into full view of Union defenses. Though Pickett was seen galloping to the left to steady his men there, and one aide is said to remember him personally ordering the division to "double-quick" at the end of the advance, his exact whereabouts during the latter stages of the assault are unknown.

As the Confederate line advanced, Union cannon on Cemetery Ridge and Little Round Top began blasting away, with Confederate soldiers continuing to march forward. One Union soldier later wrote, "We could not help hitting them with every shot . . . a dozen men might be felled by one single bursting shell."[16] By the time Longstreet's men reached Emmitsburg Road, Union artillery switched to firing grapeshot (tin cans filled with iron and lead balls), and as the Confederate troops continued to approach the Union center, Union troops positioned behind the wall cut down the oncoming Confederates, easily decimating both flanks. And while some of the men did mange to advance to the Union line and engage in hand-to-hand combat, it was of little consequence.

After about 20 minutes, the Confederates had managed to cross the shallow valley but then hit the stone fence shielding Union soldiers (in some places, two-men deep). And although Pickett's men were finally able to reach and breach the Union line on the ridge, what followed next has been categorically described as a "blood bath." While some of the men did manage to advance to the Union line and engage in hand-to-hand combat, it was of little consequence. In the midst of the fighting, as he was conferring with one of his brigadier generals, General Hancock suddenly felt a searing pain in his thigh. He had just been severely wounded when a bullet struck the pommel of his saddle and entered his inner right thigh, along with wood splinters and a large bent nail. Helped from his horse by his aides, he removed the saddle nail himself and applied a tourniquet, colorfully swearing at his own men while demanding that they not let him bleed to death. Nevertheless, he refused to remove himself to the rear until the offensive had concluded.

One of the Virginians who marched straight into Hancock's II Corps was Pickett's brigadier Lewis A. Armistead, who famously led his brigade with his hat atop his sword, serving as a visual cue for his men. They actually breached the II Corps' line, making it about as far as any Confederate got. In the fighting, Armistead was mortally wounded and captured, dying days later. One of the men in his brigade would write about the charge after the war:

> "When the advance commenced Armistead placed himself in front of the colors of the Fifty-third Regiment, and from that point watched and directed the advance until within a short distance of the enemy's line. When approximating the advance line General Kemper rode up to him and said, "General, hurry up, my men can stand no more."

> He quietly turned to the officer commanding his battalion of direction and said, "Colonel, double quick." The double quick soon quickened into a run, the run into a charge, Armistead all the time in front of his line of battle, and when the desperate effort came and the final rush for the rock fence was made he dew his sword, put his hat on the end of it, called upon his men to follow, rushed over the rock fence and was shot just as he reached the enemy's guns between the two lines in the bloody angle, thus sealing with his life's blood the high water mark of the rebellion.

---

[16]   Gaffney, P. and D. Gaffney. *The Civil War: Exploring History One Week at a Time.* Page 283.

As Armistead was carried from the field he met Hancock as he was hurrying to the front. They recognized each other, and Hancock dismounted and grasped his hand and told him how sorry he was to see him wounded. Armistead returned his kindly expression and told him the wound was mortal and that he had on his person some things that he wish to entrust to him to be returned when opportunity presented to his people in Virginia. Hancock accepted the commission and tried to persuade Armistead to look upon the bright side, that he probably was not so seriously hurt as he feared, excused himself by saying he was compelled to hurry to the front, left Armistead, promising to see him the next day. In a short time he was wounded himself and they never met again.

This was related to me as I lay on the ground back of the battle line where hundreds of wounded were carried after the fight, by one of Hancock's staff, who rode up just about dusk and found a number of men congregated about me. When he found I was a badly wounded "Johnny Reb" Colonel he dismounted, drove everybody away that I might have fresh air, and commenced a conversation.

When he found that I was of Armistead's Brigade, he said, "Armistead, Armistead. I have just left him, he is mortally wounded," and then related the above, and said, "I will have you taken care of," etc.

Armistead lingered through the 4th and died on the 5th, leaving an example of patriotism, heroism and devotion to duty which ought to be handed down through the ages."

Kemper's brigade hardly had it any easier as it moved forward, and Kemper would be seriously injured and captured at the height of the fighting. One of his men wrote about the charge after the war:

The devoted little column moved to the assault, with Garnett, and Kemper in front, and Armistead behind in close supporting distance. Soon after clearing our batteries it was found necessary to change direction to the left. While conducting the movement, which was made in perfect order under a galling flank fire from the Round Top, General Pickett, for the second time, cautioned me to be sure and keep the proper interval with General Garnett; Armistead was expected to catch up and extend the line to the left. Then we swept onward again, straight for the Golgotha of Seminary Ridge, half a mile distant, across the open plain. As we neared the Emmettsburg road, along which, behind piles of rails, the enemy's strong line of skirmishers was posted, General Kemper called to me to give attention to matters on the left, while he went to see what troops those were coming up behind us. Glancing after him, I caught a glimpse of a small body of men, compact and solid as a wedge, moving swiftly to the left oblique, as if aiming to uncover Garnett's Brigade. They were Armistead's people, and as Kemper cantered down their front on his mettlesome sorrel they greeted him with a rousing cheer, which I know made his gallant heart leap for joy. At the same moment I saw a disorderly crowd of men breaking for the rear, and Pickett, with Stuart Symington, Ned Baird, and others, vainly trying to stop the rout. And now the guns of Cushing and Abbott double-stocked by General Gibbon's express order, reinforced the terrific fire of the infantry behind the stone fence, literally riddling the orchard on the left of the now famous Cordori house, through which my regiment and some of the others passed.

Within a few steps of the stone fence, while in the act of shaking hands with General Garnett and congratulating him on being able to be with his men (he had been seriously ill a few days before), I heard some one calling me, and turning my head, saw that it was Captain Fry. He was mounted, and blood streaming from his horse's neck. Colonel Terry had sent him to stop the rush to left. The enemy in force (Stannard's Vermonters) had penetrated to our rear. He told me that Kemper had been struck down, it was feared mortally. With the help of Colonel Carrington, of the Eighteenth, and Major Bentley, of the Twenty-fourth, I hastily gathered a small band together and faced them to meet the new danger. After that everything was a wild kaleidoscopic whirl. A man near me seemed to be keeping a tally of the dead for my especial benefit. First it was Patton, then Collcote, then Phillips, and I know not how many more. Colonel Williams was knocked out of the saddle by a ball in the shoulder near the brick-house, and in falling was killed by his sword...Seeing the men as they fired, throw down their guns and pick up others from the ground, I followed suit, shooting into a flock of blue coats that were pouring down from the right, I noticed how close their flags were together. Probably they were the same people whom Hood and McLaws had handled so roughly the day before. "Used up," as General Meade said of them. Suddenly there was a hissing sound, like the hooded cobra's whisper of death, a deafening explosion, a sharp pang of pain somewhere, a momentary blank, and when I got on my feet again there were splinters of bone and lumps of flesh sticking to my clothes. Then I remembered seeing lank Tell Taliaferro, adjutant of the Twenty-fourth, jumping like a kangaroo and rubbing his crazy bone and blessing the Yankees in a way that did credit to old Jube Early's one-time law partner, and handsome Ocey White, the boy lieutenant of Company A, taking off his hat to show me where a ball had raised a whelk on his scalp and carried away one of his pretty flaxen curls, and lastly, "Old Buck" Terry, with a peculiarly sad smile on his face, standing with poor George and Val Harris and others, between the colors of the Eleventh and Twenty-fourth, near where now is the pretty monument of colonel Ward, of Massachusetts. I could not hear what he said, but he was pointing rearwards with his sword, and I knew what that meant.

As I gave one hurried glance over the field we had traversed, the thought in my mind was repeated at my side, "Oh! Colonel, why don't they support us?" It was Walker, General Kemper's orderly, unhorsed, but still unscathed and undaunted, awkward, ungainly, hard-featured, good-natured, simple-minded, stout-hearted Walker, one of the Eleventh boys, I believe; only a private doing his duty with might and main and recking no more of glory than the ox that has won the prize at a cattle show. At the storming of the Redan when Wyndham's forlorn hope tumbled into the ditch and couldn't get out, owing to the scarcity of ladders, and the few they had were too short, the men huddled together dazed and bewildered, and were mowed down like dumb beasts by the Muscovite rifles, because there were no officers left to lead them. There was a notable exception, an Irishman, scrambling up the scrap, he shouted, "Come up, boys, follow the captain." The captain fell, but Pat went on to immortality. It was not so that day at Gettysburg.

Meanwhile, Pickett's brigadier Richard Garnett, whose courage had been impugned and challenged by Stonewall Jackson unfairly in 1862, had suffered a previous leg injury and insisted on riding his horse during the charge, despite the obvious fact that riding a horse clearly indicated he was an officer. Garnett was killed during the charge, and it's unknown where he fell or where he was buried. One of the men in Garnett's brigade, C.S. Peyton of the 19th Virginia, reported on the brigade's participation in his post-battle report:

MAJOR: In compliance with instructions from division headquarters, I have the honor to report the part taken by this brigade in the late battle near Gettysburg, Pa., July 3.

Notwithstanding the long and severe marches made by the troops of this brigade, they reached the field about 9 a.m.. in high spirits and in good condition. At about 12 m. we were ordered to take position behind the crest of the hill on which the artillery, under Colonel [E. Porter] Alexander, was planted, where we lay during a most terrific cannonading, which opened at 1.30 p.m., and was kept up without intermission for one hour.

During the shelling, we lost about 20 killed and wounded. Among the killed was Lieutenant-Colonel [John T.] Ellis, of the Nineteenth Virginia, whose bravery as a soldier, and his innocence, purity, and integrity as a Christian, have not only elicited the admiration of his own command, but endeared him to all who knew him.

At 2.30 p.m., the artillery fire having to some extent abated, the order to advance was given, first by Major-General Pickett in person, and repeated by General Garnett with promptness, apparent cheerfulness, and alacrity. The brigade moved forward at quick time. The ground was open, but little broken, and from 800 to 1,000 yards from the crest whence we started to the enemy's line. The brigade moved in good order, keeping up its line almost perfectly, notwithstanding it had to climb three high post and rail fences, behind the last of which the enemy's skirmishers were first met and immediately driven in. Moving on, we soon met the advance line of the enemy, lying concealed in the grass on the slope, about 100 yards in front of his second line, which consisted of a stone wall about breast-high, running nearly parallel to and about 30 paces from the crest of the hill, which was lined with their artillery.

The first line referred to above, after offering some resistance, was completely routed, and driven in confusion back to the stone wall. Here we captured some prisoners, which were ordered to the rear without a guard. Having routed the enemy here, General Garnett ordered the brigade forward, which it promptly obeyed, loading and firing as it advanced.

Up to this time we had suffered but little from the enemy's batteries, which apparently had been much crippled previous to our advance, with the exception of one posted on the mountain, about 1 mile to our right, which enfiladed nearly our entire line with fearful effect, sometimes as many as 10 men being killed and wounded by the bursting of a single shell. From the point it had first routed the enemy, the brigade moved rapidly forward toward the stone wall, under a galling fire both from artillery and infantry, the artillery using grape and canister. We were now within about 75 paces of the wall, unsupported on the right and left, General Kemper being some 50 or 60 yards behind and to the right, and General Armistead coming up in our rear.

General Kemper's line was discovered to be lapping on ours, when, deeming it advisable to have the line extended on the right to prevent being flanked, a staff officer rode back to the general to request him to incline to the right. General Kemper not being present (perhaps wounded at the time), Captain [W. T.] Fry, of his staff, immediately began his exertions to carry out the request, but, in consequence of the eagerness of the men in pressing forward, it was impossible to have the order carried out.

Our line, much shattered, still kept up the advance until within about 20 paces of the wall, when, for a moment, it recoiled under the terrific fire that poured into our ranks both from their batteries and from their sheltered infantry. At this moment, General Kemper came up on the right and General Armistead in rear, when the three lines, joining in concert, rushed forward with unyielding determination and an apparent spirit of laudable rivalry to plant the Southern banner on the walls of the enemy. His strongest and last line was instantly gained; the Confederate battle-flag waved over his defenses, and the fighting over the wall became hand to hand, and of the most desperate character; but more than half having already fallen, our line was found too weak to rout the enemy. We hoped for a support on the left (which had started simultaneously with ourselves), out hoped in vain. Yet a small remnant remained in desperate struggle, receiving a fire in front, on the right, and on the left, many even climbing over the wall, and fighting the enemy in his own trenches until entirely surrounded; and those who were not killed or wounded were captured, with the exception of about 300 who came off slowly, but greatly scattered, the identity of every regiment being entirely lost, and every regimental commander killed or wounded.

The brigade went into action with 1,287 men and about 140 officers, as shown by the report of the previous evening, and sustained a loss, as the list of casualties will show, of 941 killed, wounded, and missing, and it is feared, from all the information received, that the majority (those reported missing) are either killed or wounded.

It is needless, perhaps, to speak of conspicuous gallantry where all behaved so well. Each and every regimental commander displayed a cool bravery and daring that not only encouraged their own commands, but won the highest admiration from all those who saw them. They led their regiments in the fight, and showed, by their conduct, that they only desired their men to follow where they were willing to lead. But of our cool, gallant, noble brigade commander it may not be out of place to speak. Never had the brigade been better handled, and never has it done better service in the field of battle. There was scarcely an officer or man in the command whose attention was not attracted by the cool and handsome bearing of General Garnett, who, totally devoid of excitement or rashness, rode immediately in rear of his advancing line, endeavoring by his personal efforts, and by the aid of his staff, to keep his line well closed and dressed. He was shot from his horse while near the center of the brigade, within about 25 paces of the stone wall. This gallant officer was too well known to need further mention.

In making the above report, I have endeavored to be as accurate as possible, but have had to rely mainly for information on others, whose position gave them better opportunity for witnessing the conduct of the entire brigade than I could have, being with, and paying my attention to, my own regiment.

After the charge, there was debate (and later controversy) over where Pickett was as his brigadiers were falling at the front of their brigades. One of Pickett's staff men discussed the way communications were going from the front back to leaders like Longstreet further to the rear:

> I found General Longstreet sitting on a fence alone; the fence ran in the direction we were charging. Pickett's column had passed over the hill on our side of the Emmettsburg road, and could not then be seen. I delivered the message as sent by General Pickett. General Longstreet said: "Where are the troops that were placed on your flank ?" and I answered: "Look over your shoulder and you will see them." He looked and saw the broken fragments. Just then an officer rode at half-speed, drawing up his horse in front of the General, and saying: "General Longstreet, General Lee sent me here, and said you would place me in a position to see this magnificent charge. I would not have missed it for the world." General Longstreet answered: "I would, Colonel Freemantle, the charge is over. Captain Bright, ride to General Pickett, and tell

hin what you have heard me say to Colonel Freemantle." At this moment our men were near to but had not crossed the Emmettsburg road. I started and when my horse had made two leaps, General Longstreet called: "Captain Bright!" I checked my horse, and turned half around in my saddle to hear, and this was what he said: "Tell General Pickett that Wilcox's Brigade is in that peach orchard (pointing), and he can order him to his assistance."

When I reached General Pickett he was at least one hundred yards behind the division, having been detained in a position from which he could watch and care for his left flank. He at once sent Captain Baird to General Wilcox with the order for him to come in; then he sent Captain Symington with the same order, in a very few moments, and last he said: "Captain Bright, you go,' and I was about the same distance behind Symington that he was behind Baird. The fire was so dreadful at this time that I believe that General Pickett thought not more than one out of the three sent would reach General Wilcox.

When I rode up to Wilcox he was standing with both hands raised waving and saying to me, "I know, I know." I said, "But, General, I must deliver my message." After doing this I rode out of the peach orchard, going forward where General Pickett was watching his left. Looking that way myself, I saw moving out of the enemy's line of battle, in head of column, a large force; having nothing in their front, they came around our flank as described above. Had our left not deserted us these men would have hesitated to move in head of column, confronted by a line of battle. When I reached General Pickett I found him too far down towards the Ennmettshurg road to see these flanking troops, and he asked of me the number. I remember answering 7,000, but this proved an over estimate. Some of our men had been faced to meet this new danger, and so doing somewhat broke the force of our charge on the left. Probably men of the 1st Virginia will remember this.

Charging to the left of Pickett's men, Trimble and Pettigrew were both wounded in the fighting, with Trimble losing a leg and Pettigrew suffering a minor wound to the hand. One of the generals in Pettigrew's part of the assault wrote about their participation:

In the numerous accounts of the battle of Gettysburg heretofore published, the writers have generally referred to the last effort made by the Confederate troops as "Pickett's charge," and in almost every instance have conveyed the idea that no troops but Pickett's division took an active part in that fierce and tremendous struggle. Disclaiming any intention to detract in the least from the glory won on that day by the gallant Virginia division, or its heroic commander, who had then been for more than twenty years one of my most valued friends, I may be permitted to say that some injustice has been done to the division commanded by General Pettigrew.

As colonel of the Thirteenth Alabama infantry, I was attached to Archer's brigade of Heth's division. That brigade opened the battle on the morning of July 1st, and during the fighting which immediately ensued General Heth was wounded, and the command of the division devolved upon Brigadier-General Pettigrew. General Archer was captured, and I succeeded him in command of the brigade.

During the forenoon of the 3d, while our division was resting in line behind the ridge and skirt of woods which masked us from the enemy, Generals Lee, Longstreet and A. P. Hill rode up, and, dismounting, seated themselves on the trunk of a fallen tree some fifty or sixty paces from where I sat on my horse at the right of our division. After an apparently careful examination of a map, and a consultation of some length, they remounted and rode away. Staff officers and couriers began to move briskly about, and a few minutes after General Pettigrew rode up and informed me that after a heavy cannonade we would assault the position in our front, and added: "They will of course return the fire with all the guns they have; we must shelter the men as best we can, and make them lie down." At the same time he directed me to see General Pickett at once and have an understanding as to the dress in the advance. I rode to General Pickett, whose division was formed on the right of and in line with ours. He appeared to be in excellent spirits, and, after a cordial greeting and a pleasant reference to our having been together in work of that kind at Chapultipec, expressed great confidence in the ability of our troops to drive the enemy after they had been "demoralized by our artillery." General Garnett, who commanded his left brigade, having joined us, it was agreed that he would dress on my command. I immediately returned and informed General Pettigrew of this agreement. It was then understood that my command should be considered the centre, and that in the assault both divisions should allign themselves by it. Soon after the two divisions moved forward about a hundred paces, and the men lay down behind our line of batteries. The cannonade which followed has been often and justly described as the most terrible of the war. In it my command suffered a considerable loss. Several officers were killed and wounded, with a number of the rank and file. I received a painful wound on the right shoulder from a fragment of shell. After lying inactive under that deadly storm of hissing and exploding missiles, it seemed a relief to go forward to the desperate assault. At a signal from Pettigrew I called my command to attention. The men sprang up with cheerful alacrity, and the long line advanced. "Stormed at with shot and shell," it moved steadily on, and even when grape, canister, and musket balls began to rain upon it the gaps were quickly closed and the allignment preserved. Strong as was the position of the enemy, it seemed that such determination could not fail. I heard Garnett give a command to his men which, amid the rattle of musketry, I could not distinguish. Seeing my look or gesture of inquiry, he called our, "I am dressing on you!" A few seconds after he fell dead. A moment later- and after Captain Williams and Colonel George had been wounded by my side- a shot through the thigh prostrated me. I was so confident of victory that to some of my men who ran up to carry me off I shouted, "Go on; it will not last five minutes longer!" The men rushed forward into the smoke, which soon became so dense that I could see little of what was going on before me. But a moment later I heard General Pettigrew, behind me, calling to some of his staff to "rally them on the left." The roll of musketry was then incessant, and I believe that the Federal troops- probably blinded by the smoke- continued a rapid fire for some minutes after none but dead and wounded remained in their front. At length the firing ceased, and cheer after cheer from the enemy announced the failure of our attack. I was of course left a prisoner.

As evidence of how close was the fighting at that part of the line, I saw a Federal soldier with an ugly wound in his shoulder, which he told me he received from the spear on the end of one of my regimental colors; and I remembered having that morning observed and laughingly commented on the fact that the color-bearer of the Thirteenth Alabama had attached to his staff a formidable-looking lance head. All of the five regimental colors of my command reached the line of the enemy's works, and many of my men and officers were killed or wounded after passing over it. I believe the same was true of other brigades in General Pettigrew's command.

It is probable that Pickett's division, which up to that time had taken no part in the battle, was mainly relied upon for the final assault; but whatever may have been the first plan of attack, the division under Pettigrew went into it as part of the line of battle, and from the commencement of the advance to the closing death grapple, his right brigade was the directing one. General Pettigrew, who I know was that day in the thickest of the fire, was killed in a skirmish a few days later. No more earnest and gallant officer served in the Confederate army.

According to Longstreet, it was Pickett who finally called retreat; after about an hour, nearly 6,500 Confederates were dead or wounded, five times that of the Union, with all 13 regimental commanders in Pickett's division killed or wounded. As Pickett's men began to stream back in a broken and disorderly, Pickett's staff member recalled one of the most famous exchanges of the battle:

I informed the General that no help was to be expected from the artillery, but the enemy were closing around us, and nothing could now save his command. He had remained behind to watch and protect that left, to put in first help expected from infantry supports, then to break the troops which came around his flank with the artillery; all had failed. At this moment our left (Pickett's Division) began to crumble and soon all that was left came slowly back, 5,000 in the morning, 1,600 were put in camp that night, 3,400 killed, wounded and missing.

We moved back, and when General Pickett and I were about 300 yards from the position from which the charge had started, General Robert E. Lee, the Peerless, alone, on Traveler, rode up and said: "General Pickett, place your division in rear of this hill, and be ready to repel the advance of the enemy should they follow up their advantage." (I never heard General Lee call them the enemy before; it was always those or these people). General Pickett, with his head on his breast, said: "General Lee, I have no division now, Armistead is down, Garnett is down, and Kemper is mortally wounded."

Then General Lee said: "Come, General Pickett, this has been my fight and upon my shoulders rests the blame. The men and officers of your command have written the name of Virginia as high to-day as it has ever been written before." (Now talk about "Glory enough for one day," why this was glory enough for one hundred years.)

In the aftermath of the repulse of Pickett's Charge, General Longstreet stated, "General Lee came up as our troops were falling back and encouraged them as well as he could; begged them to reform their ranks and reorganize their forces . . . and it was then he used the expression . . . 'It was all my fault; get together, and let us do the best we can toward saving which is left to us.'"[17] Longstreet never resisted an opportunity to distance himself from failure and direct it towards someone else, even Lee.

Today Pickett's Charge is remembered as the American version of the Charge of the Light Brigade, a heroic but completely futile march that had no chance of success. In fact, it's remembered as Pickett's Charge because Pickett's Virginians wanted to claim the glory of getting the furthest during the attack in the years after the war. The charge suffered about a 50% casualty rate while barely making a dent in the Union line before retreating in disorder back across the field. Pickett's post-battle report was apparently so bitter that Lee ordered it destroyed.

Though the charge was named Pickett's Charge by newspapers for the purpose of praising Pickett's Virginians for making the furthest progress, Pickett felt the charge had tarnished his career, and he remained upset that his name remained associated with the sharply repulsed attack. Furthermore, Pickett himself has received much criticism (both then and to this day) for surviving the battle unscathed, having established his final position well to the rear of his troops, though any charges of cowardice are strongly contradicted by his record earlier in the Civil War and in Mexico.

After the battle, Pickett wrote to Sallie offering a few details about the fateful charge. Since his official report of the battle has never been found, his letters home were his only words about the events:

"MY letter of yesterday, my darling, written before the battle, was full of hope and

---

[17]   Davis, Kenneth C. *The Civil War: Everything You Need to Know About America's Greatest Conflict but Never Learned.* Page 306.

cheer; even though it told you of the long hours of waiting from four in the morning, when Gary's pistol rang out from the Federal lines signaling the attack upon Culp's Hill, to the solemn eight-o'clock review of my men, who rose and stood silently lifting their hats in loving reverence as Marse Robert, Old Peter and your own Soldier reviewed them—on then to the deadly stillness of the five hours following, when the men lay in the tall grass in the rear of the artillery line, the July sun pouring its scorching rays almost vertically down upon them, till one o'clock when the awful silence of the vast battlefield was broken by a cannon-shot which opened the greatest artillery duel of the world. The firing lasted two hours. When it ceased we took advantage of the blackened field and in the glowering darkness formed our attacking column just before the brow of Seminary Ridge.

I closed my letter to you a little before three o'clock and rode up to Old Peter for orders. I found him like a great lion at bay. I have never seen him so grave and troubled. For several minutes after I had saluted him he looked at me without speaking. Then in an agonized voice, the reserve all gone, he said:

"Pickett, I am being crucified at the thought of the sacrifice of life which this attack will make. I have instructed Alexander to watch the effect of our fire upon the enemy, and when it begins to tell he must take the responsibility and give you your orders, for I can't."

While he was yet speaking a note was brought to me from Alexander. After reading it I handed it to him, asking if I should obey and go forward. He looked at me for a moment, then held out his hand. Presently, clasping his other hand over mine without speaking he bowed his head upon his breast. I shall never forget the look in his face nor the clasp of his hand when I said:—"Then, General, I shall lead my Division on." I had ridden only a few paces when I remembered your letter and (forgive me) thoughtlessly scribbled in a corner of the envelope, "If Old Peter's nod means death then good-by and God bless you, little one," turned back and asked the dear old chief if he would be good enough to mail it for me. As he took your letter from me, my darling, I saw tears glistening on his cheeks and beard. The stern old war-horse, God bless him, was weeping for his men and, I know, praying too that this cup might pass from them. I obeyed the silent assent of his bowed head, an assent given against his own convictions,—given in anguish and with reluctance.

My brave boys were full of hope and confident of victory as I led them forth, forming them in column of attack, and though officers and men alike knew what was before them,—knew the odds against them,—they eagerly offered up their lives on the altar of duty, having absolute faith in their ultimate success. Over on Cemetery Ridge the Federals beheld a scene never before witnessed on this continent,—a scene which has never previously been enacted and can never take place again—an army forming in line of battle in full view, under their very eyes—charging across a space nearly a mile in length over fields of waving grain and anon of stubble and then a smooth expanse—moving with the steadiness of a dress parade, the pride and glory soon to be crushed by an overwhelming heartbreak.

. . . .

Well, it is all over now. The battle is lost, and many of us are prisoners, many are dead, many wounded, bleeding and dying. Your Soldier lives and mourns and but for you, my darling, he would rather, a million times rather, be back there with his dead, to sleep for all time in an unknown grave."

Days later, Pickett wrote yet another tense letter back to Sallie, in which his angst can be felt:

General Lee's letter has been published to the division in general orders and received with appreciative satisfaction. The soldiers, one and all, love and honor Lee, and his sympathy and praise are always very dear to them. Just after the order was published I heard one of the men, rather rough and uncouth and not, as are most of the men, to the manner born, say, as he wiped away the tears with the back of his hand, "Dag-gone him, dag-gone him, dag-gone his old soul, I'm blamed ef I wouldn't be dag-gone willin' to go right through it all and be killed again with them others to hear Marse Robert, dag-gone him, say over again as how he grieved bout'n we-all's losses and honored us for we-all's bravery! Darned ef I wouldn't." Isn't that reverential adoration, my darling, to be willing to be "killed again" for a word of praise?

It seems selfish and inhuman to speak of Love—haunted as I am with the unnecessary sacrifice of the lives of so many of my brave boys. I can't think of anything but the desolate homes in Virginia and the unknown dead in Pennsylvania. At the beginning of the fight I was so sanguine, so sure of success! Early in the morning I had been assured by Alexander that General Lee had ordered that every brigade in his command was to charge Cemetery Hill; so I had no fear of not being supported. Alexander also assured me of the support of his artillery which would move ahead of my division in the advance. He told me that he had borrowed seven twelve-pound howitzers from Pendleton, Lee's Chief of Artillery, which he had put in reserve to accompany me.

In the morning I rode with him while he, by Longstreet's orders, selected the salient angle of the wood in which my line was formed, which line was just on the left of his seventy-five guns. At about a quarter to three o'clock, when his written order to make the charge was handed to me, and dear Old Peter after reading it in sorrow and fear reluctantly bowed his head in assent, I obeyed, leading my three brigades straight on the enemy's front. You never saw anything like it. They moved across that field of death as a battalion marches forward in line of battle upon drill, each commander in front of his command leading and cheering on his men. Two lines of the enemy's infantry were driven back; two lines of guns were taken—and no support came. Pendleton, without Alexander's knowledge, had sent four of the guns which he had loaned him to some other part of the field, and the other three guns could not be found. The two brigades which were to have followed me had, poor fellows, been seriously engaged in the fights of the two previous days. Both of their commanding officers had been killed, and while they had been replaced by gallant, competent officers, these new leaders were unknown to the men.

Ah, if I had only had my other two brigades a different story would have been flashed to the world. It was too late to retreat, and to go on was death or capture. Poor old Dick Garnett did not dismount, as did the others of us, and he was killed instantly, falling from his horse. Kemper, desperately wounded, was brought from the field and subsequently, taken prisoner. Dear old Lewis Armistead, God bless him, was mortally wounded at the head of his command after planting the flag of Virginia within the enemy's lines. Seven of my colonels were killed, and one was mortally wounded. Nine of my lieutenant colonels were wounded, and three lieutenant colonels were killed. Only one field officer of my whole command, Colonel Cabell, was unhurt, and the loss of my company officers was in proportion.

I wonder, my dear, if in the light of the Great Eternity we shall any of us feel this was for the best and shall have learned to say, "Thy will be done."

No castles to-day, sweetheart. No, the bricks of happiness and the mortar of love must lie untouched in this lowering gloom. Pray, dear, for the sorrowing ones."

Farnsworth's Charge

Pickett's Charge is the most memorable charge of July 3, but it wasn't the only fateful one made that day. As the Union cavalry repulsed Stuart, cavalry officer Hugh Judson Kilpatrick gave the order for some of his cavalry to charge north into the Confederates' right flank, Evander Law's brigade (which had opposed Chamberlain the day before). It's believed that the order was given as part of a plan by Meade to possibly follow up a repulse of Pickett's Charge with a flank attack that might lead to a rolling up of the Confederate line.

However, Kilpatrick was ordering the attack just as Pickett's infantry was starting the charge, not during its repulse, and he ordered an attack to be made piecemeal instead of one united assault.

West of Emmitsburg Road, Merrit's cavalry dismounted and began an attack on the Confederate flank, only to run into a brigade of Georgians, which easily repulsed the attack. The plan then called for Elon Farnsworth to attack, but this time Kilpatrick ordered a mounted cavalry charge. By now, with Merrit's attack having failed, the Confederate infantry was positioned behind a stone fence with wooden fence rails piled high above it to prevent horses from being able to jump into their lines. In essence, the Union cavalry would have to make a mounted charge, dismount right at the battle line, and then attempt a concerted attack. Historians have since accused Kilpatrick of shaming Farnsworth into making the suicidal chare, and Farnsworth allegedly told his superior, "General, if you order the charge I will lead it, but you must take the awful responsibility."

Farnsworth's charge began with a charge by the 1st West Virginia Cavalry that immediately devolved into confusion once they came under heavy fire. Eventually they dismounted near the wall, where they engaged in hand-to-hand fighting with sabers, rifles, and even rocks. The second part of the attack came from the 18th Pennsylvania, supported by companies of the 5th New York, but they were immediately repulsed.

Next, it fell upon the 400 man 1st Vermont Cavalry to charge forward, heading into a slaughter. As they rode forward, one lieutenant in an Albama regiment yelled, "Cavalry, boys, cavalry! This is no fight, only a frolic, give it to them!" All three battalions of the 1st Vermont were quickly repulsed. With that, the final attack was to be led by Farnsworth himself, which came upon the 15th Alabama. In the middle of the charge, Farnsworth fell dead from his horse, hit by 5 bullets. Kilpatrick's poorly designed attack resulted in Farnsworth and his men making a "Charge of the Light Brigade", and as it turned out, they would end up being the last major action of the Battle of Gettysburg.

Chapter 6: Controversy over Lee's Retreat

From a military perspective, Meade had made efficient use of his subordinates (particularly Generals John F. Reynolds and Winfield S. Hancock) during this three-day, course-changing battle, ultimately executing some of the most effective battleline strategies of the War. In short, Meade had successfully commanded the forces that repulsed Lee's Army and effectively won what most historians consider the battle that changed the course of the Civil War and ultimately resulted in a Confederate defeat.

While nobody questions that Meade's strategy at Gettysburg was strong, he was heavily criticized by contemporaries for not pursuing Lee's army more aggressively as it retreated. Chief-of-staff Daniel Butterfield, who would call into question Meade's command decisions and courage at Gettysburg, accused Meade of not finishing off the weakened Lee. Meade would later state that as his army's new commander, he was uncertain of his troops' capabilities and strength, especially after a battle that had just resulted in over 20,000 Union casualties. Moreover, heavy rains made pursuit almost impossible on July 4, and Lee actually invited an attack during the retreat, hoping Meade would haphazardly attack strongly fortified positions.

Though historians now mostly credit Meade with making proper decisions in the wake of the battle, Lincoln was incredibly frustrated when Lee successfully retreated south. On July 14, Lincoln drafted a letter that he ultimately put away and decided not to send to Meade, who never read it during his lifetime:

"I have just seen your despatch to Gen. Halleck, asking to be relieved of your command, because of a supposed censure of mine. I am very--very--grateful to you for the magnificent success you gave the cause of the country at Gettysburg; and I am sorry now to be the author of the slightest pain to you. But I was in such deep distress myself that I could not restrain some expression of it. I had been oppressed nearly ever since the battles at Gettysburg, by what appeared to be evidences that yourself, and Gen. Couch, and Gen. Smith, were not seeking a collision with the enemy, but were trying to get him across the river without another battle. What these evidences were, if you please, I hope to tell you at some time, when we shall both feel better. The case, summarily stated is this. You fought and beat the enemy at Gettysburg; and, of course, to say the least, his loss was as great as yours. He retreated; and you did not, as it seemed to me, pressingly pursue him; but a flood in the river detained him, till, by slow degrees, you were again upon him. You had at least twenty thousand veteran troops directly with you, and as many more raw ones within supporting distance, all in addition to those who fought with you at Gettysburg; while it was not possible that he had received a single recruit; and yet you stood and let the flood run down, bridges be built, and the enemy move away at his leisure, without attacking him. And Couch and Smith! The latter left Carlisle in time, upon all ordinary calculation, to have aided you in the last battle at Gettysburg; but he did not arrive. At the end of more than ten days, I believe twelve, under constant urging, he reached Hagerstown from Carlisle, which is not an inch over fifty-five miles, if so much. And Couch's movement was very little different.

Again, my dear general, I do not believe you appreciate the magnitude of the misfortune involved in Lee's escape. He was within your easy grasp, and to have closed upon him would, in connection with our other late successes, have ended the war. As it is, the war will be prolonged indefinitely. If you could not safely attack Lee last Monday, how can you possibly do so South of the river, when you can take with you very few more than two thirds of the force you then had in hand? It would be unreasonable to expect, and I do not expect you can now effect much. Your golden opportunity is gone, and I am distressed immeasurably because of it.

I beg you will not consider this a prosecution, or persecution of yourself As you had learned that I was dissatisfied, I have thought it best to kindly tell you why."

Still, Meade was promoted to brigadier general in the regular army and was officially awarded the Thanks of Congress, which commended Meade "... and the officers and soldiers of [the Army of the Potomac], for the skill and heroic valor which at Gettysburg repulsed, defeated, and drove back, broken and dispirited, beyond the Rappahannock, the veteran army of the rebellion."

Hancock was unquestionably one of the Union heroes at Gettysburg, but his recognition was slow in coming. In the months after the battle, the U.S. Congress thanked Meade and Howard without listing Hancock. Eventually, Major General Hancock later received the Thanks of the U. S. Congress for "gallant, meritorious, and conspicuous share in that great and decisive victory."

As usual, Hancock shared the credit with his men, writing in his post-battle report:

"To speak of the conduct of the troops would seem to be unnecessary, but still it may be justly remarked that this corps sustained its well-earned reputation on many fields, and that the boast of its gallant first commander, the late Maj. Gen. E. V. Sumner, that the Second Corps had "never given to the enemy a gun or color," holds good now as it did under the command of my predecessor, Major-General Couch. To attest to its good conduct and the perils through which it has passed, it may be stated that its losses in battle have been greater than those of any other corps in the Army of the Potomac, or probably in the service, notwithstanding it has usually been numerically weakest."

Chapter 7: Who's to Blame?

Lee?

From almost the moment the Civil War ended, Gettysburg has been widely viewed as one of the decisive turning points of the Civil War. As renowned Civil War historian described Gettysburg, "It might be less of a victory than Mr. Lincoln had hoped for, but it was nevertheless a victory—and, because of that, it was no longer possible for the Confederacy to win the war. The North might still lose it, to be sure, if the soldiers or the people should lose heart, but outright defeat was no longer in the cards." While some still dispute that labeling, Lee's Army of Northern Virginia was never truly able to take the strategic offensive again for the duration of the war.

Naturally, if Gettysburg marked an important turning point in the Civil War, then to the defeated South it represented one of the last true opportunities the South had to win the war. After the South had lost the war, the importance of Gettysburg as one of the "high tide" marks of the Confederacy became apparent to everyone, making the battle all the more important in the years after it had been fought. Former Confederate comrades like Longstreet and Jubal Early would go on to argue who was responsible for the loss at Gettysburg (and thus the war) in the following decades. Much of the debate was fueled by those who wanted to protect Lee's legacy, especially because Lee was dead and could not defend himself in writing anymore. However, on July 3, Lee insisted on taking full blame for what occurred at Gettysburg, telling his retreating men, "It's all my fault." Historians have mostly agreed, placing the blame for the disastrous Day 3 on Lee's shoulders.

Porter Alexander would later call it Lee's "worst day" of the war and further explained:

"There was one single advantage conferred by our exterior lines, and but one, in exchange for many disadvantages. They gave us the opportunity to select positions for our guns which could enfilade the opposing lines of the enemy. Enfilading fire is so effective that no troops can submit to it long. Illustrations of this fact were not wanting in the events of this day. What has been called the shank of the Federal fish-hook, extending south from the bend at Cemetery Hill toward Little Round Top, was subject to enfilade fire from the town and its flanks and suburbs. That liability should have caused special examination by our staff and artillery officers, to discover other conditions which might favor an assault. There were and are others still easily recognizable on the ground. The salient angle is acute and weak, and within about 500 yards of its west face is the sheltered position occupied by Rodes the night of July 2d, which has already been mentioned.

From nowhere else was there so short and unobstructed an approach to the Federal line, and one so free from flank fire. On the northeast, at but little greater distance, was the position whence Early's two brigades the evening before had successfully carried the east face of the same salient. Within the edge of the town between these two positions was abundant opportunity to accumulate troops and to establish guns at close ranges.

As long as Gettysburg stands and the contour of its hills remains unchanged, students of the battle-field must decide that Lee's most promising attack from first to last was upon Cemetery Hill, by concentrated artillery fire from the north and assaults from the nearest sheltered ground between the west and northeast.

That this was not realized at the time is doubtless partly due to the scarcity of trained staff and reconnoitring officers, and partly to the fact that Ewell had discontinued and withdrawn the pursuit on the afternoon of the 1st, when it was about to undertake this position. Hence the enemy's pickets were not driven closely into their lines, and the vicinity was not carefully examined. Not a single gun was established within a thousand yards, nor was a position selected which enfiladed the lines in question.

Quite by accident, during the cannonade preceding Pickett's charge, Nelson's battalion of Ewell's corps fired a few rounds from a position which did enfilade with great effect part of the 11th corps upon Cemetery Hill, but the fire ceased on being sharply replied to. Briefly the one weak spot of the enemy's line and the one advantage possessed by ours were never apprehended."

Ironically, though he had no use for post-war politics, Lee's legacy was crafted and embroiled in it. While Lee accepted the South's loss, unreconstructed rebels continued to "fight" the Civil War with the pen, aiming to influence how the war was remembered. Much of this was accomplished by the Southern Historical Society, whose stated aim was the homogenization of Southern white males. But longstanding feuds between former generals found their way into the papers, and the feuds were frequently based on regional differences. These former Confederates looked to their idealized war heroes as symbols of their suffering and struggle. Based in Richmond, the Society's ideal Southern white male embodied the "Virginian" essence of aristocracy, morality and chivalry. The Society's ideal male, of course, was Robert E. Lee. David Blight credits the Society for creating a "Lee cult" that dominates public perception to this day. Writing about this perception of Lee, Charles Osbourne described the perception as "an edifice of myth built on the foundation of truth...the image became an icon."

Still, Lee was far from perfect, despite the attempts of the Southern Historical Society to defend his war record as fault free, at the expense of some of his subordinates. Given that the Confederacy lost the war, some historians have pointed out that Lee was often too eager to engage in offensive warfare. After all, Lee scored large and smashing victories at places like Chancellorsville that deprived him of more manpower against opponents that could afford casualties more than he could. Moreover, for the engineer who used tactics to successfully defend against typical Civil War tactics, he all too often engaged in the same futile offensive tactics himself, none more costly than Pickett's Charge.

Longstreet?

However, after the war, former Confederates would not accept criticism of Lee, and blame for the loss at Gettysburg was thus placed upon other scapegoats. Although it was not immediately apparent where the blame rested for such a devastating loss, not long after the Battle of Gettysburg two names kept surfacing: cavalry leader General "Jeb" Stuart and General James Longstreet; Stuart blamed for robbing Lee of the "eyes" he needed to know of Union movement, and Longstreet for delaying his attack on Round Top Hills the second day and acting too slowly in executing the assault on the Union left flank.

Long before Gettysburg, Longstreet was characterized by his men and commanders as "congenitally resistant to hurry himself,"[18] resistant to change of orders (even from his supreme commander, Lee), and disliked to overextend his men (once bivouacked, he allowed his men to

---

[18] Dowdey, Clifford. *Lee's Last Campaign: The Story of Lee & His Men against Grant--1864.* Page 134.

prepare three-days' rations before breaking camp, even when they were supposed to stick to a timetable). In fact, his designation as Lee's "old reliable" appears to have been bestowed by someone who had never actually worked with him or had to rely upon him.

Similarly, Longstreet's clash with A. P. Hill, then Jackson, Hood and Toombs, were indicative of his unwillingness to accept that he was not the center of attention; not the one destined for greatness. And, of course, as the War progressed, Longstreet's propensity to find fault (and start feuds) with Lafayette McLaws (who he tried to have court-martialed), Evander Law (who he tried to have arrested), Charles Field, and ultimately, Lee himself, was highly indicative of the self-possessed illusion Longstreet was living (and fighting) under. While always quick to reprimand any subordinate who questioned his orders, he clearly hesitated to resist orders from his superiors on occasions. In his Gettysburg account, Longstreet had the impudence to blame Lee for "not changing his plans" based on Longstreet's "want of confidence in them."

After General Robert E. Lee died in October of 1870, a group of ex-Confederates led by General Jubal Early (who had led a division in Ewell's corps at Gettysburg) publicly criticized Longstreet for ignoring orders and delaying his attack on the second day of the Battle on July 2, 1863. But while many former Confederates held Longstreet accountable for not following orders, Early took it one step further, arguing that Longstreet -- not Lee -- was responsible for the Confederate defeat (deemed a "tactical disaster" by most) that by most accounts was the beginning of the end for the Confederacy.

In his memoirs, however, Longstreet defended himself, saying that the blistering post-War attacks concerning Gettysburg were merely "payback for supporting Black suffrage", thus shifting the blame back to Lee. He wrote, "[Lee] knew that I did not believe that success was possible . . . he should have put an officer in charge who had more confidence in his plan."[19] He went on to say that Lee should have given the responsibility to Early, thus justifying his insubordination.

On the other hand, Longstreet's reputation has mostly been on the upswing in the past few decades, due in no small part to Michael Shaara's 1974 novel *The Killer Angels*, which portrayed Longstreet in a more flattering light. That novel was the basis for the 1993 film *Gettysburg*, which has also helped rehabilitate Longstreet's legacy and helped make clear to the public how instrumental he was during the war. In 1982, Thomas L. Connolly and Barbara L. Bellows published *God and General Longstreet*, which took the Lost Cause proponents like Early to task for their blatant fabrications (such as the one that Lee ordered Longstreet to attack in the early morning of Day 2 of Gettysburg), helping make clear the extent of historical revision propagated by the Lost Cause. In doing so, they cast Longstreet as a sympathetic victim of circumstances

---

[19]   Gaffney, P., and D. Gaffney. *The Civil War: Exploring History One Week at a Time.* Page 442.

and sectional and political hostility.

It's also important to note that Lee himself never made any post-War statements to suggest that he held Longstreet responsible for the Confederacy's demise.

Stuart?

Outwardly, Stuart was the embodiment of reckless courage, magnificent manhood, and unconquerable virility; a man who could wear--without drawing suspicion of instability--the flamboyant adornments of a classic cavalier. It was once written that his black plume and hat caught up with a golden star, seemed the proper frame for a knightly face. In that same vein, people were always aware that Stuart was engaging in public relations even then, and Civil War historian Jeff Wert captured it well: "Stuart had been the Confederacy's knight-errant, the bold and dashing cavalier, attired in a resplendent uniform, plumed hat, and cape. Amid a slaughterhouse, he had embodied chivalry, clinging to the pageantry of a long-gone warrior. He crafted the image carefully, and the image befitted him. He saw himself as the Southern people envisaged him. They needed a knight; he needed to be that knight." Stuart, in effect, was the very essence of the Lost Cause.

It has been widely presumed that those same vainglorious traits led Stuart on a glory-seeking mission near the end of June 1863, which badly damaged Lee's abilities in Pennsylvania and directly led to the Army of Northern Virginia stumbling into a general battle Lee wished to avoid. Though credited with devoting his full attention to the Confederate cause upon his arrival, many historians attribute the catastrophic loss to the absence of Stuart and his cavalry. Immediately becoming the most devastating event of Stuart's military career, in his official report General Lee's wrote, " . . . the absence of the cavalry rendered it impossible to obtain accurate information. By the route [we] pursued, the Federal Army was interposed between [my] command and our main body, preventing any communication with [Stuart] until his arrival at Carlisle. The march toward Gettysburg was conducted more slowly than it would have been had the movements of the Federal Army been known." Some of Stuart's subordinates would come to his defense after the war, and Lee deserves some blame for allowing his subordinates so much discretion, which may have worked with Stonewall Jackson but backfired spectacularly with Ewell and Stuart. After the war, Stuart's subordinate, General Thomas L. Rosser stated what many were already convinced of, "On this campaign, [Stuart] undoubtedly, make the fatal blunder which lost us the battle of Gettysburg."[20]

The Army of the Potomac?

To a great extent, the Confederates' search for scapegoats is a product of the fact that they were

---

[20]   Wert, Jeffry D. *Cavalryman of the Lost Cause: A Biography of J.E.B. Stuart.* Page 300.

so used to being successful that a defeat had to be explained by a Southern failure, not a Northern success.

In casting about for Southern deficiencies, it is often overlooked that Meade and his top subordinates fought a remarkably efficient battle. Meade created an extremely sturdy defensive line anchored on high ground, he held the interior lines by having his army spread out over a smaller area, and he used that ability to shuffle troops from the right to the left on July 2. Moreover, Meade was able to rely on his corps commanders, especially Hancock, to properly use their discretion. Before the battle, Lee reportedly said that Meade "would commit no blunders on my front and if I make one ... will make haste to take advantage of it." If he said it, he was definitely right.

Perhaps none other than George Pickett himself put it best. When asked (certainly ad nauseam) why Pickett's Charge had failed, Pickett is said to have tersely replied, "I've always thought the Yankees had something to do with it."

Meade Bibliography

Catton, Bruce. *Grant Takes Command*. New York: Little, Brown and Company, 1968.
        This Hallowed Ground. Great Britain: Wordsworth, 1998.

Civil War Women website, "Margaretta Sergeant Meade" accessed via:
http://www.civilwarwomenblog.com/2009/06/margaretta-sergeant-meade.html 07.25.2012.

Davis, Kenneth C. *The Civil War: Everything You Need to Know About America's Greatest Conflict but Never Learned*. New York: William Morrow and Company, Inc., 1996.

Eicher, John H., and David J. Eicher. *Civil War High Commands*. Stanford, CA: Stanford University Press, 2001.

Gaffney, P., and D. Gaffney. *The Civil War: Exploring History One Week at a Time*. New York: Hyperion, 2011.

General Meade Society of Philadelphia website: http://www.civilwar.com/news/recent-postings/150484-the-general-meade-society-of-philadelphia.html accessed 07.20. 2012.

Historynet.com, "Day One at Chancellorsville" accessed via: http://www.historynet.com/day-one-at-chancellorsville-march-96-americas-civil-war-feature.htm 07.24.2012.

Lanning, Michael Lee. *The Civil War 100*. Illinois: Sourcebooks, Inc., 2006.

Meade George G. Jr. *The Life and Letters of George Gordon Meade*. 2 Vols. New York, 1913, accessed via: http://www.rocemabra.com/~roger/tagg/generals/general01.html 07.18.2012.

McPherson, James M. *Ordeal by Fire: The Civil War and Reconstruction*. New York: McGraw- Hill, 2001.

Porter, Horace. *Campaigning with Grant*. New York: Bonanza Books, 1961.

Sell, Bill. *Civil War Chronicles: Leaders of the North and South*. New York: MetroBooks, 1996.

Stevens, Joseph E. *1863: The Rebirth of a Nation*. New York: Bantam Books, 1999.

Hancock Bibliography

Catton, Bruce. *Grant Takes Command*. New York: Little, Brown and Company, 1968.

Davis, Kenneth C. *The Civil War: Everything You Need to Know About America's Greatest Conflict but Never Learned*. New York: William Morrow and Company, Inc., 1996.

Gaffney, P., and D. Gaffney. *The Civil War: Exploring History One Week at a Time*. New York: Hyperion, 2011.

Goodrich, Frederick Elizur. *Life of Winfield Scott Hancock, Major-General, U. S. A.* Boston: B. B. Russell, 1886. Accessed via: http://books.google.com/books?id=g1B9CIlrGbwC&pg=PA23&source=gbs_toc_r&cad=4#v=on epage&q&f=false 07.13.2012.

Kopel, David, et al. "The Hero of Gettysburg: Winfield Scott Hancock's shot straight." *National Review Online*, accessed via http://old.nationalreview.com/comment/kopel200407020018.asp 07.15.2012.

Lanning, Michael Lee. *The Civil War 100*. Illinois: Sourcebooks, Inc., 2006.

McPherson, James M. *Ordeal by Fire: The Civil War and Reconstruction*. New York: McGraw- Hill, 2001.

Porter, Horace. *Campaigning with Grant*. New York: Bonanza Books, 1961.

Tagg, Larry. *The Generals of Gettysburg*. Campbell, CA: Savas Publishing, 1998.

Tucker, Glenn. *Hancock the Superb.* Indianapolis: Bobbs-Merrill Co., 1960.

Chamberlain Bibliography

Bowdoin College Archives, accessed via: http://learn.bowdoin.edu/joshua-lawrence-chamberlain/ 06.27.2012.

Davis, Kenneth C. *The Civil War: Everything You Need to Know About America's Greatest Conflict but Never Learned.* New York: William Morrow and Company, Inc., 1996.

Desjardin, Thomas A. *Stand Firm Ye Boys from Maine: The 20th Maine and the Gettysburg Campaign.* Thomas Publications, 1995.

"Why People Admire Joshua Lawrence Chamberlain." Accessed via http://www.joshua.lurker00.com/jlcadmirers.htm 06.30.2012.

Gaffney, P., and D. Gaffney. *The Civil War: Exploring History One Week at a Time.* New York: Hyperion, 2011.

Lanning, Michael Lee. *The Civil War 100.* Illinois: Sourcebooks, Inc., 2006.

Sell, Bill. *Civil War Chronicles: Leaders of the North and South.* New York: MetroBooks, 1996.

Wallace, Willard M. *Soul of the Lion: A Biography of General Joshua L. Chamberlain.* Gettysburg, PA: Stan Clark Military Books, 1991.

Lee Bibliography

Freeman, Douglas Southall. *R.E. Lee: A Biography*, 1934-5.

Blount, Jr., Roy. *Robert E. Lee.* New York: Penguin Books, 2003.

Connelly, Thomas L. *The Marble Man: Robert E. Lee and His Image in American Society.* New York: Alfred A. Knopf, 1977.

Dowdey, Clifford (editor). *The Wartime Papers of R. E. Lee.* New York: Bramhall House, 1961.

Fellman, Michael. *The Making of Robert E. Lee*. New York: Random House, 2000.

Flood, Charles. *Lee: The Last Years*. New York: Houghton, 1981.

Horn, Stanley F. (editor). *The Robert E. Lee Reader*. New York: Konecky & Konecky, 1949.

Nagel, Paul C. *The Lee's of Virginia*. New York: Oxford University Press, 1990.

Pryor, Elizabeth Brown (October 29, 2009). "Robert Edward Lee (ca. 1806-1870)," *Encyclopedia Virginia*. Retrieved March 11, 2012.

Thomas, Emory M. *Robert E. Lee: A Biography*. New York: W. W. Norton & Company, 1995.

Van Doren Stern, Philip. *Robert E. Lee: The Man and the Soldier*. New York: Bonanza Books, 1963.

Longstreet Bibliography

Alexander, Edward P. (Gary W. Gallagher, editor). *Fighting for the Confederacy: The Personal Recollections of General Edward Porter Alexander*. Chapel Hill: University of North Carolina Press, 1989.

Catton, Bruce. *This Hallowed Ground*. New York: Doubleday & Company, Inc., 1956.

Davis, Kenneth C. *The Civil War: Everything You Need to Know About America's Greatest Conflict but Never Learned*. New York: William Morrow and Company, Inc., 1996.

Dowdey, Clifford. *Lee's Last Campaign: The Story of Lee & His Men against Grant--1864*. Lincoln: University of Nebraska Press, 1988.

Gaffney, P., and D. Gaffney. *The Civil War: Exploring History One Week at a Time*. New York: Hyperion, 2011.

Garrison, Webb. *Civil War Curiosities*. Nashville: Rutledge Hill Press, 1994.

Lanning, Michael Lee. *The Civil War 100*. Illinois: Sourcebooks, Inc., 2006.

Neely, Mark E., Holzer, Harold & Boritt, Gabor S. *The Confederate Image*. Chapel Hill: The University of North Carolina Press, 1987.

Phillips, Kevin. *The Cousins' Wars*. New York: Basic Books, 1999.

Rhea, Gordon C. *The Battle of the Wilderness May 5–6, 1864*. Baton Rouge: Louisiana State University Press, 1994.

Sanger, Donald B., & Thomas Robson Hay. *James Longstreet, I: Soldier*. Baton Rouge: Louisiana State University Press, 1952.

Sell, Bill. *Civil War Chronicles: Leaders of the North and South*. New York: MetroBooks, 1996.

Stepp, John, W. and Hill, William I. (editors). *Mirror of War, The Washington Star Reports the Civil War*. The Evening Star Newspaper Co., 1961.

Tagg, Larry. *The Generals of Gettysburg*. CA: Savas Publishing, 1998.

Wert, Jeffry D. *General James Longstreet: The Confederacy's Most Controversial Soldier: A Biography*. New York: Simon & Schuster, 1993.

Stuart Bibliography

Catton, Bruce. *This Hallowed Ground: The Story of the Union Side of the Civil War*. New York: Doubleday & Company, 1955.

Davis, Burke. *Jeb Stuart: The Last Cavalier*. New York: Random House, 1957.

Eaton, Clement. *Jefferson Davis*. New York: The Free Press, 1977.

Eicher, John H. & David, J. *Civil War High Commands*. Stanford: Stanford University Press, 2001.

Escott, Paul D. "The Uses of Gallantry: Virginians and the Origins of J. E. B. Stuart's Historical Image," *The Virginia Magazine of History and Biography*, Vol 103, No 1, 1995. Accessed via Jstor: http://www.jstor.org/discover/10.2307/4249485?uid=3739600&uid=2&uid=4&uid=3739256&sid=21100770232471 05.05.2012.

Garrison, Webb. *Civil War Curiosities*. Nashville: Rutledge Hill Press, 1994.

Howard, O. O. (Oliver Otis), *Autobiography of Oliver Otis Howard, Major General, United States Army*. New York: The Baker & Taylor Company, 1907. Accessed via http://archive.org/details/autobiographyofo01howarich 05.07.2012.

Lanning, Michael Lee. *The Civil War 100*. Illinois: Sourcebooks, Inc., 2006.

Lee, Robert E., Jr. *Recollections and Letters of General Robert E. Lee by Captain E. Lee, His Son.* Retrieved via http://www.quillspirit.org/ebooks/Letters_of_General_R_E_Lee/6.php 05.06.2012.

Mosby, John Singleton. *The Memoirs of Colonel John S. Mosby.* Boston: Little, Brown, and Company, 1917. Accessed via http://docsouth.unc.edu/fpn/mosby/menu.html 05.05.2012.

Philips, David. *Crucial Land Battles.* New York: MetroBooks, 1996.

Sears, Stephen W. *Chancellorsville.* Boston: Houghton Mifflin, 1996.
        Gettysburg. Boston: Houghton Mifflin, 2003.

Sifakis, Stewart, "Who Was Who In The Civil War." Accessed via:
http://www.civilwarhome.com/stuartbi.htm 05.07.2012.

Stuart Family Archives: http://archiver.rootsweb.ancestry.com/th/read/STUART/2006-04/1144035927 Accessed 05.04.2012.

Stepp, John W. & Hill, William I. (editors), *Mirror of War, the Washington Star Reports the Civil War.* The Evening Star Newspaper Company, 1961.

Thomas, Emory M. *Bold Dragoon: The Life of J.E.B. Stuart.* Norman: University of Oklahoma Press, 1986.

Wert, Jeffry D. *Cavalryman of the Lost Cause: A Biography of J.E.B. Stuart.* New York: Simon & Schuster, 2008.

Wright, C. M. "Flora Cooke Stuart (1836–1923)." Retrieved via Encyclopedia Virginia:
http://www.EncyclopediaVirginia.org/Stuart_Flora_Cooke_1836-1923 on 05.06.2012.

The Battle of Chickamauga

Chapter 1: The Summer of 1863

Of all the commanders who led armies during major battles of the Civil War, historians have by and large agreed that the most inept generals to face each other were the Union's William Rosecrans and the Confederacy's Braxton Bragg. The two generals' armies, the Union Army of the Cumberland and the Confederate Army of Tennessee, had already fought at the Battle of Stones River (Battle of Murfreesboro) at the end of 1862, inflicting massive casualties on each other without gaining an advantage.

Rosecrans and Bragg

During the first half of 1863, the two armies maneuvered around Chattanooga, Tennessee, one of the important railroad hubs of the theater. With Ulysses S. Grant laying siege to Vicksburg and trying to close off the Mississippi River, the Lincoln Administration hoped that a decisive campaign by Bragg in southern Tennessee would lay the groundwork for the capture of Atlanta, one of the Confederacy's most important cities.

That very thought terrorized the minds of Confederate officials and generals, even some of those fighting in the East. Early in 1863, Robert E. Lee's principal subordinate, James Longstreet, had advocated letting him take his corps west to try to relieve Vicksburg or conduct a campaign in Tennessee that would force Grant to stop his siege or send some of his men elsewhere. Lee had not wanted to detach any soldiers from his own army, given that it was badly outnumbered by the Union Army of the Potomac, but after the fall of Vicksburg and the defeat at Gettysburg, the situation had changed. Longstreet explained in his memoirs:

"To me the emergency seemed so grave that I decided to write the Honorable Secretary of War (excusing the informality under the privilege given in his request in May) expressing my opinion of affairs in that military zone. I said that the successful march of General Rosecrans's army through Georgia would virtually be the finishing stroke of the war; that in the fall of Vicksburg and the free flow of the Mississippi River the lungs of the Confederacy were lost; that the impending march would cut through the heart of the South, and leave but little time for the dissolution; that to my mind the remedy was to order the Army of Northern Virginia to defensive work, and send detachments to reinforce the army in Tennessee; to call detachments of other commands to the same service, and strike a crushing blow against General Rosecrans before he could receive reinforcing help; that our interior lines gave the opportunity, and it was only by the skilful use of them that we could reasonably hope to equalize our power to that of the better-equipped adversary; that the subject had not been mentioned to my commander, because like all others he was opposed to having important detachments of his army so far beyond his reach; that all must realize that our affairs were languishing, and that the only hope of reviving the waning cause was through the advantage of interior lines."

Longstreet

After the fall of Vicksburg, the Confederate high command had reached the same opinion, and during the end of July and into August they went about strengthening Bragg's Army of Tennessee. Bragg had about 50,000 men that summer, but Davis added the Department of East Tennessee, which included nearly 18,000 men under Maj. Gen. Simon B. Buckner, into Bragg's Department of Tennessee. Meanwhile, plans were set in motion to detach Longstreet's corps from Lee's Army of Northern Virginia and transfer it to Tennessee by rail.

As Bragg's army was being reinforced, there was another matter that Jefferson Davis had to work through: the internal squabbles among his generals. Bragg's previous campaigns (and their lack of successes) had led to harsh criticism from some of the men now nominally under his command, including the equally incompetent Lt. Gen. Leonidas Polk, as well as William Hardee and Simon Bolivar Buckner. In his official report to the Confederate government after the battle, Bragg hinted at how the mutual disdain among the senior officers in his department led to arguments over orders that summer:

"On August 20, it was ascertained certainly that the Federal army from Middle Tennessee, under General Rosecrans, had crossed the mountains to Stevenson and Bridgeport. His force of effective infantry and artillery amounted to fully 70,000, divided into four corps. About the same time General Burnside advanced from Kentucky toward Knoxville, East Tennessee, with a force estimated by the general commanding that department at over 25,000.

In view of the great superiority of numbers brought against him General Buckner concluded to evacuate Knoxville, and with a force of about 5,000 infantry and artillery and his cavalry took position in the vicinity of Loudon. Two brigades of his command (Frazer's, at Cumberland Gap, and Jackson's, in Northeast Tennessee) were thus severed from us.

The enemy having already obtained a lodgment in East Tennessee by another route, the continued occupation of Cumberland Gap became very hazardous to the garrison and comparatively unimportant to us. Its evacuation was accordingly ordered, but on the appeal of its commander, stating his resources and ability for defense, favorably indorsed by Major-General Buckner, the orders were suspended on August 31. The main body of our army was encamped near Chattanooga, while the cavalry force, much reduced and enfeebled by long service on short rations, was recruiting in the vicinity of Rome, Ga."

Hardee, in command of one of Bragg's corps, despised Bragg so greatly that he requested for a transfer out of Bragg's department in July and was replaced by D.H. Hill, brother-in-law to Stonewall Jackson and a close friend to both James Longstreet and Joseph E. Johnston. Although his military ability was well respected, he was underutilized during the second half of the Civil War due to his own falling out with Lee. Longstreet would later incur the wrath of some of his former Confederate comrades by writing that Hill was not given command of a corps in the Army of Northern Virginia because he wasn't a Virginian, which was considered an implicit criticism of Lee. Hill and Longstreet were both substantial command upgrades and among the best generals the Confederacy had, and by the time Chickamauga was over they would both harbor an intense dislike of Bragg as well.

Hill would write an account of the battle after the war that was published in the seminal *Battles & Leaders of the Civil War* series, and in it he recounted his first meeting with Bragg in years:

"On the 19th of July I reported to General Bragg at Chattanooga. I had not seen him since I had been the junior lieutenant in his battery of artillery at Corpus Christi, Texas, in 1845. The other two lieutenants were George H. Thomas and John F. Reynolds. We four had been in the same mess there. Reynolds had been killed at Gettysburg twelve days before my new assignment. Thomas, the strongest and most pronounced Southerner of the four, was now Rosecrans's lieutenant. It was a strange casting of lots that three messmates of Corpus Christi should meet under such changed circumstances at Chickamauga.

My interview with General Bragg at Chattanooga was not satisfactory. He was silent and reserved and seemed gloomy and despondent. He had grown prematurely old since I saw him last, and showed much nervousness. His relations with his next in command (General Polk) and with some others of his subordinates were known not to be pleasant. His many retreats, too, had alienated the rank and file from him, or at least had taken away that enthusiasm which soldiers feel for the successful general, and which makes them obey his orders without question, and thus wins for him other successes. The one thing that a soldier never fails to understand is victory, and the commander who leads him to victory will be adored by him whether that victory has been won by skill or by blundering, by the masterly handling of a few troops against great odds, or by the awkward use of over whelming numbers."

Hill's account suggests that the issues between Bragg and his subordinates were so well-known that it was already coloring the attitudes of men who had not yet served under him. It's likely that the only reason this situation was allowed to fester for as long as it did is because Bragg and Jefferson Davis had been close friends since their days at West Point decades earlier. Davis's loyalty to his friends presented similar problems, as he had very obvious favorites among his generals, like Lee, Bragg, and Albert Sidney Johnston. At the same time, he constantly bickered with other generals in the field, notably Joseph E. Johnston, and the discord hurt the Southern cause, especially in the West. Even after Davis reluctantly removed Bragg from command out West, he would bring Bragg to Richmond to serve as a military advisor.

While the discord among the generals clearly didn't help matters, the reinforcements gave Bragg a numbers advantage over Rosecrans, a rare situation for a Confederate army during the war. With that, Bragg was determined to take offensive operations in late August and early September, as he had been urged to do by the Confederate government.

Bragg's account noted that one of the reasons he wanted to delay moving forward was because the geographical terrain made advancing difficult, and he had hoped that it would be Rosecrans who would be forced to move forward in that same area. Sure enough, Rosecrans was hoping to avoid doing just that, but he was also being pressed to conduct offensive operations by his government. Rosecrans would thus have to march his army through the Cumberland Plateau, which would disrupt his supply lines due to poor roads and a lack of resources in the vicinity, and when he was ordered forward by Henry "Old Brains" Halleck, the general-in-chief, he described the order as being full of "recklessness, conceit and malice."

Rosecrans had managed to outmaneuver Bragg earlier in 1863 without much fighting, and he hoped to do so again in the summer. His ambitious plan called for using part of his army to pin down Bragg north of Chattanooga while the rest of his army crossed the Tennessee River well downstream and then had space to march forward on a wide front and encircle Bragg in Chattanooga or compel him to evacuate.

Rosecrans had outlined an overly ambitious marching strategy, which was made all the more bewildering by the fact that he detailed the complex difficulties associated with the movements in his post-battle report:

"It is evident from this description of the topography that to reach Chattanooga, or penetrate the country south of it, on the railroad, by crossing the Tennessee below Chattanooga was a difficult task. It was necessary to cross the Cumberland Mountains, with subsistence, ammunition, at least a limited supply of forage, and a bridge train; to cross Sand or Raccoon Mountains into Lookout Valley, then Lookout Mountain, and finally the lesser ranges, Missionary Ridge, if we went directly to Chattanooga, or Missionary Ridge, Pigeon Mountain, and Taylor s Ridge, if we struck the railroad at Dalton or south of it. The Valley of the Tennessee River, though several miles in breadth between the bases of the mountains, below Bridgeport, is not a broad, alluvial farming country, but full of barren oak ridges, sparsely settled, and but a small part of it under cultivation...

The first step was to repair the Nashville and Chattanooga Railroad, to bring forward to Tullahoma, McMinnville, Decherd, and Winchester needful forage and subsistence, which it was impossible to transport from Murfreesborough to those points over the horrible roads which we encountered on our advance to Tullahoma. The next was to extend the repairs of the main stem to Stevenson and Bridgeport, and the Tracy City branch, so that we could place supplies in depot at those points, from which to draw after we had crossed the mountains...

The crossing of the river required that the best points should be chosen, and means provided for the crossing. The river was reconnoitered, the pontoons and trains ordered forward as rapidly as possible, hidden from view in rear of Stevenson and prepared for use. By the time they were ready the places of crossing had been selected and dispositions made to begin the operation.

It was very desirable to conceal to the last moment the points of crossing, but as the mountains on the south side of the Tennessee rise in precipitous rocky bluffs to the height of 800 or 1,000 feet, completely overlooking the whole valley and its coves, this was next to impossible."

As Rosecrans was attempting the multiple crossings and aiming to concentrate his army again after doing so, the amount of time it took allowed more Confederate reinforcements to arrive from Mississippi. Adding to his challenges, there were only three suitable roads that could be used to link the several corps of his armies back together, leaving the isolated elements of his army dangerously exposed. When Bragg became aware of these dispositions, he evacuated from Chattanooga and fell back for the purpose of crushing that part of the Army of the Cumberland to his south, which included Alexander McCook's XX Corps and George H. Thomas's XIV Corps. Badly mistaking Bragg's movement as a general retreat further back into Atlanta, a joyous Rosecrans telegraphed Washington on September 9, "Chattanooga is ours without a struggle and East Tennessee is free."

Thomas

In actuality, Bragg had pulled the Army of Tennessee 20 miles back to LaFayette, which would allow him to potentially fall on the two isolated Union corps, who were way too far away from the rest of the Army of the Cumberland to receive support from them in the case of an attack. After Thomas Crittenden's XXI Corps occupied Chattanooga, Rosecrans ignored Thomas's advice to delay an advance on Bragg's army until the three Union corps could get within supporting range of each other and secure their supply lines. Instead, Rosecrans ordered one of his cavalry divisions to raid the Confederate supply lines at Resaca, have McCook's XX Corps swing further south across Lookout Mountain, push Crittenden's corps south in chase of Bragg, and move Thomas forward to LaFayette.

In other words, Rosecrans was unwittingly marching Thomas's 23,000 men straight at Bragg's entire army, just as Bragg was concentrating there for the purposes of attacking an isolated corps.

Chapter 2: Davis's Cross Roads

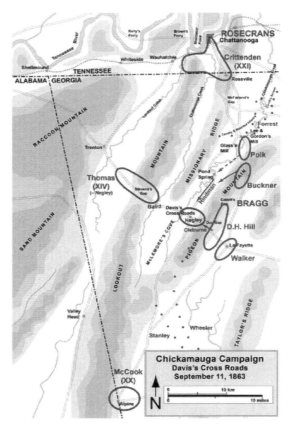

Chickamauga Campaign
Davis's Cross Roads
September 11, 1863

Given Rosecrans's orders, Thomas's corps began marching toward Dug Gap in column formation, with James Negley's division in the vanguard 12 hours ahead of the next closest division. Bragg was already aware of this forward movement on September 9, and he immediately took steps to attack Negley's division near Davis's Cross Roads by hopefully having Thomas Hindman's division march into Negley's rear near McLemore's Cove as Negley unwittingly pressed forward, thereby separating Negley from the rest of Thomas's corps:

"During the 9th it was ascertained that a column, estimated at from 4,000 to 8,000, had crossed Lookout Mountain into the cove by way of Stevens' and Cooper's Gaps. Thrown off his guard by our rapid movement, apparently in retreat, when in reality we had concentrated opposite his center, and deceived by the information from deserters and others sent into his lines, the enemy pressed on his columns to intercept us and thus exposed himself in detail.

Major-General Hindman received verbal instructions on the 9th to prepare his division to move against this force, and was informed that another division from Lieutenant-General Hill's command, at La Fayette, would join him. That evening the following written orders were issued to Generals Hindman and Hill:"

The first of several examples of incompetence among Confederate officers took place on the morning of September 10. Bragg had coordinated Hindman's division to march southwest into Negley's flank and rear as Patrick Cleburne's division of D.H. Hill's corps opposed Negley in front. As Negley kept unwittingly walking into the trap, around the time his division reached Davis's Cross Roads he heard about Hindman's movement threatening his left flank and rear and thus pulled back to take up a defensive position around McLemore's Cove, where Hindman could not flank him.

That countermarch was made possible by the fact that Cleburne's division never marched that day, which would lead to finger pointing between Bragg and D.H. Hill. Writing after the war, Hill blamed Bragg, insisting not only that the orders arrived too late but that Cleburne was ill and their proposed march would have been obstructed by physical obstacles anyway:

"As the failure of Bragg to beat Rosecrans in detail has been the subject of much criticism, it may be well to look into the causes of the failure. So far as the commanding general was concerned, the trouble with him was : first, lack of knowledge of the situation; second, lack of personal supervision of the execution of his orders. No general ever won a permanent fame who was wanting in these and elements of success, knowledge of his own and his enemy's condition, and personal superintendence of operations on the field.

The failure to attack Negley's division in the cove on September 10th, was owing to Bragg's ignorance of the condition of the roads, the obstructions at Dug Gap, and the position of the enemy."

D.H. Hill

While Hill dithered, Hindman had come within 4 miles of Negley's division but became concerned about attacking without Cleburne's division attacking in front as well. Even after being reinforced with more men from Buckner's corps, Hindman refused to make the attack on the afternoon of the 10th.

Infuriating Bragg even further, despite Hill's claims about Cleburne being sick, Cleburne was apparently well enough to order his division to start clearing the felled timber around Dug Gap and get ready to advance once he heard Hindman commence an attack on the 11th, but there seemed to have been some confusion at Hindman's headquarters over whether he was supposed to attack on the 11th. Hindman had already advised against making his attack on the 10th, only to have that advice rejected by Bragg, so naturally his attack on the 11th would be half-hearted as well. By the time the Confederates had finally coordinated an attack on Negley, a second division of the corps had reached them and taken up a defensive position, making an orderly retreat possible with a rearguard covering against Hindman's skirmishers.

Rosecrans seemed to more fully understand the situation and his dire predicament after the near disaster at Davis's Cross Roads, writing:

"On the 10th, Negley's division advanced to within a mile of Dug Gap, which he found heavily obstructed, and Baird's division came up to his support on the morning of the 11th. Negley became satisfied that the enemy was advancing upon him, in heavy force, and perceiving that if he accepted battle in that position he would probably be cut off, he fell back after a sharp skirmish, in which General Baird's division participated, skillfully covering and securing their trains, to a strong position in front of Stevens' Gap. On the 12th, Reynolds and Brannan, under orders to move promptly, closed up to the support of these two advanced divisions.

During the same day General McCook had reached the vicinity of Alpine, and, with infantry and cavalry, had reconnoitered the Broom-town Valley to Summerville, and ascertained that the enemy had not retreated on Rome, but was concentrating at La Fayette.

Thus it was ascertained that the enemy was concentrating all his forces, both infantry and cavalry, behind the Pigeon Mountain, in the vicinity of La Fayette, while the corps of this army were at Gordon's Mills, Bailey's Cross-Roads, at the foot of Stevens' Gap, and at Alpine, a distance of 40 miles, from flank to flank, by the nearest practicable roads, and 57 miles by the route subsequently taken by the Twentieth Army Corps. It had already been ascertained that the main body of Johnston's army had joined Bragg, and an accumulation of evidence showed that the troops from Virginia had reached Atlanta on the 1st of the month, and that re-enforcements were expected soon to arrive from that quarter. It was therefore a matter of life and death to effect the concentration of the army."

Chapter 3: Concentrating the Army of the Cumberland

The day after Negley avoided disaster in the south, Rosecrans began drawing up orders to link up his army. On September 12, he ordered McCook's XX Corps and his cavalry to march northeast and link up with Thomas's corps near Stevens Gap, and together they would continue marching northeast to link back up with Crittenden. As it turned out, the sheer distance between McCook and Rosecrans near Chattanooga meant it would take an entire day just for that order to reach McCook. It would then take at least three more days of hard marching to successfully link the three corps back up together.

Bragg's attempt to bag Negley's division had been a disappointment, but he still hoped to strike out at the isolated Union corps in detail, including Crittenden's corps. One of Bragg's cavalry corps, commanded by the legendary Nathan Bedford Forrest, reported Crittenden's southern movement toward Lee and Gordon's Mill, inducing Bragg to order Polk to make an attack with two of the corps under his command.

Forrest

On the night of September 12, Polk sent the order:

"Lieutenant-General POLK:

GENERAL: I inclose you a dispatch from General Pegram. This presents you a fine opportunity of striking Crittenden in detail, and I hope you will avail yourself of it at daylight to-morrow. This division crushed, and the others are yours. We can then turn again on the force in the cove. Wheeler's cavalry will move on Wilder, so as to cover your right. I shall be delighted to hear of your success."

Once again, the attack Bragg envisioned failed to materialize, this time because Bragg himself was unfamiliar with the dispositions of Crittenden's corps. Bragg had ordered Polk's men to certain points previously that would have made it impossible to reach Lee and Gordon's Mill in time to attack Crittenden before the entire corps had passed that point. This was lost on Bragg, who was infuriated at the time and complained in his post-battle report:

"Early on the 13th, I proceeded to the front, ahead of Buckner's command, to find that no advance had been made on the enemy, and that his forces had formed a junction and recrossed the Chickamauga. Again disappointed, immediate measures were taken to place our trains and limited supplies in safe positions, when all our forces were concentrated along the Chickamauga, threatening the enemy in front."

D.H. Hill pinned the blame for Bragg's lack of knowledge on what he considered a very obvious mistake, juxtaposing him with Stonewall Jackson for good measure:

"During the active operations of a campaign the post of the commander-in-chief should be in the center of his marching columns, that he may be able to give prompt and efficient aid to whichever wing may be threatened. But whenever a great battle is to be fought, the commander must be on the field to see that his orders are executed and to take advantage of the ever-changing phases of the conflict. Jackson leading a cavalry fight by night near Front Royal in the pursuit of Banks, Jackson at the head of the column following McClellan in the retreat from Richmond to Malvern Hill, presents a contrast to Bragg sending, from a distance of ten miles, four consecutive orders for an attack at daylight, which he was never to witness.

Surely in the annals of warfare there is no parallel to the coolness and nonchalance with which General Crittenden marched and counter-marched for a week with a delightful unconsciousness that he was in the presence of a force of superior strength. On the 11 we find him with two divisions (Van Cleve's and Palmer's) at Ringgold, twenty miles from Chattanooga, and with his third (Thomas J. Wood's), ten miles from Ringgold, at Lee and Gordon's Mills where it remained alone and unsupported, until late in the , day of the 12th."

Over the next several days, Rosecrans began to concentrate his army relatively unmolested and try to bring them all safely back toward Chattanooga. For their part, Bragg and his commanders decided that attacking Rosecrans in or around Chattanooga was their best available option. By the time that decision was made, the two divisions of Longstreet's corps that had been detached were just days away from arriving by rail.

On September 17, McCook's corps and Thomas's corps had linked back up, but Bragg tried to strike out north on September 18 toward Chattanooga, hoping to force a battle with Rosecrans or take the valuable city unopposed. If the Army of the Cumberland did put up a fight, Bragg figured his men would be well-positioned to turn their left flank, but in so doing he issued complex orders that would require a nearly impossible degree of coordination at 4 distinct crossing points of the Chickamauga creek.

"HEADQUARTERS ARMY OF TENNESSEE,

In the Field, Leet's Tan-yard, September 18, 1863.

1. Johnson's column (Hood's), on crossing at or near Reed's Bridge, will turn to the left by the most practicable route and sweep up the Chickamauga, toward Leo and Gordon's Mills.

2. Walker, crossing at Alexander's Bridge, will unite in this move and push vigorously on the enemy's flank and rear in the same direction.

3. Buckner, crossing at Thedford's Ford, will join in the movement to the left, and press the enemy up the stream from Polk's front at Lee and Gordon's Mills.

4. Polk will press his forces to the front of Lee and Gordon's Mills, and if met by too much resistance to cross will bear to the right and cross at Dalton's Ford, or at Thedford's, as may be necessary, and join in the attack wherever the enemy may be.

5. Hill will cover our left flank from an advance of the enemy from the cove, and by pressing the cavalry in his front ascertain if the enemy is re-enforcing at Lee and-Gordon's Mills, in which event he will attack them in flank.

6. Wheeler's cavalry will hold the gaps in Pigeon Mountain and cover our rear and left and bring up stragglers.

7. All teams, &c., not with troops should go toward Ringgold and Dalton, beyond Taylor's Ridge. All cooking should be done at the trains. Rations, when cooked, will be forwarded to the troops.

8. The above movements wall be executed with the utmost promptness, vigor, and persistence."

Naturally, these movements were full of delays on the morning of the 18th, not to mention the presence of Union cavalry in the area. Bragg later reported, "The resistance offered by the enemy's cavalry and the difficulties arising from the bad and narrow country roads caused unexpected delays in the execution of these movements. Though the commander of the right column was several times urged to press forward, his crossing was not effected until late in the afternoon."

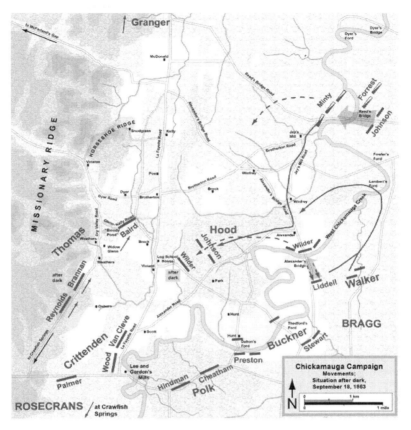

Rosecrans correctly predicted what Bragg was attempting and moved to counter it by quickly bringing up Thomas on Crittenden's left:

"Evidence accumulated during the day of the 18th that the enemy was moving to our left. Minty's cavalry and Wilder's mounted brigade encountered the enemy's cavalry at Reed's and Alexander's Bridges, and toward evening were driven into the Rossville road. At the same time the enemy had been demonstrating for 3 miles up the Chickamauga. Heavy clouds of dust had been observed 3 or 4 miles beyond the Chickamauga, sweeping to the northeast.

In view of all these facts, the necessity became apparent that General Thomas must use all possible dispatch in moving his corps to the position assigned it. He was therefore directed to proceed with all dispatch, and General McCook to close up to Crawfish Spring as soon as Thomas' column was out of the way. Thomas pushed forward uninterruptedly during the night, and at daylight the head of his column had reached Kelly's house on the La Fayette road, where Baird's division was posted. Brannan followed, and was posted on Baird's left, covering the roads leading to Reed's and Alexander's Bridges.

General Thomas ordered Brannan with two brigades to reconnoiter in that direction and attack any small force he should meet. The advance brigade, supported by the rest of the division, soon encountered a strong body of the enemy, attacked it vigorously, and drove it back more than half a mile, where a very strong column of the enemy was found, with the evident intention of turning our left and gaining possession of the La Fayette road between us and Chattanooga."

After the delays and dealing with the advanced Union defenders, several of Bragg's divisions had successfully pushed across the Chickamauga. By now, however, Thomas and Crooks were within supporting distance of Crittenden's corps. D.H. Hill faulted Bragg for being too late to make his attack orders:

"Had this order been issued on any of the four preceding days, it would have found Rosecrans wholly unprepared for it, with but a single infantry division (Wood's) guarding the crossings of the Chickamauga, and that at one point only, Lee and Gordon's - the fords north of it being watched by cavalry . Even if the order had been given twenty-four hours earlier, it must have been fatal to Rosecrans in the then huddled and confused grouping of his forces.

All that was effected on the 18th was the sending over of Walker's small corps of a little more than 5000 men near Alexander's Bridge, and Bushrod Johnson's division of 3600 men at Reed's Bridge, farther north. These troops drove off Wilder's mounted infantry from the crossings immediately south of them, so as to leave undisputed passage for Bragg's infantry, except in the neighborhood of Lee and Gordon's."

Chapter 4: September 19

Bragg's attack hadn't been carried out as expeditiously as he had hoped, but because he was unaware of the location of Thomas's corps, he planned for yet another attack on what he believed to be the Union's left flank during the morning of the 19th:

"The movement was resumed at daylight on the 19th, and Buckner's corps, with Cheatham's division, of Polk's, had crossed and formed, when a brisk engagement commenced with our cavalry under Forrest on the extreme right about 9 o'clock. A brigade from Walker was ordered to Forrest's support, and soon after Walker was ordered to attack with his whole force. Our line was now formed, with Buckner's left resting on the Chickamauga about 1 mile below Lee and Gordon's Mills. On his right came Hood with his own and Johnson's divisions, with Walker on the extreme right, Cheatham's division being in reserve, the general direction being a little east of north. The attack ordered by our right was made by General Walker in his usual gallant style, and soon developed a largely superior force opposed."

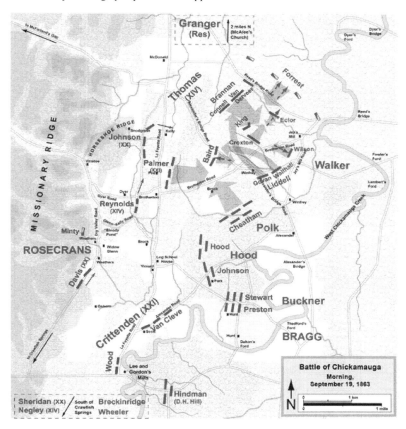

Fighting on the morning of September 19

Ironically, the first fighting of what became the Battle of Chickamauga involved Forrest's cavalry skirmishing with advanced pickets from Army of the Cumberland's Reserve Corps, commanded by Gordon Granger and stationed a couple of miles north. While those forces skirmished, it provided the Confederates evidence of the fact that the Union's left flank was not nearly as far south as Bragg had assumed it was. As the Union pickets were withdrawn north, the commander of their brigade, Daniel McCook, reported to Thomas that he assumed the fighting meant a Confederate infantry brigade was across the Chickamauga and potentially isolated. Unsure of whether McCook's report was accurate, Thomas sent orders to one of his division commanders, John Brannan, to try to find the brigade and destroy it. Thomas later reported:

"I directed General Brannan to post a brigade, within supporting distance of Baird, on the road to Alexander's Bridge, and with his other two brigades to reconnoiter the road leading to Reed's Bridge to see if he could locate the brigade reported by Colonel McCook, and, if a favorable opportunity occurred, to capture it. His dispositions were made according to instructions by 9 a.m."

McCook, of course, had skirmished with Forrest's Confederate cavalry, not a vulnerable infantry brigade. As the Union division advanced in a battle line, Forrest fought a delaying action by dismounting his cavalry troopers while requesting reinforcements from Bragg and William Walker, the commander of the two-division corps just south of Forrest's troopers. While Walker was ordering one of his brigades forward around 9:00 a.m., Bragg interpreted the advance of Brannan's division as being a major attack on his right flank, so he began the process of scrambling more and more men to his right. Thus, Thomas thought he was dealing with a Confederate brigade and had sent a division, while Bragg thought he was dealing with a major offensive by Rosecrans. Bragg later reported, "The enemy, whose left was at Lee and Gordon's Mills when our movement commenced, had rapidly transferred forces from his extreme right, changing his entire line, and seemed disposed to dispute with all his ability our effort to gain the main road to Chattanooga, in his rear. Lieutenant-General Polk was ordered to move his remaining division across at the nearest ford, and to assume the command in person on our right. Hill's corps was also ordered to cross below Lee and Gordon's Mills and join the line on the right."

By the time those movements were being made by the Confederates, the fighting between Walker's brigade and Forrest's cavalry against Brannan's division had started in earnest. Even by this early point, it was clear that the terrain around the Chickamauga would play a major role in the nature of the fighting and the ability to control the armies. Historian Steven Woodworth aptly described its effects on the fighting:

"The land between Chickamauga Creek and the LaFayette Road was gently rolling but almost completely wooded. ... In the woods no officer above brigadier could see all his command at once, and even the brigadiers often could see nobody's troops but their own and perhaps the enemy's. Chickamauga would be a classic 'soldiers battle,' but it would test officers at every level of command in ways they had not previously been tested. An additional complication was that each army would be attempting to fight a shifting battle while shifting its own position...Each general would have to conduct a battle while shuffling his own units northward toward an enemy of whose position he could get only the vaguest idea. Strange and wonderful opportunities would loom out of the leaves, vines, and gunsmoke, be touched and vaguely sensed, and then fade away again into the figurative fog of confusion that bedeviled men on both sides. In retrospect, victory for either side would look simple when unit positions were reviewed on a neat map, but in Chickamauga's torn and smoky woodlands, nothing was simple."

As the fighting started raging between Brannan's division and the Confederates, it acted like a vacuum that began sucking in nearby units on both sides, as Thomas started ordering more of his men to relieve Brannan. Thomas reported:

"General Baird was directed to throw forward his right wing, so as to get more nearly in line with Brannan, but to watch well on his right flank. Soon after this disposition of those two divisions, a portion of Palmer's division, of Crittenden's corps, took position to the right of General Baird's division. About 10 o'clock Croxton's brigade of Brannan's division, posted on the road leading to Alexander's Bridge, became engaged with the enemy, and I rode forward to his position to ascertain the character of the attack. Colonel Croxton reported to me that he had driven the enemy nearly half a mile, but that he was then meeting with obstinate resistance. I then rode back to Baird's position, and directed him to advance to Croxton's support, which he did with his whole division, Starkweather's brigade in reserve, and drove the enemy steadily before him for some distance, taking many prisoners. Croxton's brigade, which had been heavily engaged for over an hour with greatly superior numbers of the enemy, and being nearly exhausted of ammunition, was then moved to the rear to enable the men to fill up their boxes; and Baird and Brannan, having united their forces, drove the enemy from their immediate front. General Baird then halted for the purpose of readjusting his line; and hearing from prisoners that the enemy were in heavy force on his immediate right, he threw back his right wing in order to be ready for an attack from that quarter."

As Baird's division was pushing the Confederates back, St. John R. Liddell's division arrived to reinforce the Confederate line, hitting Baird's right flank and routing them. However, as Baird's brigades were breaking for the rear, the advancing Confederates were stunned and stopped by Ferdinand Van Derveer's brigade of Brannan's division. These attacks and counterattacks had inflicted steady losses, but neither side was able to hold onto the advantage for long, which all but guaranteed that both sides would send more men that way to try to achieve a decisive breakthrough.

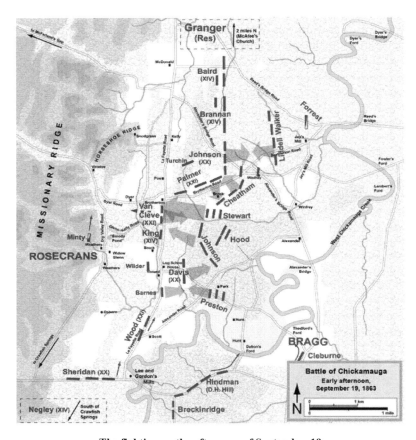

The fighting on the afternoon of September 19

The problem with this kind of fighting, as Hill noted, was that the reinforcements would go in piecemeal and make uncoordinated attacks, as opposed to reforming lines and making a general advance in larger force. Hill explained, "Unfortunately for the Confederates, there was no general advance, as there might have been along the whole line-an advance that must have given a more decisive victory on the 19th than was gained on the 20th. It was desultory fighting from right to left, without concert, and at inopportune times. It was the sparring of the amateur boxer, and not the crushing blows of the trained pugilist. From daylight on the 19th until after midday, there was a gap of two miles between Crittenden and Thomas, into which the Confederates could have poured, turning to right or left, and attacking in flank whichever commander was least prepared for the assault."

The closest the Confederates would come to a breakthrough would be in the center of the Union line during the early afternoon by men under the command of tenacious Texan John Bell Hood. A division commander in Longstreet's corps, Hood had been severely wounded at Gettysburg, recovering in time for the fighting at Chickamauga, and until Longstreet personally arrived later on the night of the 19th, Hood had command of the men in Longstreet's corps, which included his own division and Bushrod Johnson's division. As they advanced around 2:30, they began to steadily push the Union defenders back, thereby relieving a Confederate division under Alexander Stewart on their right, and for a moment they took control of the road to Chattanooga. However, a further advance was rebuffed by reinforcements in the form of four Union divisions, which pushed them back across the road, ensuring the Army of the Cumberland could keep using it to keep its own corps together.

Hood

The Union army subsequently launched a series of unsuccessful and uncoordinated counterattacks in that same sector, failing to push back the three Confederate divisions that had made about a mile of progress. Those attacks came to an end as night fell, but Bragg still intended to keep the fight going that night. Around 6:00 p.m., as it was getting dark, Bragg ordered Cleburne's division to shore up the Confederate army's right flank. Though the fighting in that sector had died down as Hood's men had pushed the action to the south, Cleburne now launched an attack that was hampered by the night and the heavily wooded underbrush. Cleburne called off the attack at 9:00 p.m., but not before having incurred about 30% casualties in his division.

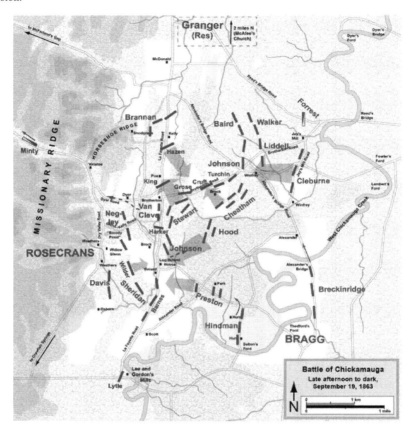

The last attacks of September 19

At the end of the fighting on September 19, some of the Confederates felt they had won a victory, particularly Bragg and Hood. Bragg was also determined to take the fight to Rosecrans again the following day:

"Night found us masters of the ground, after a series of very obstinate contests with largely superior numbers. From captured prisoners and others we learned with certainty that we had encountered the enemy's whole force, which had been moving day and night since they first ascertained the direction of our march. Orders had been given for the rapid march to the field of all re-enforcements arriving by railroad, and three additional brigades from this source joined us early next morning. The remaining forces on our extreme left, east of the Chickamauga, had been ordered up early in the afternoon, but reached the field too late to participate in the engagement of that day. They were ordered into line on their arrival, and disposed for a renewal of the action early the next morning."

Naturally, Rosecrans saw things differently, reporting:

"The roar of battle hushed in the darkness of night, and our troops, weary with a night of marching and a day of fighting, rested on their arms, having everywhere maintained their positions, developed the enemy, and gained thorough command of the Rossville and Dry Valley roads to Chattanooga, the great object of the battle of the 19th of September.

The battle had secured us these objects. Our flanks covered the Dry Valley and Rossville roads, while our cavalry covered the Missionary Ridge and the Valley of Chattanooga Creek, into which latter place our spare trains had been sent on Friday, the 18th.

We also had indubitable evidence of the presence of Longstreet's corps and Johnston's forces, by the capture of prisoners from each, and the fact that at the close of the day we had present but two brigades which had not been opportunely and squarely in action, opposed to superior numbers of the enemy, assured us that we were greatly outnumbered, and that the battle the next day must be for the safety of the army and the possession of Chattanooga."

To a degree, both of them were partly wrong. Rosecrans had not been attacked by a greatly superior force, but he was right that the Army of the Cumberland certainly hadn't suffered any consequential setbacks either. Both men have been criticized for the nature of the attacks and the counterattacks, which inflicted thousands of casualties on each other through piecemeal actions that only involved individual brigades or divisions, as opposed to concerted attacks with multiple divisions or a corps.

Bragg has been particularly criticized by historians for the failure to win anything of substance on the 19th. Thomas Connelly, who wrote a history on the Confederate Army of Tennessee, asserted, "Bragg's inability to readjust his plans had cost him heavily. He had never admitted that he was wrong about the location of Rosecrans' left wing and that as a result he bypassed two splendid opportunities. During the day Bragg might have sent heavy reinforcements to Walker and attempted to roll up the Union left; or he could have attacked the Union center where he knew troops were passing from to the left. Unable to decide on either, Bragg tried to do both, wasting his men in sporadic assaults. Now his Army was crippled and in no better position than that morning. Walker had, in the day's fighting, lost over 20 per cent of his strength, while Stuart and Cleburne had lost 30 per cent. Gone, too, was any hope for the advantage of a surprise blow against Rosecrans."

On top of that, Bragg's previous defeats had sapped the morale of the Confederate army and their belief in his abilities, something Hood noticed on the night of the 19th. Hood later noted in his memoirs, "In the evening, according to my custom in Virginia under General Lee, I rode back to Army headquarters to report to the Commander-in-Chief the result of the day upon my part of the line. I there met for the first time several of the principal officers of the Army of Tennessee, and, to my surprise, not one spoke in a sanguine tone regarding the result of the battle in which we were then engaged. I found the gallant Breckinridge, whom I had known from early youth, seated by the root of a tree, with a heavy slouch hat upon his head. When, in the course of brief conversation, I stated that we would rout the enemy the following day, he sprang to his feet, exclaiming, 'My dear Hood, I am delighted to hear you say so. You give me renewed hope; God grant it may be so.'"

One thing may have gone right for the Confederates on the night of the 19th. As Longstreet and his men marched toward Bragg's army, they may have inadvertently run into the Union army. Longstreet explained the odd encounter in his memoirs:

It was a bright moonlight night, and the woodlands on the sides of the broad highway were quite open, so that we could see and be seen. After a time we were challenged by an outlying guard, 'Who comes there?' We answered, 'Friends.' The answer was not altogether satisfying to the guard, and after a very short parley we asked what troops they were, when the answer gave the number of the brigade and of the division. As Southern brigades were called for their commanders more than by their numbers, we concluded that these friends were the enemy. There were, too, some suspicious obstructions across the road in front of us, and altogether the situation did not look inviting. The moon was so bright that it did not seem prudent to turn and ride back under the fire that we knew would be opened on us, so I said, loudly, so that the guard could hear, 'Let us ride down a little way to find a better crossing.' Riding a few rods brought us under cover and protection of large trees, sufficiently shading our retreat to enable us to ride quietly to the rear and take the road over which we had seen so many men and vehicles passing while on our first ride."

Surprisingly, by the time Longstreet and his men arrived around 11:00 p.m., Bragg was asleep. It was then that Longstreet learned he was being given command of the left wing of the army, leaving Hood in command of his corps, and that Leonidas Polk was given command of the right wing of the army.

Bragg's decision to reorganize his command structure ahead of the attack on the 20th has also come in for criticism, especially because it confused some of his own officers by adding another layer of command for orders. This was particularly a problem for the Confederates' right flank, which was manned by the corps of D.H. Hill. It was not until late that night that Hill even learned about the reorganization of the command structure, and that he had now been made one of Polk's subordinates. And if Hill is to be believed, the confusion that resulted in the reorganization led to him not receiving the attack orders that Bragg intended for him on the morning of the 20th:

> "[M]y chief-of-staff gave me a message from General Polk that my corps had been put under his command, and that he wished to see me at Alexander's Bridge. He said not a word to any of them about an attack at daylight, nor did he to General Breckinridge, who occupied the same room with him that night. I have by me written statements from General Breckinridge and the whole of my staff to that effect. General Polk had issued an order for an attack at daylight, and had sent a courier with a copy, but he had failed to find me. I saw the order for the first time nineteen years afterward in Captain Polk's letter to the Southern Historical Society."

Chapter 5: The Morning of September 20

"Taken as a whole, the performance of the Confederate right wing this morning had been one of the most appalling exhibitions of command incompetence of the entire Civil War." – Steven Woodworth

On the morning of the 20th, Bragg had anticipated that his right flank would be launching an attack on the Union left at daylight, only to discover nothing going on at daylight. Bragg reported:

> "Lieutenant-General Polk was ordered to assail the enemy on our extreme right at day-dawn on the 20th, and to take up the attack in succession rapidly to the left. The left wing was to await the attack by the right, take it up promptly when made, and the whole line was then to be pushed vigorously and persistently against the enemy throughout its extent.

> Before the dawn of day myself and staff were ready for the saddle, occupying a position immediately in rear of and accessible to all parts of the Free. With increasing anxiety and disappointment I waited until after sunrise without hearing a gun, and at length dispatched a staff officer to Lieutenant-General Polk to ascertain the cause of the delay and urge him to a prompt and speedy movement. This officer, not finding the general with his troops, and learning where he had spent the night, proceeded across Alexander's Bridge to the east side of the Chickamauga and there delivered my message.

Proceeding in person to the right wing, I found the troops not even prepared for the movement. Messengers were immediately dispatched for Lieutenant-General Polk, and he shortly after joined me. My orders were renewed, and the general was urged to their prompt execution, the more important as the ear was saluted throughout the night with the sounds of the ax and falling timber as the enemy industriously labored to strengthen his position by hastily constructed barricades and breastworks. A reconnaissance made in the front of our extreme right during this delay crossed the main road to Chattanooga and proved the important fact that this greatly desired position was open to our possession."

When Bragg found Hill around 8:00 a.m., Hill later claimed that was the first time he had heard of an attack order, after which he protested to Bragg that an attack would be unwise:

"Bragg rode up at 8 A. M. and inquired of me why I had not begun the attack at daylight. I told him that I was hearing then for the first time that such an order had been issued and had not known whether we were to be the assailants or the assailed. He said angrily, 'I found Polk after sunrise sitting down reading a newspaper at Alexander's Bridge, two miles from the line of battle, where he ought to have been fighting.' However, the essential preparations for battle had not been made up to this hour and, in fact, could not be made without the presence of the commander-in-chief. The position of the enemy had not been reconnoitered, our line of battle had not been adjusted, and par t of it was at right angles with the rest; there was no cavalry on our flanks, and no order had fixed the strength or position of the reserves."

The delay may have been fatal. Around 9:30 a.m., 4 hours after Bragg intended for the attack on the Union left to start, with Breckinridge's division and Cleburne's division of Hill's corps pushing forward. This was problematic for several reasons. First, Bragg intended that Cleburne and Breckinridge would be just the start of a coordinated series of attacks that would drive the Union's left flank to the south and southwest. Second, the delay allowed Thomas's men to dig in and erect breastworks that would greatly aid their defensive line, leading Bragg to complain that without the Confederates' delay, "our independence might have been won.

Perhaps most important of all, Bragg's attack was starting with a division that had fought late the previous night and had been sapped of nearly a third of its manpower. While Breckinridge's division had some success on the far right of the line and began pushing south along the LaFayette Road, the presence of Union breastworks had discouraged some of his men and the men in Cleburne's division. Cleburne's men went nowhere in front of several Union divisions, and the left wing of his division got mixed up with Stewart's division, which had marched to the right to close a gap in the Confederate line and inadvertently marched into the left wing of Cleburne's division. Since Stewart and Cleburne had their men tangled, Benjamin Cheatham's division, poised to advance after them, could not move forward with the Confederates in their front. Meanwhile, Hill's attempt to shore up the gap forming between Breckinridge and Cleburne was quickly savaged, and the gap remained in the line.

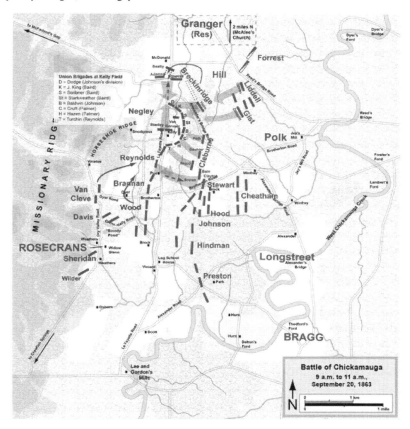

The Confederate attacks on the morning of September 20

By noon, the attack that Bragg had envisioned starting at dawn and rolling up the Union's left flank had completely fizzled out. Bragg could not hide his disgust in his official report, writing:

"The reasons assigned for this unfortunate delay by the wing commander appear in part in the reports of his subordinates. It is sufficient to say they are entirely unsatisfactory. It also appears from these reports that when the action was opened on the right about 10 a.m. the troops were moved to the assault in detail and by detachments, unsupported, until nearly all parts of the right wing were in turn repulsed with heavy losses.

Our troops were led with the greatest gallantry and exhibited great coolness, bravery, and heroic devotion. In no instance did they fail when called on to rally and return to the charge. But though invariably driving the enemy with slaughter at the points assailed, they were compelled in turn to yield to the greatly superior numbers constantly brought against them."

Chapter 6: The Union Blunder

The only good thing that can be said about the Confederates' attack on the morning of September 20 is that it set in motion a chain of miscommunications among Union officers that would ultimately produce one of the biggest blunders of the entire war.

When the attack started on the left flank, Thomas began requesting reinforcements from the generals and commands to his right. One of them was Brannan, and he sent a brigade north as reinforcements early in the morning only to be asked for more reinforcements around 10:00 a.m. At the same time, Brannan was aware that if he sent his entire division as reinforcements, it would leave a gap between Thomas Wood's division and Joseph Reynolds's division, so he initially talked the matter over with Reynolds, who suggested that Brannan withdraw his division but only after informing Rosecrans back at headquarters.

Brannan

Brannan wisely kept his division in the line, prudently waiting for Rosecrans to approve the decision and giving Rosecrans time to then reform the line and close up the gap. But somehow, Brannan's staff officer got the notion that Brannan's division was in the process of pulling out of the line and marching north as he rode back to Rosecrans. Rosecrans explained, "A message from General Thomas soon followed, that he was heavily pressed, Captain Kellogg, aide-de-camp, the bearer, informing me at the same time that General Brannan was out of line, and General Reynolds' right was exposed. Orders were dispatched to General Wood to close up on Reynolds, and word was sent to General Thomas that he should be supported, even if it took away the whole corps of Crittenden and McCook. General Davis was ordered to close on General Wood, and General McCook was advised of the state of affairs and ordered to close his whole command to the left with all dispatch."

The orders that Wood received were not what Rosecrans remembered, probably because Rosecrans did not actually review the orders before they reached Wood. Instead, his aide-de-camp, Frank Bond, wrote out the order to Wood: "The general commanding directs that you close up on Reynolds as fast as possible, and support him." Since Brannan's division was still in line, Wood could not "close up" on Reynolds's right because that spot was already filled. To "support" Reynolds meant that Wood should pull his division and organize in the rear of Reynolds's division. In other words, there was no way Wood could close up and support Reynolds at the same time unless Brannan's division had already moved out of the line.

Since it was impossible to close up on Reynolds, Wood decided to go ahead and support Reynolds, thereby pulling his division out of the Union line. Wood knew full well that he was creating a gap and thought the orders were strange, but he had already been chastised for not moving promptly after receiving orders earlier that day, so he accepted the orders. Historian Peter Cozzens noted the argument over the intent of the orders between Wood and one of the staffers:

"While Wood read the order, Starling began to explain its intent. Wood interrupted. Brannan was in position, he said, there was no vacancy between Reynold's division and his own. 'Then there is no order,' retorted Starling. There the matter should have ended. And with anyone but Tom Wood, it most assuredly would have. Rosecrans had upbraided Wood twice for failing to obey orders promptly...the dressing down just 90 minutes earlier in front of Wood's entire staff. The barbs of Rosecrans's invective pained the Kentuckian. Anger clouded his reason. No, he told Starling, the order was imperative, he would move at once."

Instead of verifying the intent with Rosecrans, whose headquarters were just 5 minutes away, Wood began to act. As he began pulling his division out of the line, Wood did not consult with his own corps commander (Crittenden) but with corps commander McCook, and though Wood later claimed McCook vowed to fill the gap, the gap essentially went unfilled. Wood was pulling out an entire division from the line, and it would only be partially filled by a single brigade.

Wood

Thus, unbeknownst to Rosecrans and McCook, a wide gap was being created right in the middle of the right wing of the Army of the Cumberland's line, and as fortune would have it, the delays brought about by Confederate confusion on their right resulted in Longstreet's left wing delaying its own attack until after 11:00. Having taken time to reform his battle lines, Longstreet had established an attacking force in 5 lines consisting of three divisions with his veterans from the Army of Northern Virginia. Bushrod Johnson's division was in front, and it was given the objective of advancing across the field of the Brotherton farm, the very part of the line that Wood's division was vacating.

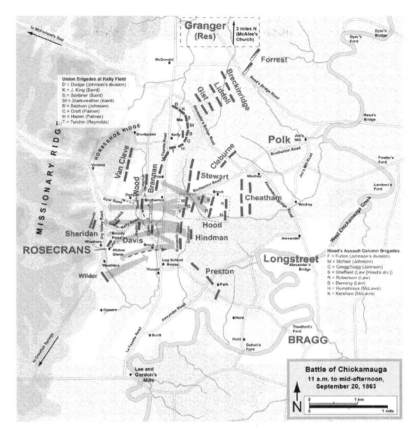

Longstreet's attack

Longstreet has often been criticized for being slow to march and form his lines before an attack, but there's no question that this time it was incredibly fortuitous. The initial attackers struck the right flank of Wood's division was it was pulling out of the line and routed them, establishing the gap for nearly 15,000 Confederates to push through. Longstreet described the initial rout in his memoirs:

"As we approached a second line, Johnson's division happened to strike it while in the act of changing position of some of the troops, charged upon and carried it, capturing some artillery, Hood's and Hindman's troops pressing in close connection. This attack forced the parts of the Twentieth and Twenty-first Corps from that part of the field, back over Missionary Ridge, in disordered retreat, and part of Negley's division of the Fourteenth Corps by the same impulsion. As our right wing had failed of the progress anticipated, and had become fixed by the firm holding of the enemy's left, we could find no practicable field for our work except by a change of the order of battle from wheel to the left, to a swing to the right on my division under General Stewart."

Bushrod Johnson was awed by the sight of the Confederates streaming through the gap, writing, "The scene now presented was unspeakably grand. The resolute and impetuous charge, the rush of our heavy columns sweeping out from the shadow and gloom of the forest into the open fields flooded with sunlight, the glitter of arms, the onward dash of artillery and mounted men, the retreat of the foe, the shouts of the hosts of our army, the dust, the smoke, the noise of fire-arms—of whistling balls and grape-shot and of bursting shell—made up a battle scene of unsurpassed grandeur."

By pushing through the gap and wheeling to the right, Longstreet had effectively cut the Army of the Cumberland in two and now fell upon the left flank of Crittenden's corps. Shortly after Longstreet's wheel to the right started, the man in charge of his corps, Hood, was nearly killed. Hood explained, "With a shout along my entire front, the Confederates rushed forward, penetrated into the wood, over and beyond the enemy's breastworks, and thus achieved another glorious victory for our arms. About this time I was pierced with a Minie ball in the upper third of the right leg; I turned from my horse upon the side of the crushed limb and fell — strange to say, since I was commanding five divisions — into the arms of some of the troops of my old brigade, which I had directed so long a period, and upon so many fields of battle." Hood's leg would be amputated nearly at the hip.

As several Union brigades began heading to the rear, one of the brigades in Wood's division, commanded by Charles Harker, managed to stay intact enough to withdraw in an orderly fashion toward Horseshoe Ridge, a naturally strong defensive spot. Luckily for Harker and the Union, the Confederates in his front, brigades led by Joseph Kershaw and Benjamin G. Humphreys, were unsupported in their advance and were unable to dislodge the brigade from Horseshoe Ridge. In the chaos and confusion, the Confederate brigades closest to Kershaw and Humphreys had become scattered in their pursuit of retreating Union brigades.

By driving through the gap and wheeling to the right, Longstreet's left flank was exposed to some of the divisions in McCook's XX Corps, but the general chaos and panic resulted in most of that corps putting up almost no fight and evacuating the field to the west. With command structure having entirely broken down, brigadier-generals were left to their own devices, and those that tried to stay and fight were dispatched by some of the Confederate attackers who had not wheeled left so as to protect the flank.

Little Phil Sheridan's division was a textbook example of the difficulties Union generals had in maintaining order. As two of his brigades, led by William Lytle and Nathan Walworth, held their ground and actually repulsed the Confederate advance, his other two brigades had quickly broken and fled to the rear. When Lytle was killed leading his men, the leaderless brigade also quickly broke. Sheridan would describe his situation in his memoirs:

"During these occurrences General Rosecrans passed down the road behind my line, and sent word that he wished to see me, but affairs were too critical to admit of my going to him at once, and he rode on to Chattanooga. It is to be regretted that he did not wait till I could join him, for the delay would have permitted him to see that matters were not in quite such bad shape as he supposed; still, there is no disguising the fact that at this juncture his army was badly crippled.

Shortly after my division had rallied on the low hills already described, I discovered that the enemy, instead of attacking me in front, was wedging in between my division and the balance of the army; in short, endeavoring to cut me off from Chattanooga. This necessitated another retrograde movement, which brought me back to the southern face of Missionary Ridge, where I was joined by Carlin's brigade of Davis's division. Still thinking I could join General Thomas, I rode some distance to the left of my line to look for a way out, but found that the enemy had intervened so far as to isolate me effectually. I then determined to march directly to Rossville, and from there effect ajunction with Thomas by the Lafayette road. I reached Rossville about 5 o'clock in the afternoon, bringing with me eight guns, forty-six caissons, and a long ammunition train, the latter having been found in a state of confusion behind the widow Glenn's when I was being driven back behind the Dry Valley road."

Rosecrans justified his leaving the field in his post-battle report:

"At the moment of the repulse of Davis' division, I was standing in rear of his right, waiting the completion of the closing of McCook's corps to the left. Seeing confusion among Van Cleve's troops, and the distance Davis' men were falling back, and the tide of battle surging toward us, the urgency for Sheridan's troops to intervene became imminent, and I hastened in person to the extreme right, to direct Sheridan's movement on the flank of the advancing rebels. It was too late. The crowd of returning troops rolled back, and the enemy advanced. Giving the troops directions to rally behind the ridge west of the Dry Valley road, I passed down it accompanied by General Garfield, Major McMichael, Major Bond, and Captain Young, of my staff, and a few of the escort, under a shower of grape, canister, and musketry, for 200 or 300 yards, and attempted to rejoin General Thomas and the troops sent to his support, by passing to the rear of the broken portion of our lines, but found the routed troops far toward the left, and hearing the enemy's advancing musketry and cheers, I became doubtful whether the left had held its ground, and started for Rossville. On consultation and further reflection, however, I determined to send General Garfield there, while I went to

Chattanooga, to give orders for the security of the pontoon bridges at Battle Creek and Bridgeport, and to make preliminary dispositions either to forward ammunition and supplies, should we hold our ground, or to withdraw the troops into good position."

However, Sheridan's sentiment about Rosecrans's disappearance was echoed by Rosecrans biographer William Lamers, who wrote, "Whether he did or did not know that Thomas still held the field, it was a catastrophe that Rosecrans did not himself ride to Thomas, and send Garfield to Chattanooga. Had he gone to the front in person and shown himself to his men, as at Stone River, he might by his personal presence have plucked victory from disaster, although it is doubtful whether he could have done more than Thomas did. Rosecrans, however, rode to Chattanooga instead."

Around the same time, one of the Union's cavalry brigades, led by John T. Wilder, was prevented from trying to attack Longstreet's flank by Assistant Secretary of War Charles Dana, who had grown so discouraged by what he had seen that he demanded to be taken back to Chattanooga, where he could inform Washington of what was going on via telegraph. Wilder had to detach part of his command to escort Dana to the city, and that afternoon Dana hysterically telegraphed Washington, "My report today is of deplorable importance. Chickamauga is as fatal a name in our history as Bull Run."

Chapter 7: The Rock of Chickamauga

By about 1:00, Longstreet's men had pushed almost all of McCook's XX Corps and Crittenden's XXI Corps off the field, including the commanding general Rosecrans along with them. As the commander and his routed Union soldiers began a panicked retreat toward Chattanooga, Longstreet met with Bragg, and according to Longstreet the commanding general was indecisive at best:

"After caring for and sending him off, and before we were through with our lunch, General Bragg sent for me. He was some little distance in rear of our new position. The change of the order of battle was explained, and the necessity under which it came to be made. We had taken some thirty or more field-pieces and a large number of small-arms, and thought that we had cut off and put to disorder the Twentieth and Twenty-first Corps that had retreated through the pass of the Ridge by the Dry Valley road. He was informed of orders given General Johnson for my left, and General Buckner for a battery on the right. I then offered as suggestion of the way to finish our work that he abandon the plan for battle by our right wing, or hold it to defence, draw off a force from that front that had rested since the left wing took up the battle, join them with the left wing, move swiftly down the Dry Valley road, pursue the retreating forces, occupy the gaps of the Ridge behind the enemy standing before our right, and call that force to its own relief.

He was disturbed by the failure of his plan and the severe repulse of his right wing, and was little prepared to hear suggestions from subordinates for other moves or progressive work. His words, as I recall them, were: 'There is not a man in the right wing who has any fight in him.' From accounts of his former operations I was prepared for halting work, but this, when the battle was at its tide and in partial success, was a little surprising. His humor, however, was such that his subordinate was at a loss for a reopening of the discussion. He did not wait, nor did he express approval or disapproval of the operations of the left wing, but rode for his Headquarters at Reed's Bridge.

There was nothing for the left wing to do but work along as best it could. The right wing ceased its active battle as the left forced the enemy's right centre, and the account of the commanding general was such as to give little hope of his active use of it in supporting us. After his lunch, General Johnson was ordered to make ready his own and Hindman's brigades, to see that those of Hood's were in just connection with his right, and await the opening of our battery. Preston's division was pulled away from its mooring on the river bank to reinforce our worn battle. "

Longstreet was beside himself at Bragg's suggestion that the battle was not being won, but Bragg was (correctly) disappointed that his ability to destroy the entire Army of the Cumberland was out of reach because his right wing's inability to advance allowed them to flee toward Chattanooga. With Bragg all but refusing to order anything out of his right wing, the work was left for Longstreet's men to try to finish the job against Thomas's Corps, which still held its defensive line.

By now, Longstreet's attack was hours old, and even if the terrain had allowed his general officers to see their entire commands, the ensuing pursuits and chaos had broken down a lot of coordination. D.H. Hill noted how unique it was that Thomas and Longstreet had become the de facto commanding generals on the field, writing "Some of the severest fighting had yet to be done after 3 P. M. It probably never happened before for a great battle to be fought to its bloody conclusion with the commanders of each side away from the field of conflict. But the Federals were in the hands of the indomitable Thomas, and the Confederates were under their two heroic wing commanders Longstreet and Polk."

While Thomas's corps held the same lines from the morning, Thomas had been going about ordering the impromptu line on Horseshoe Ridge, which was attracting small pockets of Union soldiers and allowing them to reform there. Brannan's division began forming on the ridge, while Negley's division went about directing artillery. While some Union generals, like corps commander Crittenden, declined to stick around, others like Phil Sheridan found their way to Horseshoe Ridge to take part in the defensive stand. Thomas's line was also bolstered by Gordon Granger's Reserve Corps; after listening to gunfire for hours and receiving no orders from the absent Rosecrans, Granger took it upon himself to march to the sound and somehow managed to march past Forrest's cavalry. Longstreet would later complain that he was not even informed of Granger's arrival by anyone on the right of the Confederate army.

Eventually, Longstreet's advance on the right compelled Thomas to move the rest of his defensive line gradually back toward Horseshoe Ridge. Longstreet explained:

"We were pushed back through the valley and up the slope, until General Preston succeeded in getting his brigade under Trigg to the support. Our battery got up at last under Major Williams and opened its destructive fire from eleven guns, which presently convinced General Thomas that his position was no longer tenable. He drew Reynolds's division from its trenches near the angle, for assignment as rearguard. Lieutenant-Colonel Sorrel, of the staff, reported this move, and was sent with orders to General Stewart to strike down against the enemy's moving forces. It seems that at the same time Liddell's division of the extreme right of our right wing was ordered against the march of the reserves. Stewart got into part of Reynolds's line and took several hundred prisoners. Meanwhile, Reynolds was used in meeting the attack and driving back the division of General Liddell. That accomplished, he was ordered to position to cover the retreat. As no reports came to the left from the commanding general or from the right wing, the repulse of Liddell's division was thought to indicate the strong holding of the enemy along his intrenched front line, and I thought that we should wait to finish the battle on the morrow."

It was only after the battle that Longstreet learned that the line he thought was strongly entrenched was actually empty, which only made him more disgusted with Bragg: "It is hardly possible that the Confederate commander could have failed to find the enemy's empty lines along the front of his right wing, and called both wings into a grand final sweep of the field to the capture of Thomas's command; but he was not present, and the condition of affairs was embarrassing to the subordinate commanders."

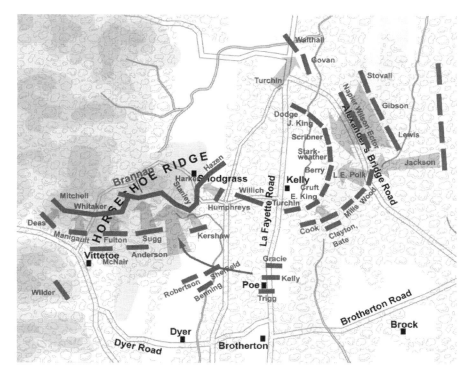

The defense of Horseshoe Ridge

Now that Thomas had all of his men back on Horseshoe Ridge, they and the scattered remnants of the other two corps who had not fled made a defiant last stand against multiple Confederate attacks. Thomas reported:

"About 2 p.m., very soon after Captain Kellogg left me, hearing heavy firing to my right and rear through the woods, I turned in that direction and was riding to the slope of the hill in my rear to ascertain the cause. Just as I passed out of the woods bordering the State road, I met Captain Kellogg returning, who reported to me that in attempting to reach General Sheridan he had met a large force in an open corn-field to the rear of Reynolds' position, advancing cautiously, with a strong line of skirmishers thrown out to their front, and that they had fired on him and forced him to return. He had reported this to Colonel Harker, commanding a brigade of Wood's division, posted on a ridge a short distance to the rear of Reynolds' position, who also saw this force advancing, but, with Captain Kellogg, was of the opinion that they might be Sheridan's troops coming to our assistance. I rode forward to Colonel Harker's position, and told him that, although I was expecting Sheridan from that direction, if those troops fired on him, seeing his flag, he must return their fire and resist their farther advance. He immediately ordered his skirmishers to commence firing, and took up a position with his brigade on the crest of a hill a short distance to his right and rear, placing his right in connection with Brannan's division and portions of Beatty's and Stanley's brigades of Negley's division, which had been retired to that point from the left, as circumstantially narrated in the reports of General John Beatty and Colonel Stanley. I then rode to the crest of the hill referred to above. On my way I met General Wood, who confirmed me in the opinion that the troops advancing upon us were the enemy, although we were not then aware of the disaster to the right and center of our army. I then directed him to place his division on the prolongation of Brannan's, who, I had ascertained from Wood, was on the top of the hill above referred to, and to resist the farther advance of the enemy as long as possible. I sent my aide, Captain Kellogg, to notify General Reynolds that our right had been turned, and that the enemy was in his rear in force.

General Wood barely had time to dispose his troops on the left of Brannan before another of those fierce assaults, similar to those made in the morning on my lines, was made on him and Brannan combined, and kept up by the enemy throwing in fresh troops as fast as those in their front were driven back, until near nightfall. About the time that Wood took up his position, General Gordon Granger appeared on my left flank at the head of Steedman's division of his corps. I immediately dispatched a staff officer, Captain Johnson, Second Indiana Cavalry, of Negley's division, to him with orders to push forward and take position on Brannan's right, which order was complied with with the greatest promptness and alacrity. Steedman, moving his division into position with almost as much precision as if on drill, and fighting his way to the crest of the hill on Brannan s right, moved forward his artillery and drove the enemy down the southern slope, inflicting on him a most terrible loss in killed and wounded. This opportune arrival of fresh troops revived the flagging spirits of our men on the right, and inspired them with new ardor for the contest. Every assault of the enemy from that time until nightfall was repulsed in the most gallant style by the whole line."

One of Rosecrans's staff officers, James Garfield, met Thomas during the afternoon, and he informed Rosecrans, "Thomas is standing like a rock." After meeting with Thomas, Garfield went so far as to suggest that Rosecrans return to the field and bring back the rest of the army to take up the fight again tomorrow, insisting "our men not only held their ground, but in many points drove the enemy splendidly. Longstreet's Virginians have got their bellies full." But Rosecrans was a beaten man, with one account claiming that he was found weeping in Chattanooga that night. Lincoln telegraphed the commanding general, "Be of good cheer. ... We have unabated confidence in you and your soldiers and officers. In the main, you must be the judge as to what is to be done. If I was to suggest, I would say save your army by taking strong positions until Burnside joins you." Lincoln, of course, knew what was truly going on, and he confided to his secretary that Rosecrans seemed "confused and stunned like a duck hit on the head."

As night fell, Thomas was able to extricate the rest of the Union defenders to Rossville Gap nearer Chattanooga right from under the nose of Bragg's army. Phil Sheridan recounted seeing Thomas near Rossville Gap that night and noted how physically and mentally exhausted he seemed:

> "The General appeared very much exhausted, seemed to forget what he had stopped for, and said little or nothing of the incidents of the day. This was the second occasion on which I had met him in the midst of misfortune, for during the fight in the cedars at Stone River, when our prospects were most disheartening, we held a brief conversation respecting the line he was then taking up for the purpose of helping me. At other times, in periods of inactivity, I saw but little of him. He impressed me now as he did in the cedars, his quiet, unobtrusive demeanor communicating a gloomy rather than a hopeful view of the situation. This apparent depression was due no doubt to the severe trial through which he had gone in the last fortyeight hours, which strain had exhausted him very much both physically and mentally. His success in maintaining his ground was undoubtedly largely influenced by the fact that two-thirds of the National forces had been sent to his succor, but his firm purpose to save the army was the main-stay on which all relied after Rosecrans left the field. As the command was getting pretty well past, I rose to go in order to put my troops into camp. This aroused the General, when, remarking that he had a little flask of brandy in his saddle-holster, he added that he had just stopped for the purpose of offering me a drink, as he knew I must be very tired. He requested one of his staff-officers to get the flask, and after taking a sip himself, passed it to me. Refreshed by the brandy, I mounted and rode off to supervise the encamping of my division, by no means an easy task considering the darkness, and the confusion that existed among the troops that had preceded us into Rossville."

Thomas, on the other hand, had just earned the eternal nickname "The Rock of Chickamauga". While there is a never ending stream of acclaim going to generals like Grant, Lee, and Sherman, General Thomas has managed to fly under the radar, despite having an unusual background as a Southerner fighting for the Union and scoring almost inconceivable successes at Missionary Ridge, Franklin, and Nashville. Thomas also skillfully fought at Perryville, Stones River, and in Sherman's Atlanta Campaign, but he has remained best known for his defense at Chickamauga on September 20, 1863.

Thomas had one of the most stellar records of any officer in the war, was instrumental in the Union's ultimate victory in the Western theater, and scored the kinds of decisive victories that eluded more celebrated generals like Lee. So why does Thomas fly under the radar? A stern military man, Thomas eschewed self-promotion and aggrandizement, and though his methodical generalship was almost always successful, it sometimes annoyed General Ulysses S. Grant. With Grant's star rising as his relationship with Thomas was cooling, Thomas was on the wrong end of history. And when he died in 1870, Thomas had burned his papers and had not written memoirs or an account of his participation in the war, missing his final opportunity to directly leave his mark and define his own legacy instead of having others write it for him.

Chapter 8: The Aftermath of Chickamauga

The Battle of Chickamauga was the second deadliest battle of the Civil War with nearly 35,000 total casualties. The Army of the Cumberland had lost over 16,000, including nearly 5,000 being captured as a result of the panic of the 20th. Bragg's army lost even more, with 2,300 killed and over 14,500 wounded, losing nearly 18,500 all told. The casualties amounted to nearly 40% of both armies, a staggering number.

Like Longstreet, D.H. Hill was shocked that Bragg had no plans to pursue Rosecrans on the 21st:

"Whatever blunders each of us in authority committed before the battles of the 19th and 20th, and during their progress, the great blunder of all was that of not pursuing the enemy on the 21st. The day was spent in burying the dead and gathering up captured stores. Forrest, with his usual promptness, was early in the saddle, and saw that the retreat was a rout. Disorganized masses of men were hurrying to the rear ; batteries of artillery were inextricably mixed with trains of wagons ; disorder and confusion pervaded the broken ranks struggling to get on. Forrest sent back word to Bragg that 'every hour was worth a thousand men.' But the commander-in-chief did not know of the victory until the morning of the 21st, and then he did not order a pursuit. Rosecrans spent the day and the night of the 21st in hurrying his trains out of town. A breathing-space was allowed him; the panic among his troops subsided, and Chattanooga - the objective point of the campaign - was held."

The day after Chickamauga ended, Rosecrans put his men to work digging defensive entrenchments around Chattanooga and waiting for Washington to send reinforcements. On September 23, Bragg's army arrived at the outskirts of Chattanooga and proceeded to seize control of the surrounding heights: Missionary Ridge (to the east), Lookout Mountain (to the southwest), and Raccoon Mountain (to the west). From these key vantage points, the Confederates could not only lob long-range artillery onto the Union entrenchments but also sweep the rail and river routes that supplied the Union army. Bragg planned to lay siege to the city and starve the Union forces into surrendering.

On September 29, U. S. Secretary of War Edwin M. Stanton ordered Union general Ulysses S. Grant, commander of the newly-created Military Division of the Mississippi, to go to

Chattanooga to bring all the territory from the Appalachian Mountains to the Mississippi River (including a portion of Arkansas) under a single command for the first time. Considering General Rosecrans's spotty record, Grant was given the option of replacing him with General Thomas. Hearing an inaccurate report that Rosecrans was preparing to abandon Chattanooga, Grant relieved Rosecrans of command and installed Thomas as commander of the Army of the Cumberland, telegraphing Thomas saying, "Hold Chattanooga at all hazards. I will be there as soon as possible." Without hesitation, Thomas replied, "We will hold the town till we starve."[21]

What followed were some of the most amazing operations of the Civil War. Grant relieved Rosecrans and personally came to Chattanooga to oversee the effort, placing General Thomas in charge of reorganizing the Army of the Cumberland. Meanwhile, Lincoln detached General Hooker and two divisions from the Army of the Potomac and sent them west to reinforce the garrison at Chattanooga. During a maneuver in which General Hooker had moved three divisions into Chattanooga Valley hoping to occupy Rossville Gap, Hooker's first obstacle was to bypass an artillery line the Confederates had established to block the movement of Union supplies. Initially, Grant merely used Hooker's men to establish the "Cracker Line", a makeshift supply line that moved food and resources into Chattanooga from Hooker's position on Lookout Mountain.

In November 1863, the situation at Chattanooga was dire enough that Grant took the offensive in an attempt to lift the siege. By now the Confederates were holding important high ground at positions like Lookout Mountain and Missionary Ridge. First Grant ordered General Sherman and four divisions of his Army of the Tennessee to attack Bragg's right flank, but the attempt was unsuccessful. Then, in an attempt to make an all out push, Grant ordered all forces in the vicinity to make an attack on Bragg's men.

On November 24, 1863 Maj. Gen. Hooker captured Lookout Mountain in order to divert some of Bragg's men away from their commanding position on Missionary Ridge. But the victory is best remembered for the almost miraculous attack on Missionary Ridge by part of General Thomas's Army of the Cumberland.

General Sheridan was part of a force sent to attack the Confederate midsection at nearby Missionary Ridge. According to several present, when Sheridan reached the base of Ridge, he stopped and toasted the Confederate gunners, shouting out, "Here's to you!"[22] In response, the Confederates sprayed his men with bullets, prompting Sheridan to quip, "That was ungenerous! I'll take your guns for that!" at which time he lit out, leading a spirited charge while screaming,

[21]   Cleaves, Freeman. *Rock of Chickamauga: The Life of General George H. Thomas*. Page 182.

[22]   Gaffney, P., and D. Gaffney. *The Civil War: Exploring History One Week at a Time*. Page 308.

"Chickamauga! Chickamauga!". The advance actually defied Grant's orders, since Grant, initially upset, had only ordered them to take the rifle pits at the base of Missionary Ridge, figuring that a frontal assault on that position would be futile and fatal. As Sheridan stormed ahead, General Grant caught the advance from a distance and asked General Thomas why he had ordered the attack. Thomas informed Grant that he hadn't; his army had taken it upon itself to charge up the entire ridge.

As it turned out, historians have often criticized Grant's orders, with acclaimed historian Peter Cozzens noting, "Grant's order to halt at the rifle pits at the base of the ridge was misunderstood by far too many of the generals charged with executing it. Some doubted the order because they thought it absurd to stop an attack at the instant when the attackers would be most vulnerable to fire from the crest and to a counterattack. Others apparently received garbled versions of the order." Sheridan later wrote, "Seeing the enemy thus strengthening himself, it was plain that we would have to act quickly if we expected to accomplish much, and I already began to doubt the feasibility of our remaining in the first line of rifle-pits when we should have carried them. I discussed the order with Wagner, Harker, and Sherman, and they were similarly impressed, so while anxiously awaiting the signal I sent Captain Ransom of my staff to Granger, who was at Fort Wood, to ascertain if we were to carry the first line or the ridge beyond. Shortly after Ransom started the signal guns were fired, and I told my brigade commanders to go for the ridge."

Regardless, to the amazement of Grant and the officers watching, the men making the attack scrambled up Missionary Ridge in a series of disorganized attacks that somehow managed to send the Confederates into a rout, thereby lifting the siege on Chattanooga. With that, the Army of the Cumberland had essentially conducted the most successful frontal assault of the war spontaneously. While Pickett's Charge, still the most famous attack of the war, was one unsuccessful charge, the Army of the Cumberland made over a dozen charges up Missionary Ridge and ultimately succeeded.

When the siege of Chattanooga was lifted, the Confederate victory at Chickamauga, the biggest battle in the Western Theater, had been rendered virtually meaningless. Not surprisingly, in the wake of Chickamauga there were recriminations among the generals involved on both sides. Chickamauga ensured Thomas continued to lead the Army of the Cumberland for the rest of the war, while the tension between Bragg and his principal subordinates bordered on outright mutiny. Longstreet discussed the unbelievable sequence of events within the Army of Tennessee's high command over the next month:

"After moving from Virginia to try to relieve our comrades of the Army of Tennessee, we thought that we had cause to complain that the fruits of our labor had been lost, but it soon became manifest that the superior officers of that army themselves felt as much aggrieved as we at the halting policy of their chief, and were calling in letters and petitions for his removal. A number of them came to have me write the President for them. As he had not called for my opinion on military affairs since the Johnston conference of 1862, I could not take that liberty, but promised to write to the Secretary of War and to General Lee, who I thought could excuse me under the strained condition of affairs. About the same time they framed and forwarded to the President a petition praying for relief.2 It was written by General D. H. Hill (as he informed me since the war).

While the superior officers were asking for relief, the Confederate commander was busy looking along his lines for victims. Lieutenant-General Polk was put under charges for failing to open the battle of the 20th at daylight; Major-General Hindman was relieved under charges for conduct before the battle, when his conduct of the battle with other commanders would have relieved him of any previous misconduct, according to the customs of war, and pursuit of others was getting warm.

On the Union side the Washington authorities thought vindication important, and Major-Generals McCook and Crittenden, of the Twentieth and Twenty-first Corps, were relieved and went before a Court of Inquiry; also one of the generals of division of the Fourteenth Corps.

The President came to us on the 9th of October and called the commanders of the army to meet him at General Bragg's office. After some talk, in the presence of General Bragg, he made known the object of the call, and asked the generals, in turn, their opinion of their commanding officer, beginning with myself. It seemed rather a stretch of authority, even with a President, and I gave an evasive answer and made an effort to turn the channel of thought, but he would not be satisfied, and got back to his question. The condition of the army was briefly referred to, and the failure to make an effort to get the fruits of our success, when the opinion was given, in substance, that our commander could be of greater service elsewhere than at the head of the Army of Tennessee. Major-General Buckner was called, and gave opinion somewhat similar. So did Major-General Cheatham, who was then commanding the corps recently commanded by Lieutenant-General Polk, and General D. H. Hill, who was called last, agreed with emphasis to the views expressed by others."

The problem for the Confederates who wanted to be done with Bragg is that he was friends with Jefferson Davis, as Longstreet was reminded when suggesting to Davis that Bragg be replaced by Joseph E. Johnston:

"In my judgment our last opportunity was lost when we failed to follow the success at Chickamauga, and capture or disperse the Union army, and it could not be just to the service or myself to call me to a position of such responsibility. The army was part of General Joseph E. Johnston's department, and could only be used in strong organization by him in combining its operations with his other forces in Alabama and Mississippi. I said that under him I could cheerfully work in any position. The suggestion of that name only served to increase his displeasure, and his severe rebuke.

I recognized the authority of his high position, but called to his mind that neither his words nor his manner were so impressive as the dissolving scenes that foreshadowed the dreadful end. He referred to his worry and troubles with politicians and non-combatants. In that connection, I suggested that all that the people asked for was success; with that the talk of politicians would be as spiders' webs before him."

Despite the negative feelings so many held about Bragg, Davis would not relieve him of command until late November 1863, well after the disastrous siege of Chattanooga was finished. By then, Bragg had successfully suspended Hindman and Polk for what he considered to be their failures during the Chickamauga campaign, and D.H. Hill was also suspended in early October.

With the failure to make anything out of the victory at Chickamauga, the Confederacy's best chance at somehow turning the tide in the West and possibly winning the war had been lost. As a result, Chickamauga became an extremely sore subject among the Confederates who had fought there, and historians still look at it as the South's last best chance in that theater.

D.H. Hill, who had played such a controversial role in the campaign, may have put it best:

There was no more splendid fighting in '61, when the flower of the Southern youth was in the field, than was displayed in those bloody days of September, '63. But it seems to me that the élan of the Southern soldier was never seen after Chickamauga - that brilliant dash which had distinguished him was gone forever. He was too intelligent not to know that the cutting in two of Georgia meant death to all his hopes. He knew that Longstreet's absence was imperiling Lee's safety, and that what had to be done must be done quickly. The delay in striking was exasperating to him; the failure to strike after the success was crushing to all his longings for an independent South. He fought stoutly to the last, but, after Chickamauga, with the sullenness of despair and without the enthusiasm of hope.

That 'barren victory' sealed the fate of the Southern Confederacy."

Bibliography

Cleaves, Freeman. Rock of Chickamauga: The Life of General George H. Thomas. Norman: University of Oklahoma Press, 1948.

Connelly, Thomas L. Autumn of Glory: The Army of Tennessee 1862–1865. Baton Rouge: Louisiana State University Press, 1971.

Cozzens, Peter. This Terrible Sound: The Battle of Chickamauga. Urbana: University of Illinois Press, 1992.

Knudsen, LTC Harold M. General James Longstreet: The Confederacy's Most Modern General. Tarentum, PA: Word Association Publishers, 2007.

Korn, Jerry, and the Editors of Time-Life Books. The Fight for Chattanooga: Chickamauga to Missionary Ridge. Alexandria, VA: Time-Life Books, 1985.

Lamers, William M. The Edge of Glory: A Biography of General William S. Rosecrans, U.S.A. Baton Rouge: Louisiana State University Press, 1961.

Tucker, Glenn. Chickamauga: Bloody Battle in the West. Dayton, OH: Morningside House, 1972.

Turchin, John Basil. Chickamauga. Chicago: Fergus Printing Co., 1888.

U.S. War Department, The War of the Rebellion: a Compilation of the Official Records of the Union and Confederate Armies. Washington, DC: U.S. Government Printing Office, 1880–1901.

Welsh, Douglas. The Civil War: A Complete Military History. Greenwich, CT: Brompton Books Corporation, 1981.

Woodworth, Steven E. Six Armies in Tennessee: The Chickamauga and Chattanooga Campaigns. Lincoln: University of Nebraska Press, 1998.

The Battle of the Wilderness

Chapter 1: Grant Comes East

Failing to secure the capture of any major northern cities, or the recognition of Great Britain or France, or the complete destruction of any northern armies, the Confederacy's last chance to survive the Civil War was the election of 1864. Democrats had been pushing an anti-war stance or at least a stance calling for a negotiated peace for years, so the South hoped that if a Democrat defeated President Lincoln, or if anti-war Democrats could retake the Congress, the North might negotiate peace with the South. In the election of 1862, anti-war Democrats made some gains in Congress and won the governorship of the State of New York. Confederates were therefore hopeful that trend would continue to the election of 1864.

Although the Army of the Potomac had been victorious at Gettysburg, Lincoln was still upset at what he perceived to be General George Meade's failure to trap Robert E. Lee's Army of Northern Virginia in Pennsylvania. When Lee retreated from Pennsylvania without much fight from the Army of the Potomac, Lincoln was again discouraged, believing Meade had a chance to end the war if he had been bolder. Though historians dispute that, and the Confederates actually invited attack during their retreat, Lincoln was constantly looking for more aggressive fighters to lead his men.

Lincoln's appreciation for aggressive fighters had made him a defender of Ulysses S. Grant as far back as 1862. In April 1862, Grant's army had won the biggest battle in the history of North America to date at Shiloh, with nearly 24,000 combined casualties among the Union and Confederate forces. Usually the winner of a major battle is hailed as a hero, but Grant was hardly a winner at Shiloh. The Battle of Shiloh took place before costlier battles at places like Antietam and Gettysburg, so the extent of the casualties at Shiloh shocked the nation. Moreover, at Shiloh the casualties were viewed as needless; Grant was pilloried for allowing the Confederates to take his forces by surprise, as well as the failure to build defensive earthworks and fortifications, which nearly resulted in a rout of his army. Speculation again arose that Grant had a drinking problem, and some even assumed he was drunk during the battle. Though the Union won, it was largely viewed that their success owed to the heroics of General William Tecumseh Sherman in rallying the men and Don Carlos Buell arriving with his army, and General Buell was happy to receive the credit at Grant's expense.

Grant

As a result of the Battle of Shiloh, General Halleck demoted Grant to second-in-command of all armies in his department, an utterly powerless position. And when word of what many considered a "colossal blunder" reached Washington, several congressmen insisted that Lincoln replace Grant in the field. Lincoln famously defended Grant, telling critics, "I can't spare this man. He fights."

Lincoln may have defended Grant, but he found precious few supporters, and the negative attention bothered Grant so much that it is widely believed he turned to alcohol again. While historians still debate that, what is known is that he considered resigning his commission, only to be dissuaded from doing so by General Sherman. While Grant was at the low point of his career, Sherman's career had been resurrected, and he was promoted to major-general the following month. With rumors that Grant was falling off the wagon with alcohol, Sherman tried to reassure Grant not to quit the war, telling him "some happy accident might restore you to favor and your true place." Sherman's appreciation of Grant's faith in his abilities cemented his loyalty and established a friendship between the two that would last a lifetime. In later years Sherman would say, "General Grant is a great general! He stood by me when I was crazy, and I stood by him when he was drunk; and now, sir, we stand by each other always."

Although Grant stayed in the army, it's unclear what position he would have held if Lincoln had not called Halleck to Washington to serve as general-in-chief in July 1862. At the same time, Halleck was given that position in large measure due to Grant's successes in the department under Halleck's command. Thankfully for the Union, Halleck's departure meant that Grant was reinstated as commander.

Lincoln's steadfastness ensured that Grant's victories out West continued to pile up, and after Vicksburg and Chattanooga, Grant had effectively ensured Union control of the states of Kentucky and Tennessee, as well as the entire Mississippi River. Thus, at the beginning of 1864, Lincoln put him in charge of all federal armies, a position that required Grant to come east.

Grant had already succeeded in achieving two of President Lincoln's three primary directives for a Union victory: the opening of the Mississippi Valley Basin, and the domination of the corridor from Nashville to Atlanta. If he could now seize Richmond, he would achieve the third.

Before beginning the Overland Campaign against Lee's army, Grant, Sherman and Lincoln devised a new strategy that would eventually implement total war tactics. Grant aimed to use the Army of the Potomac to attack Lee and/or take Richmond. Meanwhile, General Sherman, now in command of the Department of the West, would attempt to take Atlanta and strike through Georgia. In essence, having already cut the Confederacy in half with Vicksburg campaign, he now intended to bisect the eastern half.

On top of all that, Grant and Sherman were now intent on fully depriving the Confederacy of the ability to keep fighting. Sherman put this policy in effect during his March to the Sea by confiscating civilian resources and literally taking the fight to the Southern people. For Grant, it meant a war of attrition that would steadily bleed Lee's Army of Northern Virginia. To take full advantage of the North's manpower, in 1864 the Union also ended prisoner exchanges to ensure that the Confederate armies could not be bolstered by paroled prisoners.

By 1864, things were looking so bleak for the South that the Confederate war strategy was simply to ensure Lincoln lost reelection that November, with the hope that a new Democratic president would end the war and recognize the South's independence. With that, and given the shortage in manpower, Lee's strategic objective was to continue defending Richmond, while hoping that Grant would commit some blunder that would allow him a chance to seize an opportunity.

With that, the stage was set for the two most successful generals of the Civil War to finally face each other. Confederate Brigadier-General John B. Gordon, whose brigade would play a crucial role at the Battle of the Wilderness, aptly summarized the situation entering May 1864: "Grant had come from his campaigns in the Southwest with the laurels of Fort Donelson, Shiloh, Vicksburg, and Missionary Ridge on his brow. Lee stood before him with a record as military executioner unrivalled by that of any warrior of modern times. He had, at astoundingly short intervals and with unvarying regularity, decapitated or caused the official 'taking off' of the five previously selected commanders-in-chief of the great army which confronted him…This advance by General Grant inaugurated the seventh act in the 'On to Richmond' drama played by the armies of the Union."

Chapter 2: Entering the Wilderness

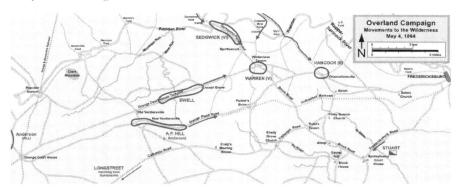

As usual, the Army of the Potomac had a large numbers advantage over Lee's Army of Northern Virginia, with Grant bringing an estimated 100,000 into the Wilderness to face Lee's 60,000. Although George Meade was nominally in command of the Union army, the fact that Grant marched with the army essentially meant that he would be making the overall decisions.

The Army of the Potomac was organized into three infantry corps, John Sedgwick's VI Corps, Winfield Scott Hancock's II Corps, and Gouverneur Warren's V Corps, along with a cavalry corps led by Phil Sheridan, who Grant brought east with him. Sedgwick was considered one of the most competent and aggressive corps commanders in the Union, and Hancock's heroics during the last two days of the Battle of Gettysburg more than demonstrated his ability to lead a corps. Warren had been a staff officer who alertly manned Little Round Top on the second day at Gettysburg, but he was relatively new to commanding a corps, and it would show. Ambrose Burnside's IX Corps was an independent command in the vicinity, but it would not fight in the Wilderness.

The Army of Northern Virginia started the Overland Campaign with the same structure as it had after losing Stonewall Jackson at Chancellorsville in May 1863. Lee's army was also divided into three corps commanded by James Longstreet, A.P. Hill and Richard S. Ewell. Longstreet was perhaps the best corps commander on either side during the Civil War, but Hill and Ewell struggled leading their corps at Gettysburg after having distinguished themselves in charge of smaller commands earlier in the war. The Confederate cavalry was led by their flamboyant but skilled cavalier, JEB Stuart, who was nearly as competent as he was vainglorious.

While the Union's advantage in manpower colored Grant's attritional strategy, on a tactical level it would not help the Army of the Potomac in the Wilderness because of the terrain. Grant explained why in his memoirs:

"The country over which the army had to operate, from the Rapidan to the crossing of the James River, is rather flat, and is cut by numerous streams which make their way to the Chesapeake Bay. The crossings of these streams by the army were generally made not far above tide-water, and where they formed a considerable obstacle to the rapid advance of troops even when the enemy did not appear in opposition. The country roads were narrow and poor. Most of the country is covered with a dense forest, in places, like the Wilderness and along the Chickahominy, almost impenetrable even for infantry except along the roads. All bridges were naturally destroyed before the National troops came to them."

Moreover, the Confederate soldiers' faith in their own abilities and General Lee ensured that they were constantly up to the challenge when facing the bigger Army of the Potomac. Gordon described the mood in camp that spring, "The reports of General Lee's scouts were scarcely necessary to our appreciation of the fact that the odds against us were constantly and rapidly increasing: for from the highland which bordered the southern banks of the Rapidan one could almost estimate the numbers that were being added to Grant's ranks by the growth of the city of tents spreading out in full view below. The Confederates were profoundly impressed by the situation, but they rejected as utterly unworthy of a Christian soldiery the doctrine that Providence was on the side of the heaviest guns and most numerous battalions."

When Grant began marching the army on May 4, he actually hoped to avoid a general battle against Lee in the Wilderness, given that the heavy forestry and thick underbrush would make infantry coordination impossible and artillery practically unusable. To avoid fighting on this ground, Grant needed to move the army southeast as quickly as he could, and he hoped to reach Spotsylvania Court House before fighting Lee.

As it turned out, Grant would fight Lee at Spotsylvania Court House, but it would be the second pitched battle of the campaign. The sheer size of the army made it difficult to move everything, especially its supplies. Grant's army was marching with just 10 days of rations, so a lot of live cattle had to be brought along to be butchered along the way, not to mention the thousands of wagons and ambulances as well. By some counts the rear of the marching army would've extended over 60 miles if marching down a single road. Grant wrote about all the work and necessities that went into provisioning his large army:

> "There never was a corps better organized than was the quartermaster's corps with the Army of the Potomac in 1864. With a wagon-train that would have extended from the Rapidan to Richmond, stretched along in single file and separated as the teams necessarily would be when moving, we could still carry only three days' forage and about ten to twelve days' rations, besides a supply of ammunition. To overcome all difficulties, the chief quartermaster, General Rufus Ingalls, had marked on each wagon the corps badge with the division color and the number of the brigade. At a glance, the particular brigade to which any wagon belonged could be told. The wagons were also marked to note the contents: if ammunition, whether for artillery or infantry; if forage, whether grain or hay; if rations, whether, bread, pork, beans, rice, sugar, coffee or whatever it might be. Empty wagons were never allowed to follow the army or stay in camp. As soon as a wagon was empty it would return to the base of supply for a load of precisely the same article that had been taken from it. Empty trains were obliged to leave the road free for loaded ones. Arriving near the army they would be parked in fields nearest to the brigades they belonged to. Issues, except of ammunition, were made at night in all cases. By this system the hauling of forage for the supply train was almost wholly dispensed with."

To alleviate the logistical issues, Grant intended to have his three corps march separately on two different roads toward their objective, as he explained in his memoirs:

> "The 5th corps, General Warren commanding, was in advance on the right, and marched directly for Germania Ford, preceded by one division of cavalry, under General J. H. Wilson. General Sedgwick followed Warren with the 6th corps. Germania Ford was nine or ten miles below the right of Lee's line. Hancock, with the 2d corps, moved by another road, farther east, directly upon Ely's Ford, six miles below Germania, preceded by Gregg's division of cavalry, and followed by the artillery. Torbert's division of cavalry was left north of the Rapidan, for the time, to picket the river and prevent the enemy from crossing and getting into our rear. The cavalry seized the two crossings before daylight, drove the enemy's pickets guarding them away, and by six o'clock A.M. had the pontoons laid ready for the crossing of the infantry and artillery. This was undoubtedly a surprise to Lee. The fact that the movement was unopposed proves this.
>
> Burnside, with the 9th corps, was left back at Warrenton, guarding the railroad from Bull Run forward to preserve control of it in case our crossing the Rapidan should be long delayed. He was instructed, however, to advance at once on receiving notice that the army had crossed; and a dispatch was sent to him a little after one P.M. giving the

information that our crossing had been successful.

The country was heavily wooded at all the points of crossing, particularly on the south side of the river. The battle-field from the crossing of the Rapidan until the final movement from the Wilderness toward Spottsylvania was of the same character. There were some clearings and small farms within what might be termed the battle-field; but generally the country was covered with a dense forest. The roads were narrow and bad. All the conditions were favorable for defensive operations."

Lee hadn't opposed the crossings because he had dispersed his army to prepare for several avenues of attack that Grant might choose. In fact, he anticipated that Grant would cross exactly how he did, using the Germanna and Ely Fords across the Rapidan River, but he hadn't concentrated his army until he knew for sure. As a result, Ewell's corps and Hill's corps were within marching distance of the Wilderness, but Longstreet was about 20 miles southwest near Gordonsville.

Grant's march intended to turn Lee's right flank, but once Lee realized which way Grant was marching on May 4, he began swiftly moving to meet the Union army in the Wilderness, since it was ideal for defense and negated the artillery advantage enjoyed by the Army of the Potomac. And as a result of the manner in which Grant's army was marching down separate roads, Lee was being given a chance to strike the Union's right flank instead of vice-versa. Ewell's corps and Hill's corps were close enough to fight in the Wilderness, but it would take a day for Longstreet's corps to come up.

Lee's intentions were assisted by the nature of the terrain, which allowed his two corps to march almost entirely undetected, as well as the Union's misuse of their cavalry. While cavalry was typically used to screen the infantry's advance and to conduct reconnaissance, Sheridan's cavalry was east of the army responding to a report that JEB Stuart's cavalry was near Fredericksburg, presumably with the intention of harassing the Union army's rear. The only problem was that the report was completely inaccurate; Stuart was actually southeast near Spotsylvania, where his cavalry would be in a position to ride north and intercept Warren's advancing V Corps.

As the armies' movements progressed on May 4, Grant and Meade had no clue that Lee's army was in close proximity, so they ultimately decided to camp near Chancellorsville, giving their gigantic wagon trains a chance to stay close. It had only taken a day for everything to fall Lee's way. Two of his corps were in position to intercept the Army of the Potomac from the west as it was marching south, and one of the Union army's three corps was marching on a separate road and wouldn't be able to immediately come to the other two corps' assistance in the event of a surprise attack.

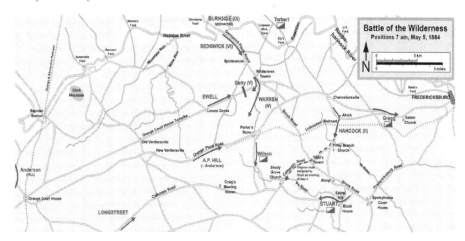

The armies' dispositions on the morning of May 5

Although Grant did not realize that Lee's army was closing in on his, he did have the wherewithal to face his army west when it wasn't marching south, aware that if an attack did come, it would come from that direction. Indeed, it wouldn't take long for the armies to run into each other on May 5.

As Warren's column started marching south around dawn on the 5th, it ran into Ewell's corps heading east on the Orange Turnpike toward him around 6:00 a.m. Shortly after that, Union cavalry reported Confederate infantry (Hill's Corps) marching in force east down the Orange Plank Road. In response, Grant immediately scrambled to form a battle line on both of Warren's flanks while preparing to attack whatever force was in his front, but with Hancock's II Corps too far away, Grant had to order up one of the divisions in Sedgwick's corps to advance and join Warren's left flank while the rest of the VI Corps formed on Warren's right flank:

"My orders were given through General Meade for an early advance on the morning of the 5th. Warren was to move to Parker's store, and Wilson's cavalry—then at Parker's store—to move on to Craig's meeting-house. Sedgwick followed Warren, closing in on his right. The Army of the Potomac was facing to the west, though our advance was made to the south, except when facing the enemy. Hancock was to move south-westward to join on the left of Warren, his left to reach to Shady Grove Church.

At six o'clock, before reaching Parker's store, Warren discovered the enemy. He sent word back to this effect, and was ordered to halt and prepare to meet and attack him.

Wright, with his division of Sedgwick's corps, was ordered, by any road he could find, to join on to Warren's right, and Getty with his division, also of Sedgwick's corps, was ordered to move rapidly by Warren's rear and get on his left. This was the speediest way to reinforce Warren who was confronting the enemy on both the Orange plank and turnpike roads."

Grant's aide, Theodore Lyman, would later describe just how difficult the Wilderness was to maneuver around near the Orange Plank Road: "The very worst of it is parallel with Orange plank and upper part of the Brock road. Here it is mostly a low, continuous, thick growth of small saplings, fifteen to thirty feet high and seldom larger than one's arm. The half-grown leaves added to the natural obscurity, and there were many places where a line of troops could with difficulty be seen at fifty yards. This was the terrain on which we were called to manoeuvre a great army."

As Grant's orders were put into motion and Warren started to prepare a battle line, Ewell's corps started going about digging in, building earthworks and fortifications to the west near Saunders Field, a small clearing in the dense woods near the Turnpike. Though Lee obviously wanted to block Grant's march and ensnare him in the Wilderness, he also didn't want to give battle himself until he could get Longstreet up. When Longstreet received orders to march, it was nearly 1:00 p.m. and his corps would have to march nearly 30 miles. Luckily for the Confederates, Hancock's II Corps would also not be in position to link up with Getty's division on Warren's left until the middle of the afternoon at the earliest.

Grant and Meade initially believed that Ewell's corps was not an entire corps but merely an advance guard, an assumption that was dispelled when Warren's men approached Saunders Field only to find the Confederates' defensive line extended past his right flank. Warren suggested to Meade that his assault on the Confederate line not take place until Sedgwick's VI Corps joined his right, but delays in their march eventually induced the frustrated Meade into ordering an attack at 1:00 p.m. regardless of Sedgwick's positioning.

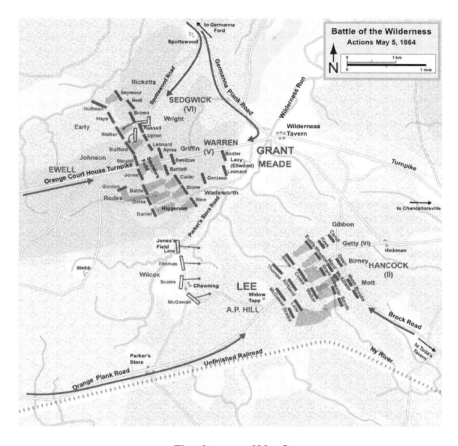

The afternoon of May 5

It didn't take long for Warren's men to suffer for the decision. Although the clearing actually allowed for a cohesive line to form and advance, the outflanked Union soldiers experienced devastating enfilades from Confederate soldiers on their right, compelling Romeyn Ayres's brigade to halt its forward movement even as the brigades to their left kept moving forward. In fact, Joseph Bartlett's brigade managed to pierce the Confederate line by overrunning a Confederate brigade led by John M. Jones, who was killed during the fight. Unfortunately, this breakthrough could not be exploited due to the fact that the inability of Ayres to move his brigade forward opened up Bartlett's right flank to the same kind of enfilade that pinned down Ayres in the first place.

As the general fight continued, Lyman described what it was like behind the lines, as general officers from the various Union corps were trying to get their commands to their respective positions.

I found General Getty at the plank road (a spot I shall remember for some years) and gave him instructions. He told me the whole of Hill's Corps was in his front and the skirmishers only 300 yards from us. For all I could see they might have been in Florida, but the occasional wounded men who limped by, and the sorry spectacle of two or three dead, wrapped in their blankets, showed that some fighting had already taken place. I got back and reported a little before one o'clock, and had scarcely got there when B-r-r-r-r wrang went the musketry, in front of Griffin and of Wright, which for the next hour and a half was continuous — not by volley, for that is impossible in such woods; but a continuous crackle, now swelling and now abating, and interspersed with occasional cannon. Very soon the ambulances began to go forward for their mournful freight. A little before two, I was sent with an order to a cavalry regiment, close by. The pike was a sad spectacle indeed; it was really obstructed with trains of ambulances and with the wounded on foot; all had the same question, over and over again; 'How far to the 5th Corps' hospital?'"

Although Bartlett's advance was repulsed by the shooting on his right flank, the Iron Brigade continued advancing on the left. Although this was one of the hardest and most famous brigades of the entire war, it had been so badly devastated at Gettysburg that the brigade needed to be refilled with raw recruits, to the extent that the character of the Iron Brigade in 1864 was no longer what it was in 1862 and 1863. But for a time, it didn't seem like that would matter, because the Iron Brigade made a steady advance that sent a Confederate brigade under Cullen Battle into a disorderly retreat.

The Confederates were fortunate enough to have John B. Gordon's brigade behind the line. Indicative of the confusion that both sides were experiencing in the early fighting, Gordon's brigade found itself in position to reinforce the line simply because it had marched in the direction where the gunfire sounded heaviest. Gordon recalled the scene as his men were coming up to provide reinforcements:

"Alternate confidence and apprehension were awakened as the shouts of one army or the other reached our ears. So distinct in character were these shouts that they were easily discernible. At one point the weird Confederate 'yell' told us plainly that Ewell's men were advancing. At another the huzzas, in mighty concert, of the Union troops warned us that they had repelled the Confederate charge; and as these ominous huzzas grew in volume we know that Grant's lines were moving forward. Just as the head of my column came within range of the whizzing Miniés, the Confederate yells grew fainter, and at last ceased; and the Union shout rose above the din of battle. I was already prepared by this infallible admonition for the sight of Ewell's shattered forces retreating in disorder. The oft-repeated but spasmodic efforts of first one army and then the other to break through the opposing ranks had at last been ended by the sudden rush of Grant's compact veterans from the dense covert in such numbers that Ewell's attenuated lines were driven in confusion to the rear. These retreating divisions, like broken and receding waves, rolled back against the head of my column while we were still rapidly advancing along the narrow road. The repulse had been so sudden and the confusion so great that practically no resistance was now being made to the Union advance; and the elated Federals were so near me that little time was left to bring my men from column into line in order to resist the movement or repel it by countercharge."

Gordon

As his men were coming up, Gordon ran into Ewell himself, who told Gordon that the fate of the day rested on his men's shoulders. With that, Gordon ordered his men forward, producing what he called the "strangest" scene he saw during the Civil War:

. " At this moment of dire extremity I saw General Ewell, who was still a superb horseman, notwithstanding the loss of his leg, riding in furious gallop toward me, his thoroughbred charger bounding like a deer through the dense underbrush…'General Gordon, the fate of the day depends on you, sir,' he said. 'These men will save it, sir,' I replied, more with the purpose of arousing the enthusiasm of my men than with any well-defined idea as to how we were to save it. Quickly wheeling a single regiment into line, I ordered it forward in a counterttcharge, while I hurried the other troops into position. The sheer audacity and dash of that regimental charge checked, as I had hoped it would, the Union advance for a few moments, giving me the essential time to throw the other troops across the Union front. Swiftly riding to the centre of my line, I gave in person the order: 'Forward!' With a deafening yell which must have been heard miles away, that glorious brigade rushed upon the hitherto advancing enemy, and by the shock of their furious onset shattered into fragments all that portion of the compact Union line which confronted my troops.

At that moment was presented one of the strangest conditions ever witnessed upon a battle-field. My command covered only a small portion of the long lines in blue, and not a single regiment of those stalwart Federals yielded except those which had been struck by the Southern advance. On both sides of the swath cut by this sweep of the Confederate scythe, the steady veterans of Grant were unshaken and still poured their incessant volleys into the retreating Confederate ranks. My command had cut its way through the Union centre, and at that moment it was in the remarkably strange position of being on identically the same general line with the enemy, the Confederates facing in one direction, the Federals in the other. Looking down that line from Grant's right toward his left, there would first have been seen a long stretch of blue uniforms, then a short stretch of gray, then another still longer of blue, in one continuous line. The situation was both unique and alarming…

As soon as my troops had broken through the Union ranks, I directed my staff to halt the command; and before the Union veterans could recover from the shock, my regiments were moving at double-quick from the centre into file right and left, thus placing them in two parallel lines, back to back, in a position at a right angle to the one held a moment before. This quickly executed manoeuvre placed one half of my command squarely upon the right flank of one portion of the enemy's unbroken line, and the other half facing in exactly the opposite direction, squarely upon the left flank of the enemy's line."

Gordon's counterattack had saved the Confederate line in that spot, but the Confederate line to his right was also being attacked by Union brigades led by Roy Stone and James C. Rice. As those attacks were being repulsed, Warren tried to bring up artillery to help the advance, only to have the Confederates surge forward and initiate hand-to-hand fighting for control of the two guns in the field. In the melee, Saunders Field caught fire, consigning some of the unfortunate injured men lying on the field to literally watch flames creep up to them before burning them to death. One of the soldiers, Private Frank Wilkeson, later recalled, "I saw many wounded soldiers in the Wilderness who hung on to their rifles, and whose intention was clearly stamped on their pallid faces. I saw one man, both of whose legs were broken, lying on the ground with his cocked rifle by his side and his ramrod in his hand, and his eyes set on the front. I knew he meant to kill himself in case of fire—knew it is surely as though I could read his thoughts."

Warren's assault had failed to exploit any of its breakthroughs, but just as his V Corps was ending its fighting, Sedgwick's VI Corps came up on their right around 3:00 p.m. and started attacking Ewell's left. Sedgwick made the attack up the Spottswood Road, but Ewell's line forced him to try to align a battle line well into the Wilderness off the road as well. For the next hour, Sedgwick's corps tried to dislodge Ewell's line, but the inability to keep a line moving forward with any semblance of coordination doomed the attempts of Union and Confederates alike to attack and counterattack. After just an hour, Sedgwick's attack began to peter out.

About a mile to the southeast, A.P. Hill's corps was confronting Getty's division, which had come up on Warren's left to hold the crossroad where the east-west Orange Plank Road intersected the north-south Brock Road. It was essential for the Union to hold that intersection to make sure that Hancock could rejoin the other two corps by marching northwest up the Brock Road toward the now pitched battle. Getty was assisted in holding the spot with some a brigade of cavalry, keeping Hill's soldiers a few hundred yards to the west while Hancock's men began to trickle up.

Some of Hancock's men came up around 4:00 p.m., and with their arrival in mind, Getty's division was ordered to attack Hill. Lyman described the scene on the Union left that afternoon:

At 3.15 I was sent with an order to General Getty to attack at once, and to explain to him that Hancock would join also. He is a cool man, is Getty, quite a wonder; as I saw then and after. 'Go to General Eustis and General Wheaton,' he said to his aides, 'and tell them to prepare to advance at once.' And so we were getting into it! And everybody had been ordered up, including Burnside, who had crossed that very morning at Germanna Ford. General Grant had his station with us (or we with him); there he took his seat on the grass, and smoked his briarwood pipe, looking sleepy and stern and indifferent. His face, however, may wear a most pleasing smile, and I believe he is a thoroughly amiable man. That he believes in his star and takes a bright view of things is evident. At 4.15 P. M. General Meade ordered me to take some orderlies, go to General Hancock (whose musketry we could now hear on the left) and send him back reports, staying there till dark. Delightful! At the crossing of the dotted cross-road with the plank sat Hancock, on his fine horse — the preux chevalier of this campaign — a glorious soldier, indeed! The musketry was crashing in the woods in our front, and stray balls — too many to be pleasant — were coming about. It's all very well for novels, but I don't like such places and go there only when ordered. 'Report to General Meade,' said Hancock, 'that it is very hard to bring up troops in this wood, and that only a part of my Corps is up, but I will do as well as I can.' Up rides an officer: 'Sir! General Getty is hard pressed and nearly out of ammunition!' 'Tell him to hold on and

General Gibbon will be up to help him.' Another officer: 'General Mott's division has broken, sir, and is coming back.' 'Tell him to stop them, sir!!' roared Hancock in a voice of a trumpet. As he spoke, a crowd of troops came from the woods and fell back into the Brock road. Hancock dashed among them. 'Halt here! halt here! Form behind this rifle-pit. Major Mitchell, go to Gibbon and tell him to come up on the double-quick!' It was a welcome sight to see Carroll's brigade coming along that Brock road, he riding at their head as calm as a May morning. 'Left face — prime — forward,' and the line disappeared in the woods to waken the musketry with double violence. Carroll was brought back wounded. Up came Hays's brigade, disappeared in the woods, and, in a few minutes, General Hays was carried past me, covered with blood, shot through the head.

As Lyman's account indicates, the fighting was back-and-forth, with both Hill's corps and Hancock's corps entangled in underbrush and forest near a small stream called the Ny River. Lee had made his headquarters at the Widow Tapp's house in a small clearing just behind Hill's defensive line, and at one point some Union soldiers came streaming out of the woods and into the clearing, coming into eyesight of Lee while he was discussing the fighting with Hill and JEB Stuart. Thankfully for the three Confederate officers, the Union soldiers were just as confused as they were, and when they realized there were Confederates in their front they turned right back around and reentered the forest.

When the fighting ended that night, both lines had maintained their respective positions, and the soldiers on both sides immediately started digging in and preparing strong defensive fortifications. There was still a gap separating the two armies from completely forming one line, something Grant would attempt to remedy the next day by bringing up Burnside's IX Corps and something that Lee could do nothing about other than to gamble that the confusing Wilderness would protect Hill's left flank and Ewell's right flank.

"After the close of the battle of the 5th of May my orders were given for the following morning. We knew Longstreet with 12,000 men was on his way to join Hill's right, near the Brock Road, and might arrive during the night. I was anxious that the rebels should not take the initiative in the morning, and therefore ordered Hancock to make an assault at 4.30 o'clock. Meade asked to have the hour changed to six. Deferring to his wishes as far as I was willing, the order was modified and five was fixed as the hour to move.

Hancock had now fully one-half of the Army of the Potomac. Wadsworth with his division, which had arrived the night before, lay in a line perpendicular to that held by Hill, and to the right of Hancock. He was directed to move at the same time, and to attack Hill's left.

Burnside, who was coming up with two divisions, was directed to get in between

Warren and Wadsworth, and attack as soon as he could get in position to do so. Sedgwick and Warren were to make attacks in their front, to detain as many of the enemy as they could and to take advantage of any attempt to reinforce Hill from that quarter. Burnside was ordered if he should succeed in breaking the enemy's centre, to swing around to the left and envelop the right of Lee's army. Hancock was informed of all the movements ordered."

Despite being outnumbered and not gaining any ground, Lee had kept Grant's army in the Wilderness, and he could count on Longstreet arriving at some point to fight tomorrow. Lee reported back to Richmond:

"The enemy crossed the Rapidan yesterday at Ely's and Germanna Fords. Two corps of this army moved to oppose him: Ewell's, by the old turnpike, and Hill's, by the plank road. They arrived this morning in close proximity to the enemy's line of march. A strong attack was made upon Ewell, who repulsed it, capturing many prisoners and four pieces of artillery. The enemy subsequently concentrated upon General Hill, who, with Heth's and Wilcox's divisions, successfully resisted repeated and desperate assaults. A large force of cavalry and artillery on our right flank was driven back by Rosser's brigade. By the blessing of God we maintained our position against every effort until night, when the contest closed."

Gordon summed up Confederate sentiments on the night of May 5:

"Both sides labored all night in the dark and dense woodland, throwing up such breastworks as were possible--a most timely preparation for the next day's conflicts. My own command was ordered during the night to the extreme left of Lee's lines, under the apprehension that Grant's right overlapped and endangered our left flank.

Thus ended the 5th of May, which had witnessed the first desperate encounter between Grant and Lee. The fighting had not involved the whole of either army, but it was fierce and bloody. It would be unjust to claim that either of the famous leaders had achieved a signal victory. Both sides had left their dead scattered through the bullet-riddled underbrush. The Confederates drew comfort from the fact that in the shifting fortunes of the day theirs was the last advance, that the battle had ended near where it had begun, and that the Union advance had been successfully repulsed."

Chapter 4: May 6

At the beginning of May 6, Grant was hoping that his advantage in manpower would make it possible for Burnside's IX Corps to interpose itself between Hill and Ewell, making it possible to cut Lee's army in half and destroy them. But he wasn't the only one intending to make an attack; the characteristically aggressive Lee had decided to keep Hill's outnumbered men in position and even use them to attack Hancock's corps, operating under the assumption that Longstreet's corps would be up in the morning and could sustain the momentum of the advance.

Naturally, things would not go according to plan for either Grant or Lee. Due to miscommunications, or due to the understanding that they would be used to attack the following morning, multiple divisions in Hill's corps decided not to dig in and build defensive fortifications on the night of May 5. While that may have been understandable and normal in 1862, experience had taught both sides by 1864 that the first thing to do once they had an established line was to start digging in and building earthworks that would protect them during an attack. By the end of the war, the Civil War had become a forerunner to the trench warfare of World War I, and if an army was given 24 hours to entrench, their position became practically unassailable. Grant described the process in his memoirs:

"[I]n every change of position or halt for the night, whether confronting the enemy or not, the moment arms were stacked the men intrenched themselves. For this purpose they would build up piles of logs or rails if they could be found in their front, and dig a ditch, throwing the dirt forward on the timber. Thus the digging they did counted in making a depression to stand in, and increased the elevation in front of them. It was wonderful how quickly they could in this way construct defences of considerable strength. When a halt was made with the view of assaulting the enemy, or in his presence, these would be strengthened or their positions changed under the direction of engineer officers."

Moreover, Lee had expected that Longstreet's men would be up at dawn, allowing him to slide Hill's corps to the left and eventually link up with Ewell, which would have put Hill in the gap that Grant intended to push Burnside's IX Corps through. However, the nature of the night marching, the nature of the roads, and the nature of the terrain all delayed Longstreet's marching during the early morning hours of May 6. Longstreet expressed some of the causes of the inevitable delays:

"About eleven o'clock in the night the guide reported from General Lee to conduct my command through the wood across to the Plank road, and at one o'clock the march was resumed. The road was overgrown by the bushes, except the side-tracks made by the draft animals and the ruts of wheels which marked occasional lines in its course. After a time the wood became less dense, and the unused road was more difficult to follow, and presently the guide found that there was no road under him; but no time was lost, as, by ordering the lines of the divisions doubled, they were ready when the trail was found, and the march continued in double line. At daylight we entered the Plank road, and filed down towards the field of strife of the afternoon of the 5th and daylight of the 6th."

Longstreet's men would be advancing down the Orange Plank Road toward Hill's corps and the Union line by the break of dawn, but by then Hancock's attack, which began at Grant's appointed time of 5:00 a.m., was already starting to steadily drive Hill's corps back. Even several decades later, Longstreet's frustration with Hill's corps was evident when explaining what happened in his memoirs:

"R. H. Anderson's division of the Third Corps, marching on the Plank road, had rested at Verdierville during the night, and was called to the front in the morning. The divisions of Heth and Wilcox rested during the night of the 5th where the battle of that day ceased, but did not prepare ammunition nor strengthen their lines for defence, because informed that they were to be relieved from the front. Both the division commanders claim that they were to be relieved, and that they were ordered not to intrench or replenish supplies. So it seems that they were all night within hearing of the voices of Hancock's men, not even reorganizing their lines so as to offer a front of battle! General Heth has stated that he proposed to arrange for battle, but was ordered to give his men rest. While Hancock was sending men to his advanced line during the night and intrenching there and on his second line, the Confederates were all night idle."

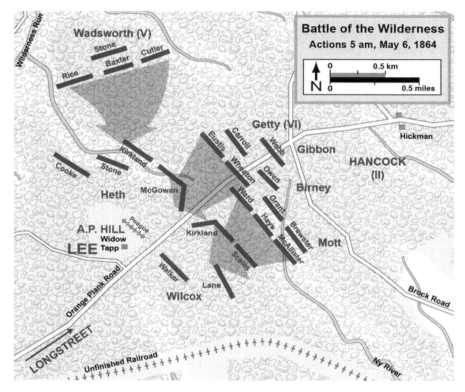

Longstreet wouldn't be the only one frustrated. One of the reasons Meade had lobbied Grant to push back the time for Hancock's assault was concern that Burnside wouldn't be in position yet. While that convinced Grant to push back the attack to 5:00, that still wasn't enough time for Burnside's IX Corps to be in position, something that at least a few of his comrades anticipated. Lyman was ordered to ride over to Hancock and keep Meade and Grant informed of the attack's results, and he later recalled the morning attack:

> "It was after five when I mounted, and already the spattering fire showed that the skirmishers were pushing out; as I rode down the crossroad, two or three crashing volleys rang through the woods, and then the whole front was alive with musketry. I found General Hancock at the crossing of the plank: he was wreathed with smiles. 'We are driving them, sir; tell General Meade we are driving them most beautifully. Birney has gone in and he is just cleaning them out be-au-ti-fully!' This was quite apparent from the distance of the receding firing and the absence of those infernal minie balls. 'I

am ordered to tell you, sir, that only one division of General Burnside is up, but that he will go in as soon as he can be put in position.' Hancock's face changed. 'I knew it!' he said vehemently. 'Just what I expected. If he could attack now, we would smash A. P. Hill all to pieces!' And very true were his words. Meantime, some hundreds of prisoners were brought in; all from Hill's troops. Presently, however, the firing seemed to wake again with renewed fury; and in a little while a soldier came up to me and said: 'I was ordered to report that this prisoner here belongs to Longstreet's Corps.' 'Do you belong to Longstreet?' I hastened to ask. 'Ya-as, sir,' said grey-back, and was marched to the rear. It was too true!

Writing in his memoirs, Grant later expressed the belief that it was the Wilderness, not Longstreet, that would prove Hancock's undoing:

"I believed then, and see no reason to change that opinion now, that if the country had been such that Hancock and his command could have seen the confusion and panic in the lines of the enemy, it would have been taken advantage of so effectually that Lee would not have made another stand outside of his Richmond defences.

Gibbon commanded Hancock's left, and was ordered to attack, but was not able to accomplish much.

On the morning of the 6th Sheridan was sent to connect with Hancock's left and attack the enemy's cavalry who were trying to get on our left and rear. He met them at the intersection of the Furnace and Brock roads and at Todd's Tavern, and defeated them at both places. Later he was attacked, and again the enemy was repulsed.

Hancock heard the firing between Sheridan and Stuart, and thinking the enemy coming by that road, still further reinforced his position guarding the entrance to the Brock Road. Another incident happened during the day to further induce Hancock to weaken his attacking column. Word reached him that troops were seen moving towards him from the direction of Todd's Tavern, and Brooke's brigade was detached to meet this new enemy; but the troops approaching proved to be several hundred convalescents coming from Chancellorsville, by the road Hancock had advanced upon, to join their respective commands. At 6.50 o'clock A.M., Burnside, who had passed Wilderness Tavern at six o'clock, was ordered to send a division to the support of Hancock, but to continue with the remainder of his command in the execution of his previous order. The difficulty of making a way through the dense forests prevented Burnside from getting up in time to be of any service on the forenoon of the sixth."

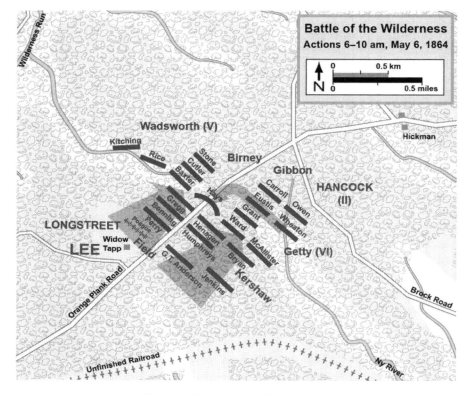

Longstreet's counterattack

Longstreet's late arrival meant Lee could not slide Hill's corps to the left, but it meant that his corps was in just the right place to blunt Hancock's assault and launch a fierce counterattack itself. As Longstreet's column came marching up, Lee was so excited that he began riding at the head of the column, acting as though he intended to lead the counterattack himself. Writing about the episode decades later, Longstreet quipped that if Lee was going to lead the charge, he'd like to move farther behind the lines to safety:

"Hancock advanced and struck the divisions before sunrise, just as my command reported to General Lee. My line was formed on the right and left of the Plank road, Kershaw on the right, Field on the left. As the line deployed, the divisions of Heth and Wilcox came back upon us in disorder, more and more confused as their steps hurried under Hancock's musketry. As my ranks formed the men broke files to give free passage for their comrades to the rear. The advancing fire was getting brisk, but not a shot was fired in return by my troops until the divisions were ready. Three of Field's brigades, the Texas, Alabama, and Benning's Georgia, were formed in line on the left of the road, and three of Kershaw's on the right. General Lee, appalled at the condition of affairs, thought to lead the Texas brigade alone into desperate charge, before my lines were well formed. The ordeal was trying, but the steady troops, seeing him off his balance, refused to follow, begged him to retire, and presently Colonel Venable, of his staff, reported to me General Lee's efforts to lead the brigade, and suggested that I should try to call him from it. I asked that he would say, with my compliments, that his line would be recovered in an hour if he would permit me to handle the troops, but if my services were not needed, I would like to ride to some place of safety, as it was not quite comfortable where we were."

Of course, Lee would not end up leading the charge, and he wouldn't need to. Longstreet has often been criticized for being reluctant to move, and slow when he did, but once he put his corps into action, he was one of the best generals the Civil War had. As one Confederate soldier put it, "Like a fine lady at a party, Longstreet was often late in his arrival at the ball. But he always made a sensation and that of delight, when he got in, with the grand old First Corps sweeping behind him as his train."

Longstreet's counterattack also had the advantage of coming at a time when the Union charge had progressed a mile and inevitably resulted in soldiers getting intermingled with other commands and unit cohesion becoming relatively impossible. The Wilderness also hid Longstreet's impending attack until his men were within just a few hundred yards, but it also caused Longstreet some difficulty as well. Longstreet explained, "As full lines of battle could not be handled through the thick wood, I ordered the advance of the six brigades by heavy skirmish lines, to be followed by stronger supporting lines. Hancock's lines, thinned by their push through the wood, and somewhat by the fire of the disordered divisions, weaker than my line of fresh and more lively skirmishers, were checked by our first steady, rolling fire, and after a brisk fusillade were pushed back to their intrenched line, when the fight became steady and very firm, occasionally swinging parts of my line back and compelling the reserves to move forward and recover it."

While the counterattack blunted Hancock's momentum and also kept some of the men from Burnside's IX Corps occupied, Longstreet had heard about an unfinished railroad bed south of the Plank Road that his troops might be able to travel through and come up on Hancock's left flank by surprise. When the four brigades traveled through the railroad cut and hit Hancock's left flank at 11:00, it completely rolled up Hancock's battle line. Hancock would later claim that his line was rolled up "like a wet blanket", but Longstreet's men were still advancing as Hancock's men retreated. Longstreet wrote:

"As soon as the troops struck Hancock his line began to break, first slowly, then rapidly. Somehow, as they retreated, a fire was accidentally started in the dry leaves, and began to spread as the Confederates advanced. Mahone's brigade approached the burning leaves and part of it broke off a little to get around, but the Twelfth Virginia was not obstructed by the blaze and moved directly on. At the Plank road Colonel Sorrel rode back to join us. All of the enemy's battle on the right of the Plank road was broken up, and General Field was fighting severely with his three brigades on the left against Wadsworth and Stevenson, pushing them a little.

General Smith then came and reported a way across the Brock road that would turn Hancock's extreme left. He was asked to conduct the flanking brigades and handle them as the ranking officer. He was a splendid tactician as well as skilful engineer, and gallant withal. He started, and, not to lose time or distance, moved by inversion, Wofford's left leading, Wofford's favorite manoeuvre. As Wofford's left stepped out, the other troops moved down the Plank road, Jenkins's brigade by the road, Kershaw's division alongside. I rode at the head of the column, Jenkins, Kershaw, and the staff with me. After discussing the dispositions of their troops for reopening battle, Jenkins rode closer to offer congratulations, saying, 'I am happy; I have felt despair of the cause for some months, but am relieved, and feel assured that we will put the enemy back across the Rapidan before night." Little did he or I think these sanguine words were the last he would utter.'"

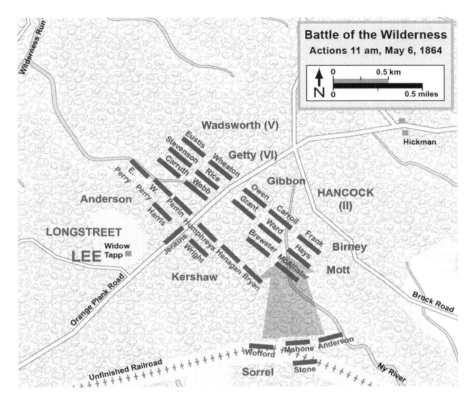

Battle of the Wilderness
Actions 11 am, May 6, 1864

On May 2, 1863, almost a year to the day that the battle was raging in the Wilderness, Stonewall Jackson had been mortally wounded by his own men while leading a successful flank attack after being mistaken for advancing Union soldiers. On May 6, 1864, less than 5 miles to the west, Longstreet nearly suffered the same fate.

"As the Twelfth Regiment marched back to find its place on the other side of the Plank road, it was mistaken, in the wood, for an advance of the enemy, and fire was opened on it from the other regiments of the brigade. The men threw themselves to the ground to let the fire pass. Just then our party of officers was up and rode under the fire. General Jenkins had not finished the expressions of joyful congratulations which I have quoted when he fell mortally wounded.

Captain Doby and the orderly, Bowen, of Kershaw's staff, were killed. General Kershaw turned to quiet the troops, when Jenkins's brigade with levelled guns were in the act of returning the fire of the supposed enemy concealed in the wood, but as Kershaw's clear voice called out 'F-r-i-e-n-d-s!' the arms were recovered, without a shot in return, and the men threw themselves down upon their faces.

At the moment that Jenkins fell I received a severe shock from a minie ball passing through my throat and right shoulder. The blow lifted me from the saddle, and my right arm dropped to my side, but I settled back to my seat, and started to ride on, when in a minute the flow of blood admonished me that my work for the day was done. As I turned to ride back, members of the staff, seeing me about to fall, dismounted and lifted me to the ground."

Longstreet's day was done, and so was his involvement in the Overland Campaign as a whole. He would have to spend the next 5 months convalescing and wouldn't return to Lee's army until October, several months into the siege of Petersburg. To say his loss at this juncture would be an understatement, something acknowledged by both sides. Grant claimed, "His loss was a severe one to Lee, and compensated in a great measure for the mishap, or misapprehensions, which had fallen to our lot during the day." The leader of the artillery in Longstreet's corps, Porter Alexander, went even further, arguing, "I have always believed that, but for Longstreet's fall, the panic which was fairly underway in Hancock's Corps would have been extended and have resulted in Grant's being forced to retreat back across the Rapidan."

The delays and confusion brought about by Longstreet's injury hampered the effectiveness of his counterattack. Richard Anderson succeeded him, but he was unfamiliar with the entire corps' dispositions and needed to try to confer with the grievously wounded Longstreet to get the information after the corps commander had been shot through the throat. Lee would also be forced to take a more active role on his right, personally directing the line.

How much of a difference Longstreet's loss made continues to be debated, but there's no question that Hancock's defensive line ultimately held because of the defensive fortifications his men had constructed the night before. Although the Confederates were able to get into their rifle pits, the II Corps eventually repulsed them, forcing Lee to take time to reform his lines and prepare another attack for later in the afternoon.

Grant later wrote in his memoirs, "After Longstreet's removal from the field Lee took command of his right in person. He was not able, however, to rally his men to attack Hancock's position, and withdrew from our front for the purpose of reforming. Hancock sent a brigade to clear his front of all remnants that might be left of Longstreet's or Hill's commands. This brigade having been formed at right angles to the intrenchments held by Hancock's command, swept down the whole length of them from left to right. A brigade of the enemy was encountered in this move; but it broke and disappeared without a contest…Firing was continued after this, but with less fury. Burnside had not yet been able to get up to render any assistance. But it was now only about nine in the morning, and he was getting into position on Hancock's right."

When Burnside arrived, Anderson had to swing part of Longstreet's corps to face that new threat, until the corps had practically formed at a right angle. Burnside's arrival and Hancock's defensive fortifications ensured that the Army of the Potomac's left would remain secure throughout the day.

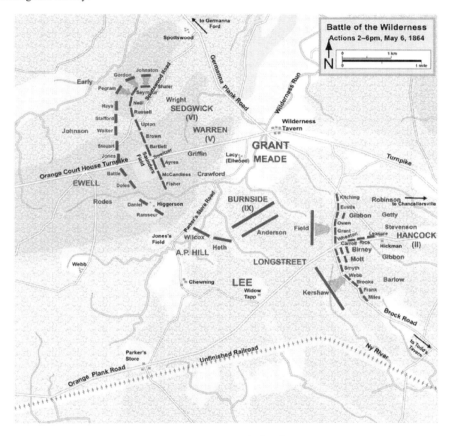

The afternoon of May 6

Grant's left flank had come close to disaster as a result of a surprise flank attack, and it turned out that his right would suffer nearly the same fate later in the day. While the fighting was going on south of them, John Gordon's scouts on the extreme left of the Confederate line reported the potential of turning Sedgwick's right flank. Gordon verified the situation for himself, and later wrote of his great surprise:

"THE night of the 5th of May was far spent when my command reached its destination on the extreme Confederate left. The men were directed to sleep on their arms during the remaining hours of darkness. Scouts were at once sent to the front to feel their way through the thickets and ascertain, if possible, where the extreme right of Grant's line rested. At early dawn these trusted men reported that they had found it: that it rested in the woods only a short distance in our front, that it was wholly unprotected, and that the Confederate lines stretched a considerable distance beyond the Union right, overlapping it. I was so impressed with the importance of this report and with the necessity of verifying its accuracy that I sent others to make the examination, with additional instructions to proceed to the rear of Grant's right and ascertain if the exposed flank were supported by troops held in reserve behind it. The former report was not only confirmed as to the exposed position of that flank, but the astounding information was brought that there was not a supporting force within several miles of it.

Much of this scouting had been done in the late hours of the night and before sunrise on the morning of the 6th. Meantime, as this information came my brain was throbbing with the tremendous possibilities to which such a situation invited us, provided the conditions were really as reported. Mounting my horse in the early morning and guided by some of these explorers, I rode into the unoccupied woodland to see for myself. It is enough to say that I found the reports correct in every particular. Riding back toward my line, I was guided by the scouts to the point near which they had located the right of the Union army. Dismounting and creeping slowly and cautiously through the dense woods, we were soon in ear-shot of an unsuppressed and merry clatter of voices. A few feet nearer, and through a narrow vista, I was shown the end of General Grant's temporary breastworks. There was no line guarding this flank. As far as my eye could reach, the Union soldiers were seated on the margin of the rifle-pits, taking their breakfast. Small fires were burning over which they were boiling their coffee, while their guns leaned against the works in their immediate front.

No more time was consumed in scouting. The revelations had amazed me and filled me with confident anticipations of unprecedented victory. It was evident that General Grant had decided to make his heaviest assaults upon the Confederate right, and for this purpose had ordered his reserves to that flank. By some inconceivable oversight on the part of his subordinates, his own right flank had been left in the extremely exposed condition in which my scouts had found it. Undoubtedly the officer who located that battle line for General Grant or for General Sedgwick was under the impression that there were no Confederates in front of that portion of it; and this was probably true at the time the location was made. That fact, however, did not justify the officer in leaving his flank (which is the most vulnerable part of an army) thus unguarded for a whole night after the battle…

During the night, while the over-confident Union officer and his men slept in fancied security, my men stole silently through the thickets and planted a hostile line not only in his immediate front, but overlapping it by more than the full length of my command. All intelligent military critics will certainly agree that such an opportunity as was here presented for the overthrow of a great army has rarely occurred in the conduct of a war."

Once he was certain of the Union line's situation, Gordon began forming the plan that he thought could destroy the entire Army of the Potomac:

"As later developments proved, one brigade on the flank was all that was needed for the inauguration of the plan and the demonstration of its possibilities. The details of the plan were as follows: While the unsuspecting Federals were drinking their coffee, my troops were to move quickly and quietly behind the screen of thick underbrush and form squarely on Sedgwick's strangely exposed flank, reaching a point far beyond that flank and lapping around his rear, so as to capture his routed men as they broke to the rear. While my command rushed from this ambush a simultaneous demonstration was to be made along his front. As each of Sedgwick's brigades gave way in confusion, the corresponding Confederate brigade, whose front was thus cleared on the general line, was to swing into the column of attack on the flank, thus swelling at each step of our advance the numbers, power, and momentum of the Confederate forces as they swept down the line of works and extended another brigade's length to the unprotected Union rear. As each of the Union brigades, divisions, and corps were struck by such an absolutely resistless charge upon the flank and rear, they must fly or be captured. The effective force of Grant's army would be thus constantly diminished, and in the same proportion the column of attack would be steadily augmented."

Despite the fact Gordon had determined the state of Sedgwick's flank in the early morning hours of May 6, the flank attack did not start until the late afternoon. As Gordon anticipated, the flank attack was decisive from the very beginning:

"The Georgia brigade (Gordon's) was directed to make the assault, and the North Carolina brigade (Johnson's) was ordered to move farther to the Union rear and to keep as nearly as possible in touch with the attacking force and to gather up Sedgwick's men as they broke to the rear. As the sun went down these troops were ordered forward. In less than ten minutes they struck the Union flank and with thrilling yells rushed upon it and along the Union works, shattering regiments and brigades, and throwing them into wildest confusion and panic. There was practically no resistance. There could be none. The Georgians, commanded by that intrepid leader, Clement A. Evans, were on the flank, and the North Carolinians, led by a brilliant young officer, Robert Johnson, were sweeping around to the rear, without a shot in their front. There was nothing for the brave Federals to do but to fly. There was no time given them to file out from their works and form a new line of resistance. This was attempted again and again; but in every instance the swiftly moving Confederates were upon them, pouring a consuming fire into their half-formed ranks and shivering one command after another in quick succession. The gallant Union leaders, Generals Seymour and Shaler, rode among their panic-stricken troops in the heroic endeavor to form them into a new line. Their brave efforts were worse than unavailing, for both of these superb officers, with large numbers of their brigades, were quickly gathered as prisoners of war in the Confederate net; and nearly the whole of Sedgwick's corps was disorganized.

It will be seen that my troops were compelled to halt at last, not by the enemy's resistance, but solely by the darkness and the cross-fire from Confederates. Had daylight lasted one half-hour longer, there would not have been left an organized company in Sedgwick's corps. Even as it was, all accounts agree that his whole command was shaken. As I rode abreast of the Georgians, who were moving swiftly and with slight resistance, the last scene which met my eye as the curtain of night shut off the view was the crumbling of the Union lines as they bravely but vainly endeavored to file out of their works and form a new line under the furious onset and withering fire of the Confederates."

Gordon's flank attack on Sedgwick also led to one of Grant's most famous quotes of the war, as remembered by Union general Horace Porter. Porter recalled the scene at headquarters when Sedgwick's line began to unravel:

"It was now about sundown; the storm of battle which had raged with unabated fury from early dawn had been succeeded by a calm . . . . . Just then the stillness was broken by heavy volleys of musketry on our extreme right, which told that Sedgwick had been assaulted and was actually engaged with the enemy. The attack against which the general-in-chief during the day had ordered every precaution to be taken had now been made . . . . . Generals Grant and Meade, accompanied by me and one or two other staff officers, walked rapidly over to Meade's tent, and found that the reports still coming in were bringing news of increasing disaster. It was soon reported that General Shaler and part of his brigade had been captured; then that General Seymour and several hundred of his men had fallen into the hands of the enemy; afterward that our right had been turned, and Ferrero's division cut off and forced back upon the Rapidan . . . . . Aides came galloping in from the right, laboring under intense excitement, talking wildly and giving the most exaggerated reports of the engagement. Some declared that a large force had broken and scattered Sedgwick's entire corps. Others insisted that the enemy had turned our right completely and captured the wagon-train. . . . A general officer came in from his command at this juncture and said to the general-in-chief, speaking rapidly and laboring under considerable excitement:'General Grant, this is a crisis that cannot be looked upon too seriously; I know Lee's methods well by past experience; he will throw his whole army between us and the Rapidan and cut us off completely from our communications.'

The general rose to his feet, took his cigar out of his mouth, turned to the officer, and replied, with a degree of animation which he seldom manifested: 'Oh, I am heartily tired of hearing about what Lee is going to do. Some of you always seem to think he is suddenly going to turn a double somersault, and land in our rear and on both of our flanks at the same time. Go back to your command, and try to think what we are going to do ourselves, instead of what Lee is going to do.' The officer retired rather crestfallen, and without saying a word in reply. This recalls a very pertinent criticism regarding his chief once made in my presence by General Sherman. He said: 'Grant always seemed pretty certain to win when he went into a fight with anything like equal numbers. I believe the chief reason why he was more successful than others was that while they were thinking so much about what the enemy was going to do, Grant was thinking all the time about what he was going to do himself.'"

Ultimately, Gordon's flank attack was conducted too late in the day to achieve the result he had hoped for. It would have been difficult enough in the Wilderness to conduct such an attack during the day, but with night falling and reinforcements brought up, Gordon's flank attack ultimately lost its momentum.

While Gordon obviously gave a rosy projection of what his flank attack could have achieved, the real historical question is why there was a delay of nearly 9 hours before the attack started. Gordon later blamed Ewell and his division commander, Jubal Early:

"When the plan for assault was fully matured, it was presented, with all its tremendous possibilities and with the full information which had been acquired by scouts and by my own personal and exhaustive examination. With all the earnestness that comes from deep conviction, the prompt adoption and vigorous execution of the plan were asked and urged. General Early at once opposed it. He said that Burnside's corps was immediately behind Sedgwick's right to protect it from any such flank attack; that if I should attempt such movement, Burnside would assail my flank and rout or capture all my men. He was so firmly fixed in his belief that Burnside's corps was where he declared it to be that he was not perceptibly affected by the repeated reports of scouts, nor my own statement that I myself had ridden for miles in rear of Sedgwick's right, and that neither Burnside's corps nor any other troops were there. General Ewell, whose province it was to decide the controversy, hesitated. He was naturally reluctant to take issue with my superior officer in a matter about which he could have no personal knowledge, because of the fact that his headquarters as corps-commander were located at considerable distance from this immediate locality. In view of General Early's protest, he was unwilling to order the attack or to grant me permission to make it, even upon my proposing to assume all responsibility of disaster, should any occur."

Early explained why he was hesitant to support making the flank attack in his own memoirs, and why the attack was made when it was:

"In the meantime General Gordon had sent out a scouting party on foot, which discovered what was supposed to be the enemy's right flank resting in the woods, in front of my division; and, during my absence while posting Johnston's brigade, he reported the fact to General Ewell, and suggested the propriety of attacking this flank of the enemy with his brigade, which was not engaged. On my return, the subject was mentioned to me by General Ewell, and I stated to him the danger and risk of making the attack under the circumstances, as a column was threatening our left flank and Burnside's corps was in rear of the enemy's flank, on which the attack was suggested. General Ewell concurred with me in this opinion, and the impolicy of the attempt at that time was obvious, as we had no reserves, and, if it failed, and the enemy showed any enterprise, a serious disaster would befall, not only our corps, but General Lee's whole army. In the afternoon, when the column threatening our left had been withdrawn, and it had been ascertained that Burnside had gone to Grant's left, on account of the heavy fighting on that flank, at my suggestion, General Ewell ordered the movement which Gordon had proposed...

Gordon succeeded in throwing the enemy's right flank into great confusion, capturing two brigadier generals (Seymour and Shaler), and several hundred prisoners, all of the 6th corps, under Sedgwick. The advance of Pegram's brigade, and the demonstration of Johnston's brigade in the rear, where it encountered a part of the enemy's force and captured some prisoners, contributed materially to the result. It was fortunate, however, that darkness came to close this affair, as the enemy, if he had been able to discover the disorder on our side, might have brought up fresh troops and availed himself of our condition. As it was, doubtless, the lateness of the hour caused him to be surprised, and the approaching darkness increased the confusion in his ranks, as he could not see the strength of the attacking force, and probably imagined it to be much more formidable than it really was. All of the brigades engaged in the attack were drawn back, and formed on a new line in front of the old one, and obliquely to it."

While Early may have been accurate in the belief that Burnside was behind Sedgwick early in the morning of May 6, it's also true that Burnside had been given orders to march further south and post himself on Sedgwick's left and Hancock's right. For his part, Grant pointed to the fact that he was sending reinforcements in his memoirs and also cited Early's memoirs, writing, "The defence, however, was vigorous; and night coming on, the enemy was thrown into as much confusion as our troops, engaged, were. Early says in his Memoirs that if we had discovered the confusion in his lines we might have brought fresh troops to his great discomfort. Many officers, who had not been attacked by Early, continued coming to my headquarters even after Sedgwick had rectified his lines a little farther to the rear, with news of the disaster, fully impressed with the idea that the enemy was pushing on and would soon be upon me."

Regardless, Gordon's attack brought an end to the fighting. On May 7, with the two armies in the same lines staring each other down, Grant issued marching orders to his army, beginning the process of delicately pulling out of his defensive lines in the face of Lee's army. The two days had produced nearly 30,000 casualties, with over 17,000 Union soldiers killed, wounded or captured and over 11,000 Confederates suffering the same fate.

Chapter 5: The Campaign Continues

The battle was over, but who had won it? Grant would later call the Battle of the Wilderness a Union victory, writing, "Our victory consisted in having successfully crossed a formidable stream, almost in the face of an enemy, and in getting the army together as a unit. We gained an advantage on the morning of the 6th, which, if it had been followed up, must have proven very decisive. In the evening the enemy gained an advantage; but was speedily repulsed. As we stood at the close, the two armies were relatively in about the same condition to meet each other as when the river divided them. But the fact of having safely crossed was a victory."

Naturally, Lee saw it from a different perspective, telling Richmond at the end of May 6, " Early this morning as the divisions of General Hill, engaged yesterday, were being relieved, the enemy advanced and created some confusion. The ground lost was recovered as soon as the fresh troops got into position and the enemy driven back to his original line. Afterward we turned the left of his front line and drove it from the field, leaving a large number of dead and wounded in our hands, among them General Wadsworth. A subsequent attack forced the enemy into his intrenched lines on the Brock road, extending from Wilderness Tavern, on the right, to Trigg's Mill. Every advance on his part, thanks to a merciful God, has been repulsed. Our loss in killed is not large, but we have many wounded; most of them slightly, artillery being little used on either side. I grieve to announce that Lieutenant-General Longstreet was severely wounded and General Jenkins killed. General Pegram was badly wounded yesterday. General Stafford, it is hoped, will recover."

Both sides claimed victory, but who was right? In a sense, they were both right and wrong. For the third straight year, Lee's army had successfully defended an advance toward Richmond by the Army of the Potomac and inflicted more casualties upon them. Moreover, it would be Grant who disengaged from the battle and left the field to Lee. But while these suggest the Confederates had won a tactical victory, the Battle of the Wilderness would not be a strategic victory because it would not end Grant's campaign.

Although Grant had suffered more casualties, he and Lee had both lost about 17% of their armies. This worked in Grant's favor not only because his army remained much larger than Lee's but also because he could replenish his manpower much more easily. While the casualties would astound and mortify the American public, it was all part of Grant's plan to grind down the Army of Northern Virginia until it could put up no resistance. This was evident to Lee, who became increasingly more desperate to score some kind of dramatic victory that would destroy the Army of the Potomac later in the Overland Campaign.

Ultimately, if there's any legacy to come out of the Battle of the Wilderness, or any way in which it was a turning point, it was enshrined in Grant's official orders on May 7.

"Make all preparations during the day for a night march to take position at Spottsylvania C. H. with one army corps, at Todd's Tavern with one, and another near the intersection of the Piney Branch and Spottsylvania road with the road from Alsop's to Old Court House. If this move is made the trains should be thrown forward early in the morning to the Ny River.

I think it would be advisable in making the change to leave Hancock where he is until Warren passes him. He could then follow and become the right of the new line. Burnside will move to Piney Branch Church. Sedgwick can move along the pike to Chancellorsville and on to his destination. Burnside will move on the plank road to the intersection of it with the Orange and Fredericksburg plank road, then follow Sedgwick to his place of destination.

All vehicles should be got out of hearing of the enemy before the troops move, and then move off quietly.

It is more than probable that the enemy concentrate for a heavy attack on Hancock this afternoon. In case they do we must be prepared to resist them, and follow up any success we may gain, with our whole force. Such a result would necessarily modify these instructions."

Unlike McClellan, Burnside and Hooker before him, Grant's orders directed the Army of the Potomac to continue heading south. The Battle of the Wilderness had only been a beginning, not an ending. As Grant would famously telegraph Washington, D.C. a few days later, "I propose to fight it out on this line, if it takes all summer."

If the Battle of the Wilderness had been a Confederate victory, that was an opinion lost on Grant's men when they learned the new marching orders. Grant himself would recount one such scene as he put his army into motion on May 7:

"Soon after dark Warren withdrew from the front of the enemy, and was soon followed by Sedgwick. Warren's march carried him immediately behind the works where Hancock's command lay on the Brock Road. With my staff and a small escort of cavalry I preceded the troops. Meade with his staff accompanied me. The greatest enthusiasm was manifested by Hancock's men as we passed by. No doubt it was inspired by the fact that the movement was south. It indicated to them that they had passed through the 'beginning of the end' in the battle just fought. The cheering was so lusty that the enemy must have taken it for a night attack. At all events it drew from him a furious fusillade of artillery and musketry, plainly heard but not felt by us."

With that, Grant began marching his army toward Spotsylvania Court House, the area he had hoped to reach before fighting Lee in a pitched battle. Things hadn't gone according to plan in the Wilderness, but Grant and Lee would have their battle at Spotsylvania soon enough.

Bibliography

Alexander, Edward P. Military Memoirs of a Confederate: A Critical Narrative. New York: Da Capo Press, 1993.

Bonekemper, Edward H., III. A Victor, Not a Butcher: Ulysses S. Grant's Overlooked Military Genius. Washington, DC: Regnery, 2004.

Grant, Ulysses S. Personal Memoirs of U. S. Grant. 2 vols. Charles L. Webster & Company, 1885–86.

Grimsley, Mark. And Keep Moving On: The Virginia Campaign, May–June 1864. Lincoln: University of Nebraska Press, 2002.

Jaynes, Gregory, and the Editors of Time-Life Books. The Killing Ground: Wilderness to Cold Harbor. Alexandria, VA: Time-Life Books, 1986.

Longstreet, James. From Manassas to Appomattox: Memoirs of the Civil War in America. New York: Da Capo Press, 1992. First published in 1896 by J. B. Lippincott and Co.

Lyman, Theodore. With Grant and Meade: From the Wilderness to Appomattox. Edited by George R. Agassiz. Lincoln: University of Nebraska Press, 1994.

Rhea, Gordon C. The Battle of the Wilderness May 5–6, 1864. Baton Rouge: Louisiana State University Press, 1994.

Rhea, Gordon C. The Battles of Wilderness & Spotsylvania. National Park Service Civil War series. Fort Washington, PA: U.S. National Park Service and Eastern National, 1995.

Rhea, Gordon C. In the Footsteps of Grant and Lee: The Wilderness Through Cold Harbor. Baton Rouge: Louisiana State University Press, 2007.

Trudeau, Noah Andre. Bloody Roads South: The Wilderness to Cold Harbor, May–June 1864. Boston: Little, Brown & Co., 1989.

U.S. War Department, The War of the Rebellion: a Compilation of the Official Records of the Union and Confederate Armies. Washington, DC: U.S. Government Printing Office, 1880–1901.

The Battle of Spotsylvania Court House

Chapter 1: Racing to Spotsylvania

When Grant ordered Meade on the night of May 7 to have the Army of the Potomac march to Spotsylvania Court House, he did so for several reasons. In addition to disengaging from Lee at the Wilderness and bring him out into the open, Grant hoped that swift marching might get his army inbetween Lee and Richmond, which would make the Confederates even more desperate. But there was also another reason, as Grant noted in his memoirs:

"On the afternoon of the 7th I received news from Washington announcing that Sherman had probably attacked Johnston that day, and that Butler had reached City Point safely and taken it by surprise on the 5th. I had given orders for a movement by the left flank, fearing that Lee might move rapidly to Richmond to crush Butler before I could get there.

My object in moving to Spottsylvania was two-fold: first, I did not want Lee to get back to Richmond in time to attempt to crush Butler before I could get there; second, I wanted to get between his army and Richmond if possible; and, if not, to draw him into the open field. But Lee, by accident, beat us to Spottsylvania. Our wagon trains had been ordered easterly of the roads the troops were to march upon before the movement commenced. Lee interpreted this as a semi-retreat of the Army of the Potomac to Fredericksburg, and so informed his government. Accordingly he ordered Longstreet's corps—now commanded by Anderson—to move in the morning (the 8th) to Spottsylvania. But the woods being still on fire, Anderson could not go into bivouac, and marched directly on to his destination that night. By this accident Lee got possession of Spottsylvania. It is impossible to say now what would have been the result if Lee's orders had been obeyed as given; but it is certain that we would have been in Spottsylvania, and between him and his capital. My belief is that there would have been a race between the two armies to see which could reach Richmond first, and the Army of the Potomac would have had the shorter line. Thus, twice since crossing the Rapidan we came near closing the campaign, so far as battles were concerned, from the Rapidan to the James River or Richmond. The first failure was caused by our not following up the success gained over Hill's corps on the morning of the 6th, as before described: the second, when fires caused by that battle drove Anderson to make a march during the night of the 7th-8th which he was ordered to commence on the morning of the 8th. But accident often decides the fate of battle."

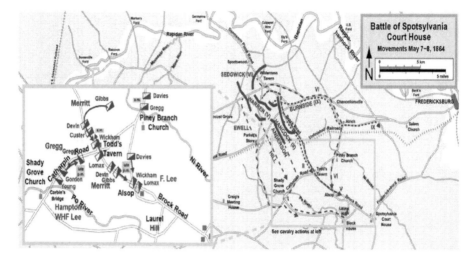

Grant's route to Spotsylvania Court House had been opened by Phil Sheridan's cavalry in the days before, due to the fact that Grant had initially intended to march there before engaging in battle. Sheridan's cavalry had been holding important spots, including crossings of the Ny and Po Rivers, in anticipation of that movement, but when Hancock's left was turned by Longstreet's corps on May 6, the cavalry had been hurried back north. As a result, when Grant issued the orders to march toward Spotsylvania on May 7, it was once again incumbent on the Union cavalry to ride to those spots and hold them for the infantry advance. Sheridan explained in his memoirs:

"On the 7th of May, under directions from headquarters, Army of the Potomac, the trains were put in motion to go into park at Piney Branch Church, in anticipation of the movement that was about to be made for the possession of Spottsylvania Court House. I felt confident that the order to move the trains there had been given without a full understanding of the situation, for Piney Branch Church was now held by the enemy, a condition which had resulted from the order withdrawing the cavalry on account of the supposed disaster to Hancock's left the day before; but I thought the best way to remedy matters was to hold the trains in the vicinity of Aldrich's till the ground on which it was intended to park them should be regained.

This led to the battle of Todd's Tavern, a spirited fight for the possession of the crossroads at that point, participated in by the enemy's cavalry and Gregg's division, and two brigades of Torbert's division, the latter commanded by Merritt, as Torbert became very ill on the 6th, and had to be sent to the rear. To gain the objective point — the crossroads — I directed Gregg to assail the enemy on the Catharpen road with Irvin

Gregg's brigade and drive him over Corbin's bridge, while Merritt attacked him with the Reserve brigade on the Spottsylvania road in conJunction with Davies's brigade of Gregg's division, which was to be put in on the Piney Branch Church road, and unite with Merritt's left. Davies's and Irvin Gregg's brigades on my right and left flanks met with some resistance, yet not enough to deter them from executing their orders. In front of Merritt the enemy held on more stubbornly, however, and there ensued an exceedingly severe and, at times, fluctuating fight. Finally the Confederates gave way, and we pursued them almost to Spottsylvania Court House; but deeming it prudent to recall the pursuers about dark, I encamped Gregg's and Merritt's divisions in the open fields to the east of Todd's Tavern."

As previously noted by Grant in his memoirs, the Confederates were not idle on May 7. The movements of the Union Army's logistics train had suggested to him that Grant was either moving east toward Fredericksburg or south toward Spotsylvania. Either way, Lee needed to hold the crossroads at Spotsylvania, so he gave orders to Richard Anderson's corps to occupy Spotsylvania Court House on May 8. Luckily for the Confederates, however, the desperate fighting of the 6th by that corps had sparked fires in the area of the fighting, and the putrid smells of the burning and death compelled Anderson and his soldiers to go ahead and march to Spotsylvania that night, rather than try to bivouac near the burning and dying. By 10:00 p.m., Anderson's corps was on the march toward Spotsylvania.

The same fires that had compelled the Confederates to march that night were also causing logistical problems for the Army of the Potomac's movement. In addition to the inevitable traffic jams on the roads, the Union's unfamiliarity with the area caused fits and starts, as Grant mentioned in his memoirs:

"Meade and I rode in advance. We had passed but a little way beyond our left when the road forked. We looked to see, if we could, which road Sheridan had taken with his cavalry during the day. It seemed to be the right-hand one, and accordingly we took it. We had not gone far, however, when Colonel C. B. Comstock, of my staff, with the instinct of the engineer, suspecting that we were on a road that would lead us into the lines of the enemy, if he, too, should be moving, dashed by at a rapid gallop and all alone. In a few minutes he returned and reported that Lee was moving, and that the road we were on would bring us into his lines in a short distance. We returned to the forks of the road, left a man to indicate the right road to the head of Warren's column when it should come up, and continued our journey to Todd's Tavern, where we arrived after midnight."

While the infantry struggled to get underway in the right direction, the poor relationship between Meade and Sheridan played an important role on the night of the 7th. After Sheridan's cavalry had taken up their posts to hold the necessary ground for the infantry, Meade lost his temper when he and Grant arrived near Todd's Tavern and found Sheridan's cavalry troopers sleeping near their posts. At that point, Meade ordered part of Sheridan's cavalry to help clear the road for the infantry's march, which incensed Sheridan. Sheridan later claimed that this decision prevented his cavalry from blocking the Confederates at Spotsylvania, writing:

"Had Gregg and Merritt been permitted to proceed as they were originally instructed, it is doubtful whether the battles fought at Spottsylvania would have occurred, for these two divisions would have encountered the enemy at the Po River, and so delayed his march as to enable our infantry to reach Spottsylvania first, and thus force Lee to take up a line behind the Po. I had directed Wilson to move from the left by 'the Gate' through Spottsylvania to Snell's bridge, while Gregg and Merritt were to advance to the same point by Shady Grove and the Block House. There was nothing to prevent at least a partial success of these operations; that is to say, the concentration of the three divisions in front of Snell's bridge, even if we could not actually have gained it. But both that important point and the bridge on the Block House road were utterly ignored, and Lee's approach to Spottsylvania left entirely unobstructed, while three divisions of cavalry remained practically ineffective by reason of disjointed and irregular instructions.

On the morning of the 8th, when I found that such orders had been given, I made some strong remonstrances against the course that had been pursued, but it was then too late to carry out the combinations I had projected the night before, so I proceeded to join Merritt on the Spottsylvania road. On reaching Merritt I found General Warren making complaint that the cavalry were obstructing his column, so I drew Merritt off the road, and the leading division of the Fifth Corps pushed up to the front. It got into line about 11 o'clock, and advanced to take the village, but it did not go very far before it struck Anderson's corps, and was hurled back with heavy loss. This ended all endeavor to take Spottsylvania that day."

As Sheridan's account indicates, Anderson's corps eventually forced the advanced elements of his cavalry to fall back up the road. At the same time, it's unclear whether Sheridan's two divisions of cavalry could have held off an entire Confederate corps of infantry long enough for Warren's V Corps to beat Anderson's corps to the spot. For his part, Grant later insisted it would have been likely, writing, "Wilson, who was ordered to seize the town, did so, with his division of cavalry; but he could not hold it against the Confederate corps which had not been detained at the crossing of the Po, as it would have been but for the unfortunate change in Merritt's orders. Had he been permitted to execute the orders Sheridan gave him, he would have been guarding with two brigades of cavalry the bridge over the Po River which Anderson had to cross, and must have detained him long enough to enable Warren to reinforce Wilson and hold the town."

If Grant was going to occupy Spotsylvania, he now needed to dislodge Anderson's corps or destroy it on May 8 before the rest of the Confederate army joined him.

Chapter 2: May 8

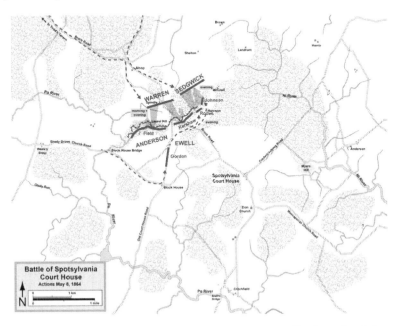

As soon as the sun came up on May 8, the Union cavalry busied itself trying to break through the Confederate defenses on Brock Road just north of Spotsylvania. If Sheridan's cavalry could dislodge the Confederates there, it would prevent the rest of the Confederate army from being able to march northeast toward Spotsylvania along the Old Court House Road, which would have required Lee's army to fall back several miles south to the next natural defensive line along the Po River. While Wesley Merritt's division skirmished with Fitzhugh Lee's Confederate cavalry on the Brock Road, Anderson's corps and Warren's corps marched toward the action, both intending to hold Brock Road for their respective armies.

While Fitzhugh Lee's cavalry fought a delaying action around the Alsop farm, two brigades from Anderson's corps marched north to arrive at Laurel Hill, just south of the farm. As those men pulled into position on the ridge of Laurel Hill, they spotted men from Warren's V Corps just 100 yards away.

Warren was operating under the assumption that the men he saw on Laurel Hill were just Confederate cavalry, unaware that an entire corps of Confederate infantry was in the vicinity.

While Warren's men prepared for that assault, Joseph Kershaw's division of Anderson's corps was clearing away a brigade of Union cavalry south of Laurel Hill, ensuring that the rear was safe and then allowing the rest of Anderson's corps to march up to the impromptu line at Laurel Hill. Perhaps due to his incorrect belief that he was only dealing with a small number of Confederate cavalry, Warren's initial attacks consisted of piecemeal maneuvers by separate divisions. Grant discussed the morning fighting in his memoirs, as well as a candid appraisal of Warren, whose strengths as an engineer led to frequent criticism that he was too slow and cautious as an infantry corps commander:

"Anderson soon intrenched himself—if indeed the intrenchments were not already made—immediately across Warren's front. Warren was not aware of his presence, but probably supposed it was the cavalry which Merritt had engaged earlier in the day. He assaulted at once, but was repulsed. He soon organized his men, as they were not pursued by the enemy, and made a second attack, this time with his whole corps. This time he succeeded in gaining a position immediately in the enemy's front, where he intrenched. His right and left divisions—the former Crawford's, the latter Wadsworth's, now commanded by Cutler—drove the enemy back some distance.

At this time my headquarters had been advanced to Piney Branch Church. I was anxious to crush Anderson before Lee could get a force to his support. To this end Sedgwick who was at Piney Branch Church, was ordered to Warren's support. Hancock, who was at Todd's Tavern, was notified of Warren's engagement, and was directed to be in readiness to come up. Burnside, who was with the wagon trains at Aldrich's on our extreme left, received the same instructions. Sedgwick was slow in getting up for some reason—probably unavoidable, because he was never at fault when serious work was to be done—so that it was near night before the combined forces were ready to attack. Even then all of Sedgwick's command did not get into the engagement. Warren led the last assault, one division at a time, and of course it failed.

Warren's difficulty was twofold: when he received an order to do anything, it would at once occur to his mind how all the balance of the army should be engaged so as properly to co-operate with him. His ideas were generally good, but he would forget that the person giving him orders had thought of others at the time he had of him. In like manner, when he did get ready to execute an order, after giving most intelligent instructions to division commanders, he would go in with one division, holding the others in reserve until he could superintend their movements in person also, forgetting that division commanders could execute an order without his presence. His difficulty was constitutional and beyond his control. He was an officer of superior ability, quick perceptions, and personal courage to accomplish anything that could be done with a small command."

Gouverneur Warren

While Warren was miscalculating the force in his front, the confusion of the marches and the armies' relative dispositions led to an encounter further north at the intersection of Brock Road and Catharpin Road, where a division of Jubal Early's corps encountered Winfield Scott Hancock's II Corps protecting the rear of the Union army. The aggressive Early tested Barlow's division of Hancock's corps but ultimately chose not to test the rearguard. Grant took this as evidence that Lee was unaware of Grant's intentions and movements, and that Anderson's arrival at Spotsylvania had thus been by chance, not due to Lee's skill: "Lee had ordered Hill's corps—now commanded by Early—to move by the very road we had marched upon. This shows that even early in the morning of the 8th Lee had not yet become acquainted with my move, but still thought that the Army of the Potomac had gone to Fredericksburg. Indeed, he informed the authorities at Richmond he had possession of Spottsylvania and was on my flank. Anderson was in possession of Spottsylvania, through no foresight of Lee, however. Early only found that he had been following us when he ran against Hancock at Todd's Tavern. His coming detained Hancock from the battle-field of Spottsylvania for that day; but he, in like manner, kept Early back and forced him to move by another route."

As a result of Warren's inability to push Anderson's men at Laurel Hill, men from Ewell's corps were able to slide into the line to the right of Anderson before John Sedgwick's VI Corps was in position on Warren's left. The two Union corps attempted a coordinated assault on the night of May 8, with Warren finally willing to put in all his men, but by then they were surprised to find Ewell's men in position and the assault was quickly and sharply repulsed.

May 8 had not been a good day for the Union. Delays in their marches and countermanded cavalry orders had let Anderson occupy the crossroads at Spotsylvania in force, Warren's inability to initially beat back two brigades on Laurel Hill allowed those defenders to allow two whole corps to take up positions there, and Sedgwick's inability to get up quickly enough prevented the Union from launching a decisive assault that night. Grant wrote about what he may have been able to do differently that day in his memoirs, both noting that he was still not familiar enough with the army's corps commanders and weighing the risks and rewards:

"Had I ordered the movement for the night of the 7th by my left flank, it would have put Hancock in the lead. It would also have given us an hour or earlier start. It took all that time for Warren to get the head of his column to the left of Hancock after he had got his troops out of their line confronting the enemy. This hour, and Hancock's capacity to use his whole force when necessary, would, no doubt, have enabled him to crush Anderson before he could be reinforced. But the movement made was tactical. It kept the troops in mass against a possible assault by the enemy. Our left occupied its intrenchments while the two corps to the right passed. If an attack had been made by the enemy he would have found the 2d corps in position, fortified, and, practically, the 5th and 6th corps in position as reserves, until his entire front was passed. By a left flank movement the army would have been scattered while still passing the front of the enemy, and before the extreme right had got by it would have been very much exposed. Then, too, I had not yet learned the special qualifications of the different corps commanders. At that time my judgment was that Warren was the man I would suggest to succeed Meade should anything happen to that gallant soldier to take him from the field. As I have before said, Warren was a gallant soldier, an able man; and he was beside thoroughly imbued with the solemnity and importance of the duty he had to perform."

Meanwhile, Meade was in his notorious "snapping turtle" mode, with his short temper long gone by the end of the day. He was irate at Warren's caution, Sedgwick's slowness, and Sheridan's command of the cavalry, over which they had serious philosophical differences of opinion. Meade preferred having his cavalry perform traditional duties like screening army movements and reconnaissance, but Sheridan was a soldier who had previously commanded infantry and spoiled for a fight. Sheridan explained the roots of the friction between the two of them in his memoirs:

"Before and at the review I took in this situation, and determined to remedy it if possible; so in due time I sought an interview with General Meade and informed him that, as the effectiveness of my command rested mainly on the strength of its horses, I thought the duty it was then performing was both burdensome and wasteful. I also gave him my idea as to what the cavalry should do, the main purport of which was that it ought to be kept concentrated to fight the enemy's cavalry. Heretofore, the commander of the Cavalry Corps had been, virtually, but an adjunct at army headquarters — a sort of chief of cavalry-and my proposition seemed to stagger General Meade not a little. I knew that it would be difficult to overcome the recognized custom of using the cavalry for the protection of trains and the establishment of cordons around the infantry corps, and so far subordinating its operations to the movements of the main army that in name only was it a corps at all, but still I thought it my duty to try.

At first General Meade would hardly listen to my proposition, for he was filled with the prejudices that, from the beginning of the war, had pervaded the army regarding the importance and usefulness of cavalry, General Scott then predicting that the contest would be settled by artillery, and thereafter refusing the services of regiment after regiment of mounted troops. General Meade deemed cavalry fit for little more than guard and picket duty, and wanted to know what would protect the transportation trains and artillery reserve, cover the front of moving infantry columns, and secure his flanks from intrusion, if my policy were pursued. I told him that if he would let me use the cavalry as I contemplated, he need have little solicitude in these respects, for, with a mass of ten thousand mounted men, it was my belief that I could make [194] it so lively for the enemy's cavalry that, so far as attacks from it were concerned, the flanks and rear of the Army of the Potomac would require little or no defense, and claimed, further, that moving columns of infantry should take care of their own fronts. I also told him that it was my object to defeat the enemy's cavalry in a general combat, if possible, and by such a result establish a feeling of confidence in my own troops that would enable us after a while to march where we pleased, for the purpose of breaking General Lee's communications and destroying the resources from which his army was supplied.

The idea as here outlined was contrary to Meade's convictions, for though at different times since he commanded the Army of the Potomac considerable bodies of the cavalry had been massed for some special occasion, yet he had never agreed to the plan as a permanency, and could not be bent to it now. He gave little encouragement, therefore, to what I proposed, yet the conversation was immediately beneficial in one way, for when I laid before him the true condition of the cavalry, he promptly relieved it from much of the arduous and harassing picket service it was performing, thus giving me about two weeks in which to nurse the horses before the campaign opened.

The interview also disclosed the fact that the cavalry commander should be, according to General Meade's views, at his headquarters practically as one of his staff, through whom he would give detailed directions as, in his judgment, occasion required.

Meade's ideas and mine being so widely divergent, disagreements arose between us later during the battles of the Wilderness, which lack of concord ended in some concessions on his part after the movement toward Spottsylvania Court House began, and although I doubt that his convictions were ever wholly changed, yet from that date on, in the organization of the Army of the Potomac, the cavalry corps became more of a compact body, with the same privileges and responsibilities that attached to the other corps-conditions that never actually existed before."

On the night of May 8, Meade and Sheridan continued arguing over the use of cavalry, when Sheridan suggested that his cavalry be massed and allowed to find and engage JEB Stuart's cavalry in mass. While Meade was against it, Grant held his former Western subordinate in higher regard and acceded to Sheridan's request, stating, "Well, he generally knows what he is talking about. Let him start right out and do it." As a result, Sheridan's entire force of 10,000 cavalry left the Army of the Potomac and would end up missing the most important fighting of the battle on May 12. Although they fought Stuart's cavalry at the Battle of Yellow Tavern on May 11 and mortally wounded the iconic Confederate cavalry chieftain in the process, most modern historians have since sided with Meade's side of the argument, with Overland Campaign historian Gordon Rhea going so far as to write, "In the larger picture, Sheridan's raid proved to be a costly mistake. Chasing Stuart was another side show for the campaign, which would be decided by what the armies did at Spotsylvania. By abandoning the main theater of conflict to pursue his whimsical raid south, Sheridan deprived Grant of an important resource. His victory at Yellow Tavern offered scant solace to the blue-clad soldiers hunkering in trenches above the courthouse town. Sheridan's absence hurt Grant at Spotsylvania in much the same way that Stuart's absence from Gettysburg had handicapped Lee."

Chapter 3: Digging In

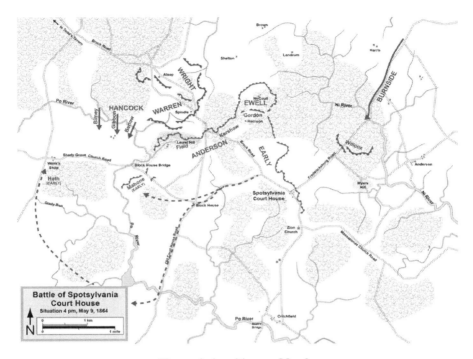

The armies' positions on May 9

By the end of the war, the Civil War had become a forerunner to the trench warfare of World War I, and if an army was given 24 hours to entrench, their position became practically unassailable. Grant described the process in his memoirs:

> "[I]n every change of position or halt for the night, whether confronting the enemy or not, the moment arms were stacked the men intrenched themselves. For this purpose they would build up piles of logs or rails if they could be found in their front, and dig a ditch, throwing the dirt forward on the timber. Thus the digging they did counted in making a depression to stand in, and increased the elevation in front of them. It was wonderful how quickly they could in this way construct defences of considerable strength. When a halt was made with the view of assaulting the enemy, or in his presence, these would be strengthened or their positions changed under the direction of engineer officers."

Thus, the Army of the Potomac's inability to clear Brock Road on May 8 allowed the Confederates to begin the process of digging in, a crucial advantage. By the end of the Civil War, some generals who fought in it had come to believe that a well-entrenched defensive line could only be taken if there were 4 times as many attackers as defenders. John Gordon, who led a brigade in Early's corps, discussed the nature of the line as the Confederates dug in on the night of May 8:

"As the heads of the columns collided, the armies quickly spread into zigzag formation as each brigade, division, or corps struck its counterpart in the opposing lines. These haphazard collisions, however, rapidly developed a more orderly alignment and systematic battle, which culminated in that unparalleled struggle for the possession of a short line of Lee's breastworks. I say unparalleled, because the character of the fighting, its duration, and the individual heroism exhibited have no precedent, so far as my knowledge extends, in our Civil War, or in any other war.

During these preliminary and somewhat random engagements, General Lee, in order to secure the most advantageous locality offered by the peculiar topography of the country, had placed his battle line so that it should conform in large measure to the undulations of the field. Along the brow of these slopes earthworks were speedily constructed. On one portion of the line, which embraced what was afterward known as the 'Bloody Angle,' there was a long stretch of breastworks forming almost a complete semicircle. Its most advanced or outer salient was the point against which Hancock made his famous charge.

My command had been withdrawn from position in the regular line, and a role was assigned me which no officer could covet if he had the least conception of the responsibilities involved. I was ordered to take position in rear of that salient, and as nearly equidistant as practicable from every point of the wide and threatened semicircle, to watch every part of it, to move quickly, without waiting for orders, to the support of any point that might be assaulted, and to restore, if possible, any breach that might be made. We were reserves to no one command, but to all commands occupying that entire stretch of works. It will be seen that, with no possibility of knowing when or where General Grant would make his next effort to penetrate our lines, the task to be performed by my troops was not an easy one, and that the tension upon the brain and nerves of one upon whom rested the responsibility was not light nor conducive to sleep."

As the Confederates dug in, they were well aware that a salient was being created in the line at the Mule Shoe, which jutted out nearly a mile in front of the rest of their defensive line. Civil War armies always tried to avoid creating a salient in the line because it allowed the salient to be attacked in multiple directions. In this case, despite the fact the Mule Shoe was a salient, the Confederates dug in there to hold onto the nearest high ground in the area, hoping to prevent Union soldiers from occupying it and disrupting the rest of their line.

At the same time, the Army of the Potomac began digging in and erecting earthworks along their own lines, just as aware of their importance. With that, the two armies hunkered down into the kind of trench warfare that would've seemed foreign to the soldiers and generals in 1861. With sharpshooters among the lines, which were about half a mile away from each other, soldiers were afraid to even show their heads above their trenches for fear of being sniped.

While this process was going on during the morning of May 9, Union VI Corps commander John Sedgwick was placing his artillery and directing the men in his line when scattered shots from snipers started coming in from several hundred yards away. The soldiers in his corps had been harassed by the sharpshooters all morning, and one bullet had already knocked one of Sedgwick's brigadier-generals off his horse. Nevertheless, Sedgwick projected calm as he went about his business, even acting amused when some of his staff joined the soldiers in taking cover. Sedgwick mocked them, "What? Men dodging this way for single bullets? What will you do when they open fire along the whole line? I am ashamed of you. They couldn't hit an elephant at this distance." After one bullet whizzed by, one of his soldiers told Sedgwick that he had already nearly had his own head taken off by an artillery shell, to which Sedgwick reassured him and told him to stay in his position. His men would note that Sedgwick kept repeating, "I'm ashamed of you, dodging that way. They couldn't hit an elephant at this distance."

Sedgwick

Just then, another shot whizzed through the air, the unmistakable sound of a bullet fired by a .451 caliber Whitworth rifle. But this one found a mark, as noted by one of the soldiers in the vicinity, Lieutenant Colonel Martin McMahon, who wrote, "For the third time the same shrill whistle, closing with a dull, heavy stroke." Far from being unable to hit an elephant, a Confederate sharpshooter had just hit Sedgwick right in the face, killing him almost instantly. McMahon would later note that as he tried to catch Sedgwick from falling, blood spurted out just below his left eye, and that Sedgwick died so quickly that he still had a smile on his face.

Sedgwick was the highest ranking Union officer to die during the war (though James McPherson died while commanding an army during Sherman's Atlanta campaign that same year). When news reached Grant's headquarters, Grant was so shocked that he repeatedly asked, "Is he really dead?" Grant later wrote, "His loss was a severe one to the Army of the Potomac and to the Nation. General H. G. Wright succeeded him in the command of his corps." According to Grant's aide, Horace Porter, the grief-stricken Grant was telling those around him, "His loss to this army is greater than the loss of a whole division of troops."

Meanwhile, Burnside's IX Corps, which had been late to show up at the Battle of the Wilderness, marched southwest along the Fredericksburg Road and came up on the far left of the Union line, leaving a gap between his men and Wright's VI Corps. When Burnside's corps were confronted by cavalry led by Fitzhugh Lee, the cautious Burnside stopped moving forward and began digging in. That skirmish induced Grant into thinking that Lee might be trying to turn his left flank, when Lee had no such plan. As a result, Grant prepared Hancock's II Corps to make an attack on the Confederates' left flank, figuring that would be the weaker part of their line, while Lee was actually shifting some of Early's corps along his left in the hopes of attacking Hancock's flank.

Grant had no idea that Burnside's corps was poised to strike Lee's right flank and had only been opposed by cavalry, and he would not realize it until after the war, much to his consternation.

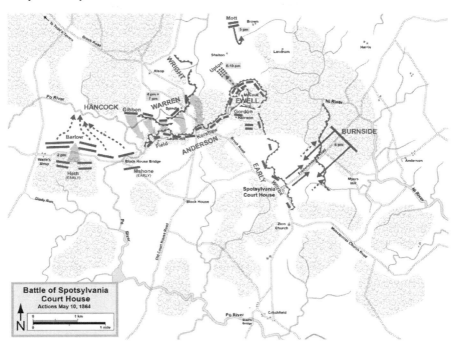

The action on May 10

On several occasions throughout the Overland Campaign, Grant ordered general attacks out of a sense that he could break Lee's army, and he had conceived of such an attack for May 10:

"Accordingly in the morning, orders were issued for an attack in the afternoon on the centre by Warren's and Wright's corps, Hancock to command all the attacking force. Two of his divisions were brought to the north side of the Po. Gibbon was placed to the right of Warren, and Birney in his rear as a reserve. Barlow's division was left south of the stream, and Mott of the same corps was still to the left of Wright's corps. Burnside was ordered to reconnoitre his front in force, and, if an opportunity presented, to attack with vigor."

Grant's plan actually started to go haywire on the evening of May 9, when the Confederates noticed some of Hancock's II Corps shifting their position that night. This allowed Lee to counter the perceived threat by trying to outflank Hancock's corps with Early's corps, which led the Union high command to mistakenly assume that Early's men were being shifted to the Confederates' right flank. By the morning of May 10, Grant realized his mistake, but when he pulled back most of Hancock's corps behind the Po River, he left Francis Barlow's division on the other side to keep manning the earthworks there, which all but invited a Confederate attack.

Sure enough, that attack came at 2:00 p.m., with Henry Heth's division of Early's corps and William Mahone's division in support on the right. Early noted in his memoirs:

"Our line was then north of the Po, with its left, Fields' division of Longstreet's corps, resting on that stream, just above the crossing of the Shady Grove road. The whole of the enemy's force was also north of the Po, prior to this movement of his. Mahone's division was sent to occupy the banks of the Po on Fields' left, while with Heth's division and a battalion of artillery I moved to the rear, crossing the Po on the Louisa Court-House road, and then following that road until we reached one coming in from Waite's Shop on the Shady Grove road. After moving about a mile on this road, we met Hampton gradually falling back before the enemy, who had pushed out a column of infantry considerably to the rear of our line. This column was in turn forced back to the posi tion on Shady Grove road which was occupied by what was reported to be Hancock's corps. Following up and crossing a small stream just below a mill pond, we succeeded in reaching Waite's Shop, from whence an attack was made on the enemy, and the entire force, which had crossed the Po, was driven back with a loss of one piece of artillery, which fell into our hands, and a considerable number in killed and wounded. This relieved us from a very threatening danger, as the position the enemy had attained would have enabled him to completely enfilade Fields' position and get possession of the line of our communications to the rear, within a very short distance of which he was, when met by the force which drove him back. In this affair Heth's division behaved very handsomely, all of the brigades (Cook's, Davis', Kirkland's and Walker's) being engaged in the attack. General H. H. Walker had the misfortune to receive a severe wound in the foot, which rendered amputation necessary, but otherwise our loss was slight. As soon as the road was cleared, Mahone's division crossed the Po, but it was not practicable to pursue the affair further, as the north bank of the stream at this point was covered by a heavily entrenched line, with a number of batteries, and night was approaching."

While Hancock was trying to extricate Barlow's division, it left Warren in command of the general attack that Grant intended to make on the center. Warren was eager to make the assault, still smarting from perceived criticism over his timidity the previous two days, but in so doing he ended up ordering an attack that was uncoordinated with Hancock's men on the right or Wright's men on the left. Despite having tried to reconnoiter in force twice and being pushed back both times, Warren recommended making an assault on the Confederate center, and his uncoordinated attack was quickly repulsed at 4:00 p.m.

As Warren began reforming his lines, this time to make a coordinated attack, one of the divisions in Wright's VI Corps did not realize that the general attack at 5:00 p.m. had been delayed. Gershom Mott, whose division had performed poorly at the Wilderness, had even less luck when it made an uncoordinated attack at that hour.

When Early's two divisions had shifted to the left to attack Hancock, it left Cadmus Wilcox's division on the right flank, where it opposed Burnside's entire corps. Luckily for the Confederates, Grant had thought that the Confederates had been shifting more soldiers to their right instead of their left, leaving the Union high command with no idea that Burnside so heavily outnumbered the enemy in his front. Since Burnside was only ordered to reconnoiter in force, he stopped advancing down the road almost as soon as he came into contact with Wilcox's division, and at that point Grant started to worry about the gap between Wright's corps and Burnside's corps. Had Grant kept Sheridan's cavalry with him, such a reconnaissance might have already been done by the cavalry, and he would have had a better idea of what was in Burnside's front. But since he had allowed Sheridan to leave the army with no cavalry, later that night he pulled Burnside back to close the gap with Wright's corps, losing a chance to overwhelm Lee's right flank. It was something he greatly regretted after the war, writing, "Burnside on the left had got up to within a few hundred yards of Spottsylvania Court House, completely turning Lee's right. He was not aware of the importance of the advantage he had gained, and I, being with the troops where the heavy fighting was, did not know of it at the time. He had gained his position with but little fighting, and almost without loss. Burnside's position now separated him widely from Wright's corps, the corps nearest to him. At night he was ordered to join on to this. This brought him back about a mile, and lost to us an important advantage. I attach no blame to Burnside for this, but I do to myself for not having had a staff officer with him to report to me his position."

There had been fighting by all of the Union corps along each sector of the lines, but the most famous assault on the 10th was made by 12 regiments under the command of 24 year old Colonel Emory Upton, consisting of mixed elements of Wright's corps. This "storming party" was sent out at 6:00 p.m. with the intention of quickly rushing into the Confederate trenches and creating at least a minor breakthrough in the Confederate lines that could then be further breached by reinforcements. By using an unusual battle formation and not pausing to stop and fire, Upton's small attack force gained a surprising success, at least at first. Grant explained:

"Wright also reconnoitred his front and gained a considerably advanced position from the one he started from. He then organized a storming party, consisting of twelve regiments, and assigned Colonel Emory Upton, of the 121st New York Volunteers, to the command of it. About four o'clock in the afternoon the assault was ordered, Warren's and Wright's corps, with Mott's division of Hancock's corps, to move simultaneously. The movement was prompt, and in a few minutes the fiercest of struggles began. The battle-field was so densely covered with forest that but little could be seen, by any one person, as to the progress made. Meade and I occupied the best position we could get, in rear of Warren.

Warren was repulsed with heavy loss, General J. C. Rice being among the killed. He was not followed, however, by the enemy, and was thereby enabled to reorganize his command as soon as covered from the guns of the enemy. To the left our success was decided, but the advantage was lost by the feeble action of Mott. Upton with his assaulting party pushed forward and crossed the enemy's intrenchments. Turning to the right and left he captured several guns and some hundreds of prisoners. Mott was ordered to his assistance but failed utterly. So much time was lost in trying to get up the troops which were in the right position to reinforce, that I ordered Upton to withdraw; but the officers and men of his command were so averse to giving up the advantage they had gained that I withdrew the order. To relieve them, I ordered a renewal of the assault. By this time Hancock, who had gone with Birney's division to relieve Barlow, had returned, bringing the division with him. His corps was now joined with Warren's and Wright's in this last assault. It was gallantly made, many men getting up to, and over, the works of the enemy; but they were not able to hold them. At night they were withdrawn. Upton brought his prisoners with him, but the guns he had captured he was obliged to abandon. Upton had gained an important advantage, but a lack in others of the spirit and dash possessed by him lost it to us. Before leaving Washington I had been authorized to promote officers on the field for special acts of gallantry. By this authority I conferred the rank of brigadier-general upon Upton on the spot, and this act was confirmed by the President. Upton had been badly wounded in this fight."

Had Upton's successful assault been made in a coordinated fashion along with Mott's previous attack at 5:00 p.m. or Warren's attack at 4:00 p.m., it's possible that there would have been a much bigger breakthrough that wouldn't have allowed Lee to flush Upton's attack party out with reinforcements. But as it was, Upton's success in reaching the western side of the Mule Shoe salient had established both the model for attacking the line and the point at which the Confederate line should be attacked.

Chapter 5: May 11

Every attack made by the Army of the Potomac on May 10 had been repulsed, and the lines had barely moved since the end of fighting on May 8, but Grant had reason for optimism. On May 11, he began plans to conduct another attack in the innovative style Upton had used, but with Hancock's entire II Corps instead of just 5,000 men. He also continued to believe that Lee's army was on the verge of being broken, partly the result of overestimating how many casualties he had inflicted on the Army of Northern Virginia and underestimating the Confederates. That day, he telegraphed Washington:

"We have now ended the 6th day of very hard fighting. The result up to this time is much in our favor. But our losses have been heavy as well as those of the enemy. We have lost to this time eleven general officers killed, wounded and missing, and probably twenty thousand men. I think the loss of the enemy must be greater—we having taken over four thousand prisoners in battle, whilst he has taken from us but few except a few stragglers. I am now sending back to Belle Plain all my wagons for a fresh supply of provisions and ammunition, and propose to fight it out on this line if it takes all summer.

The arrival of reinforcements here will be very encouraging to the men, and I hope they will be sent as fast as possible, and in as great numbers. My object in having them sent to Belle Plain was to use them as an escort to our supply trains. If it is more convenient to send them out by train to march from the railroad to Belle Plain or Fredericksburg, send them so.

I am satisfied the enemy are very shaky, and are only kept up to the mark by the greatest exertions on the part of their officers, and by keeping them intrenched in every position they take.

Up to this time there is no indication of any portion of Lee's army being detached for the defence of Richmond.

U. S. GRANT,

Lieut.-General."

After a couple of days in which Grant's incorrect assumptions had cost him chances for success, Lee made a terrible mistake on May 11 while reacting to movements by the Union army. Grant's plan for Hancock's assault required pulling his men out of the line and assembling them about a mile north of the Mule Shoe. By having Hancock attack the north face of the Mule Shoe while Wright advanced on the west face and Burnside advanced on the east face, the salient in the Confederate line would be as exposed as possible. Hancock's men would be advancing over open ground, while the part in the line they pulled out of was woody, which would keep Lee from fully understanding the movements and prevent the Confederates from launching a potentially devastating attack in the gap while Warren shifted to the left to replace Hancock's men.

Even worse, the movements of Hancock's corps and intelligence reports that Lee received convinced him that Grant was actually starting to retreat. Thinking this was the case, Lee intended to try to attack Grant's army while it was most vulnerable on the move, and since that would require improving the Army of Northern Virginia's mobility, he started withdrawing his artillery from around the salient for the purpose of having it prepared to advance more quickly. His nephew Fitzhugh Lee explained, "On the 11th he thought Grant was preparing for another move, and that night ordered most of the cannon out of the salient so as to be ready for a counter move, all of which a deserter from [Allegheny] Johnson's line reported, and which may account for the assault which, though favored by a climatic condition, was courageously executed."

Though Fitzhugh Lee credited that Confederate deserter for the assault, it was apparent that Grant already had it in mind. As Hancock's men began moving to their staging ground at the Brown farm, thunderstorms provided a torrential downpour, making it that much harder to truly understand the purpose of the movement. That was of little comfort to Allegheny Johnson and his division, who were defending the salient in the line and watching Hancock's men marching north in their front even while their artillery was being withdrawn. Johnson pleaded with corps commander Richard Ewell to bring the guns back to his line, but by the time Ewell accepted the request and the orders reached the artillery units, it was 3:30 a.m. on the morning of May 12. Hancock's assault was scheduled to come crashing right into Allegheny Johnson's division just half an hour later.

Allegheny Johnson

Chapter 6: The Bloody Angle

"I fancy this war has furnished no parallel to the desperation shown here by both parties. It must be called, I suppose, the taking of the Salient." – Theodore Lyman, George Meade's aide-de-camp

The ugly weather conditions had slowed Hancock's men to the extent that they reached the Brown farm around midnight, and then had to spend most of the next 4 hours forming their battle lines. The attack was delayed half an hour, back to 4:30 a.m., and Grant ordered Burnside to attack the east face of the Mule Shoe at the same time in force.

As if Grant's attack hadn't already been aided by Lee pulling the artillery away from the salient, there was a dense fog over the battlefield when Hancock's men stepped off to begin their assault. Hancock's men would not have come into view until they were within 300 yards of the Confederate lines, and now they would be obscured by mist.

At 4:30 a.m. that morning, nobody could have believed what the salient would look like 24 hours later. Gettysburg hero Rufus Dawes, Colonel of the 6th Wisconsin in the Iron brigade, described the final approach to the salient and the nature of the entrenchments:

"We stood perhaps one hundred feet from the enemy's line, and so long as we maintained a continual fire they remained hidden in their entrenchments. But if an attempt to advance was made, an order would be given and they would all rise up together and fire a volley upon us. They had constructed their works by digging an entrenchment about four feet deep, in which at intervals there were traverses to protect the flanks. This had the effect of making a row of cellars without drainage, and in them was several inches of mud and water. To protect their heads, they had placed in front logs which were laid upon blocks, and it was intended to put their muskets through the chinks under the head logs, but in the darkness this became impracticable and the head log proved a serious obstruction to their firing."

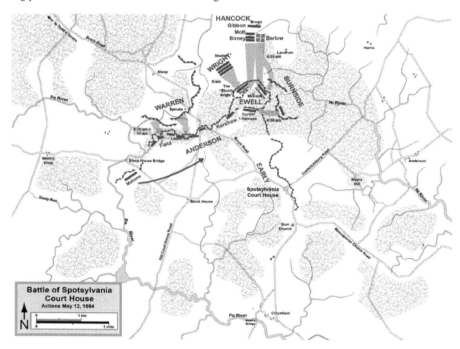

Hancock's corps, nearly 15,000 strong, quickly overwhelmed the salient and almost immediately destroyed the initial defenders comprised of William Witcher's brigade. As Hancock's men entered the Confederate trenches, Barlow's division fanned out to their left and flanked George Steuart's brigade facing Burnside's men on the eastern face of the Mule Shoe, capturing both Steuart and Allegheny Johnson. Meanwhile, David Birney's division advanced along the western part of the Mule Shoe until confronting the old Stonewall Brigade, once commanded by the legendary Stonewall Jackson but now commanded by James Walker.

Within half an hour, Hancock's corps had breached the Confederates' main line, capturing nearly 4,000 men and 20 guns, including their horses and ammunition. As the men kept advancing, Hancock had the captured Confederate guns turned around and began firing them down the Confederate lines, providing a devastating enfilade. Around this time, news of the initial success was making its way back to Grant's headquarters, and Theodore Lyman described the scene:

"At a little after five o'clock, General Williams approached from the telegraph tent; a smile was on his face: Hancock had carried the first line! Thirty minutes after, another despatch: he had taken the main line with guns, prisoners and two generals! Great rejoicings now burst forth. Some of Grant's Staff were absurdly confident and were sure Lee was entirely beaten. My own experiences taught me a little more scepticism. Hancock presently sent to ask for a vigorous attack on his right, to cover and support his right flank. General Wright was accordingly ordered to attack with a part of the 6th Corps. As I stood there waiting, I heard someone say, 'Sir, this is General Johnson.' I turned round and there was the captured Major-General, walking slowly up. He was a strongly built man of a stern and rather bad face, and was dressed in a double-breasted blue-grey coat, high riding boots and a very bad felt hat. He was most horribly mortified at being taken, and kept coughing to hide his emotion. Generals Meade and Grant shook hands with him, and good General Williams bore him off to breakfast. His demeanor was dignified and proper. Not so a little creature, General Steuart, who insulted everybody who came near him, and was rewarded by being sent on foot to Fredericksburg, where there was plenty of mud and one stream up to his waist."

Horace Porter also recounted a rather tense exchange between Steuart and Hancock: "General George H. Steuart was also captured, but was not sent in to general headquarters on account of a scene which had been brought about by an unseemly exhibition of temper on his part. Hancock had known him in the old army, and in his usual frank way went up to him, greeted him kindly, and offered his hand. Steuart drew back, rejected the offer, and said rather haughtily, 'Under the present circumstances, I must decline to take your hand.' Hancock, who was somewhat nettled by this remark, replied, 'Under any other circumstances, general, I should not have offered it.'"

Burnside's men had attacked in concert with Hancock's and had greatly assisted in destroying the Confederate line on the eastern face of the Mule Shoe, but in the process his men had lost contact with the faster advancing II Corps. When Burnside informed Grant that his men had lost contact with Hancock's men, Grant responded, "Push the enemy with all your might; that's the way to connect."

Now, with a breach in the Confederate line nearly half a mile wide, both sides began quickly reacting by ordering more men to the fighting. For Grant, this meant that Wright's corps would support Hancock on the right, but because Grant had only planned for Wright to remain in a defensive posture during the initial assault, it required time for Wright's men to prepare for a similar kind of advance.

Meanwhile, Lee was so desperate that as he was ordering up reinforcements from John Gordon's division, he rode to the front of their marching column as though he was going to lead the charge himself. Fitzhugh Lee recalled the scene, writing, "On this occasion the general rode to the head of the column forming for the charge, took off his hat, and pointed to the captured line; but General John B. Gordon proposed to lead his own men, and no one in the army could do it better, for he was in dash and daring inferior to none. 'These are Virginians and Georgians who have never failed,' said Gordon. 'Go to the rear, General Lee.' And appealing to his men, he cried: 'Is it necessary for General Lee to lead this charge?' 'No, no,' they exclaimed; 'we will drive them back if General Lee will go to the rear.'

Gordon was unquestionably one of the toughest soldiers in the South. He had led a desperate flank attack at the Battle of the Wilderness on May 6, and he had been wounded several times at Antietam. But not even Gordon was ready for his division's initial contact with Hancock's corps:

"So rapidly and silently had the enemy moved inside of our works-- indeed, so much longer time had he been on the inside than the reports indicated--that before we had moved one half the distance to the salient the head of my column butted squarely against Hancock's line of battle. The men who had been placed in our front to give warning were against that battle line before they knew it. They were shot down or made prisoners. The sudden and unexpected blaze from Hancock's rifles made the dark woodland strangely lurid. General Johnson, who rode immediately at my side, was shot from his horse, severely but not, as I supposed, fatally wounded in the head. His brigade was thrown inevitably into great confusion, but did not break to the rear. As quickly as possible, I had the next ranking officer in that brigade notified of General Johnson's fall and directed him at once to assume command. He proved equal to the emergency. With great coolness and courage he promptly executed my orders. The Federals were still advancing, and every movement of the North Carolina brigade had to be made under heavy fire. The officer in charge was directed to hastily withdraw his brigade a short distance, to change front so as to face Hancock's lines, and to deploy his whole force in close order as skirmishers, so as to stretch, if possible, across the entire front of Hancock. This done, he was ordered to charge with his line of skirmishers the solid battle lines before him. His looks indicated some amazement at the purpose to make an attack which appeared so utterly hopeless, and which would have been the very essence of rashness but for the extremity of the situation. He was, however, full of the fire of battle and too good a soldier not to yield prompt and cheerful obedience. That order was given in the hope and belief that in the fog and mists which concealed our numbers the sheer audacity of the movement would confuse and check the Union advance long enough for me to change front and form line of battle with the other brigades. The result was not disappointing except in the fact that Johnson's brigade, even when so deployed, was still too short to reach across Hancock's entire front. This fact was soon developed: not by sight, but by the direction from which the Union bullets began to come."

As Gordon's account indicated, the fog and damp conditions made musket volleys and firing far more ineffective than they otherwise would have usually been. Moreover, the nature of the Confederate lines, which were composed of trenches that were upwards of 4 feet deep in some positions, made it all but impossible for Hancock's corps to reform their battle lines once they had stormed the Confederates' positions. With men getting mixed up in the chaos, it became impossible for officers to control their commands, and the fighting around the breached salient began to devolve into hand-to-hand fighting.

As Hancock was proudly boasting, "I have used up Johnson and am going into Early", Gordon's division came countercharging into the breach and checked Hancock's progress with a series of desperate attacks. As they began to push back Hancock's now-exhausted attackers on the eastern portion of the Mule Shoe, division commander Robert Rodes was reestablishing the Confederate line on the western part of the Mule Shoe.

The Confederates had just desperately stopped Hancock's momentum, but the worst was yet to come. By the time the Confederates had fought off Hancock, Wright's entire corps was ready to press forward around 6:30 a.m., and Grant had also ordered Warren's corps to attack the Confederates on their left and pin them down. By now, the steady rain that was still coming down had combined with the mud and the blood of the fighting soldiers to produce a nauseating stream in the trenches near the salient that one soldier recalled being half-way up to his knees. It was only about to get worse.

Around 6:30 a.m., Wright's corps had been assembled in a similar manner to Upton's assault, and they rushed forward into the salient even while some of Hancock's men were streaming to the rear. G. Norton Galloway, a member of the 95th Pennsylvania in Wright's corps, described the scene:

"Under cover of the smoke-laden rain the enemy was pushing large bodies of troops forward, determined at all hazards to regain the lost ground. Could we hold on until the remainder of our brigade should come to our assistance? Regardless of the heavy volleys of the enemy that were thinning our ranks, we stuck to the position and returned the fire until the 5th Maine and the 121st New York of our brigade came to our support, while the 96th Pennsylvania went in on our right ; thus reenforced, we redoubled our exertions. The smoke, which was dense at first, was intensified by each discharge of artillery to such an extent that the accuracy of our aim became very uncertain, but nevertheless we kept up the fire in the supposed direction of the enemy. Meanwhile they were crawling forward under cover of the smoke, until, reaching a certain point, and raising their usual yell, they charged gallantly up to the very muzzles of our pieces and reoccupied the Angle.

Upon reaching the breastwork, the Confederates for a few moments had the advantage of us, and made good use of their rifles. Our men went down by the score; all the artillery horses were down ; the gallant Upton was the only mounted officer in sight. Hat in hand, he bravely cheered his men, and begged them to 'hold this point.' All of his staff had been either killed, wounded, or dismounted.

At this moment, and while the open ground in rear of the Confederate works was choked with troops, a section of Battery C, 5th United States Artillery, under Lieutenant Richard Metcalf, was brought into action and increased the carnage by opening at short range with double charges of canister. This staggered the apparently exultant enemy. In the maze of the moment these guns were run up by hand close to the famous Angle, and fired again and again, and they were only abandoned when all the drivers and cannoneers had fallen. The battle was now at white heat.

The rain continued to fall, and clouds of smoke hung over the scene. Like leeches we stuck to the work, determined by our fire to keep the enemy from rising up. Captain John D. Fish, of Upton's staff, who had until this time performed valuable service in conveying ammunition to the gunners, fell, pierced by a bullet. This brave officer seemed to court death as he rode back and forth between the caissons and cannoneers with stands of canister under his 'gum' coat. 'Give it to them , boys! I'll bring you the canister,' said he; and as he turned to cheer the gunners, he fell from his horse, mortally wounded. In a few moments the two brass pieces of the 5th Artillery, cut and hacked by the bullets of both antagonists, lay unworked with their muzzles projecting over the enemy's works, and their wheels half sunk in the mud. Between the lines and near at hand lay the horses of these guns, completely riddled. The dead and wounded were torn to pieces by the canister as it swept the ground where they had fallen."

Earthworks near the Bloody Angle

With Wright's VI Corps crashing into the line, the Confederates were forced to quickly bring in more reinforcements, beginning with William Mahone's division. Mahone had been near the extreme left the previous day while Heth's division was attacking the Union's right flank, and now he was forced to quickly countermarch two of his brigades from the extreme left to the Mule Shoe. By 9:30 a.m., all of the VI Corps had been committed and were desperately fighting to hold on as more Confederates streamed to the breach.

Grant had hoped to avoid allowing massive reinforcements by having Warren's corps pin down the Confederate left. Given that Mahone was able to march his entire division from that sector to the Mule Shoe, it was apparent that Warren's assault was a failure. Warren's men had been ordered to attack near Laurel Hill multiple times the past few days, and the failures of the previous days had demoralized them. Despite the fact that Warren's entire corps was opposed by just one division of Anderson's corps, their attack completely stalled in under an hour. When Warren had to tell Meade that he could not advance, the short-tempered Meade exploded and ordered him to attack "at once at all hazards with your whole force, if necessary." Once again, Warren's men made a half-hearted advance that was quickly bogged down, and by now Grant was so frustrated that he authorized Meade to relieve Warren of command. Although Warren technically avoided being relieved, one of his divisions was placed under Wright's command and another was placed under Hancock's, leaving him with only one division. For the one division still nominally under Warren's command, Meade had his chief of staff, General Humphreys, attached to Warren's division and the authority to give it orders in his name. Grant would ruefully note in his memoirs, "If the 5th corps, or rather if Warren, had been as prompt as Wright was with the 6th corps, better results might have been obtained."

As Lee kept pulling men from his left to reinforce the Mule Shoe, a stalemate developed in which neither side could fully dislodge the other. For Lee, this meant that Union artillery positions made his current defensive line precarious, while Grant was still holding out hope of achieving a decisive breakthrough that would cut Lee's army in two, separating Ewell and Early from Anderson. As a result, both commanders kept ordering more and more men forward into the salient.

By the mid-afternoon, the Union and Confederate soldiers had been fighting at the salient for over 10 hours. Galloway discussed the nature of the fighting at the Bloody Angle during this time:

"The great difficulty was in the narrow limits of the Angle, around which we were fighting, which precluded the possibility of getting more than a limited number into action at once. At one time our ranks were crowded in some parts four deep by reenforcements. Major Henry P. Truefitt, commanding the 119th Pennsylvania, was killed, and Captain Charles P. Warner, who succeeded him, was shot dead. Later in the day Major William Ellis, of the 49th New York, who had excited our admiration, was shot through the arm and body with a ramrod during one of the several attempts to get the men to cross the works and drive off the enemy. Our losses were frightful. What remained of many different regiments that had come to our support had concentrated at this point and planted their tattered colors upon a slight rise of ground close to the Angle, where they staid during the latter part of the day.

To keep up the supply of ammunition pack mules were brought into use, each animal carrying three thousand rounds. The boxes were dropped close behind the troops engaged, where they were quickly opened by the officers or file-closers, who served the ammunition to the men. The writer fired four hundred rounds of ammunition, and many others as many or more. In this manner a continuous and rapid fire was maintained, to which for a while the enemy replied with vigor.

Finding that we were not to be driven back, the Confederates began to use more discretion, exposing themselves but little, using the loop-holes in their works to fire through, and at times placing the muzzles of their rifles on the top logs, seizing the trigger and small of the stock, and elevating the breech with one hand sufficiently to reach us."

However, while more and more men packed into the tight lines, Lee was busy creating a new defensive line south of the Mule Shoe that would prevent him from having to defend a salient. All throughout the afternoon Confederate engineers began shuffling men south of the fighting and digging in, so that there would be a new set of entrenchments for the Confederates to use once the new line was established.

By the time the Confederates were ready to dislodge Wright's corps, the men from Hancock's corps had been reformed and ordered back to the salient, keeping the fight going throughout the night. It was not until 4:00 a.m. on the 13th, nearly 24 hours after Hancock's assault began, that the Confederates at the salient began to pull back to the newly formed trenches a few hundred yards south. Nearly 9,000 Union soldiers had been killed or wounded, while 5,000 Confederates had been killed or wounded and 3,000-4,000 had been captured.

When dawn broke on the 13th, the Bloody Angle produced a sight unlike anything the battle hardened soldiers had seen before. Theodore Lyman recounted injured men being pulled out from under multiple corpses, and seeing one corpse that looked like it had been shot 80 times. Dawes, who had fought at Antietam and Gettysburg, was so horrified by the Bloody Angle that he ordered his men to pull out so they wouldn't have to sleep near the spot, writing, "In the morning the rebel works presented an awful spectacle. The cellars were crowded with dead and wounded, lying in some cases upon each other and in several inches of mud and water. I saw the body of a rebel soldier sitting in the corner of one of these cellars in a position of apparent ease, with the head entirely gone, and the flesh burned from the bones of the neck and shoulders. This was doubtless caused by the explosion of a shell from some small Cohorn mortars within our lines."

Grants aide, Horace Porter, was astounded by what he saw: "The appalling sight presented was harrowing in the extreme. Our own killed were scattered over a large space near the "angle," while in front of the captured breastworks the enemy's dead, vastly more numerous than our own, were piled upon each other in some places four layers deep, exhibiting every ghastly phase of mutilation. Below the mass of fast-decaying corpses, the convulsive twitching of limbs and the writhing of bodies showed that there were wounded men still alive and struggling to extricate themselves from the horrid entombment. Every relief possible was afforded, but in too many cases it came too late. The place was well named the 'Bloody Angle.'"

Galloway noted one morbid way that the Union soldiers still holding the salient went about burying the dead: "Hundreds of Confederates, dead or dying, lay piled over one another in those pits. The fallen lay three or four feet deep in some places, and, with but few exceptions, they were shot in and about the head. Arms, accouterments, ammunition, cannon, shot and shell, and broken foliage were strewn about. With much labor a detail of Union soldiers buried the dead by simply turning the captured breastworks upon them. Thus had these unfortunate victims unwittingly dug their own graves. The trenches were nearly full of muddy water. It was the most horrible sight I had ever witnessed."

Grant was more circumspect, writing, "Lee massed heavily from his left flank on the broken point of his line. Five times during the day he assaulted furiously, but without dislodging our troops from their new position. His losses must have been fearful. Sometimes the belligerents would be separated by but a few feet. In one place a tree, eighteen inches in diameter, was cut entirely down by musket balls. All the trees between the lines were very much cut to pieces by artillery and musketry. It was three o'clock next morning before the fighting ceased. Some of our troops had then been twenty hours under fire. In this engagement we did not lose a single organization, not even a company. The enemy lost one division with its commander, one brigade and one regiment, with heavy losses elsewhere. Our losses were heavy, but, as stated, no whole company was captured. At night Lee took a position in rear of his former one, and by the following morning he was strongly intrenched in it."

Chapter 7: Lee Lives to Fight Another Day

"The enemy are obstinate, and seem to have found the last ditch." – Ulysses S. Grant, May 12 telegraph to Washington.

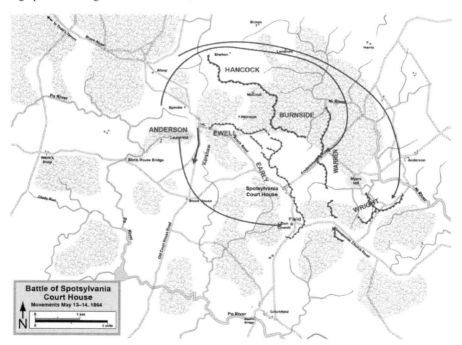

Movements on May 13-14

Lee's army had barely escaped disaster on the 12th, leaving Grant anxious to continue offensive operations, but he was also well aware that an attack against the newly entrenched line would be suicidal. Thus, he began the delicate process of marching the men on his right flank to come up on the left flank of the army, requiring them to countermarch and then head south and southeast. From May 13-14, he accomplished this by having the VI Corps and the remaining men of the V Corps move behind Hancock's men and march to the left of Burnside's IX Corps. The steady rains, which had now continued for nearly 4 days, slowed the progress and bogged them down. In response to these movements, Lee shifted Anderson's corps from his left to his right to counter them.

On May 16, Grant telegraphed Washington to explain that the rain had all but halted his campaign: "We have had five days almost constant rain without any prospect yet of it clearing up. The roads have now become so impassable that ambulances with wounded men can no longer run between here and Fredericksburg. All offensive operations necessarily cease until we can have twenty-four hours of dry weather. The army is in the best of spirits, and feel the greatest confidence of ultimate success."

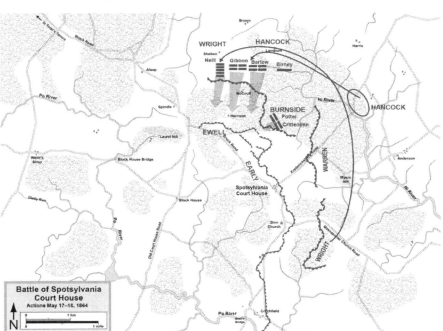

The attack on May 18

The following day, Grant devised plans for another assault, hoping to catch the Confederates by surprise. Since Grant had been marching men from his right to his left, he hoped and guessed that Lee was countering that by building up that flank to meet the new threat, so he decided to try to attack Lee's left flank with Hancock's men and Burnside's men, near the Mule Shoe. The problem with the plan was that Lee was still fearful that an assault might come at any time, so the Confederates were alert. Moreover, Ewell's men had been in the same defensive lines for several days, which had allowed them to dig in so effectively that their line was all but impregnable. When Hancock's corps led this attack, the felled trees (abates) bogged them down and made them sitting ducks for Confederate artillery, which had not been withdrawn this time. The Union attack was repulsed without Ewell's infantry having to fire a single musket.

With that, Grant had finally been convinced of the hopelessness of striking a decisive blow at Spotsylvania Court House, noting in his memoirs, "I immediately gave orders for a movement by the left flank, on towards Richmond, to commence on the night of the 19th. I also asked Halleck to secure the cooperation of the navy in changing our base of supplies from Fredericksburg to Port Royal, on the Rappahannock."

On May 19, as Grant was getting ready to march south by pulling his right flank out of the lines, Lee ordered Ewell's corps to conduct a reconnaissance in force that would probe the Union's right flank. This was the kind of reconnaissance that would have been assigned to JEB Stuart's cavalry in previous years, but Stuart's badly outnumbered cavalry had their hands full with Sheridan, and the famous cavalier had been mortally wounded in a skirmish at the Battle of Yellow Tavern on May 11. As a result, two of Ewell's divisions pushed forward until they came across some of Hancock's corps at Harris Farm, a skirmish that lasted most of the 19th. By the time Lee withdrew Ewell's men, they had suffered 900 casualties. Meanwhile, Grant was disappointed by Warren yet again, writing, "Warren had been ordered to get on Ewell's flank and in his rear, to cut him off from his intrenchments. But his efforts were so feeble that under the cover of night Ewell got back with only the loss of a few hundred prisoners, besides his killed and wounded. The army being engaged until after dark, I rescinded the order for the march by our left flank that night."

After Harris Farm, the last major fighting of the Battle of Spotsylvania Court House was finished. From May 8-21, the two armies had inflicted nearly 32,000 casualties on each other. Grant had lost over 18,000 killed, captured or wounded, meaning he had lost over 35,000 since entering the Wilderness less than three weeks earlier. Meanwhile, Lee had lost another 13,000 soldiers, over 20% of his entire army. It was the deadliest battle of the Overland Campaign and one of the 5 bloodiest battles of the entire Civil War.

At Spotsylvania, just like at the Battle of the Wilderness, Lee's army had skillfully defended against Grant's attacks and had inflicted more casualties than they suffered. But once again, the

Confederates had suffered a larger % of casualties within their army and failed to stop Grant's campaign. The Army of the Potomac and Army of Northern Virginia would continue to move south, destined to meet again along the North Anna River.

Bibliography

Alexander, Edward P. Military Memoirs of a Confederate: A Critical Narrative. New York: Da Capo Press, 1993.

Bonekemper, Edward H., III. A Victor, Not a Butcher: Ulysses S. Grant's Overlooked Military Genius. Washington, DC: Regnery, 2004.

Grant, Ulysses S. Personal Memoirs of U. S. Grant. 2 vols. Charles L. Webster & Company, 1885–86.

Grimsley, Mark. And Keep Moving On: The Virginia Campaign, May–June 1864. Lincoln: University of Nebraska Press, 2002.

Jaynes, Gregory, and the Editors of Time-Life Books. The Killing Ground: Wilderness to Cold Harbor. Alexandria, VA: Time-Life Books, 1986.

Longstreet, James. From Manassas to Appomattox: Memoirs of the Civil War in America. New York: Da Capo Press, 1992. First published in 1896 by J. B. Lippincott and Co.

Lyman, Theodore. With Grant and Meade: From the Wilderness to Appomattox. Edited by George R. Agassiz. Lincoln: University of Nebraska Press, 1994.

Rhea, Gordon C. The Battle of the Wilderness May 5–6, 1864. Baton Rouge: Louisiana State University Press, 1994.

Rhea, Gordon C. The Battles of Wilderness & Spotsylvania. National Park Service Civil War series. Fort Washington, PA: U.S. National Park Service and Eastern National, 1995.

Rhea, Gordon C. In the Footsteps of Grant and Lee: The Wilderness Through Cold Harbor. Baton Rouge: Louisiana State University Press, 2007.

Trudeau, Noah Andre. Bloody Roads South: The Wilderness to Cold Harbor, May–June 1864. Boston: Little, Brown & Co., 1989.

U.S. War Department, The War of the Rebellion: a Compilation of the Official Records of the Union and Confederate Armies. Washington, DC: U.S. Government Printing Office, 1880–1901.

Made in the USA
San Bernardino, CA
20 October 2013